FRAMING MARI

MW00577073

# Framing Mary

## The Mother of God in Modern, Revolutionary, and Post-Soviet Russian Culture

EDITED BY
AMY SINGLETON ADAMS
AND VERA SHEVZOV

NIU PRESS / DEKALB, IL

Northern Illinois University Press, DeKalb 60115
© 2018 by Northern Illinois University Press
All rights reserved

27  26  25  24  23  22  21  20  19  18        2  3  4  5
978-0-87580-776-8 (paper)
978-1-60909-235-1 (e-book)
Book and cover design by Yuni Dorr

Library of Congress Cataloging-in-Publication Data is available online
at http://catalog.loc.gov

TO JOHN, NINA, AND ANYA

for their tireless patience and support. *VS*


TO BILL, BEN, ALEC,

AND, OF COURSE, MARY CATHERINE

with love. *ASA*

# Contents

# Illustrations

# Acknowledgments

If there is one lesson to be learned from this volume, it is that there is no one way to study the image of Mary in Russia. Indeed, our own work on the subject over the years has consistently revealed the enormity of the subject and the limitations of approaching it from a single perspective or discipline. Thus, we are immensely grateful for the community of scholars who grew up around this project and to those people who were willing to devote their time and effort to help us realize it.

We give deep thanks to the Northern Illinois University Press and especially to Interim Co-Director and Acquisitions Editor Amy Farranto, who guided the publication of this project through its many stages. We give deep thanks also to Nathan Holmes, Yuni Dorr, Lori Propheter, Cara Carlson, Pat Yenerich, and Bola Balogun. We would also like to thank our anonymous reader and Robert H. Greene for their careful review of the manuscript and their supportive comments and suggestions.

We are deeply grateful to the hosts and sponsors of the 2011 Working Symposium on the Mother of God in Russian culture, which launched the Framing Mary project. We thank the Rev. Michael C. McFarland, S.J. Center for Religion, Ethics, and Culture at the College of the Holy Cross and the generosity and support of Director Thomas M. Landy, PhD, Associate Director for Communications Danielle Kane, and Administrative Assistant Patricia Hinchliffe. We would also like to thank the Rev. Michael C. McFarland, S.J., for his interest and attendance at the event. We are likewise extremely appreciative of the Museum of Russian Icons in Clinton, Massachusetts, for their co-sponsorship of the 2011 Working Symposium, and their long-term support, expertise, and assistance. We are indebted to President and Founder Gordon B. Lankton, CEO and Curator Kent Russell, Registrar Laura Garrity-Arquit, and Deputy Director Tara Young.

We would also like to express our appreciation to the Information Technology Services department at Holy Cross. This talented and creative team helped us realize our vision of a truly collaborative writing experience by designing, building, and maintaining an interactive web site for our Framing

Mary symposium and beyond. We thank Robert Allen, Denise Davies, Ellen Keohane, Harold Knapp, James Noonan, and Greg Rodenhiser.

We are also grateful to Laura Garrity-Arquit at the Museum of Russian Icons and James L. Jackson, president and CEO of Jackson's International Auctioneers and Appraisers, who were generous with both permission and time as we struggled to locate images of icon types. We also thank Rachel E. Bauer, Carol A. Leadenham, and Stephanie E. Stewart of the Hoover Institution Archives for their help in locating and reproducing images from Hoover's rich poster collection. A special thanks is also due Elena Volkova, deputy chair of the English Language Department at St. Petersburg University of Humanities and Social Sciences, who went out of her way to provide the image of Petrov-Vodkin's Mother of God icon on the façade of the Orthopedic Clinic in Aleksandrovskii Park. Likewise a warm thanks to photographer Dick Fish of Smith's Imaging Center, who has been supporting faculty in their various imaging-related needs for more than fifty years. For funding to support the reproduction of the volume's images so integral to the volume, we thank the Committee on Faculty Scholarship at Holy Cross and Bill E. Peterson, Associate Provost and Dean of Academic Development and the Committee for Faculty Compensation and Development at Smith College.

Finally, to our family, friends, and colleagues for their patience, support, and good humor through the various obstacles that periodically delayed this project—our warmest and deepest gratitude.

# Note on Transliteration

We use the modified Library of Congress system to transliterate Russian words, names, and phrases. However, in cases where common usage dictates otherwise, we observe that convention. For example, instead of Dostoevskii and Gor'kii, we write Dostoevsky and Gorky.

# FRAMING MARY

FIGURE 0.1 Vladimir icon of the Mother of God, 15th century, tempera on wood, Tretiakov Gallery, Moscow. Photo courtesy of Stanislav Koslovskii.

## INTRODUCTION

# At Every Time and In Every Place
## The Mother of God in Modern Russian Culture

VERA SHEVZOV AND AMY SINGLETON ADAMS

O Birthgiver of God ... reigning helper, strengthen this land that you have blessed against its enemies; as you once saved Constantinople from the incursion of heathens, so now save Russia from the onslaught of adversaries, from civil strife ... the land of Russia glorifies you, a helper of people.

(Service in honor of the Vladimir Icon of the Mother of God)[1]

In times of nationwide misfortune
Your image, raised over Rus',
Through the darkness of the centuries showed us the way
And in prison—a secret exit.
The horrific history of Russia
All passed before your face.

(From Maximilian Voloshin, "The Vladimir Mother of God")

THROUGHOUT RUSSIA'S LONG HISTORY, ONE woman stands out among all others. Her life is legendary and her image is easily recognized. She was born neither Russian nor Orthodox, but many of the country's villages, towns, and cities—such as Kazan, Tikhvin, and Vladimir—historically have claimed her as their own, and she has been described as the "heart" of the Russian Orthodox Church.[2] In the minds of the faithful, her almost militant love for them is unwavering. Her inspiration in the realm of Russian spiritual, cultural, and political life is widely acknowledged; she is also revered as an untiring advocate for the downtrodden, the marginalized, and the voiceless. Although first and foremost an intercessor and protectress, she is known by many names in Russia—most often the Birthgiver of God (*Bogoroditsa*), the Mother of God (*Bogomater'*) and, with less frequency, the Virgin Mary (*Deva Mariia*).[3]

Mary's undeniable popularity in Russia stems from a perceived identity and from stories of miracles similar to those that gained her fame in the Christian West, resulting in comparable legacies in the worlds of art, religion, and politics. Scholarship on the Marian phenomenon in the Christian West has burgeoned in the past several decades, in particular with regard to her cultural, social, and political influence in the modern and contemporary world.[4] Her continued influence in modern Eastern Orthodox Christian cultures, however, has drawn significantly less attention, especially with respect to Russia.[5] Most major comprehensive scholarly English-language studies of Mary in recent decades have barely acknowledged her influence in Russia's medieval religious and civic culture, let alone her place in Russia's modern and post-Soviet contexts.[6] Similarly, scholars of modern and contemporary Russia—especially art historians, historians, sociologists, and literary scholars—have for the most part devoted only sporadic attention to Mary in the context of their broader studies.[7] Even scholars in Russia who have made enormous strides in reviving the academic study of Orthodoxy after seventy years of Soviet rule have only relatively recently turned their attention to the highly influential figure of the Mother of God.[8]

This volume introduces readers to the cultural life of Mary from the seventeenth century to the post-Soviet era through an array of disciplinary lenses and, as historian Henry Adams expressed it, "track[s] [her] energy" in a country where her influence is both essential and often overlooked.[9] Informed by the Christian East and West since the tenth century, Russia's perception of Mary has been shaped as much (if not more) by believers' relationship with her as by any prescriptive teachings. Within the context of who she was and the perceived role she played and continues to play in Russian Orthodox conceptions of history, Mary in Russia might best be approached as a relational notion.[10] As Robert Orsi has observed, the image of Mary above all engages those who turn to her.[11] Her lasting cultural and historical impact rests largely on response—of her devotees (and detractors) to her as well as her's to them, as they imagined it. Accordingly, Mary in Russia became inseparable from the stories and visual images associated with believers' reported encounters with her and from the more enigmatic realm of sensibilities and emotions that often generated, and were generated by, such experiences. As much a symbol of national identity as Mexico's Virgin of Guadalupe or Poland's Lady of Częstochowa, Russia's Mary facilitates a wide range of relationships among individuals and groups within Russian society.[12]

The essays in this volume examine a broad spectrum of engagements among a wide array of people—pilgrims, poets, and painters; clergy and laity; women and men; politicians and political activists—and the woman they knew as the *Bogoroditsa*. Our authors trace Mary's irrepressible pull and inexhaustible promise, which even the most avid atheists and secularists who sought to cast away old ways in light of modernity and revolution often found too great to ignore. Although written nearly a century ago, Soviet ethnographer Nikolai Matorin's observation that "the gravity of the Marian cult ... in Orthodoxy is still so great that it must be taken into account even in the most prominent proletarian centers" is no less relevant today.[13] It might even be argued that the strength of Mary's image pushed a once obscure group of female Russian activists—whom we now know as Pussy Riot—onto the world stage.

Taking place from the seventeenth through the twenty-first centuries, many of the engagements with Mary that these essays examine might be regarded from a contemporary point of view as little more than ethnographic curiosities, if not obstacles to Russia's modernization. Yet again as Robert Orsi has argued, labels such as "premodern," "modern," and "postmodern" do little to help us understand and appreciate peoples' sensibilities concerning the sacred and the profound influence these sensibilities exert on behavior.[14] From this perspective, the volume documents the relentless tenacity and pervasiveness of a subculture whose making in any given period cannot be easily traced to those of any particular social, political, or economic standing, educational level, gender, or age. As the following essays illustrate, the figure of Mary often defies such conventional boundaries and demands demarcations of her own.

## RUSSIA'S MARY: BETWEEN CHRISTIAN EAST AND WEST

Although nourished by emotions and sentiments that inspired her devotees elsewhere in the world—hope, despair, desire, fear, and gratitude—Russia's Orthodox Marian culture has enjoyed its own characteristic traits. Mary's humanity and motherhood, for example, tended to be emphasized in Russia more than her virginity, which was reflected in the fact that Mary was widely referred to as "Mother" or "Birthgiver" rather than "Virgin" or the later Renaissance term "Our Lady" (Madonna, *Gospozha*).[15] As Russian philologist and literary theorist Sergei Averintsev notes, Russia's Orthodox Mary remained untouched by the culture of courtly love and chivalry with which her image became so intimately intertwined in the medieval West.[16] Instead, as the essays in this volume illustrate, as mother, Russia's Mary is primarily a protectress and intercessor, to whom people appeal especially during times of crisis.

Moreover, devotion to Mary in Russia has historically focused on dreams and icons rather than the apparitions reported more commonly in the West, which may partially explain why her "appearances" in Russia have often eluded Western scholars.[17] While in this volume Stella Rock describes believers speaking of Mary as having walked in Russia as she had through Western European lands, Russia's Marian devotees have generally experienced and imagined her presence primarily by means of icons. Through her icons, as authors in this volume agree, Russia's believers related to Mary as if to a living person. Not surprisingly, her icons often graced private homes in numbers far greater than those of Christ or other saints.[18] Over time, consequently, Marian icons have played a key role in actualizing the special relationship Mary was perceived to have established with believers. As one Orthodox priest explained in 1908, miracle-working icons were regarded as both a sign of Mary's desire to relate to the faithful and a means through which to communicate her "presence," a presence whose influence often spread beyond the boundaries of institutionalized Orthodoxy.[19]

Russia's Marian heritage stems from a two-fold source that by the nineteenth century was as European as it was Byzantine. Beginning in the ninth century, missionaries, monastics, and clergy from Byzantium and the south-Slavic regions of Bulgaria and Serbia introduced the Orthodox veneration of Mary to Rus'. Stories about her life as well as her physical appearance were gradually introduced to the newly converted territory through a variety of genres, including scriptural and apocryphal texts, homilies, liturgical commemorations, and iconography. By the end of the Kievan era in the twelfth and thirteenth centuries, Rus' was well aware of Mary as both the mother of Jesus, so faintly sketched in the gospel texts, and the doctrinally laden "bearer" or "birthgiver" of God (*Theotokos; Bogoroditsa*) promulgated in fourth- and fifth-century Christological controversies. Yet she was also known through engaging legends about her life, death, and even afterlife, including the enduringly popular *Visitation to the Torments by the Mother of God* (Khozhdenie Bogoroditsy po mukam).[20] Even what would become one of Russia's most cherished Marian feasts, the Protection of the Most Holy Birthgiver of God (Pokrov Presviatoi Bogoroditsy), established as early as the twelfth century, was based on the tenth-century Byzantine story of the fool-for-Christ Andrew's vision of Mary in the Church of Blachernae in Constantinople.[21]

The unsystematic flow of texts and images into Rus' helps to explain the character that Marian devotion in Russia acquired over time. The introduction of Christianity's literary heritage to Rus' defied neat categories of "canonical" and "uncanonical," "history" and "legend." Ancient manuscripts reveal that monastic compilers of sacred texts often made little qualitative distinction between biblical texts and homilies, apocryphal stories (including excerpts from the *Protevangelium of James*), and lives of saints. As a result, New Testament references to Mary and the details of her life as depicted in the *Protevangelium* and in later apocryphal accounts, visions, and well-known homilies often blended together under the canopy of "sacred writings."[22]

Liturgical celebrations and iconographic depictions of non-scripturally based events in Mary's life—including her birth, entry into the Temple, and death—were well established in Eastern and Western Christian communities before the Christianization of Rus'. Such visual and textual sources encouraged a creative impulse to imagine Mary's life and death in ways that not only shaped the nature of Russia's Marian culture, but continued to inform Russia's social and cultural ideals well into modern and even post-Soviet times. Scenes from the apocryphal life of Mary, for instance, adorned the private prayer room of Peter the Great's sister, the regent Sofiia Alekseevna (1682–1689), and bolstered notions of female sovereignty.[23] Indeed, Mary's primary role as intercessor (*zastupnitsa*), which accounts for her persistent appeal, found its validation in apocryphal stories rather than in scripture. According to the ancient apocryphal account of her death that entered the Eastern Orthodox tradition through liturgy and iconography, Mary encourages believers to seek her out: "At every time and in every place where there is a memorial of my name, sanctify that place and glorify those who glorify you through my name, accepting every offering and every supplication and prayer."[24] With her intercessory role so sanctioned, Mary's name and image remained firmly embedded in the storytelling that gave shape to Russia's Marian culture, especially from the Muscovite period through contemporary times.

In addition to this profusion of apocryphal stories and other texts, Rus' inherited Byzantine Marian iconographic types—the Blachernitissa, Eleousa, Hodegetria, and Nikopoios—which generated a highly diverse and ever-expanding array of indigenous Marian iconographic prototypes. In the early twentieth century, the well-known art historian Nikodim Kondakov noted that while images of Christ had become more or less fixed in Eastern Christian iconography, those of Mary—especially in Russia—continued to multiply.[25] Storytelling traditions associated with these specially revered Marian icons experienced parallel development. Scattered throughout Rus's ancient chronicles, lives of saints, narratives of military victories, and the founding of monasteries, many of these stories included accounts of Mary's intercession and healing power. Beginning in the twelfth century, these icon-related stories began to be told in their own genre—the icon narrative, or *skazanie*.[26]

Although frequently based on existing oral histories, the *skazaniia* are difficult to classify as a genre. Against the background of both historical and hagiographic sensibilities that are not well conveyed by the terms "tale" or "legend" often used to translate this term, the written accounts of an icon's *life*—often a tangle of lore and fact—became one of the most characteristic and persistent features of Russia's Marian culture.[27]

Most of the essays in this volume are informed by Russia's Marian icon stories, which concern Mary's perceived activities in the lives of individuals, local communities, or the country as whole. This was a fluid, open-ended genre, with a single icon often possessing several versions of a *life* that continued to evolve through time as new "events" or occurrences associated with it were attributed to Mary's intercession. The *life* of Russia's perhaps most widely recognizable Marian icon—the Vladimir icon—is a case in point. The earliest known icon-related *skazanie* in Rus', a twelfth-century record of miracles associated with this image, frames Mary in universal terms, describing how her icon radiates protective light over Rus' and all nations.[28] As Wil van den Bercken has argued, following their Christianization, the Rus' imagined themselves as "accepted among the Christian nations" and incorporated into God's salvific plan.[29] Early accounts of Mary's presence in Rus' echoed this universalism, depicting her as a "wall, protectress [*pokrov*], and haven for all Christians," among whom the relatively newly converted Rus' were now a part.[30]

Prince Andrei Bogoliubskii (1110–1174) of Vladimir and Suzdal reportedly attempted to draw parallels between his rule and that of the imperial court in Constantinople, and to view the Vladimir icon as Rus's counterpart to Byzantium's honored Hodegetria icon of the Mother of God.[31] But the earliest account of the Vladimir icon contains no hint of such political ambitions; it details no military victories or state-related miracles. Even Bogoliubskii, as the protagonist of the account, makes only a limited appearance and his authority is not in Mary's purview. Instead, Mary's intercessory power via her icon is confirmed by more commonplace miracles, such as healings that affect women as often as men. Such healings involve the combination of prayer and the consumption of water in which the icon had been immersed, a practice that Christine Worobec's essay confirms continued in modern Russia.[32]

By the late fifteenth and early sixteenth centuries, after the fall of Byzantium (1453) and the dissolution of the Golden Horde (1480), monastic scribes retold the story of the Vladimir icon in order to emphasize the induction of Muscovy (and Russia) into Mary's favored lands.[33] As Muscovy's new "master symbol," the Vladimir icon inspired a more detailed story, which appeared in the historical narrative *Book of Degrees of the Royal Genealogy* (Stepennaia kniga tsarskogo rodosloviia).[34] This updated version of the icon's *skazanie* follows major geopolitical shifts in Russia's history; it traces the icon's origins to the evangelist Luke and tracks its movement from Palestine to Constantinople, Kiev, Vladimir, and finally to Moscow.[35] The focus of the icon's narrative shifts from common people to the interests of princes and metropolitans. Stories of earlier military victories are incorporated and describe the defeat of the Volga Bulgars (1165), the Mongol ruler Batu Kahn (1207–1255) in 1238 and, in 1395, the Turkic-Mongolian conqueror Tamerlane (1336–1405), who was purportedly frightened by a vision of Mary as a woman clothed in a purple robe, radiating light, and surrounded by regiments that "served her like a queen." In this account, Mary's supplicants gaze at her icon "with their hearts," addressing her image as if it were alive. Similar to the biblical theme of the Israelites repeatedly reminding God of their covenant, so here the people of the city of Vladimir remind Mary of her self-appointed role as intercessor, her blessing of chosen icons, and her choice "to live" in the "newly enlightened land of Rus," thereby acknowledging her full agency in their future fate.[36] By the late seventeenth century, the well-known artist-iconographer Simon Ushakov (1626–1686) visually enshrined the Vladimir icon of the Mother of God as the palladium of Russia in his well-known work The Tree of the Muscovite State (Drevo gosudarstva Moskovskogo), a sign of Moscow's own covenant with Mary.[37]

Not all of Russia's medieval and early modern Marian icon stories concerned nation-building, however. Marian icons were often linked to the founding of monastic communities and the construction of churches, credited with relief from illness, drought, and epidemics, and provided the basis for morality tales. The late fifteenth-century account of the Koloch icon of the Mother of God, for instance, focuses on Luke, a common man who was "blessed" by finding a miracle-working image of the Mother of God. Because of his discovery, Luke is treated as a "prophet" and "apostle" and, as he travels with the icon from the village of Koloch to Mozhaisk, Moscow, and other towns, he is received with respect and given alms. Celebrated by bishops, princes, and "all the people," Luke succumbs to the temptation of fame and fortune and turns to a life of excess. Despite such recklessness, even the local ruling prince of Mozhaisk, Andrei Dmitrievich, defers to Luke because the Mother of God has supposedly favored him with her icon. A close brush with death results in Luke's change of heart, however, leading to his tonsure and the founding of a monastic community at the site where he had originally found the icon.[38] Such stories of miracles, faith, and morality became the mainstay of Russia's Marian devotional culture into modern and contemporary times.

Finally, speculating on the ancient roots of Russia's Marian culture, modern scholars from Russia and the West have sought the existence of pre-Christian cults of goddess figures in Rus' that may have influenced the reception and assimilation of the figure of Mary. Although the culture of ancient Rus' lacks a defined pantheon as in the Greco-Roman goddess figures such as Cybele, Demeter, Isis, Rhea, and Tyche—in whom scholars have seen precursors to Mary in late antiquity—both prerevolutionary Russian and contemporary Western scholars have sought pre-Christian sacred figures that may have served as indigenous prototypes for Russia's "Mary."[39] Nineteenth- and twentieth-century Russian ethnographers and folklorists who pursued this line of inquiry generally assumed, as had the ethnographer Sergei Maksimov (1831–1901), that even when "Christ's teaching seemingly permeated to the [peasant] bone," it remained but a thin veneer.[40] While this approach has faced resistance from historians and philologists, many of Russia's ethnographers and folklorists continued to seek Mary's cultural roots in the divine feminine principle of "Mother Damp Earth" (*mat' syra zemlia*)—personified, according to some scholars, as an earth goddess—or with the Slavic goddesses of fertility, such as Lada, Mokosh, or perhaps even Simargl.[41] This contested view, which became intertwined with the equally problematic notion of "dual-faith" (*dvoeverie*), proved expedient during Soviet times as a means of minimizing Orthodoxy's historical influence in Russia's past and of undercutting its future potential in the promised new socialist order.[42] The Soviet ethnographer Nikolai Matorin (1898–1936), for instance, cast the study of Marian devotion in Russia as a form of cultural paleontology that led inevitably to pre-Christian beliefs.[43] In more recent times, this line of inquiry among Western scholars of Russia has dovetailed well with the feminist search for ancient matriarchal cultures and the feminist attempts to construct neo-pagan goddess cults.[44]

Since the seventeenth century, which marks the starting point of this volume, three major cultural revolutions have influenced the framing and reframing of Russia's Mary: the Westernization and modernization of the eighteenth and nineteenth centuries, the Bolshevik Revolution and subsequent exodus of Russian émigrés to the West, and the fall of communism. These political and cultural shifts played a formidable role in shaping cultural self-perception and, as modernity and secularism offered viable alternatives, in creating new roles for Mary. Through trade routes in the north and strong cultural ties with the southwestern territories that constitute today's Ukraine and Belarus, Russia encountered Western aesthetic sensibilities and Western forms of Christian devotion. The result was a visual and narrative reorientation with regard to Mary that drew on European influences as much as earlier Byzantine ones, in many ways marking Russia's increasingly complex cultural relationship with Europe.[45] If prior to the sixteenth century Russia's church and state elite eyed primarily Constantinople and its Marian legacy as sources for inspiration and identity-formation, now Europe and "the West" served that function as both a cultural kin that Russia often sought to emulate and a civilizational Other whose influences Russia sought to regulate or resist. The result was a modern Marian culture fraught with ambiguity and deep paradoxes. At the same time, negotiations between its Byzantine and Western aesthetic forms also produced numerous brilliant examples of fusion between "the essence of an alien culture" and Russia's native one, as Sarah Pratt's essay on Alexander Pushkin's Mary so vividly demonstrates.

Visually, Russia's turn to the West in the seventeenth century marks the beginning of Mary's makeover in iconographic depictions. Emperor Peter the Great's short-lived efforts to regulate Orthodox iconographic production and the subsequent role of the Imperial Academy of Arts (founded in 1757) in setting the standards of "good" iconography resulted in a varied palette of iconographic styles. Mary might be depicted as lighter European (the "Italian" or "Frankish" style) or in the darker-toned, traditional "Greek" style, typical of rural Old Believer iconographic workshops. Simon Ushakov promoted the *friazh'* style of iconography, which combined traditional Byzantine and Western forms and styles. Using examples from the turn of the twentieth century, Wendy Salmond notes how this creative integration of "icon" and "art" continued throughout the imperial period, producing new, revitalized sacred styles among artist-iconographers of the Silver Age (1890s to the early 1920s) such as Viktor Vasnetsov (1848–1926), Mikhail Nesterov (1862–1942), and Kuzma Petrov-Vodkin (1878–1939). Roy Robson traces the same impulse in the work of the traditionally trained Old Believer iconographer Pimen Sofronov, who, as an iconographer in emigration, creatively integrated features of Roman Catholic iconography without compromising the iconicity of Orthodox Marian works.

A church council in 1551 maintained that the work of fifteenth-century master Andrei Rublev should be the iconographic standard in Russia. But the fact that in the late nineteenth century Western reproductions of Michelangelo and Leonardo da Vinci were readily found in Russia's rural, predominantly peasant, iconographic workshops indicates that Mary enjoyed a wide array of "looks" in prerevolutionary Russian churches and homes. It might indeed be argued that by the eighteenth and nineteenth centuries, Raphael's Sistine Madonna was more influential than any of Rublev's icons in Russia's conception of Mary.[46] No enforced Orthodox iconographic canon existed that could certify her appearance, despite guidelines offered by iconographer manuals (*podlinniki*) and periodic synodal directives. Indeed, Roy Robson's essay

FIGURE 0.2 Aleksei Venetsianov (1780–1847), The Intercession of the Mother of God for the Students of the Smolny Institute (1832–1835), painted for a side altar in the Cathedral of the Resurrection of Christ the Savior (Smolny Cathedral) in St. Petersburg. State Russian Museum, St. Petersburg. The script at the left side of the icon is a verse from Psalm 80—"Look down from heaven, O God, and behold, and visit this vine, and the vineyard which thy right hand hath planted"—the motto of the Society for the Education of Noble Maidens.

on Sofronov demonstrates that the unexpected flexibility of these guidelines may have been a function of the wide-ranging influences on the iconographer, especially as the icon painter emigrated westward.

Lighter, Europeanized images of Mary, along with scenes from her life that had at one time typified the Christian West (such as her coronation) now found homes in Russia's sacred spaces (see fig. 0.2). The growing demand for affordable icons in Russia eventually led to new methods of mass production. To save cost and time, Mary was only partially depicted (usually only her face and hands) and covered with a metal or foil plate setting or depicted on paper prints. While the iconicity of prints was a contested issue among church officials as early as the seventeenth century, for many believers print icons of Mary were the most affordable. Some clergy, laity, and eventually icon experts may have periodically questioned the iconicity of images painted in the "Italian taste" and those printed on paper, but believers for the most part prayed indiscriminately before a wide variety of images of a woman they saw as Mary.

Elena Boeck shows how, despite the changes in iconography that the seventeenth and eighteenth centuries brought to Russia's Mary, many Orthodox clergy and laity continued to rely on her icons and miracles for historical orientation, as had their counterparts in Rus' centuries earlier. Drawing on an early modern Western propensity to collect and display "the marvelous" and a Counter-Reformation focus on Marian devotion, Orthodox churchmen reaffirmed their belief in Russia's place among the nations.[47] Visual and literary compendia of Marian icons and their stories often made no confessional distinction between Western and Eastern Christian accounts of encounters with Mary, again illustrating how porous the cultural boundaries were between Russia and its Western European neighbors. Like their predecessors in ancient Rus', many modern Orthodox churchmen emphasized Mary's favor toward Russia not so much in terms of exceptionalism as in universal terms that presented Russia as no less favored than her European counterparts.

By the nineteenth century, the veneration of Russia's Marian miracle-working icons had grown to proportions unknown in other Eastern Orthodox countries, spurred, in part, by their sheer number. The mass production of inexpensive icons and an Orthodox ritual culture that liturgically honored specially revered icons led to a veritable cottage industry in the cataloging and celebration of their stories.[48] By 1893, some four hundred and fifty specially revered icons of the Mother of God, which included more than seventy-five distinct visual types, traveled Russia's remote back roads, visiting urban and remote localities. Usually requested by local communities that prepared annually for such a visit, the most well-known of these icons spent only a fraction of any given year "at home" in monasteries and urban cathedrals.[49] Keeping in mind that the Orthodox Church at the time only nationally celebrated some twenty-eight icons of the Mother of God, such visitations (*poseshcheniia*) testified to a broader, laity-driven Marian subculture within Orthodoxy. Using sources still largely unexplored by scholars, William Wagner traces the rituals and liturgical culture that facilitated the sense of bonding and belonging that these visitations cultivated. Illustrating how such rituals often reinforced existing hierarchical structures, Wagner's essay also suggests that those visitations inherently deflected the gravity of authority from the very same official ecclesiastical and state governance structures, encouraging instead shared, collective encounters with Mary. The fact that by the nineteenth century the subjects of stories associated with newly revered Marian icons were no longer predominantly Russia's social or ecclesiastical elite also confirms the populist underpinning of modern Russia's Marian subculture. Indeed, as Amy Singleton Adams argues, in the late nineteenth and early twentieth centuries, even artists and activists who, like Maxim Gorky, actively cultivated alternatives to Orthodox spirituality, recognized and attempted to redirect the energy inherent in this subculture in their own efforts to "transform and transfigure faith" in the new revolutionary context.

Ironically, the very engagement with the West that had promoted the cataloging and celebration of Mary's miracles also led to the rise of a philosophical disposition in Russia that challenged Mary's identity as an active agent in peoples' lives. Starting with church and civil legislation crafted during the reign of Peter the Great, institutional thinking about miracles was based on the ill-defined project of freeing Orthodoxy from all that was "superfluous and not essential to salvation."[50] Influenced by Counter-Reformation efforts to tackle ecclesiastical corruption, and strengthened by both Enlightenment-era rationalism and Orthodox clerical distrust of lay devotional sensibilities, this legislation subjected spontaneous veneration of Marian icons to a new level of bureaucratic scrutiny and censure. At a time when doubt became increasingly understood as progressive and the miracle as a disdained "phantom of this age," believers were often left defending a way of seeing that modernity had discarded as obsolete.[51]

Perhaps most significantly, Russia's complex engagement with the West ushered in a world of art—painting, literature, music, dance, and theater—that flourished far beyond the ecclesiastically defined semantic frame of Orthodoxy. Especially in the eighteenth and early nineteenth centuries, Russia's professional academy-trained artists produced Marian images that were sometimes difficult to distinguish from that of their Western counterparts. These artists' works often became known abroad. Aleksei Egorov (1776–1851), professor of art history at the Academy of Art, for instance, won accolades as a

"Russian Raphael" for his religious works.[52] While no less spiritual or at times even "religious" in its inspiration—and indeed, the work of many of these academically trained artists adorned the walls of Russia's urban cathedrals—Russia's secular artistic world established a context in which artists, poets, and writers could draw on Mary's Eastern and Western Christian legacies and move beyond them, engaging her anew.

In their creative engagement of both the "Western" and the "native" in Marian aesthetics, Russia's artists and authors nevertheless often distinguish the West's Madonna from Russia's *Bogoroditsa*. In the nineteenth and early twentieth centuries, the work of Mikhail Lermontov, Fyodor Dostoevsky, and Anna Akhmatova, for example, cast the Russian Mother of God as protectress, bestower of mercy and succor in death, and the kenotic female sufferer. At the same time, paragons of the Italian Renaissance, such as the Sistine Madonna and the Madonna da Settignano, in the work of Dostoevsky and Alexander Blok tended to represent the ideals of aesthetic beauty or the poet's creative processes.[53] As Sarah Pratt observes, even the whimsical, sometimes bawdy verse about the European Madonna by Alexander Pushkin—the "cultural conduit" from Europe to Russia and "translator" par excellence of European culture into native Russian sensibilities—remained a "Western model made quintessentially Russian, keeping the Orthodox *Bogoroditsa* at bay."

In their search for distinctly Russian forms that either shed or engaged European influences in new ways, many writers, artists, and poets of the Silver Age turned to the ancient icon as a source of inspiration. The populist underpinnings of Russia's realist and avant-garde art, the Silver Age's attraction to iconographic language—its color, form, and perspective—and the revolutionary fervor that sought to harness the energy of "the people" all helped to secure a place for Mary in Russia's burgeoning secular culture. While mostly working outside the boundaries of the institutional church, the work of Russia's Silver Age writers, poets, artists, and philosophers nevertheless often proceeded from an insider's knowledge of lived Orthodoxy and the craft of iconography. During a period of intense religious reflection at the outset of the twentieth century, for example, the poet Alexander Blok—who, according to his mother, "locked himself in a church to pray"—even considered writing a dissertation on miracle-working icons of the Mother of God.[54] The deep religious and spiritual foundation of the Silver Age, which coincided with what historians of Russian thought have since termed the "Russian Religious Renaissance," often found its inspiration in the work of philosopher Vladimir Solov'ev.[55] As Natalia Ermolaeva reminds us in her essay, Solov'ev's religious engagement with modernity and the often mystical undertones of his writings (especially those dedicated to Divine Sophia) deeply influenced Silver Age writers, poets, and artists working beyond the enclaves of the institutional church, as well as academically trained Orthodox thinkers.

The explosion of creativity that marked Russia's Silver Age was accompanied by an almost breathless search for ways to express the social, cultural, and spiritual renewal that the highly charged revolutionary atmosphere promised. Painters such as Kuzma Petrov-Vodkin drew on iconic forms and on the image of Mary to tap the energy often generated by her familiar image in order to serve their broader cultural or social agendas, like highlighting the plight of the poor. Reminding us of Petrov-Vodkin's training in iconographic workshops, Wendy Salmond presents his painting *1918 in Petrograd (The Petrograd Madonna)* as an "icon-painting" that simultaneously reflected an "evangelical desire" to speak to an audience "hungry for spiritual as well as physical food" and represented "the most complete visual manifestation" of the twentieth-century Russian philosophy of "aesthetic Christianity."

In addition to Vladimir Solov'ev's Divine Sophia, other female forms, like poet Alexander Blok's Beautiful Lady (Prekrasnaia dama), represented Symbolist ideas about spiritual unity, Sophiology, and Godmanhood. For many artists and thinkers, however, the image of the *Bogoroditsa* continued to act as a defining, symbolic text. The impetus to find non-transcendent but still spiritual means of expressing the meaning and values of the revolutionary and post-revolutionary world was often expressed in the idea of the "living icon." For poet Marina Tsvetaeva, whom Alexandra Smith describes as a "spiritual truth-seeker" in more a theosophical sense, Moscow itself becomes a "living" icon of what seems to be four dimensions, a space "imbued by divine truth" and protected by the Mother of God. Maxim Gorky's "living" literary icons, as Amy Singleton Adams shows, display both the writer's search for a collective human spirituality and his struggle to inject into Lenin's revolutionary project certain humane values—love, compassion, tenderness—that might engender cultural renewal.

Gorky's novel *Mother* was heralded as the first work of Soviet Socialist Realism; although successive editions gradually scrubbed religious imagery from it, the first iteration was dominated by the figure of the eponymous mother-cum-Madonna.[56] However, if some Silver Age and early Soviet artists and writers recognized the spiritual fervor that Mary's image traditionally commanded and attempted to harness it for their own purposes, for others, the iconic woman seemed to have little to offer a society with a new vision. Instead, she appeared as an obstacle to the rapid modernization this vision presupposed. In his story, "The Homeland of Electricity" ("Rodina elektrichestva"), for instance, the proletarian writer Andrei Platonov (1899–1951) presents Orthodoxy's Mary as a symbol of a faith misplaced and worn by centuries of now meaningless habits of religious ritual that cannot evoke any hope. Represented as a solitary young woman whose premature wrinkles and dull, unresponsive eyes betray first-hand knowledge of the hardship and bitterness of everyday life, Platonov's Mary (and the institution that had produced her) had little to offer believers. Her purposeless gaze held no spark of faith; such eyes, observed Platonov, "tired quickly."[57]

Such a Mary had no place in an atheistic society driven by the project to create the New Soviet Person (*novyi chelovek*). In the broader context of Soviet culture, therefore, Mary met a variety of fates. Artists and writers such as Kuzma Petrov-Vodkin and Maxim Gorky attempted to free Mary from ecclesiastical trappings and transform her image into that of a new proletarian mother, while others were convinced that such a "freeing" was ultimately impossible. Countless Western-style or folk icons of Mary from the eighteenth and nineteenth centuries, along with other imperial-age artifacts, were viewed as worthless clutter and destroyed. State officials confiscated Mary's more ancient images from churches and monasteries, which the art world had deemed most valuable, and either safely preserved them in museums as cultural artifacts or sold them abroad for much needed state revenue. With thousands of churches and monasteries destroyed or closed, the narratives that had once so informed Russia's Marian culture lost their vitality and were largely forgotten. Only the clandestine efforts of believers—often without the participation of clergy—kept Russia's Marian storytelling culture alive.

Nevertheless, in their communist-building efforts, anti-religious propagandists strategically appropriated familiar Marian iconic forms that recast and frequently degraded their traditional uses while fulfilling their own social and political purposes. While the female figure may have been rare in nascent Soviet political art, even during these years Mary's image proved useful for anti-Orthodox propaganda.[58] For instance, linking Mary (and thus Orthodoxy) with counterrevolutionary forces during Russia's Civil War (1917–1922), communist satirist Viktor Deni based his 1919 lithograph *The Village Birthgiver of God* (Selianskaia Bogoroditsa; see fig. 0.3) on the easily recognizable form of the Hodegetria icon of the Mother of God. In this image, the well-known anti-Bolshevik Socialist Revolutionary Viktor Chernov (1873–1952) is cast as Mary, White Army leader Admiral Alexander Kolchak (1874–1920) as the Christ child, and White Army generals Anton Denikin (1872–1947) and Nikolai Yudenich (1862–1933) as angels.

By the mid-1920s and 1930s, the face of Mary in Soviet visual, especially antireligious, propaganda became more prominent. A 1927 sketch from the

FIGURE 0.3 Viktor Deni, *The Village Birthgiver of God* (Selianskaia Bogoroditsa), 1919. The image is signed "Iconographer Deni." The scroll held by Alexander Kolchak, who is pictured in the place of the Christ child, reads: "Shoot every tenth worker and peasant." Archive, Poster Collection, Hoover Institute, Stanford University.

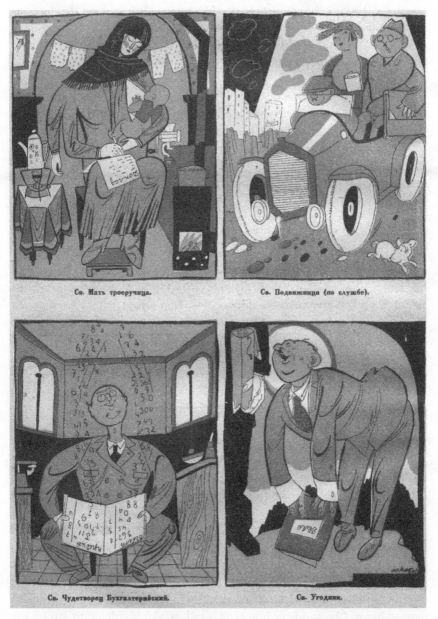

Св. Мать троеручница.

Св. Подвижница (по службе).

Св. Чудотворец Бухгалтерийский.

Св. Угодник.

FIGURE 0.4 Iurii Ganfa, *The New Saints*. Clockwise from top left, the "Holy three-handed Mother"; the "Holy female ascetic (at work)"; the "Miracle-working accountant"; and "the Holy god-pleaser." *Smekhach* [The Jokester], no. 8 (1927).

satirical journal *Smekhach* (The Jokester), for instance, utilized the Three-Handed (Troeruchitsa) image of the Mother of God to laud the working mother among the "new saints" of Soviet society. In this image, a veiled woman resembling the *Bogoroditsa* breastfeeds a child while doing housework and preparing a lecture; her multitasking is miraculously aided by a third hand (see fig. 0.4).[59]

Similarly, Vsevolod Pudovkin's 1926 film based on Gorky's novel *Mother* (Mat', 1906) drew on familiar images to promote the sufferings and joys of Soviet collective motherhood.[60] With a certain irony, Valentin Rasputin's 1974 novel *Live and Remember* (Zhivi i pomni) seems to close out the era of Soviet Socialist Realism with both the overturning of its archetype of the heroic war veteran and a return to a Marian heroine who embodies the values of compassion, mercy, and self-sacrifice.[61]

Because the new Soviet state associated her with the tsarist regime and "enemies of the people," Orthodoxy's Mary remained mostly hidden from public view. In the post-Stalin decades, some of Russia's dissidents focused on this Mary as part of Russia's "forbidden past," as they searched for cultural meaning in Soviet society.[62] Virtually each of the fourteen volumes of dissident Zoia Krakhmalnikova's journal *Nadezhda* (Hope; published between 1976 and 1983) began with a chapter dedicated to Mary—an excerpt from her apocryphal life, a well-known homily, or a prayer in honor of one of her icons. Similarly, as Elizabeth Skomp's essay recounts, dissident Tatiana Goricheva reclaimed Mary as a countercultural feminine symbol in her discovery of liberation in Orthodox Christianity in the 1970s. Doing so, she marked the emergence of two parallel forms of feminism in Russia—secular and religious—that have characterized the feminist movement in the West as well. In the same figure that the Soviet state deemed a symbol of institutional and political oppression, Goricheva found not only a personal spiritual "home," but also a source of inspiration that, in Skomp's estimation, could liberate contemporary Soviet women from their "passivity, silence, and slavish dependency on home and family."

Following the Bolshevik Revolution, émigrés fleeing Russia carried the image of Mary with them. Like Roman Catholic Italian immigrants a half century earlier and Cuban and Haitian exiles a half century later, Russia's Orthodox exiles living on virtually every continent turned to Mary as a way of making sense of their fate.[63] An akathist composed in Paris in the 1930s likened her to "the abode of homeless wanderers" (*Svetlaia obitel' strannikov bezdomnykh*) as Mary's role as protectress took on new meaning.[64] Sought for her maternal mercy, for guidance and light in "the darkness of sorrowful days" of banishment in a foreign land, the image of Mary helped not only to maintain collective identity among scattered immigrants, but also to forge a "diasporic nationalism" that persists to this day.[65] According to this hymn, she was "the mother of the Russian people" (*Mat' roda russkago*) and thus acted as a beacon of hope and help. Carried by émigrés to such cities as Chicago and New York, well-known miracle-working icons of Mary like the Tikhvin and Kursk-Root icons of the Mother of God helped to sacralize immigrant experiences and emotions, which included longing for the homeland, the traumas of displacement, and the hope for eventual return.[66]

The *Bogoroditsa*'s role in the negotiation of Russian identity abroad varied as widely as it had in Russia. European Catholic communities, especially in Spain and Italy, had their own "moving Madonnas" that processed through streets. But for some, like émigré poet Alla Golovina, Russia's itinerant Mary remained tenaciously distinct from Europe's museum-bound Madonna. Golovina could not reconcile her childhood memory of a Mary who, through visitations, seemed to seek out her devotees as often as they did her, with a Mary whose terms of engagement were primarily aesthetic. Speaking of Russia's Mary, she wrote:

> Your sister—the Sistine Madonna
> Is not carried to villages, like you.
> She is sought in galleries, in a catalog
> A conventional number for tranquil eyes.
> But you, along country roads,
> Sought us out in meadowed hinterlands.[67]

For others, such as Old Believer iconographer Pimen Sofronov, the distinctions between icon and art—*Bogoroditsa* and Madonna—were not so categorical with regard to lived experience. Without reservation, he incorporated features from traditional Roman Catholic depictions of Mary into his highly acclaimed Orthodox frescoes and icons. As Roy Robson shows, Sofronov was, ironically, dubbed "the Madonna Painter" by his Western colleagues. At the same time, he understood the value of the Mary of museums and the role they played in keeping her image alive in a modern and postmodern age. Indeed, it might be argued that, despite its intentions, the "museumification" of Mary in Soviet Russia re-sacralized her image in a new setting, allowing for those born and living in an atheistic society to engage with her icon in unpredictable ways.[68]

The 1988 millennial celebration of the Christianization of Rus' and the collapse of the Soviet Union three years later marked a resurgence of Orthodox Christianity both at the grassroots and the institutional levels, launching the Church into the public sphere with unexpected speed. Initially viewed by many believers as a providential act, this turn in history inspired hopes among believers of a new, "resurrected Rus," which would "emerge from the ashes, from a sin-filled abyss, and shine in truth and love to the world."[69] But the rapid and turbulent transition in the state's ideology, economy, and geographical makeup of Russia engendered a new crisis of national identity. Initially, the crisis lent Orthodoxy and its symbols—first and foremost the *Bogoroditsa*—relevance, lure, and power. But what Orthodox clergy might have conceived as a missionizing effort soon morphed in the eyes of many citizens into a clericalization of society that drew resistance, and more recently, aversion. As the essays by Stella Rock and Vera Shevzov illustrate, in their struggles to formulate and express their competing views of Russia's past and future, Russia's citizens—including statesmen and church leaders, social and political activists, and artists, as well as common believers—have often sought, in the words of sociologist Alek Epshtein, to "mobilize Mary."[70]

## FRAMING MARY

*Framing Mary* is a title with several meanings. On one level, it suggests that the Mother of God has been somehow "set up," taking the blame for an outcome not of her own creation. In this sense, for instance, leading Western feminist scholars often indict traditional institutional images of Mary for their perpetuation of women's subservience to God and men. "For the first time in the history of mankind," Simone de Beauvoir writes in a well-known passage in *A Second Sex*, "a mother kneels before her son and acknowledges, of her own free will, her inferiority. The supreme victory of masculinity is consummated in Mariolatry: it signifies the rehabilitation of woman through the completeness of her defeat."[71] Building on de Beauvoir's work, Mary Daly sharpens the critique of Roman Catholic Mariology in particular as the worship of a domesticated goddess and the acceptance of motherhood as a confining loss of selfhood.[72] For Marina Warner, Mary becomes an unreachable goal for women, all of whom inevitably fall short of her perceived perfect purity.[73] In the case of Russia, Joanna Hubbs sees similar processes at work in the tenth-century conversion of Rus'. At that time, in her estimation, Christianity reoriented the cultural priorities of Rus' from family to state, and from goddess figures to a male God, which resulted in the subjugation of women.[74]

Frames indeed can be restrictive. They can limit the roles of women solely to birth-givers and mothers; they can deny them agency and exclude them from public spheres.[75] More broadly, frames are often politically motivated and enforced in order to buttress regimes and institutional authorities, ecclesiastical and secular alike. And yet, as this volume shows, Mary has been and remains a complex image in modern Russia that transcends hegemonic discourse and enters into the fray of politics, art, and philosophy. Indeed, while the view that, historically, the image of Mary reinforced male-dominated social structures and cultural motifs in some traditional Christian cultures may be true, it is not the only truth. In fact, the power of Mary resides in the paradoxes of her perceived identities—the uniqueness of a virgin mother yet, especially in the Russian cultural context, a model of all humanity. In her discussion of Western Marian cultural discourse, French feminist philosopher Julia Kristeva can only approximate the paradoxical power of Mary's image. "What is *it*," Kristeva asks, "which in this maternal figure ... allowed her to become both an object with whom women wished to identify and an object that those responsible for maintaining the social and symbolic order felt it necessary to manipulate?"[76] Although addressed primarily to the Catholic West, Kristeva's work reminds us that Mary's complex role in Russian culture can also negotiate core tensions inherent in her image.

Thus we come to the second understanding of "framing." In Russia, Mary is most frequently depicted in or with reference to her icons. Unlike a painting, the icon does not require a conventional frame to designate the boundaries of represented reality or to convey its semiotic significance. Instead, as Boris Uspensky argues, the icon's unique composition creates a natural border between the sometimes contradictory internal and external points of view.[77] Thus, the "frame" of an icon is also established as a matter of interpretation, a fluid category that can be simultaneously prescribed and freely formulated.

Broadly speaking, the religious, aesthetic, and social contexts in which an icon "lives" create an interpretive framework that, like any other paradigm, can shift. Interpretations of the Mother of God as an icon and symbol often indicate the boundary between an Orthodox understanding of her image and a secular appropriation and transformation of that image that may be no less "sacred." "Framing" Mary, then, refers also to the narrative frame, whether written or spoken.[78] Often these narratives involve dreams, visions, and miracles that focus our attention on issues of authority and alternative power structures. Such narrative frames can guide contemporary views on such complex issues as national identity, the role of women, or the cultural meaning of motherhood. Giving shape to an ever-changing cultural landscape, these narrative frames again demonstrate the power of Mary as a defining symbolic "text" in modern and contemporary Russia. One of the main struggles of working with the image of the Mother of God in any genre is maintaining an awareness of reductionist readings. While the various understandings of her "frame" help us better understand the wide range of meanings and functions of the image of the Mother of God, it is important to appreciate that no single interpretive frame can contain her.

In many instances, as these essays repeatedly testify, Mary herself functions as a framing device that defines and structures discourse on Russian identity, women and gender roles, and the roles of art and religion in society. Although theories of framing developed and took shape primarily in the fields of social psychology and media studies, they provide a useful context in which to discuss and understand potent cultural symbols.[79] Social framing is a system of communication (and in that way overlaps with semiotics and reception theory); it affects how people respond to the ways in which information is shaped and delivered.[80] Like the "relational" experience of Mary, this process is essentially subjective, since any kind of framing includes and excludes, thus creating or conveying only certain perspectives.[81] While it may seem manipulative (news reporting and political rhetoric are frequent subjects of framing studies), the selection of certain frames and cultural symbols as "salient" or "primary" becomes an act of cultural self-definition.[82] Inasmuch as culture can be conceived as a way to explain and locate oneself in a universe of phenomena, framing can be regarded as a way of generating cultural meaning. As frames, the Mother of God and her icon, as well as their associated narratives and their reworking in literature, art, and contemporary Russian media, become a vital source of cultural discourse.

The chapters in this study trace the means by which Mary has framed and has been framed in modern Russian culture with respect to two broad issues: space and place; and women and motherhood. As historian of religion in America Thomas Tweed has argued, among their various functions, religions and their symbols orient people by providing cognitive maps, "socially constructed spatial codes," and a sense of belonging that can be personally healing or socially transformative.[83] Mary in Russia provided such orientation individually and collectively, locally and nationally. As Alexandra Smith and Stella Rock's essays illustrate, Mary's perceived presence demarcated particular urban and rural spaces into iconic realms—transcendent "no places," "not-made-by-human-hands"—drawing in those in search of renewal and strength and ultimately Mary's coveted protection. Largely because of Mary's perceived relationship with her icons, Mary's presence was mobile; carried in processions, her image could overcome separations that often came with geographic distance.

Images of Mary and believers' stories about their encounters with her framed what Elena Boeck has termed "geographies of the sacred." In turn, these personal and local encounters were often collectively reframed by linking them to other more well-known, yet often geographically distant, Marian images. As William Wagner describes in his essay, the abbess of the Convent of the Exaltation of the Cross, Dorofeia, helped to consolidate her convent's standing and her personal authority in the early nineteenth century by promoting the veneration of a local image of the Iveron icon of the Mother of God, whose prototype was associated with the highly revered, male Iveron monastic community on Mount Athos. Similarly, in post-Soviet times, the eighteenth-century Akhtyrka icon of the Mother of God (the subject of Christine Worobec's essay) has become a source for visually legitimizing the specially revered post-Soviet icon of the Mother of God named Holy Cross. As Vera Shevzov's essay shows, this depiction is based on an apparition of Mary during the 1995 siege of a hospital by terrorists in the town of Budyonnovsk, located seventy miles north of Russia's border with Chechnya.

In the eighteenth century, as Elena Boeck's essay notes, Russian churchmen and believers began reframing Russia's Marian images within a more universal context that included Western European images of Mary. In so doing, they affirmed—for those who may have doubted or had not considered it—the place of Russia in sacred history. Such transnational Marian links were a characteristic feature of Russia's modern Marian culture. Eventually, they helped to promote a sense of collective identity among Russia's émigrés following the Bolshevik Revolution, allowing them to imagine a Russia outside of Russia.

At the same time, as her *omophorion* or protective veil suggests, Mary's image could signify borders and boundaries as much as centers. In her essay, Christine Worobec shows how, despite its Western "look," the Akhtyrka icon was embraced as a protectress in Ukrainian border regions against the inroads of Catholic Poland. As Vera Shevzov argues in her essay, post-Soviet Marian mappings of Russia have offered a symbolic means to demarcate Russia from her Western and Eastern neighbors and to promote a sense of national solidarity despite ethnic, religious, and social diversity in the face of perceived "Others." Here, Mary's ancient theological and more modern folkloric associations with land and soil assume geopolitical connotations, dovetailing with patriotic and nationalist sentiments conjured by the notion of motherland.[84] The most notable example of such Marian framing was the 2005 institution of a new national holiday—the Day of National Unity (Den' narodnogo edinstva; 4 November)—chosen in large part because of its correlation with the celebration of the feast of the Kazan icon of the Mother of God on the same date. As Vera Shevzov's essay illustrates, by strategically aligning Russia's celebration of national unity with an image of Mary, church and state officials simultaneously distanced Russia from its Soviet past (the holiday replaced the 7 November anniversary of the Bolshevik Revolution as Russia's national holiday) and mythically reforged its ties with a prerevolutionary past, thus fueling the culture wars that have defined post-Soviet Russia.

As Shevzov's essay argues, clergy and laity have routinely inserted Mary into the cultural market place—the contemporary domain of "the people"— in an effort to rehabilitate Orthodoxy and the Orthodox Church in a society that was not only highly secularized after seventy years of Soviet rule but also "amnesiatic."[85] Doing so, they contributed to the commodification of Mary as an identity marker for all of Russia's citizens. As a result, the Moscow Patriarchate abdicated any perceived exclusive "rights" to Mary as a sacred symbol, and, like Petrov-Vodkin a century before, in effect freed her from dogmatically and institutionally defined frames. Pussy Riot's choice to frame their social and political protest of "Punk Prayer" in Marian terms, for example, confirmed that, in post-Soviet Russia's culture wars, Mary often confounds the secular/religious divide, belonging to no one and everyone.[86]

In addition to the Marian framing of place and space, the essays in this volume also examine her role in shaping Russian cultural discourse about women and motherhood. While Orthodoxy has historically emphasized Mary's motherhood and her pivotal role as a mother in securing the salvation of humankind, it has also traditionally emphasized Mary as a model for all of humanity.[87] Yet despite this feature of Orthodox thought, many of Russia's churchmen, as well as modern, more liberal religious philosophical thinkers, including Sergei Bulgakov and Nikolai Berdiaev, could not escape the cultural and religious mores—especially those related to understandings of sex and sin—in their consideration of Mary. Consequently, as Natalia Ermolaev's essay shows, despite their creative associations between Mary and the figure of Divine Sophia, and despite the Russian religious philosophical striving to reconcile dichotomies in their search for wholeness (*tsel'nost'*) or total-unity (*vseedinstvo*), Mary in these metaphysical constructs often remained disconnected from the realities of most women's (and men's) daily lives. By correlating Mary's Sophianic qualities with those of the ideals of virginity, many of Russia's religious thinkers, including Pavel Florenskii, conceived of Mary foremost in ascetic terms—as a "kind that is predisposed to the virginity of the soul."[88] In this sense, Mary was not "alone of all her sex," but a type of person—male or female—who, as Florenskii argued, from the womb possesses "a special organization of the soul."[89]

At the same time, such views represent only one among several currents of thought in Russia's Marian culture concerning women and gender roles. As essays by Amy Singleton Adams, Alexandra Smith, and Wendy Salmond illustrate, Silver Age artists were inspired by alternate understandings of Mary that contributed to and reflected the empowering features of Russia's cult of motherhood, which was not associated exclusively with family. Artist Kuzma Petrov-Vodkin, for instance, associated motherhood in general—and Mary's motherhood in particular—with a "cosmic electric spark" that could help ignite a spiritual revolution in Russia, while Maxim Gorky, according to Adams, turned to Mary as the central metaphor in his God-building philosophy. Echoing the yearning of her lover, poet Sophia Parnok (1885–1933), for an "alternative" and "feminine" church, poet Marina Tsvetaeva's encounters with the sacred image of Mary, Smith writes, "might be seen as an embodiment of the Solov'evean model of active involvement in the salvation of the world" through the contemplation of her icon-poems. As Vera Shevzov's essay reminds us, the Silver Age thirst for "living" icons found resonance with some contemporary Russian women almost a century later in Pussy Riot's call for the *Bogoroditsa* to become a feminist.

Essays in this volume challenge Soviet ethnographer Nikolai Matorin's observation in 1931 that devotion to the Mother of God distracted women from the kind of social activism that gave women a voice and a place in the social sphere.[90] The two abbesses who are the subject of William Wagner's essay (Dorofeiia [Martynova, d. 1830] and Taisiia [Solopova, d. 1915]) consolidated their authority among their female monastics and in the wider community in large part because of their special devotion to Mary. Both women used their authority to establish and engage in education, health, and welfare programs, which further increased the prominence and power of the convents. Inspired by Mary, these women used a different model of Mary's motherhood than their male counterparts, who often emphasized her modesty, meekness, and obedience.

Similarly, Ermolaev argues, as a mother, émigré activist and theologian Mother Maria Skobtsova drew on Mary's motherhood as a model of radical love necessary for the genuine mending of a fragmented world. Elizabeth Skomp shows how, in response to social and political realities that differed from that of their Western feminist counterparts, some of Russia's most active feminists in the 1970s and 1980s turned to the image of Mary in their struggle against the "equality among genderless slaves" that the Soviet state propagated as equality between the sexes.[91] They imagined Mary "descending into the hell of Russian life" and traveling through Russia in the guise of a simple Russian woman. Indeed, similar to Leila Ahmed's observations regarding ways of knowing in Islamic cultures, these essays imply that women's understandings of Mary often differed from that of (especially clerical) men and proved no less culturally and politically formative.[92] Goricheva's pull toward Mary's motherhood remains fundamentally distinct from ideals of motherhood that, as the essay by Vera Shevzov relates, have characterized often male and clerically driven public discourse about women on family values, reproductive rights, and family planning in post-Soviet society.[93]

Twenty-five years after the fall of communism and a millennium after her introduction into Rus', Mary is back in the news. She has entered the public sphere with people from various sides of the post-Soviet cultural and political fronts that invoke her image to support their various causes. Church and state officials have staked their wagers on her traditional image as a legitimizing "protectress of statehood," only to stir nationalist sentiments and fuel political opposition.[94] In 2015, for example, a fringe group of Russian nationalists composed a prayer modeled on Nikolai Gogol's 1846 poetic paean to the *Bogoroditsa*, "A Prayer (To You, O Mother Most Holy)" (Molitva [K Tebe, o Mater' Presviataia]) in honor of Vladimir Putin's sixtieth birthday. In place of Mary, however, the wildly pro-Putin activist group calling itself the National Committee +60 (Natsional'nyi komitet +60) appeals to *Putin* as the "protector of the unfortunate" to "free [the supplicant's] spirit from evil and harm."[95] Putin's critics have also drawn on the image of Mary to market a different message. In 2012, in the wake of the Pussy Riot affair, the embattled artist Artem Loskutov painted an image of the icon of the Mother of God named the Sign (Znamenie) wearing a balaclava in a show of support for the imprisoned women, for which he was accused of fomenting religious divisions.[96] That same year, designer Katia Dobriakova, inspired by the well-known ancient Iveron icon of the Mother of God, created a tee shirt that featured the then anti-Putin social and political commentator Ksenia Sobchak as Mary to mark the launch of Sobchak's women's magazine, *Style, News, Commentary*.[97] Not surprisingly, both sides of the civil conflict in Ukraine have also claimed Mary as their vanguard, with her image firmly entrenched on the barricades of Maidan and fastened to riot shields.

The essays in this volume show how these wide-ranging appropriations of the image of Mary are all part of a rich and complex heritage that has imagined her as a lovely maiden, an enticing beauty, a personal manifestation of divine femininity and wisdom, a reprimanding disciplinarian, a revolutionary, a warrior, and a political activist. Simon Coleman has aptly noted that, as a symbol, Mary is "able to sustain a range of referents within the same form."[98] Thus, she endures as Russia's most cherished cultural resource, and will remain valued for reasons both of faith and beyond faith for a long time to come.

## NOTES

1. Please consult the glossary at the end of this volume for more detailed information concerning stories related to the various Mother of God icons to which this volume refers. The title of the introduction refers to words from an ancient apocryphal story that describes Mary's death. See

J. K. Elliott, ed., "The Discourse of St. John the Divine Concerning the Falling Asleep of the Holy Mother of God," in *The Apocryphal New Testament* (New York: Oxford University Press, 1993), 706–7. The first quotation comes from a liturgical service, composed in the late fifteenth or early sixteenth century, in honor of the Vladimir icon of the Mother of God (*Sretenie chudotvornyia ikony Presviatyia Bogoroditse, iazhe naritsaetsia "Vladimirskaia"*) celebrated annually on 3 June (21 May, O.S.). *Mineia. Mai. Chast' vtoraia* (Moscow: Moscow Patriarchate, 1987), 320.

2. Sergei Bulgakov, *The Orthodox Church* (Crestwood, NY: St. Vladimir's Seminary Press, 1988), 133.

3. For an overview of the history of the well-known titles of Mary "Birthgiver of God" or "God Bearer" (*Theotokos, Bogoroditsa*) and "Mother of God" (*Meter Theou, Bogomater'*), see Ioli Kalavrezou, "Images of the Mother: When the Virgin Mary Became *Meter Theou*," *Dumbarton Oaks Papers*, no. 44 (1990): 165–72.

4. Scholarship on Mary in the West has grown significantly since Marina Warner's now classic study *Alone of All of Her Sex: The Myth and Cult of the Virgin Mary* (New York: Alfred A. Knopf, 1976). Examples of recent social and cultural studies of the modern Marian phenomenon include: Chris Maunder, *Our Lady of the Nations: Apparitions of Mary in Twentieth-Century Catholic Europe* (New York: Oxford University Press, 2016); Lisa M. Bitel, *Our Lady of the Rock: Vision and Pilgrimage in the Mojave Desert* (Ithaca, NY: Cornell University Press, 2015); Jalane D. Schmidt, *Cachita's Streets: The Virgin of Charity, Race, and Revolution in Cuba* (Durham, NC: Duke University Press, 2015); Joseph P. Laycock, *The Seer of Bayside: Veronica Lueken and the Struggle to Define Catholicism* (NY: Oxford University Press, 2014); Alicia Gaspar de Alba and Alma López, *Our Lady of Controversy: Alma López's Irreverent Apparition* (Austin, TX: University of Texas Press, 2011); Elaine A. Peña, *Performing Piety: Making Space Sacred with the Virgin of Guadalupe* (Berkeley: University of California Press, 2011); Anna-Karina Hermkens, Willy Jansen, and Catrien Notermans, *Moved by Mary: The Power of Pilgrimage in the Modern World* (Burlington, VT: Ashgate, 2009); Apolito Paolo, *The Internet and the Madonna: Religious Visionary Experience on the Web*, trans. Antony Shugaar (Chicago: University of Chicago Press, 2005); Thomas A. Tweed, *Our Lady of the Exile: Diasporic Religion at a Cuban Catholic Shrine in Miami* (New York: Oxford University Press, 1997).

5. For examples of recent scholarship on Mary in late antiquity and Byzantium, see Stephen J. Shoemaker, *Mary in Early Christian Faith and Devotion* (New Haven, CT: Yale University Press, 2016); Leslie Brubaker and Mary B. Cunningham, eds., *The Cult of the Mother of God in Byzantium: Texts and Images* (Burlington, VT: Ashgate, 2011); Chris Maunder, ed., *The Origins of the Cult of the Virgin Mary* (London: Burns and Oates, 2008); Bissera V. Pentcheva, *Icons and Power: The Mother of God in Byzantium* (University Park: Pennsylvania State University Press, 2006); Maria Vassilaki, *Images of the Mother of God: Perceptions of the Theotokos in Byzantium* (Burlington, VT: Ashgate, 2005); Nicholas Constas, *Proclus of Constantinople and the Cult of the Virgin in Late Antiquity* (Leiden: Brill, 2003); Stephen J. Shoemaker, *Ancient Traditions of the Virgin Mary's Dormition and Assumption* (New York: Oxford University Press, 2002). For studies of the Mother of God in modern Eastern Christian cultures, see Jill Dubisch, *In a Different Place: Pilgrimage, Gender, and Politics at a Greek Island Shrine* (Princeton, NJ: Princeton University Press, 1995).

6. As examples, see Miri Rubin, *Mother of God: A History of the Virgin Mary* (New Haven, CT: Yale University Press, 2009); Sarah Jane Boss, ed., *Mary: The Complete Resource* (New York: Oxford University Press, 2007); Jaroslav Pelikan, *Mary through the Centuries: Her Place in the History of Culture* (New Haven, CT: Yale University Press, 1996); Sandra Zimdars-Swartz, *Encountering Mary: From La Salette to Medjugorje* (Princeton, NJ: Princeton University Press, 1991).

7. Examples of more focused studies on the Marian phenomenon in modern and contemporary Russia include Vera Shevzov, "Mary and Women in Late Imperial Russian Orthodoxy," in *Women in Nineteenth-Century Russia: Lives and Culture*, ed. Wendy Rosslyn and Alessandra Tosi (Cambridge: Open Book Publishers, 2012), 63–90; Elena Boeck, "Claiming and Acclaiming Peter I: Ukrainian Contributions to the Visual Commemorations of Petrine Victories," in *Poltava 1709: The Battle and the Myth*, ed. Serhii Plokhy, *Harvard Papers in Ukrainian Studies* 31 (Cambridge, MA: Ukrainian Research Institute of Harvard University, 2012): 271–308; Elena Boeck, "Strength in Numbers or Unity

in Diversity? Compilations of Miracle-Working Virgin Icons," in *Alter Icons: The Russian Icon and Modernity*, ed. Jefferson J. A. Gatrall and Douglas Greenfield (University Park: Pennsylvania State University Press, 2010), 27–49; Vera Shevzov, "Scripting the Gaze: Liturgy, Homilies and the Kazan Icon of the Mother of God in Late Imperial Russia," in *Sacred Stories: Religion and Spirituality in Modern Russia*, ed. Mark D. Steinberg and Heather J. Coleman (Bloomington: Indiana University Press, 2007), 61–92; "Between Popular and Official: Akafisty Hymns and Marian Icons in Late Imperial Russia," in *Letters from Heaven: Popular Religion in Russia and Ukraine*, ed. John-Paul Himka and Andriy Zayarnyuk (Toronto: University of Toronto Press, 2006), 251–77; Eugene Clay, "The Church of the Transfiguring Mother of God and Its Role in Russian Nationalist Discourse, 1984–1999," *Novo Religio: The Journal of Alternative and Emergent Religions* 3, no. 2 (April 2000): 320–49; Julie de Sherbinin, *Chekhov and Russian Religious Culture: The Poetics of the Marian Paradigm* (Evanston, IL: Northwestern University Press, 1997); Sergei S. Averintsev, "The Image of the Virgin Mary in Russian Piety," *Gregorianum* 75, no. 4 (1994): 611–22; Joanna Hubbs, *Mother Russia: The Feminine Myth in Russian Culture* (Bloomington: Indiana University Press, 1993).

8. Most publications regarding Mary the Mother of God in post-Soviet Russia remain quasi-confessional and limited in academic rigor. Of notable exception is the attention that has been given to the critical examination of aspects of Russia's Marian culture by art historians, anthropologists, ethnographers, sociologists, and scholars of feminism. As examples, see M. B. Pliukhanova, *"Kipenie Sveta": Russkie Odigitrii v liturgicheskoi poezii i v istorii* (St. Petersburg: Pushkinskii Dom, 2016); V. G. Chentsova, *Ikona Iverskoi Bogomateri: Ocherki istorii otnoshenii Grecheskoi tserkvi s Rossiei v seredine XVII v. po dokumentam RGADA* (Moscow: Indrik, 2010); D. I. Lebedev, *Istoriia sobornykh khramov Feodorovskogo i Uspenskogo v gorode Kostrome: V sviazi s povest'iu o Feodorovskoi ikone Bogomateri, kratkoi istoriei i topografiei drevnego goroda* (Kostroma: Kostromaizdat, 2010); I. V. Samsonova, *Ikonograficheskaia traditsiia izobrazheniia Akafista Bogomateri v russkoi kul'ture XV–XVIII vekov* (Shuia: Shuiskii gosudarstvennyi pedagogicheskii universitet, 2010); V. M. Kirillin, *Skazanie o Tikhvinskoi ikone Bogomateri "Odigitriia": Literaturnaia istoriia pamiatnika do XVII veka, ego soderzhatel'naia spetsifika v sviazi s kul'turnoi epokhi* (Moscow: Iazyki slavanskikh kul'tur, 2007); Olga Lipovskaya, "The Mythology of Womanhood in Contemporary 'Soviet' Culture," in *Women in Russia: A New Era in Russian Feminism*, ed. Anastasia Posadskaya-Vanderbeck et al. (New York: Verso, 1994), 123–34.

9. Henry Adams, *Mont-Saint-Michel and Chartres* (London: Constable, 1936), 17.

10. For a discussion of relationality and sacred presence in history, see Robert A. Orsi, "Abundant History: Marian Apparitions as Alternative Modernity," in Hermkens, Jansen, and Notermans, eds, *Moved by Mary*, 215–25.

11. Robert A. Orsi, *Between Heaven and Earth: The Religious Worlds People Make and the Scholars Who Study Them* (Princeton, NJ: Princeton University Press, 2005), 62.

12. On Mary's function as "master symbol" within societies, see Eric R. Wolf, "Aspects of Group Relations in a Complex Society: Mexico," *American Anthropologist* 58, no. 6 (1956): 1065–78; and "The Virgin of Guadalupe: A Mexican National Symbol," *The Journal of American Folklore* 71, no. 279 (January–March 1958): 34–39; Cathelijne de Busser and Anna Niedźwiedź, "Mary in Poland: A Polish Master Symbol," in Hermkens, Jansen, and Notermans, eds, *Moved by Mary*, 87–100.

13. Nikolai Matorin, *Zhenskoe bozhestvo v pravoslavnom kul'te: Piatnitsa-bogoroditsa* (Moscow: Moskovskii rabochii, 1931), 8–10.

14. Orsi, *Between Heaven and Earth*, 51.

15. Dubisch, *In a Different Place*, 236; Hubbs, *Mother Russia*, 100, 102; Judith Kornblatt, *Divine Sophia: The Wisdom Writings of Vladimir Solovyov* (Ithaca, NY: Cornell University Press, 2009), 52. When Russia's well-known poets wrote about the "Madonna," they usually did so in reference to a Western work of art. See, for instance, E. A. Boratynskii, "Madonna," A. N. Maikov, "Madonna," and K. D. Bal'mont, "Spiashchaia Madonna." For emphasis on Mary's motherhood in Russian culture rather than on her virginity, see examples of more recent studies: Adele Barker, *The Mother Syndrome in the Russian Folk Imagination* (Columbus, OH: Slavica, 1986), 48; O. G. Isupova, "The Social Meaning of Motherhood in Russia Today," *Russian Social Science Review* 43, no. 5 (September–October 2002): 23–43.

16. Sergei Averintsev, "Gorizont sem'i: O nekotorykh konstantakh traditsionnogo russkogo soznaniia," *Novi mir*, no. 2 (2000): 171.

17. See, for instance, E. Ann Matter, "Apparitions of the Virgin Mary in the Late Twentieth Century: Apocalyptic, Representation, Politics," *Religion* 31, no. 2 (2001): 125–53. Also see the map of Marian sightings in the 2015 feature article, "The World's Most Powerful Woman," by Maureen Orth in *National Geographic*, December 2015, 40–41.

18. Daniel H. Kaiser, "Icons and Private Devotion among Eighteenth-Century Moscow Townsfolk," *Journal of Social History* 45, no. 1 (2011): 128–29. The observation that the image of Mary was more dominant than even that of Jesus in Russian Orthodoxy has been repeatedly noted. For example, see D. Samarin, "Bogoroditsa v russkom narodnom pravoslavii," *Russkaia mysl'* 3–4 (1918): 1–3; Nikolai Berdiaev, *Dusha Rossii* (1915; repr., Leningrad: Skaz, 1990), 10.

19. V. V. Doronikin, *O Tikhvinskoi chudotvornoi ikone Bozhiei Materi, nakhodiashcheisia v Ranenburgskoi Petropavlovskoi pustyne, Riazanskoi eparkhii* (Kasimov, 1911), 1.

20. A good example of the lasting cultural impact of such stories can be seen in Dostoevsky's allusion to the well-known Byzantine apocryphal tale of "The Wanderings of the Mother of God through Hell" in his novel *The Brothers Karamazov*. Fyodor Dostoevsky, *The Brothers Karamazov*, trans. Constance Garnett (New York: Barnes & Noble Classics, 2004), 229. For the Byzantine *Apocalypse of the Theotokos*, composed between the ninth and eleventh centuries, see Jane Baun, *Tales from Another Byzantium: Celestial Journey and Local Community in the Medieval Greek Apocrypha* (New York: Cambridge University Press, 2007). For this text's introduction into ancient Rus' with the title *Khozhdenie Bogoroditsy po mukam*, see V. V. Mil'kov, *Drevnerusskie apokrify* (St. Petersburg: Izd-vo Russkogo Khristianskogo gumanitarnogo instituta, 1999), 21–24. For a history of the apocryphal story of Mary's death, see Shoemaker, *The Ancient Traditions*. For a discussion of the ancient genre of Mary's *Life* in modern Russian culture, see Shevzov, "Mary and Women."

21. The origins of this Marian feast are murky and, though they involve supposed events in tenth-century Constantinople, the feast was indigenous to Orthodoxy in Russia. For a detailed history of this feast, see Mariia Pliukhanova, *Siuzhety i simvoly Moskovskogo tsarstva* (St. Petersburg: Akropol, 1995), 23–62.

22. For a historical overview of this transmission process, see Mil'kov, *Drevnerusskie apokrify*, 18–45.

23. A German painter participated in the decoration of this prayer room. Isolde Thyrêt, "The Queen of Heaven and the Pious Maiden Ruler: Mariological Imagery in the Iconographic Program of Sofiia Alekseevna's Prayer Room," *Harvard Ukrainian Studies* 28, nos. 1–4 (2006): 629; 633–34.

24. Elliott, "The Discourse of St. John the Divine." For the history of the Dormition narrative, see Shoemaker, *The Ancient Traditions*.

25. N. P. Kondakov, *Ikonografiia Bogomateri* (St. Petersburg: Tipografiia imperatorskoi akademii nauk, 1914), 1:3.

26. For a detailed study of the *skazanie* with respect to icons of the Mother of God, see Andreas Ebbinghaus, *Die altrussischen Marienikonen-Legenden* (Wiesbaden: Harrassowitz, 1990).

27. A. A. Turilov, "Skazaniia o chudotvornykh ikonakh v kontekste istorii ikh pochitanii na Rusi," in *Relikvii v iskusstve i kul'ture vostochnokhristianskogo mira*, ed. A. M. Lidov (Moscow: Radunitsa, 2000), 64–67.

28. V. A. Kuchkin and T. A. Sumnikova, "Drevneishaia redaktsiia skazaniia ob ikone Vladimirskoi Bogomateri," in *Chudotvornaia ikona v Vizantii i drevnei Rusi*, ed. A. M. Lidov (Moscow: Martis, 1996), 476–509; V. O. Kliuchevskii, *Skazanie o chudesakh Vladimirskoi ikony Bozhiei Materi* (St. Petersburg, 1878); L. A. Shchennikova, "Chudotvornaia ikona 'Bogomater' Vladimirskaia' kak 'Odigitriia' Evangelista Luki," in Lidov, *Chudotvornaia ikona*, 252.

29. Wil van den Bercken, *Holy Russia and Christian Europe: East and West in the Religious Ideology of Russia*, trans. John Bowden (London: SCM Press, 1999), 37–38.

30. See, as an example, the mid-fourteenth-century account that describes the battle between the Novgorodians and the Suzdalians in the year 1170 and the role of the icon of the Mother of God of the Sign in that battle. "Skazanie o bitve novogorodtsev s suzdal'tsami" (also known as "Slovo o

znamenii sviatoi Bogoroditsy v god 6677 (1169))," in *Biblioteka literatury Drevnei Rusi*, ed. D. S. Likhachev et al., (Leningrad: Nauka, 1987), 6: 444–49.

31. G. Iu. Filippovskii, "Skazanie o pobede nad volzhskimi Bolgarami 1164," in *Slovar' knizhnikov i knizhnosti drevnei Rusi XI–pervaia polovina XIV v.*, ed. D. S. Likhachev (Leningrad: Nauka, 1987), 411–12.

32. "Skazanie o chudesakh Vladimirskoi ikony Bozhiei Materi," in *Biblioteka literatury drevnei Rusi* (St. Petersburg: Nauka, 2004), 4:218–25; Kuchkin and Sumnikova, "Drevneishaia redaktsiia," 476–509. Regarding the practice of immersing icons and relics in water, see Shchennikova, "Chudotvornaia ikona," 259.

33. For examples of accounts regarding Mary's protection of Rus' cities, including during times of civil strife, see Pliukhanova, *Siuzhety i simvoly*, 31–44; 48.

34. Gail Lenhoff, "Novgorod's *Znamenie* Legend in Moscow's *Stepennaia kniga*," in *Moskovskaia Rus: Spetsifika razvitiia*, ed. Gyula Szvák (Budapest: Magyar Ruszisztkai Intézet, 2003), 175–82.

35. "Povest' na sretenie chudotvornago obraza Prechistyia Vladichitsy nasheia Bogoroditsy i Prisnodevy Marii," in *Polnoe Sobranie Russkikh Letopisei* (St. Petersburg: Tip. Eduarda Pratsa, 1913), 424–40.

36. "Povest' na sretenie," 435; Shchennikova, "Chudotvornaia ikona"; Gail Lenhoff, "Temir Aksak's Dream of the Virgin as Protectress of Muscovy," *Die Welt der Slaven* 49 (2004): 39–64; David B. Miller, "Legends of the Icon of Our Lady of Vladimir: A Study of the Development of Muscovite National Consciousness," *Speculum* 43, no. 4 (October 1968): 657–70.

37. E. M. Saenkova and S. V. Sverdlova, *Simon Ushakov: Drevo gosudarstva Moskovskogo* (Moscow: Gosudarstvennaia Tret'iakovskaia galeria, 2015).

38. *Polnoe sobranie russkikh letopisei (Patriarshaia ili Nikonovskaia letopis')* (1897; repr. Moscow: Nauka, 1965), 11: 221–23.

39. Stephen Benko, *The Virgin Goddess: Studies in the Pagan and Christian Roots of Mariology* (Leiden: Brill, 2004); Philippe Borgeaud, *Mother of the Gods: From Cybele to the Virgin Mary*, trans. Lysa Hochroth (Baltimore, MD: The Johns Hopkins University Press, 2004); Vasiliki Limberis, *Divine Heiress: The Virgin Mary and the Creation of Christian Constantinople* (New York: Routledge, 1994). For scholars who have followed a similar line of inquiry for Russia, see, for example, Hubbs, *Mother Russia*, 99–101, 110–16; Moshe Lewin, "Popular Religion in Twentieth-Century Russia," in *The World of the Russian Peasant: Post-Emancipation Culture and Society*, ed. Ben Eklof and Stephen P. Frank (Boston: Unwin Hyman, 1990), 155–57; Linda J. Ivanits, *Russian Folk Belief* (New York: M. E. Sharpe, 1989).

40. Sergei Maksimov, *Nechistaia, nevedomaia i krestnaia sila* (St. Petersburg: Golike i Vil'borg, 1903), 221.

41. Philologist Aleksei Popov argued, for instance, that upon their conversion to Christianity, the Rus' did not identify the figure of Mary with previous goddess figures or divine feminine symbols, but understood her as a distinct figure in her own right. In his estimation, the illiterate acquired their main understanding of Mary though liturgy, sermons, prayers, lives of saints, and stories associated with Marian icons. Aleksei Popov, *Vliianie tserkovnago ucheniia i drevnerusskoi dukhovnoi pis'mennosti na mirosozertsanie russkago narod i v chastnosti na narodnuiu slovesnost', v drevnii do Petrovskii period* (Kazan: Tip. imp. universiteta, 1883), 152–72. For an example of those who sought the foundations of modern Marian devotion in pre-Christian beliefs, see Aleksandr Afanas'ev, *Poeticheskie vozzreniia slavian na prirodu*, 3 vols. (Moscow: K. Soldatenkov, 1865–1869). Some scholars, however, have maintained that "Mother Damp Earth" was associated more with the goddess Piatnitsa. I. K. Kondrovskii, "Ostatki kul'ta bogini-materi v nastoiashchee vremia," *Izvestiia Tavricheskogo obshchestva istorii, arkheologii i etnografii* 11, no. 59 (1928): 77–85.

42. For a study of the notion of "dual faith" or "dual belief" in Russia, see Stella Rock, *Popular Religion in Russia: "Double Belief" and the Making of an Academic Myth* (New York: Routledge, 2007).

43. Matorin, *Zhenskoe bozhestvo*.

44. As examples, see Mary Daly, *Beyond God the Father: Toward a Philosophy of Women's Liberation* (Boston, MA: Beacon Press, 1973); Starhawk, *The Spiral Dance: A Rebirth of the Ancient Religion of the Goddess* (San Francisco, CA: Harper and Row, 1989); Cynthia Eller, *Living in the Lap of the Goddess:*

*The Feminist Spirituality Movement in America* (Boston, MA: Beacon Press, 1995); Carol P. Christ, *Rebirth of the Goddess: Finding Meaning in Feminist Spirituality* (Reading, MA: Addison-Wesley, 1997).

45. James Cracraft, *The Petrine Revolution in Russian Imagery* (Chicago: University of Chicago Press, 1997).

46. On the Sistine Madonna as a key symbol of Dostoevsky's religious-aesthetic philosophy of art, for example, see Robert Louis Jackson, *Dostoevsky's Quest for Form* (New Haven, CT: Yale University Press, 1966), 40–70; and Joseph Frank, *Dostoevsky: The Mantle of the Prophet, 1871–1881* (Princeton, NJ: Princeton University Press, 2003), 463–64.

47. A well-known example of this trend is the Ukrainian churchman Ioannikii Galiatovskii's *Nebo novoe s novymi zvezdami sotvorennoe, t.e. Preblagoslovennaia Deva Mariia s chudami Svoimi*, first published in Polish (Lvov: Tip. Mikhaila Slezki, 1665). The work was translated into Russian in 1677. N. F. Sumtsov, *Ocherki istorii iuzhno-russkikh apokrificheskikh skazanii i pesen'* (Kiev: Tip. A. Davidenko, 1888), 3–4. Also see I. I. Ogienko, *Legendarno-apokrificheskii element v "Nebe Novom" Ioannikiia Goliatovskago, iuzhno-russkago propovednika VII-go veka* (Kiev: Tip. T. G. Meinandera, 1913); Gary Marker, "Narrating Mary's Miracles and the Politics of Location in Late 17th-Century East Slavic Orthodoxy," *Kritika: Explorations in Russian and Eurasian History* 15, no. 4 (Fall 2014): 695–727. Greek churchmen penned similar compendia, but as a genre, compendia of miracle stories associated with Marian icons became much more popular in Russia. V. V. Lepakhin, *Skazaniia o chudotvornykh ikonakh v drevenrusskoi slovesnosti* (Moscow: Palomnik, 2012), 163–94. For an analysis of the Marian compendia phenomenon in Russia, see Boeck, "Strength in Numbers," and Marker, "Narrating Mary's Miracles."

48. Sergii (Spasskii), *Russkaia literatura ob ikonakh Presviatyia Bogoroditsy v XIX v.* (St. Petersburg, 1900).

49. The akathist in honor of Mary, "The Bright Abode of Homeless Wanderers" ("Akafist Presviatoi Bogoroditse, Svetloi Obiteli strannikov bezdomnykh") was reportedly written by the priest Georgii Spasskii in the 1930s. *Akafist Presviatei Bogoroditse, Svetloi Obiteli strannikov bezdomnykh* (New York: Zarubezhnaia Rus', 1971).

50. Alexander V. Muller, ed. and trans., *The Spiritual Regulation of Peter the Great* (Seattle: University of Washington Press, 1972), 15. Also see P. V. Znamenskii, "Zakonodatel'stvo Petra Velikago otnositel'no chistoty very i blagochestiia tserkovnago," *Pravoslavnyi sobesednik*, no. 12 (December 1864): 290–340. For more recent discussions, see Paul Bushkovitch, "Popular Religion in the Time of Peter the Great," in *Letters from Heaven: Popular Religion in Russia and Ukraine*, ed. John-Paul Himka and Andriy Zayarnyuk (Toronto: University of Toronto Press, 2006),146–64; Simon Dixon "Superstition in Imperial Russia," *Past and Present* 199, Supplement 3 (2008): 209, 218; Eve Levin, "False Miracles and Unattested Dead Bodies: Investigations into Popular Cults in Early Modern Russia," in *Religion and the Early Modern State: Views from China, Russia, and the West*, ed. James D. Tracy and Marguerite Ragnow (Cambridge: Cambridge University Press, 2004), 260.

51. E. I. Loviagin, "Sobytiia voskreseniia Iisusa Khrista," *Khristianskoe chtenie*, no. 4 (1869): 559.

52. "Egorov, Aleksei Egorovich," Artcyclopedia.ru, http://artcyclopedia.ru/egorov_aleksej_egorovich.htm.

53. See, for instance, Mikhail Lermontov's "Prayer" ("Molitva"), Anna Akhmatova's "July 1914" ("Iiul' 1914") and *Requiem* (Rekviem), and Blok's *Italian Poems* (Italianskie stikhi). The image of the Mother of God in Dostoevsky's work is ubiquitous, most notably in "The Landlady" ("Khoziaka," 1847), "A Gentle Creature" ("Krotkaia," 1876), "The Peasant Marey" ("Muzhik Marei," 1876), *Demons/The Possessed* (Besy, 1871–1872), *The Brothers Karamazov* (Brat'ia Karamazovy, 1879–1880) and *The Idiot* (Idiot, 1868–1869). For the role of the Madonna in Blok's work, see Jenifer Presto, *Beyond the Flesh: Alexander Blok, Zinaida Gippius, and the Symbolist Sublimation of Sex* (Madison: University of Wisconsin Press, 2008), 70–105. S. L. Konstantinova considers Blok's treatment of the Virgin Mary in "'Bogorodichnye motivy' v 'Ital'ianskikh stikhakh' A. Bloka," in *Aleksandr Blok i mirovaia kul'tura*, ed. V. V. Musatov and T. V. Igosheva (Velikii Novgorod: Novgorodskii gosudarstvennyi universitet imeni Iaroslava Mudrogo, 2000), 62–68.

54. Sergei Solov'ev, "Vospominaniia ob Aleksandre Bloke," in *Pis'ma Aleksandra Bloka* (Leningrad: Kolos, 1925), 12.

55. Kornblatt, *Divine Sophia*, 51–55. Also see the classic work of Nicolas Zernov, *The Russian Religious Renaissance of the Twentieth Century* (New York: Harper & Row Publishers, 1963).

56. A history of Gorky's reworking of *Mother* to weaken the role of religious imagery in the novel can be found in S. V. Kastorskii, *Povest' M. Gor'kogo "Mat'": Ee obshchestvenno-politicheskoe i literaturnoe znachenie* (Leningrad: Gosudarstvennoe uchebno-pedagogicheskoe izd-vo, 1954), 60–69; 70–104. By the 1980s, *Mother* was widely accepted by Soviet critics as a work of pure Social-ist Realism. See D. M. Stepaniuk, "Ob otnoshenii M. Gor'kogo k antireligioznoi teme v literature," *Voprosy russkoi literatury* 2, no. 24 (1974): 26–32, and Andrei Siniavskii, "Roman M. Gor'kogo *Mat'*—kak ranii obrazets sotsialisticheskogo realizma," *Cahiers du Monde russe et soviétique* 29, no. 1 (1988): 33–40.

57. Andrei Platonov, "Rodina elektrichestva," in *Sobranie sochinenii* (Moscow: Sovetskaia Ros-siia, 1984), 1:63.

58. Victoria E. Bonnell, *Iconography of Power: Soviet Political Posters under Lenin and Stalin* (Berkeley: University of California Press, 1997), 66. See also Elizabeth Waters, "The Female Form in Soviet Political Iconography, 1917–32," in *Russia's Women: Accommodation, Resistance, Transforma-tion*, eds. Barbara Evans Clements, Barbara Alpern Engel, and Christine D. Worobec (Berkeley: Uni-versity of California Press, 1991), 225–42.

59. *Smekhach* (The Jokester), no. 8, 1927.

60. Lynne Attwood, "'Rodina-Mat'' and the Soviet Cinema," in *Gender Restructuring in Russian Studies*, eds. Marianne Liljeström, Eila Mäntysaari, Arja Rosenholm (Tampere, Finland: University of Tampere, 1993), 17.

61. On the Marian imagery in Rasputin's novel, see Gerald E. Mikkelson, "Religious Symbolism in Valentin Rasputin's *Live and Remember*," in *Studies in Honor of Xenia Gasiorowska*, ed. Lauren G. Leighton (Columbus, OH: Slavica Publishers, 1983), 172–87.

62. Although the Madonna figures in Liudmila Petrushevskaia's work of the Stagnation and Perestroika eras are highly problematized, they clearly raise the issue of cultural restoration. On that topic, see Helena Goscilo, "Inscribing the Female Body in Women's Fiction: Cross-Gendered Passion à la Holbein," in *Gender Restructuring in Russian Studies*, 73–86; and Amy Singleton Adams, "The Blood of Children: Petrushevskaia's 'Our Crowd' and the Russian Easter Tale," *Slavic and East European Jour-nal* 56, no. 4 (2012): 612–28.

63. Robert Orsi, *The Madonna of 115th Street: Faith and Community in Italian Harlem, 1880–1950* (New Haven, CT: Yale University Press, 1985); Tweed, *Our Lady of the Exile*; Paul DiMaggio and Patricia Fernández-Kelly, eds., *Art in the Lives of Immigrant Communities in the United States* (New Brunswick, NJ: Rutgers University Press, 2010), 234–38.

64. *Akafist Presviatoi Bogoroditse.*

65. Tweed, *Our Lady of the Exile*, 5.

66. For discussion of the role of religion in the formation of diasporic identities, see Tweed, *Our Lady of the Exile*, 91–98.

67. A. S. Golovina, "Nerukotvornaia," in *Bogoroditsa v russkoi poezii, XVII–XX vv.*, ed. B. N. Romanov (Moscow: Novyi kliuch, 2010), 299–300.

68. For a discussion of sacred objects and museums, see Ronald L. Grimes, "Sacred Objects in Museum Spaces," *Studies in Religion/Sciences Religieuses* 21, no. 4 (1992): 419–30; Crispin Paine, ed., *Godly Things: Museums, Objects and Religion* (London: Leicester University Press, 2000).

69. Patriarch of Moscow and All Rus' Alexei II, Speech at the first meeting of the World Rus-sian People's Council, Stenogramma 1-ogo Vsemirnnogo Russkogo Narodnogo Sobora, 26 May 1993, accessed 29 December 2016, http://www.vrns.ru/documents/54/1283/.

70. Alek Epshtein, "Mobilizovannaia Bogoroditsa: Pank-moleben gruppy 'Pussy Riot' v khrame Khrista Spasitelia," *Neprikosnovennyi zapas* 83 (2012), accessed 29 December 2016, http://www.nlobooks.ru/node/2285.

71. Simone de Beauvoir, *The Second Sex* (New York: Random House, 2012), 180.

72. For Daly, the subordination of humans to God is something negative, especially when this state of affairs is expressed in a feminine symbol such as Mary. See Mary Daly, *Gyn/Ecology: The*

*Metaethics of Radical Feminism* (Boston, MA: Beacon Press, 1978), 84–85. A more recent study on Catholic Poland, however, suggests that certain sectors of contemporary Polish society associate qualities such as responsibility, strength, and independence with the symbol of Mary, thus challenging traditional representations that deprive her of agency and free will. See Agnieszka Koscianska, "Obraz pol'skoi materi i Bogoroditsa: novoe ispol'zovanie simvoliki materinstva," *Gosudarstvo, religiia, tserkov' v Rossii i za rubezhom*, no. 3 (2016): 95–115.

73. Warner, *Alone of All Her Sex*, 161.

74. Hubbs, *Mother Russia*, 87–90.

75. On the idea of "framing" as an expression of women's social and political isolation and exclusion in art and narrative, see Shirley Neilsen Blum, "The Open Window: A Renaissance View," in *The Window in Twentieth-Century Art*, ed. Suzanne Delehanty (Purchase, NY: Neuberger Museum, State University of New York, 1986), 13; and Nehama Aschkenasy, *Woman at the Window: Biblical Tales of Oppression and Escape* (Detroit, MI: Wayne State University Press, 1998), 14, 17–18.

76. Julia Kristeva, "Stabat Mater," *Poetics Today* 6, nos. 1–2 (1985): 147–48.

77. Boris Uspensky, *The Semiotics of the Russian Icon* (Lisse, Belgium: Peter de Ridder Press, 1976), 39–41.

78. For an extensive consideration of the effect, dynamics, and relationships among visual elements of framing, see Theo van Leeuwen, *Introducing Social Semiotics* (London: Routledge, 2004).

79. On the ways that cultural objects function as frames, see Michael Schudson's "How Culture Works: Perspectives from Media Studies on the Efficacy of Symbols," *Theory and Society* 18, no. 2 (1989): 153–80.

80. See especially Robert Entman, "Framing: Toward Clarification of a Fractured Paradigm," *Journal of Communication* 43, no. 4 (1993): 52–53.

81. On the subjectivity of framing, see Titus Ensink, "Transformational Frames: Interpretive Consequences of Frame Shifts and Frame Embeddings," in *Framing and Perspectivising in Discourse*, ed. Titus Ensink and Christoph Sauer (Philadelphia, PA: John Benjamins Publishing, 2003); Entman, "Framing," 53–55.

82. This kind of cultural communication among social groupings is key to the understanding of framing as Erving Goffman describes it in his foundational work on the subject, *Frame Analysis: An Essay on the Organization of Experience* (New York: Harper and Row, 1974). In *Framing Public Life: Perspectives on Media and Our Understanding of the Social World* (Mahwah, NJ: Lawrence Erlbaum, 2001), Stephen D. Reese et al. discuss the social function of framing, its relationship with culture, and the production of meaning.

83. Thomas A. Tweed, *Crossing and Dwelling: A Theory of Religion* (Cambridge, MA: Harvard University Press, 2006), 74–75.

84. A. N. Parshin, "'Bogoroditsa—mat' syra zemlia...' (o trekh lektsiiakh v Moskovskoi dukhovnoi akademii)," in *Filosofiia, bogoslovie i nauka kak opyt tsel'nogo znaniia*, ed. O. M. Sedykh (Moscow: Maks Press, 2012), 295–309.

85. On history and amnesia in post-Soviet society, see Alexander Agadjanian, "Exploring Russian Religiosity as a Source of Morality Today," in *Multiple Moralities and Religions in Post-Soviet Russia*, ed. Jarrett Zigon (New York: Berghahn Books, 2011), 19. Also see historian Andrei Zubov's comments in "Tserkov' mozhet sodeistvovat' stanovleniiu grazhdanskogo obshchestva," *Mir religii*, 1 February 2002, http://www.religio.ru/arch/01feb2002/news/3073.html.

86. See comment by Pussy Riot member Katya Samutsevich in her closing statement during her trial, "Closing Courtroom Statement by Katya," in *Pussy Riot!: A Punk Prayer for Freedom* (New York: The Feminist Press at the City University of New York, 2013), 89.

87. See the observation by sociologist O. G. Isupova in "The Social Meaning of Motherhood," 26–27.

88. Pavel Florenskii, *The Pillar and Ground of the Truth: An Essay in Orthodox Theodicy in Twelve Letters*, trans. Boris Jakim (Princeton, NJ: Princeton University Press, 1997), 258.

89. Florenskii, *The Pillar*, 258.

90. Matorin, *Zhenskoe bozhestvo*, 8.

91. Alla Mitrofanova, "Leningradskii feminism 70-x gg," *Livejournal* (blog), accessed 29 December 2016, http://philologist.livejournal.com/1446235.html.

92. Leila Ahmed, "A Border Passage: From Cairo to America—A Woman's Journey," in *Women's Studies in Religion: A Multicultural Reader*, ed. Kate Bagley and Kathleen McIntosh (Upper Saddle River, NJ: Prentice Hall, 2007), 35–47.

93. As examples, see Irina Aristarkhova, "Trans-lating Gender into the Russian (Con)Text," in *The Making of European Women's Studies*, ed. Rosi Braidotti, Esther Vonk, Sonja van Wichelen (Utrecht: Athena, 2000), 2–74; Arja Rosenholm and Irina Savkina, "'We must all give birth: That's an order': The Russian Mass Media Commenting on V. V. Putin's Address," in *Russian Mass Media and Changing Values*, ed. Arja Rosenholm, Kaarle Nordenstreng, and Elena Trubina (New York: Routledge, 2010), 93.

94. "Putin posetil Uspenskii sobor v Astane," *RIA Novosti*, 15 October 2015, accessed 29 December 2016, http://ria.ru/religion/20151015/1302343837.html.

95. For a copy of the "prayer" to mark Putin's sixtieth birthday, which received wide coverage in the press, see "Patriarkha Kirilla prosiat utverdit' 'Molitvu Putinu,'" *Rossiiskoe informatsionnoe agentstvo*, 8 December 2015, accessed 29 December 2016, http://ura.ru/news/1052233161; "Patriarkha Kirilla prosiat utverdit' 'Molitvu Putinu,'" *Radio Ekho Moskvy*, 9 December 2015, accessed 29 December 2016, http://echo.msk.ru/news/1673778-echo.html. For the text on which this "prayer" was based, see N. V. Gogol', *Sobranie sochinenii v deviati tomakh* (Moscow: Russkaia kniga, 1994), 6:547.

96. Kharym Omarova, "Khudozhnik oshtrafovan za ikony s uchastnitsami gruppy Pussy Riot," *Novye izvestiia*, no. 99, 9 June 2012, 3.

97. "Ksenia Sobchak primerila na sebia obraz Bogoroditsy," *Izvestiia*, 13 September 2012, accessed 29 December 2016, http://izvestia.ru/news/535147; "Ksenia Sobchak predstala v obraze Bogoroditsy na glamurnykh futbolkakh," *Spletnik*, 14 September 2012, accessed 29 December 2016, http://www.spletnik.ru/blogs/pro_zvezd/61347_kseniya-sobchak-predstala-v-obraze-bogoroditcy-na-glamurnykh-futbolkakh.

98. Simon Coleman, "Mary: Images and Objects," in Boss, *Mary*, 400.

# 1

# More Numerous Than the Stars in Heaven

## An Early Eighteenth-Century Multimedia Compendium of Mariology

ELENA N. BOECK[1]

AN ENORMOUS, HANDWRITTEN VOLUME PRESERVES a rich trove of narratives devoted to geographies of the sacred. This illustrated compendium of Mariology testifies to the tremendous cultural ferment of seventeenth-century Russia. Although in most historical narratives this period is consistently overshadowed by the intellectual output generated in the age of Peter the Great, it is important to recall that Russia's intellectual dialogue with distant knowledge, print culture, and encyclopedic scholarship began well before his reign. Orthodox intellectuals from Ukraine and Belarus served as a conduit for connecting literate Russians to Counter-Reformation discourses about the sacred. Well before the intense cultural exchanges that were carried out forcefully, often forcibly, by Peter, Russian intellectuals confronted and contested Western narratives that accorded little recognition to Russia in either the divine plan or the republic of letters.

By copying, arranging, and illustrating narratives about the miraculous appearances of the Mother of God, an unknown patron commissioned the most extensive premodern compilation of Mariology in Russia.[2] The remarkable volume, which heretofore has escaped scholarly notice, is kept in the Moscow State University library (Ms. Slav. 302/Ms. 10536-7-71; *1). The handwritten, mammoth compilation of nearly nine hundred folios is dedicated to the icons and miracles of the Mother of God. Diverse texts of

East Slavic origin celebrate Mary's accomplishments in wide expanses of time and space, but the volume as a whole emphasizes her particular bestowal of grace upon Russia.

This article examines the structure of the compilation and explores its strategies for elevating Russia within a universal framework. By exploring a productive encounter between Russian and "foreign" geographies of the miraculous, as well as the interrelationship between texts and images, this article seeks to highlight an unacknowledged seventeenth-century contribution to the framing of Marian discourse. Although this volume escaped the attention of Andreas Ebbinghaus, whose foundational study *Die altrussischen Marienikonen-Legenden* remains unsurpassed, the anonymous compiler of this volume was interested in a number of the same icons that intrigued his scholarly successor.


THE CONTENT AND CONTEXT OF THE MANUSCRIPT

The volume's biography is incomplete and the manuscript is mute about its intended message. No title page survives. No preface offers verbal rationalization for the volume and its structure. It was "discovered" in the course of a book- and manuscript-collecting expedition conducted by the Moscow State University between 1970 and 1972 in the village of Perevoz (old Starodub), in the Briansk region, which was known for its extensive Old Believer community.[3] In the latter part of the seventeenth century, this area was situated in Polish territory along Russia's western border. Landlords in the area provided a safe haven for religious dissidents and runaway peasants. The Starodub region attracted so many Russian dissidents that it was occasionally referred to as "The Old Believer Capital" in the mid-eighteenth century.[4]

The manuscript's modern discovery in an Old Believer community does not necessarily correlate with its place of production. Paleography dates the manuscript to no later than the first decades of the eighteenth century. The selection of texts, emphasis on particular icons of the Mother of God, and expansive structure of the volume are comparable to the kind of intellectual output that was being generated in Moscow around the end of the seventeenth and beginning of the eighteenth centuries.[5] As the discussion below will demonstrate, the overarching purpose of the volume was to assemble a comprehensive collection of evidence for the continuing grace of the Mother of God to her people by means of miraculous icons and their spectacular miracles.

The volume still retains its original binding of dark brown embossed leather. Bottom corners of pages are consistently greasy and quite dirty, suggesting that the manuscript was frequently read over the centuries. The manuscript consists of eight hundred fifty-three folios that were copied by three different scribal hands.[6] None of its contents can be categorized as original texts written exclusively for this volume. Instead this was an editorial project, the statement of a collector who desired to bring together multiple messages of Marian benevolence. As shown below, an integral component of the volume's larger message can be discerned in a dialogue between different media: texts versus images.

The volume opens with two encyclopedic compilations of miracles performed by the Mother of God in various times and places.[7] The first text is *Nebo novoe* (New heaven); it lacks the title heading, and starts with the first chapter, "The Miracles of the Most Holy Mother of God among the Pagan Seer Sibyls" ("Chudesa Presviatyia Bogoroditsy v sivilakh prorochishchakh iazycheskikh"). It is the longest text in the compilation, which occupies the first 118 folios.[8] The next longest narrative, *Zvezda presvetlaia* (The most brilliant star), follows (fols. 128r–223v).[9] Both texts were composed in the second part of the seventeenth century in east Slavic lands outside of Russia, and both became incredibly popular in Russia due to their linguistic accessibility and reassuringly consistent structure. The former text was written by Ioannikii Galiatovskii and first published in 1665 in Lvov. The authorship of *Zvezda presvetlaia* remains unknown, and, unlike *Nebo novoe*, it circulated only in manuscript format.

The pairing of *Nebo novoe* and *Zvezda presvetlaia* under a single cover is not unusual. Both texts celebrate the miracles produced by the images of the Mother of God. Other manuscripts containing the two texts collated in that order were produced in the late seventeenth century (such as the one in the Russian State Library manuscript division, *fond* 722, number 746), and continued to circulate and be copied well into the nineteenth century. Each of these texts was also very popular in Russia in its own right and actively circulated independently, starting from the latter seventeenth century and continuing well into the nineteenth century (for example, Russian State Library manuscript division, *fond* 722, number 123).[10] However, this manuscript of *Nebo novoe* is remarkable for its rich illustrations, which will be analyzed below, and which remain unique in the corpus of the known manuscripts of the text.

The remainder of the volume consists of twenty-nine narratives, principally of Russian origin, that are dedicated to icons of the Mother of God. It also features five sermons that highlight aspects of the Virgin's biography and one text primarily devoted to the history of a monastery. As discussed below, the visual program of the compilation is overwhelmingly devoted to the Mother of God and her icons. Over 90 percent of the images include a representation of Mary (fifty-five out of sixty-four illustrations). The selection and arrangement of texts reveals that the volume's aim was a collation of universalizing, historically rooted, geographically expansive Marian miracles, which revealed Russia's preferred place in the divine plan.

COMPILATION AS COMPETITION: EXPANDING THE GEOGRAPHY
OF MARIOLOGY

*Nebo novoe* and *Zvezda presvetlaia* were both beguiling and disconcerting texts for a Russian audience. On the one hand, these texts revealed a sweeping, majestic, hitherto unknown geography of miracles performed by the Mother of God and systematically cataloged the continuously ongoing manifestations of her involvement in the human world since the time of Christ. On the other hand, though presented in Orthodox guise, their universal and ecumenical defense of Marian imagery challenged assumptions about the Mother of God's special favor toward Russia.

The compiler of this volume could not have known the complex and fascinating story of how the intellectual ferment of the Counter-Reformation in the Polish-Lithuanian Commonwealth stimulated a new Orthodox impulse to collect, codify, and collate testimonies about religious imagery. *Nebo novoe* and *Zvezda presvetlaia* were Orthodox answers to the encyclopedic Counter-Reformation volumes that started to appear in force from the beginning of the seventeenth century. Their Catholic antecedents were dedicated to the defense of the veneration of the Virgin Mary in the Catholic (and the lost Catholic) lands against the Protestant challenges ranging from the denial of her diverse miraculous manifestations to outright iconoclasm.[11] These works were infused with a universalistic ideology of the presence of the divine and melded together the encyclopedic and collecting interests of the age.[12]

*Nebo novoe* provides a provocative case for considering the nexus between the universal and the particular in Marian devotion. The text is divided into twenty-eight chapters of widely varied length. Each chapter begins with a clearly demarcated standardized title written in red ink: "The Miracles of the Most Holy Mother of God among . . ." The rigidly consistent chapter headings clearly signal that the overarching narrative emphasis belongs to the Mother of God, while the evidence of her miraculous deeds is divided among various categories of sentient beings ranging from monks to evil spirits. No place is singled out as the special locus of her favor. Most chapters feature a range of miracles that happened in various places and at various times. Although the range of examples suggests a wide chronology ranging over several centuries, actual dates are rarely supplied.

The expansive geographies and diverse beneficiaries of divine miracles presented in *Nebo novoe* testified that the Mother of God was working miracles in all places, in all times, among all kinds of people. A catalogue of miracles from a single chapter, chapter 14, folios 23v–32v—organized around the miracles "for those who pray" will demonstrate the point. The following persons and locations are mentioned in the chapter in the order of their appearance: Maria in the city of Taraskona (presumably the Spanish Tarragona); the French city of Skesion; a certain pious woman in Marsilii (presumably the French Marseilles); the city of Ankona; the city of Evora; Father Daniil Skitskii; Foma, archbishop of Kantuaria (presumably Cantabria); Genovefa daughter of the prince of Brabant; Temir (*sic* Timur) who assailed *Velikaia Rossiia* (great Russia); Rome; *grechestyi* (*sic* Greek) Tsar Iraklii; Constantinople attacked by a Persian Sarvar; another *grechestyi* (*sic* Greek) Tsar Constantine Pogonat; brothers Goratsii and Mutsii in a neighborhood of Rome; someone living in Koln (Cologne); Alfons the bishop of Toleto (Toledo); Bonet, the bishop of Alverena; Eronim in the city of Papia; Marko in Little Russia's region of *Galitsia* (Galicia); the island of Tumba (*sic* Cuba) on "*mori okianskom*" (ocean sea); Stephan, king of Hungary (twice); Ioanna, queen of France; Maria Zegniia; Indians (*indiane*) in the city of Antipol; Antonii in the Albingensian land; Dikadus in the city of Dokmentsiia in Spain; Peter who reached the city of Ruan in Flanders; and a ship traveling from Aeziutaniia (presumably Lusitania, Portugal) to Spain. Furthermore, St. Catherine (twice) and St. John of Damascus also become beneficiaries of the miracles in this chapter.

Such passages both expanded and challenged Russians' understanding of sacred topography. Almost all of these miracles would have been unknown in seventeenth-century Russia. Most of the geography was strange and unfamiliar, as demonstrated by the curious transformations introduced by the translator. Only attentive Russian readers of translated European cosmographies could have possessed even a vague sense how these various locations related to one another. Among the thirty-two miracles that were compiled for this chapter, at least twenty-five took place in Catholic territories. Providential benevolence even reached as far as the Spanish transatlantic possessions. Only seven of the thirty-two miracles could be remotely associated with the Orthodox world.

More importantly, these compilations challenged local notions of Russia's controlling share of Marian benediction. In chapter after chapter, catalogues of miracles suggested that the Mother of God showed no particular favor to

Russia. A moment of productive confrontation between multiple modes of Mariology explains the genesis of our compilation. Galiatovskii's encounter with Catholic polemical literature provoked a desire to incorporate Orthodox examples into an existing universalistic narrative framework that was heavily weighted toward the Catholic world. The unknown late seventeenth-century Russian compiler admired Galiatovskii's effort, but desired to elevate Russia's place within the universal geography of Marian devotion. His compilation became a competition with the work of Galiatovskii. While admiring and privileging *Nebo novoe* as the foundational text of the compilation, the Russian bookman strove to outshine his predecessor by creating a monumental testimonial to Russia's particular favor in the divine plan. As the essay by Vera Shevzov in this volume suggests, similar patriotic impulses still motivate Russian attempts to "imagine the wide expanse of Russia's geography in Marian terms."[13]

The creator of this compilation countered his predecessors with a compilation of his own. Although he assigned *Nebo novoe* (fols. 1–116r) and *Zvezda presvetlaia* (fols. 128r–223v) an honored place at the beginning of his Marian anthology, these catalysts for his work would only comprise a quarter of the new collection. In his collection the particular would prevail over the universal. Narratives primarily centered on Russia account for over 60 percent of the compilation, substantially more if cases that are partially associated with Russia are included in the count.

Although *Nebo novoe* and *Zvezda presvetlaia* remained the longest compositions, with the former occupying 13.6 percent of the compilation and the latter occupying 11.13 percent, a narrative dedicated to the Shuia icon is the third longest text in the compilation. Its ninety-two folios (fols. 652r–744r) comprise 10.78 percent of the compilation. The inclusion of this interesting narrative reveals more about the creator of the compilation than it might seem to at first glance.

The Shuia icon tale was relatively new and its miracles had become a source of controversy in the 1660s. The compilation includes one of the very earliest copies of "The Narrative of the Smolensk Mother of God icon in Shuia, in the church of the Resurrection of Christ, which is located in the merchant quarter." Dated by Ebbinghaus to the eighteenth century, Bulanin has recently proposed that it was written soon after a series of miraculous healings that took place in 1666.[14] Its inclusion in the compilation, however, excludes the possibility that the tale was written to promote or revive the icon's cult in the mid-eighteenth century.

The narrative celebrates the miracles of the "newly painted"[15] (*novopisannyia*) icon of the Smolensk Mother of God (see fig. 1.1). Because this was a new image,

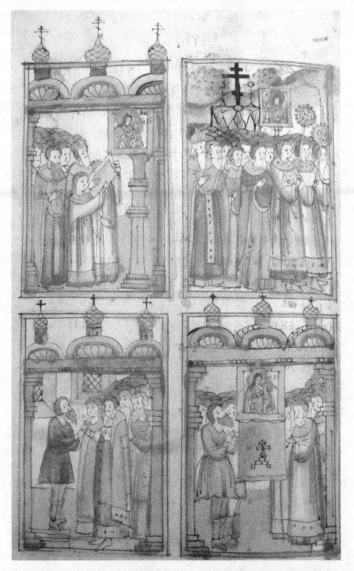

FIGURE 1.1 Smolensk Icon of the Mother of God, *Nebo novoe* manuscript, early eighteenth century (Ms. Slav. 302/Ms. 10536-7-71; *1, fol. 651v), Moscow State University, Moscow. Photo by Elena N. Boeck.

its narrative was generated in connection with a campaign for acknowledgment and official recognition of the miraculous image by the authorities in Moscow. The narrative unfolds in clearly defined stages: divine wrath and its wake, the desire of the populace to propitiate God, the commission of the icon as a thank offering, followed by numerous miracles produced by the icon. The narrative begins with a vivid, emotional account of the terrible plague that befell all of Russia, including Shuia, in 1654:

> Here in the city of Shuia when this terrible destruction came and started to reap people … and all people saw their impending deadly demise, they were filled with great fear and terror and depression and sadness and bewilderment: awash in tears and bitterly crying.[16]

Emotional intensity was followed by the next stage of grief—bargaining. Fervent communal prayers in the cathedral culminated in the expansive attempt to propitiate the divine power:

> … [Some of the people] promised to found new churches, others to restore the old churches, yet others promised to restore icons of Christ; and to paint new icons of the Mother of God and of those pleasing to God and to offer revetments to others … and others promised to adorn churches with all sorts of church furnishings … and to give alms to the poor … in order to build the beneficial order so that they might somehow beseech the most benevolent Pantocrator Lord God and to turn him to benevolence.[17]

Communal soul searching culminated in action—an anonymous resident suggested that a new image of the Smolensk Mother of God be painted as a collective offering. This idea was jubilantly taken up, for, according to the pious inhabitants, the Mother of God "visits us with constant favor and covers us with her honest *amforom* [*sic* maphorion] and relieves us of the great misfortunes and evils that come upon us and [the Mother of God] pleads for us and intercedes for us before God, [she is] defender and helper to us."[18]

Thus inspired, the urban residents set to the task of finding a worthy icon painter without delay: "in the same hour they started to work on this with great diligence and to look for a good *izograf*, that is icon painter, and found a good person, icon painter and talented master, resident of the merchant quarters of the same town, by the name Gerasim Tikhonov, son of an icon painter."[19] While the icon was being expeditiously painted, the inhabitants prayed, confessed their sins, and received forgiveness and the Eucharist. The finished icon was then carried to the Church of the Resurrection in a festive and solemn ceremony. When the icon entered the church, the church "was illuminated by that miraculous and most pure icon of the Mother of God, more than from the rise of the rays of the sun."[20] Following another wave of the plague epidemic, the icon reportedly performed the miracle of granting recovery to some people of the parish; recovery in the rest of the city ensued shortly thereafter.

The Shuia narrative above all reinforces the central idea of the compilation, that the Mother of God is always present in the world, and confirms the notion that local initiative and veneration of her cult result in miracles. This might seem uncontroversial, but a series of reforms designed to bring Russian rituals into line with international Orthodox practice provoked decades of turmoil within Russia. Although Patriarch Nikon, the author of these reforms, was deposed, his efforts to introduce uniformity across all parishes and assert central control over popular piety, righteous initiatives, and religious iconography were continued by his successors. The renewal of miraculous activity in Shuia after a ten-year-long hiatus was viewed suspiciously by church authorities in Moscow.

Patriarch Ioasaf sent a special commission to Shuia in 1667. The commission was headed by the archbishop of Suzdal, Stefan. The archbishop Stefan reported to the patriarch that his commission

> ...took testimony from the priests...and parish people about the miracles from the icon of the Most Holy Mother of God about the cures of the populace and of the people [referenced] against the list of those who were cured by the image of the Most Pure Sovereign Lady; we found them, and put the witnesses in front of us [and] we asked them—what illnesses possessed them, how many years ... they were possessed by these illnesses, and did they receive the cure from the image of the Most Pure Mother of God, and if they have these illnesses now, and if they continue to suffer; and that, Lord Patriarch, about that they testified, and in the inquiry about illnesses and about cures from the icon of the Most Pure Sovereign Lady they testified, and who they could reference in that [that is, who could corroborate their testimony]; and what their neighbors and nearby local residents said in the presence of their confessors, in the inquiry, about their sufferings, and about the cures from the icon of the Most Holy Sovereign Lady; and about that we compiled books with their signatures. And those books I send to you, Lord Patriarch with this [letter].[21]

Remarkably, the commission's systematic investigation would become one of the first of many systematic, critical attempts by the official church to control popular piety and to curtail grassroots efforts to endorse miraculous icons that potentially bypassed the church hierarchy. This theme has featured prominently in the work of Gregory Freeze and Vera Shevzov on the church and Orthodoxy in the imperial era and is further explored in the essays by William Wagner and Christine Worobec in this volume.[22] When the commission was not able to independently verify all of the purported miracles, further veneration of the Shuia icon seems to have been discouraged.[23] Suddenly the miracles stopped and did not resume until the 1760s.

There is no way to know whether or not the compiler was aware of the results of the commission, but his actions suggest that he would not have been sympathetic to its results. He believed that a newly manifested icon and its miracles merited inclusion among the venerable, pedigreed images of Russian icons featured in other parts of the compilation. Moreover, the absence of other seventeenth-century copies demonstrates that the Shuia text did not circulate widely after the commission's investigation. In the world of Marian miracles it was a collector's item. This was, in fact, just one of a number of rare texts included in the volume. Its inclusion reveals the compiler to be a connoisseur, someone who was not satisfied to possess only common knowledge (such as the narratives about the Vladimir or Tikhvin icons). The inclusion of this text in the volume therefore functions as an endorsement of the miraculous image and the veracity of its miracles.

The Shuia narrative also reinforces one of the larger goals of the compilation: to commemorate the particular miraculous fecundity of Marian imagery in seventeenth-century Russia. This chronological emphasis is prevalent in several texts that were selected for the compilation, including the miraculous activities of the Feodorov icon, the liberation of Ustiug by the Mother of God, the miracles of the icon of the Smolensk Mother of God in Shuia, the miracles of the Abalak icon (near Tobolsk) and several other texts. Although the astounding generosity of the Mother of God in the seventeenth century is admirable, the inclusion of such texts also demonstrates doubt about post-Nikonian skepticism in regard to miraculous icons.

The compilation presents a case not only for the inclusion of Russia in the divine plan, but also its elevation. By expanding the geographical scope of the compilation, the compiler simultaneously expanded his own understanding of the expansive range of the Mother of God in Russia. With the exception of the two Ruthenian texts that open the volume, Russian geography is dominant: in addition to Moscow's prominence, notable locations include Ustiug (two narratives), Kostroma (two narratives), and Kazan (two narratives). Other Russian locations that feature in single narratives of greater or lesser length include Tikhvin, Tolga, Shuia, the river Iuga, Suzdal, Arkhangelsk, and Tobolsk. The geography of the sacred seems to favor the heartland and two centers of Russian expansion (Kazan and Tobolsk). Russia's southern frontier is curiously absent from the miraculous geography, most likely because this region had an underdeveloped Orthodox infrastructure and low levels of book culture. Vulnerability to Tatar raids meant that fewer monasteries were founded here than in other parts of Russia and the ones that were founded were generally more impoverished since peasant populations were largely absent.[24] The Russian cities featured in the compilation became part of the universal story and part of the international geographies of Orthodoxy alongside Constantinople, Jerusalem, and Mt. Athos.

## VISUAL ADAPTATION AS DIALOGUE

In addition to its literary rarities, the compilation features intriguing imagery. It incorporates diverse forms of imagery: sixty-four hand-painted illustrations of various sizes, several decorated initials, and three glued-in, hand-colored fragments of Baroque floral engravings.[25] These multiple, simultaneous interventions in the fabric of the manuscript provide significant evidence about its patron, since even the layout of the manuscript was transformed to facilitate the process of visual adaptation.[26] The images provide a parallel message to the text that can be decoded to reveal hierarchies of prioritization among the selected texts.

Since the images are distributed very unevenly in the compilation, they communicate an alternate hierarchy of prioritization. The decision to allocate images unevenly indicates a planned process of prioritization and exclusion. The person who created the manuscript therefore provided additional information about his preferences and preoccupations.

The preferences of the verbal medium were adjusted in the visual adaptation. The pairing of *Nebo novoe* and *Zvezda presvetlaia* was torn asunder in the visual program. *Nebo novoe* was illustrated with fifty-nine images, *Zvezda presvetlaia* received not a single image. Patterns of visual prioritization within the Russian texts of the compilation are also intriguing. Some of the best-known Russian icons, such as the Vladimir and Tikhvin icons, were ignored in the visual program; hundreds of miracles merited no images, while simultaneously some awesome (but arguably foreign) miracles and the recently manifested Russian icons were represented.

Even in its approach to *Nebo novoe* there appears to be no single consistent principle in allocation of imagery. Nine chapters have no illustrations at all,[27] nine chapters have one illustration per chapter,[28] four chapters have two illustrations per chapter,[29] three chapters have three illustrations per chapter,[30] one chapter has four illustrations,[31] one chapter has six illustrations,[32] and one chapter has twenty-three illustrations.[33]

Patterns of exclusion from the visual program are extremely revealing about the patron. Collectively, the biographical chapters of the Mother of God display a very low level of illustration: two of the six chapters are unillustrated, three contain only one image (in each case extremely generic), and one chapter has two illustrations. It is also notable that chapters dedicated to the touch-relics were left virtually unillustrated: there are no images in the chapter dedicated to the ring of the Virgin, her maphorion, and girdle.[34] These important tangible memories of the Mother of God were ascribed to her lifetime. Thus touch-relics were mundane objects that became sacred relics by virtue of their putative physical contact with the Mother of God.[35] In contrast the vast majority of icons were assumed to have come into being or to have manifested the divine power following the Dormition. Since it was firmly believed at the time that St. Luke had painted an image of the Virgin and Christ child directly from living sacred persons, various miraculous icons, including the Vladimir Mother of God, were ascribed to the hand of the saint.[36] This pattern clearly indicates that the icons in Russia were elevated over important Marian relics that resided outside of Russia.

The extraordinary prioritization of a single chapter is also revealing. While hundreds of folios generated no illustrations, a mere sixteen folios included twenty-three illustrations. Chapter 22, devoted to miracles performed by icons of the Mother of God, is also the longest chapter in *Nebo novoe*, containing the greatest number of miracles (sixty). This means that 38.3 percent of miracles in this chapter were chosen for illustration. The emphatic visual prioritization of a chapter pertaining to images clearly correlates with the six hundred folios of text added from the compiler's own collection. Notably, the exceptional attention to the miracles performed by the icons of the Mother of God also correlates with the purpose of the compilation as a whole.

The visual program vigorously defends image veneration, rallies against heresy, celebrates miraculous iconic manifestations, emphasizes proximity of the divine by means of dreams and prayers, and promises reward and recognition to good Christians. A few of the iconographic features and stylistic elements in the illustrations of *Nebo novoe* either derive from or were inspired by Western European (Catholic) printed sources. These include such features as turrets and crenellations of urban cityscapes (fol. 56v, fol. 58v; see fig. 1.2). Some of the borrowings could have also come from Ukrainian printed books. For instance, the Renaissance-inspired architectural setting of a miraculous icon on folio 28r even includes the suggestion of perspective (the checkered floor; see fig 1.3). These features bear close resemblance to the iconographic elements (such as the checkered floor, the lines of which converge below the icon of the Mother of God, simultaneously indicating perspective and the central element in the composition) in the image that opens "A word of praise

FIGURE 1.2 Illustration from the chapter in *Nebo novoe* on the miracles performed by icons of the Mother of God; a miracle-working image of the Mother of God in Rome (Ms. Slav. 302/Ms. 10536-7-71; *1 fol. 58v), Moscow State University, Moscow. Photo by Elena N. Boeck.

московскїй сомно́жествомь люде́й срѣ-
шоша ю̑ моля́щеся прч҃той бц҃ѣ. дɑ̀зɑ
стꙋ́питъ и̑хъ ю̑непрїа́телꙗ благо. и̑ю
дѣ́йствова сіѐ прч҃тал бц҃а. и̑ꙗ́кꙍ тача
рове ю̑страши́шасꙗ. и̑дале разɑ́ни немого
ша нимало постꙋ̑пи́ти. Чꙋ́до.

Пꙋсви́шрїе въ кри́мѣ вели́кое. моля́хꙋсꙗ
рима́не прч҃той бц҃ѣ. просꙗ́ще ю̑ней помощи
и̑зɑстꙋ̑пленїа. и̑възе́мше ю̑́браз҃ еꙗ̑. ношахꙋ̑
ю̑крть гра́да.

вꙿто́й чаеть въ
двиша наве́тхꙋ̑
зда́нїи а̑ндреа̑
нокомъ прєчею̑
днагома́нца
и̑жевлага́ше
въпо́хвы мечь
ппровїю ново

ю̑мо́ченный. в̑ɑ̑шебото́й а̑́гг҃лъ вою̑бра́з҃
ю̑ноши. и̑жехода́тай ствомъ прч҃тыꙗ
бц҃ы преста морь люде́й кри́мъ ю̑бивɑ́ти.
сего рɑ́ди положи мечь въпо́хвы. Чꙋдо д҃.

Прɑ̑йрɑклїй цр҃ь грꙿчєстꙋ̑юмъ. сɑрвɑрь
коево́дɑ пєрєскїй; и̑кага́нь коево́дɑ скиꙋ̑.
скїй, своиннеꙗквы вели́кими. мо́ремъ и̑з̑
мɑ́ею̑ прїидо́ша под҃ цɑ́рь гра́дъ. в̑то́й чаеть

to the Most Pure Mother of God" in the tome of Lazar Baranovych, *Truby sloves propovednykh na narochitye dni prazdnikov* (1674).[37]

These conclusions highlight the dialogical nature of the illustrations. Creation of images was an active and thoughtful process. This process required negotiation between multiple visual and intellectual stimuli by selectively accepting, rejecting, synthesizing, filtering, and suppressing them in the production of these images.[38]


CONCLUSION

The systematic compilation of narratives designed to define and defend the power of the Mother of God was not an invention of early modern Russia. Late seventeenth-century efforts to assemble evidence for the Mother of God's preference for Russia would initiate, and eventually culminate in, multiple forms of cultural production ranging from patriotic catalogs to compendium icons. By entering into a competitive dialogue with the more distant forms of knowledge displayed in *Nebo novoe* and *Zvezda presvetlaia*, this compiler embraced Mariology as a universal endeavor that did not preclude him from devoting his intellectual efforts to one particularly preferred space. By assembling texts testifying to the activity of Mary and her icons in seventeenth-century Russia, our bookman advanced a sustained claim for the ongoing benevolence of the Mother of God toward Russia, despite troubles ranging from marauding Poles to the plague.

For the compiler of this volume *Nebo novoe* was a valiant but failed attempt to catalog the universal presence of the Mother of God. It could not live up to its aim because it was unaware of so much of the Marian presence that was known to and cherished by Russians. Because the miraculous geographies of *Nebo novoe* framed Mary primarily within an unfamiliar world, the visual program strove to modulate its message.

The last image of the compilation is anomalous in its exceptional execution and the mystery of its message (see fig. 1.4). An image that was supposed to summarize the narrative of the Novopechera Mother of God in the Svenskii Monastery near Briansk for some reason lacks unambiguous features of the surrounding narrative. On several levels this is one of the most interesting and enigmatic images in the compilation. Its unusual composition and absence of any religious referents makes it unique.[39]

In order to appreciate this visual puzzle, it is important to present its verbal counterpart (transcribed on folios 786r–789v). According to the pious text, a miraculous image of the Mother of God was residing in Kiev, where it was

FIGURE 1.4 Illustration of the narrative of the Novopechera icon of the Mother of God in the Svenskii Monastery near Briansk (Ms. Slav. 302/Ms. 10536-7-71; *1, fol. 789v), Moscow State University, Moscow. Photo by Elena N. Boeck.

producing numerous spectacular miracles (the blind could see, the lame could walk, the deaf could hear, etc.). At a later point, during the reign of Tsar Ivan Vasilievich (Tsar Ivan III or IV ["the Terrible"]), the icon chose to travel to Moscow, where it again produced numerous miracles of the same awesome caliber. The image, however, did not choose to reside in Moscow. Soon afterwards, it decided to return to Kiev, to its "old holy place."[40] The grand prince, the unnamed metropolitan, the boyars, merchants, and all the people naturally respected the will of the Mother of God. They fervently prayed to the icon one more time and accompanied it until it was some distance away from Moscow.[41] The icon then uneventfully returned to Kiev, where it again produced numerous miracles. A little later, a certain prince built a monastery for the icon a considerable distance away. The prince then came to Kiev to woo the icon with the gift of a pearl (*biser*) revetment and implored local residents to allow him to take the icon with him and to install it in his monastery. Kievans gave him the icon without opposition, and the prince began the return journey by sailing on the river Sven'. According to the narrative, an awesome miracle took place en route, in a location a considerable distance from Kiev and the intended point of arrival: the river stopped running for three days and four nights and the princely boat could move no further. The prince quickly realized that he was witnessing a miracle and that the icon wanted to stay in this wilderness. The prince submitted to divine will, built a chapel on the spot chosen by the icon, installed the icon in the newly built chapel, and built the Svenskii Monastery (Briansk region). Awesome healing miracles resumed.

However, some time later a Tatar raid was sent upon the region as punishment for the sins of humanity. The legend narrates with pathos how the evildoers robbed the church of its treasures, killed the brethren, and left the monastery desecrated. But the Mother of God purportedly asserted awesome power over the evildoers, who were miraculously blinded. Realizing that they were afflicted by divine punishment, they returned all of the robbed treasure back to the Mother of God and to the monastery. The monastery was never again molested and the great miracles resumed.

This curious story includes several standard preoccupations of pious narratives: manifestations of the divine nature of the miraculous images of the Mother of God, human submission to divine will, and repeated reinforcement of divine power over temporal authority. The narrative also exhibits historical, geographical, and geopolitical concerns: geographies of old and new centers of power (Kiev and Moscow); preoccupations with measurable distances (location of Tsar Ivan's prayer to the Virgin before the icon leaves Moscow, location of the new residence of the icon once it leaves Kiev); importance of the Muscovite autocracy (the only named human actor in the narrative is

Ioan Vasilievich, while other participants are anonymous); and vulnerability to Tatar raids.

The image stands out within the entire compilation due to the absence of either the Mother of God or her miracles. The stunning image is beautifully symmetrical, carefully balancing two fortified cities and two armies along diagonals in a large composition (fol. 789v). The fortified cities appear in the bottom right and in the upper left corners, while the two armies approach each fortress with flags unfurled from the two remaining corners. The larger, more prominent, fortified city of the bottom right appears to be deliberately site-specific: the double-headed eagle surmounting the red defensive tower and an exceptionally tall, three-tiered bell tower identify it as the Moscow Kremlin. The heroic ruler could also be a Muscovite: he wears a fur-lined red hat, red robe, and red boots and carries in his left hand a very tall object, perhaps a whip. The vivid, extraordinary image stands apart from the text, and thrusts a vibrant, detailed, and lively political world into a manuscript that is otherwise singularly dedicated to cataloging heavenly glory.

How can the unique disconnect between the text and the image be explained? Did the compiler of the volume intend to suggest that Moscow was the most favored among cities in the Russian landscape of Marian devotion? Or is this a critique of Muscovite power? After all, the icon is depicted neither in Moscow nor the other city, which perhaps is meant to represent Kiev. Did the compiler intend to signal that the Mother of God favors all of Russia, not any single political center or ruler? Or did he deploy absence to suggest that the divine is continually on the move? Given this final mystery, it is eerily appropriate that the manuscript repeated one of the icon's journeys in reverse. It was transferred to Moscow by a team of scholars who retrieved it from Briansk.

## Notes

1. I would like to thank the editors, Amy Singleton Adams and Vera Shevzov, for their thoughtful comments and helpful suggestions.

2. This study primarily cites publications that discuss the content of this volume. A larger study will provide more extensive connections to the secondary literature that explores broader questions of icons and their narratives. I. V. Pozdeeva, in the only publication that discussed this volume, called it "a peculiar and very complete encyclopedia of Russian Mariology." Pozdeeva, "Arkheograficheskie raboty Moskovskogo universiteta v raione drevnei Vetki i Staroduba," in *Pamiatniki kul'tury: Novye otkrytiia; Pis'mennost', Iskusstvo, Arkheologiia 1975* (Moscow: Nauka, 1976), 59.

3. Pozdeeva, "Arkheograficheskie raboty," 52.

4. M. I. Lileev, ed., *Novye materialy dlia istorii raskola na Vetke i v Starodub'i XVII–XVIII vv.* (Kiev: Tip. G. T. Korchak-Novitkago, 1893).

5. The encyclopedic Marian interests of this volume are akin to the volume produced by Simeon Mokhovikov ca. 1715–1716, which contained images and descriptions of numerous Marian icons. Mokhovikov had been a guard of the Moscow Annunciation Cathedral. See further I. Pozdeeva, "Vnov' naidennyi sbornik Simeona Mokhovikova s graviurami G. P. Tepchegorskogo," in *Narodnaia graviura i fol'klor v Rossii XVII–XIX vv.* (Moscow: Sovetskii khudozhnik, 1976), 175–76; I. A. Kochetkov, "Svod chudotvornykh ikon Bogomateri na ikonakh i graviurakh XVIII–XIX vekov," in *Chudotvornaia ikona v Vizantii i Drevnei Rusi*, ed. A. M. Lidov (Moscow: Martis, 1996), 409–10.

6. It is worth revisiting the content of the volume, for its description by Pozdeeva contains some problems and inaccuracies. For instance, the first text is not identified as *Nebo novoe*.

7. For additional discussion of Marian miracle tales, see Gary Marker, "Narrating Mary's Miracles and the Politics of Location in Late 17th-Century East Slavic Orthodoxy," *Kritika: Explorations in Russian and Eurasian History* 15, no. 4 (2014): 695–727.

8. Though *Nebo novoe* has not attracted much attention in historiography, its compiler Ioannikii Galiatovskii has. For *Nebo novoe*, see I. I. Ogienko, "Otrazhenie v literature 'Neba Novogo' Ioannikiia Galiatovskogo, iuzhno-russkogo propovednika XVII veka," *Filologicheskie zapiski* 51, no. 6 (1911): 857–74; and 52, no. 1 (1912): 1–8; Ogienko, "Legendarno-apokrificheskii element v 'Nebe Novom' Ioannikiia Galiatovskogo, iuzhno-russkogo propovednika XVII veka," *Chteniia v Istoricheskom Obshchestve Nestora Letopistsa* 24, no. 1 (1913): 41–98; Ogienko, "Izdaniia 'Neba Novogo' Ioannikiia Galiatovskogo: Iz istorii staropechatnykh knig," *Iskusstvo, zhivopis', grafika* (n.p., 1912). For a good introduction to Galiatovskii and his oeuvre, see D. M. Bulanin, "Ioannikii Galiatovskii (Goliatovskii)," in *Slovar' knizhnikov i knizhnosti Drevnei Rusi*, vol. 3, *XVII v.*, part 4, T-Ia, Dopolneniia (St. Petersburg: Dmitrii Bulanin, 2004), 438–49.

9. For the still unresolved questions about the origins and the date of translation of this text, as well as an introduction to the state of the question, see M. R. Poklonskaia, "Rukopisnaia traditsiia sbornika Zvezda Presvetlaia," in *Literatura i klassovaia bor'ba epokhi pozdnego feodalizma v Rossii*, ed. E. K. Romodonovskaia (Novosibirsk: Nauka, 1987): 175–92. Even though its Ukrainian or (perhaps) Belarussian original has not been identified, from the translator's note it is known that the text was translated in Moscow. Ibid., 176.

10. A recent count put the number of known copies of *Zvezda presvetlaia* at 115 (forty-three of which circulated as independent manuscripts, rather than as compendia). Ibid., 179, 185.

11. For further discussion, see Elena Boeck, "Strength in Numbers or Unity in Diversity? Compilations of Miracle-Working Virgin Icons," in *Alter Icons: The Russian Icon and Modernity*, ed. Jefferson J. A. Gatrall and Douglas Greenfield (University Park: Pennsylvania State University Press, 2010), 35–37.

12. Compare, for instance, to *Atlas Marianus*, which, in reporting the miracles, identifies recipients of the divine grace as well as their location with an almost scientific attention to detail.

13. See also Vera Shevzov, *Russian Orthodoxy on the Eve of Revolution* (New York: Oxford University Press, 2004).

14. For an introduction to this text and bibliography, see D. M. Bulanin, "Skazanie o ikone Bogomateri Shuiskoi," in *Slovar' knizhnikov i knizhnosti Drevnei Rusi*, vol. 3, *XVII v.*, part 4, T-Ia, Dopolneniia (St. Petersburg: Dmitrii Bulanin, 2004), 600–603. See also Andreas Ebbinghaus, *Die altrussischen Marienikonen-Legenden* (Wiesbaden: Harrassowitz, 1990), 94, 128. The recent publication of N. I. Nikonov, *Shuisko-Smolenskaia ikona Presviatoi Bogoroditsy* (St. Petersburg: Ladan, 2008), belongs to the category of pious, rather than academic works.

15. Fol. 657v; fol. 660r.

16. Fol. 653v.

17. Fol. 654v.

18. Fol. 656r.

19. Fol. 656v. The text published by Nikonov is a reprint of a nineteenth-century publication that incorrectly identifies the icon painter as Gerasim Tikhonov Ikonnikov (thus conflating his profession as icon painter with his last name). Nikonov, *Shuisko-Smolenskaia ikona*, 123.

20. Fol. 657v.

21. The text is republished in Nikonov, *Shuisko-Smolenskaia ikona*, 214, from a 2002 reprint of a publication by V. A. Borisov, *Opisanie goroda Shui i ego okrestnostei*, vol. 1 (Moscow, 1851).

22. See Gregory Freeze, "Institutionalizing Piety: The Church and Popular Religion, 1750–1850," in *Imperial Russia: New Histories for the Empire*, ed. Jane Burbank and David L. Ransel (Bloomington: University of Indiana Press, 1998), 210–49; Vera Shevzov, "Icons, Miracles, and the Ecclesial Identity of Laity in Late Imperial Russian Orthodoxy," *Church History* 69, no. 3 (2000): 610–31; Vera Shevzov, "Miracle-Working Icons, Laity, and Authority in the Russian Orthodox Church, 1861–1917," *Russian Review* 58, no. 1 (1999): 26–48.

23. See Bulanin, "Skazanie o ikone Bogomateri Shuiskoi," 601. This manuscript is kept in the State Historical Museum, Moscow (Uvarov collection, number 1724 [196]). The author has not yet been able to see this manuscript.

24. For further information on the cultural dynamic of the southern frontier, see Brian Davies, *State Power and Community in Early Modern Russia: The Case of Kozlov, 1635–1649* (Houndmills, Basingstoke: Palgrave Macmillan, 2004). The author thanks Brian J. Boeck for sharing with me his understanding of the ecclesiastical situation along the southern frontier.

25. The glued-in, hand-colored engraved fragments serve as decorative frontispieces on fols. 224r and 371r. On fol. 482v part of a glued-in engraving covers the entire page. The original engraving contained an extensive text in Cyrillic in the cartouche, which has been scratched off.

26. Dudley Andrew noted: "Adaptation is . . . both a leap and a process. It can put into play the intricate mechanism of its signifiers only in response to a general understanding of the signified it aspires to have constructed at the end of its process." Dudley Andrew, "Adaptation," in *Film Adaptation*, ed. James Naremore (New Brunswick, NJ: Rutgers University Press, 2000), 29.

27. These chapters are as follows: chapter 1—miracles of the most holy Mother of God among the sibyls; chapter 2—in the church of Solomon; chapter 7—miracles of the most holy Mother of God by the name Maria; chapter 8—miracles from the maphorion (*riza*) and girdle of the most holy Mother of God; chapter 9—miracles of the most holy Mother of God from her ring; chapter 11—miracles of the most holy Mother of God during war; chapter 12—miracles of the most holy Mother of God over sinners; chapter 17—miracles of the most holy Mother of God over the dead; chapter 21—miracles of the most holy Mother of God among the evil spirits.

28. These chapters are as follows: chapter 3—miracles of the most holy Mother of God during the birth of Christ; chapter 4—miracles of the most holy Mother of God during the flight to Egypt; chapter 6—miracles of the most holy Mother of God during her Dormition; chapter 10—miracles of the most holy Mother of God from her spring; chapter 13—miracles of the most holy Mother of God over those who keep their virginity; chapter 16—miracles of the most holy Mother of God over those who are incapacitated; chapter 19—miracles of the most holy Mother of God among the Jews; chapter 26—miracles of the most holy Mother of God of Pechersk; chapter 27—miracles of the most holy Mother of God of Kupiatich.

29. These chapter are as follows: chapter 5—miracles of the most holy Mother of God during her life; chapter 18—miracles of the most holy Mother of God among the pagans; chapter 24—miracles of the most holy Mother of God among the monks; chapter 25—miracles of the Iveron most holy Mother of God.

30. These chapters are as follows: chapter 15—miracles of the most holy Mother of God over *neumeiushchie* (those not in possession of their mind); chapter 20—miracles of the most holy Mother of God among the heretics; chapter 28—miracles of the most holy Mother of God in different places.

31. This is chapter 23—miracles of the most holy Mother of God in her churches.

32. This is chapter 14—miracles of the most holy Mother of God for those who pray.

33. This is chapter 22—miracles of the most holy Mother of God from her icons.

34. This omission is quite interesting, since representations of the maphorion were popular in Russian icons and frescos .

35. For a good discussion of representations of the Virgin's maphorion and girdle in Byzantine and Russian images, see I. A. Shalina, *Relikvii v vostochnokhristianskoi ikonografii* (Moscow: Indrik, 2005), 293–331.

36. L. A. Shchennikova, "Chudotvornaia ikona 'Bogomater' Vladimirskaia' kak 'Odigitriia Evangelista Luki,'" in *Chudotvornaia ikona v Vizantii i Drevnei Rusi*, ed. A. M. Lidov (Moscow: Martis, 1996), 274. For the sources as early as the sixth century, see Hans Belting, *Likeness and Presence: A History of the Image before the Era of Art* (Chicago: University of Chicago Press, 1994), 57–59.

37. This book was published in Kiev, dedicated to Tsar Aleksei Mikhailovich, subsidized by the tsar (who paid for the paper), and produced for the Russian market. This publication was one of several that Baranovich aimed directly at a Russian audience. See Serhii Plokhy, *The Origins of the Slavic Nations: Premodern Identities in Russia, Ukraine, and Belarus* (Cambridge: Cambridge University Press, 2006), 259–60; Plokhy, *Tsars and Cossacks: A Study in Iconography* (Cambridge, MA: Harvard University Press, 2002), 36–39; N. F. Sumtsov, *K istorii iuzhnorusskoi literatury semnadtsatogo stoletiia*, vol. 1, *Lazar' Baranovich* (Kharkov: Tip. M. F. Zil'berberga, 1883); A. Stradomskii, *Lazar' Baranovich: arkhiepiskop Chernigovskii i Novgorod-severskii* (Moscow, 1852). For a discussion of illustrations produced for Baranovich and his circle, see Elena Boeck, "Claiming and Acclaiming Peter I: Ukrainian Contributions to the Visual Commemoration of Petrine Victories," in *Poltava 1709: The Battle and the Myth*, ed. Serhii Plokhy, Harvard Papers in Ukrainian Studies 31 (Cambridge, MA: Ukrainian Research Institute of Harvard University, 2012), 271–308.

38. For a recent overview of Russian responses to Western European iconographies in the seventeenth century, see I. L. Buseva-Davydova, *Kul'tura i iskusstvo v epokhu peremen: Rossiia semnadtsatogo stoletiia* (Moscow: Indrik, 2008), 100–116.

39. Although stylistically distinct, iconographically this image is related to illustrations of Russian historical manuscripts, the most famous of which is *Litsevoi svod*. For a recent discussion of that illustrated corpus, see V. V. Morozov, *Litsevoi svod v kontekste otechestvennogo letopisaniia XVI veka* (Moscow: Indrik, 2005).

40. Fol. 786v.

41. Fol. 787r.

# 2

# The Akhtyrka Icon of the Mother of God

## A Glimpse of Eighteenth-Century Orthodox Piety on a Southwestern Frontier

CHRISTINE D. WOROBEC[1]

ON 2 JULY 1739 FATHER Daniil Vasiliev of the Pokrov Church in the regimental town of Akhtyrka/Okhtyrka (located in southwestern Belgorod/Bilhorod diocese, which in 1775 became Kharkov/Kharkiv diocese and province) was about to try out a new scythe when he noticed in the hayfield an icon "shining brightly as if it were the sun." Once he overcame his awe, he paid tribute to the Virgin Mary, whose image adorned the icon, by "inton[ing] the *kondak* [special hymn] honoring the Mother of God's birth." According to the icon's founding legend, Father Daniil put the icon in a special place in his home because of the powerful radiance that it emitted. None of Father Daniil's servants could spend the night at home if he were not present, the cleric noted, due to the fear and dread that overcame them.[2] It would appear that, as far as the priest was concerned, this disturbing image that signified a divine presence to him and others was not yet ready for worshipers to wonder over and venerate.

More than three years passed before another momentous event having to do with the icon occurred. In early 1743, Father Daniil dreamed that the Birthgiver of God was washing her face and putting on her outer robes. Her face mirrored her portrait on the icon. Obeying the order that he believed Mary gave him in the dream, he washed the icon with water. When Father Daniil went to throw the runoff in the nearby Vorskla River, however, he again saw Mary. His description of her as "a beautiful maiden" once more pointed to the icon's depiction of the Virgin, this time with an emphasis on her hair being uncovered and down over her shoulders as befit a "maiden." According to the cleric's recollections, Mary asked him, "Where are you going?" "Take that water home with you," she commanded, "and keep it in a dish; this water will be curative for those people ill with fever." On 16 January 1743, Father Daniil gave his feverish daughter Maria some of the water. Upon waking, Maria reported that she had seen "the most holy Mother of God in beautiful multicolored attire," referring to the bejeweled clothing that Mary wore on the Akhtyrka icon. Afterwards, the daughter recovered her health. Yet, even this cure (which Father Daniil and his daughter believed to be miraculous through Mary's intercession) and another cure of fever on the same day that the cleric attributed to the icon water's healing powers did not prompt him to display the icon in public as church law required.[3]

The event that finally forced his hand had to do with circumstances surrounding the icon's image. On the day of the two healings Father Daniil summoned the local icon painter Ivan to his home, asking him to repair small markings on the icon. Washing the icon, presumably in preparation for its restoration, the iconographer gave his own feverish child some of the runoff water, and the child recovered. After the icon has been at the painter's home for three days, Ivan maintained that he heard a voice in his sleep tell him it was time to return the icon to Father Daniil as he, Ivan, would be unable to improve the icon's image. The painter's dream coincidently occurred during the week of the Publican and Pharisee, an Orthodox commemoration celebrating humility. In returning what he perceived to be a miraculous image, Ivan told Father Daniil about his dream and what he understood to be the Mother of God's desires and authority.[4]

As word spread of the cures that had supposedly occurred through the intercession of the Akhtyrka Mother of God, worshipers came to venerate the icon. Penitents' reports of new miracles they attributed to the icon occurred steadily from mid-February 1743 onward. By the end of the month, the icon was housed in the parish church.[5] Between 1743 and 1774 a total of 376 miracles of a variety of types attributed to the Akhtyrka icon of the Mother of God were recorded, affecting 392 people directly and producing many hundreds of witnesses to the unusual events.[6] Not all of these healings occurred before the icon itself. Indeed, many of the cures believers ascribed to the Akhtyrka Mother of God took place at home. Individuals noted that they either had a dream in which her image appeared or prayed directly to her on behalf of themselves or a relative (usually a child).[7]

But what was it about the portrayal of the Akhtyrka Mother of God that made it so unusual? First, it is important to take into account the icon's epiphanic

FIGURE 2.1 A 1778 copy of the Akhtyrka icon of the Mother of God by Aleksei Afanasiev. The script at the bottom of the icon reads, "The true representation and measure of the Akhtyrka icon of the Mother of God, which appeared in the year 1739, month of July, 2nd day." It is nonetheless possible that embellishments or changes were made to the original version, which disappeared in the early twentieth century. Courtesy of Jackson's International Auctioneers and Appraisers.

nature or its mysterious appearance in a field. As Vera Shevzov explains, believers perceived such an icon's epiphany to be "providential—God, as well as the saint [or in this case the Mother of God] depicted, intended for the icon to appear at that particular place and time."[8] However, the Holy Synod, the bureaucratic arm of the Russian Orthodox Church established in 1721, had become uneasy about such "newly manifested icons" due to the possibility of false miracles and other superstitions attached to them as well as clerical fraud, a charge to which Father Daniil was susceptible. The icon's image also presented a new prototype for a Mother of God miracle-working icon, which by law required the Holy Synod's approval. As the above descriptions suggest, the Virgin was depicted in an Italian Renaissance style, with her hair loose and not covered with the traditional wimple and mantle. Even more startling from a Russo-Byzantine Orthodox perspective were the juxtaposition of the young Virgin and a crucified Christ within the same frame, where the main theme was not the Crucifixion itself but rather a young Mary's premonition of her son's fate (see fig. 2.1).

A case study of the eighteenth-century cult of the Akhtyrka icon of the Mother of God illuminates a changing Orthodox landscape within the eighteenth-century Russian Empire. Historians have tended to emphasize Russian Orthodoxy's lack of inventiveness; it adopted a religion that was formed within the ancient Byzantine Empire and prided itself on hewing to the doctrines of the Eastern Church Fathers. Nonetheless, changes did take place. The mid-seventeenth-century reforms that produced a church schism present a case in point. While the Akhtyrka icon did not represent such a dramatic change, its history demonstrates the ways in which influences from the West, politics, empire, and popular apocryphal notions converged. An image of Mary that would have been rejected in the early eighteenth century by the Holy Synod as having Catholic influences had become acceptable to that governing body by mid-century. Royal patronage of the icon, as discussed below, was a factor in the Synod's acquiescence. Most important, the imprimatur that the icon received from political and religious officials signified empire-building, the incorporation of a loyal Ukrainian area into the empire.

The miracle stories connected to the Akhtyrka icon also reveal how the image's veneration developed and broadened over time. As more types of illnesses were reportedly cured with the Akhtyrka Mother of God's intercession, more people from outside Akhtyrka came to venerate the icon. Pilgrims traveled from all over Left-Bank Ukraine, the city of Kiev in Right-Bank Ukraine, and the non-Ukrainian areas of Orel, Kursk, Mtsensk, St. Petersburg, and Kazan. What began as a local cult providing succor to military men and their families in garrison Ukrainian towns spread nationwide. Although most of the reported stories of healings are brief, some testimonies provide first-person and third-person narratives that illuminate understandings of the divine, representations of the Mother of God, forms of personal piety, and personal experiences with adversity and what was understood to be divine grace. As in the case of seventeenth-century icons and narratives of the Mother of God, which Elena Boeck discusses in the present volume, divine authority required the submission of human will or miracles could be withheld or withdrawn.

INVESTIGATIONS OF THE AKHTYRKA ICON AND THE POLITICS
OF MIRACLES

The attention that the Akhtyrka icon received from ecclesiastical authorities between 1743 and 1751—which involved four investigations of the icon cult and the role Father Daniil played in promoting the cult—must be viewed within the context of decrees that attempted to eradicate excessive or even fraudulent popular practices. With the growth of rival Old Believer and sectarian movements as well as influences of the Reformation and Counter-Reformation, the 1721 Spiritual Regulation and subsequent legislation advised bishops to guard against superstitious practices that included false miracles, false icons, as well as Catholic practices in icon painting and veneration rituals. Although the clerical elite accepted the Orthodox veneration of icons, they worried that "it too often turned into idolatry among the ignorant." On 21 February 1722 the Holy Synod accordingly "ordered the removal of miracle-working icons from private homes to cathedral churches or monasteries, where their cults could be overseen," a ruling that Father Daniil had violated by keeping the Akhtyrka icon in his home for several years. The Synod's continuing concerns about epiphanic or "newly manifested icons" resulted in a 1737 decree demanding inquiries once again into "false miracles," and "all sorts of shameful customs involving holy icons."[9] Finally, numerous eighteenth-century decrees, in the spirit of legislation dating back to the sixteenth century, forbade the production of icons that "violated traditional iconographic canons" and that constituted bad art.[10] The fact that decrees had to be repeated suggest that they were in most cases ignored and that the new church bureaucracy created by Peter the Great in 1721 lacked the resources to police effectively such popular and clerical practices. Indeed, in spite of its demands that newly manifested icons be investigated, the Holy Synod subjected relatively few to intense scrutiny in the eighteenth century.[11] Most specially revered and miracle-working icons did not receive official sanction but gradually became recognized without official investigation and decrees.[12] Ultimately more important than official scrutiny was the succor these icons provided worshipers who, believing the images to be miracle-working in a non-medical age, expected something miraculous to occur.

The inquiries into the popular cult that developed around the Akhtyrka icon stemmed in part from the actions of Father Daniil, who not only found the epiphanic icon but also became its clerical sponsor. In the cures believers ascribed to the icon, he administered to the infirm the curative water from the icon's periodic washings and directed those suffering from impaired or lack of vision to distinguish between various colored cloths he presented to them in the icon's presence. Father Daniil also counseled the sick and their relatives, conducted prayer services before the icon, and collected donations that worshipers gave for those services as well as offerings to the icon. According to local lore, the initial 1743 investigation was sparked not by the cleric's violation of the law forbidding the placement of miracle-working icons in private spaces, but rather by the suspicion of another cleric in Akhtyrka that the Akhtyrka icon and miracles attributed to it were fraudulent.[13]

On 24 July 1743 Archpriest Simeon Sadovskii informed Metropolitan Antonii of Belgorod about the icon cult. The metropolitan set up what turned out to be the initial inquiry, wherein Sadovskii served as an investigator. In the course of questioning, military officers in Akhtyrka confirmed the existence of miracles.[14] The report to the Holy Synod attracted the attention of the devout empress Elizaveta Petrovna, who, according to local lore, in August 1744 secretly made a pilgrimage (accompanied by her lady-in-waiting and confidante Mavra Egorovna Shuvalova [née Sheleva, 1708–1759]) to Akhtyrka to venerate the icon.[15]

Whether the empress made the visit or not, she did order a second inquiry into the icon cult on 26 November 1744 that excluded any locals as investigators. When commissioners examined the list of miracles that Father Daniil had recorded and took depositions under sacred oath from witnesses, a few individuals in Akhtyrka voiced suspicions about discrepancies in Father Daniil's accounting of donations to the icon. In response, the Belgorod Consistory replaced the cleric and placed him under arrest on 12 February 1745. After two months imprisonment, Father Daniil was allowed to return to Akhtyrka for Easter under surety of his family and the town's inhabitants but within two days he disappeared. He was not heard of again for a year and a half, during which time he traveled to Jerusalem without proper documents or ecclesiastical permission.[16] A decree of the Holy Synod mentions the sojourn to Jerusalem, but not the reason behind it.[17] One local historian of Akhtyrka concludes that Father Daniil went on pilgrimage, while another suggests that the cleric sought an audience with the patriarch of Jerusalem to complain about the Russian Orthodox ecclesiastics' actions and the Belgorod Consistory's seizure of donations that worshipers gave to the Akhtyrka icon.[18]

The claim that Father Daniil wished to launch an official complaint can only be speculation at this point, but it is included here for two reasons. First, Father Daniil had been uneasy about publicly showing the icon until he was sure of its extraordinary powers, perhaps because of a concern that ecclesiastical authorities might question the icon's authenticity or its unusual composition. Second, after two more investigations into the Akhtyrka icon cult, the Holy Synod on 31 May 1751 declared the miracles to have been genuine and recognized the Akhtyrka Mother of God as a miracle-working icon, setting 2 July as its official feast day. It also exonerated Father Daniil for making false claims in some of the miracles he recorded and recommended that Bishop Ioasaf (Gorlenko) of Belgorod be lenient in his treatment of Father Daniil. The decree pointed out that Father Daniil had already served sufficient jail time (which also included incarcerations in monasteries after his return from Jerusalem), that many of his written testimonies corresponded with the findings of the investigations, and that miracles from the Akhtyrka icon were still occurring. No mention was made of his having improperly used donations to the icon.[19] And his failings were insufficient to deter him from arranging an audience with the empress; unfortunately, he died on the road to St. Petersburg.[20] Surprisingly, there was also nothing in the Holy Synod's decrees that mentioned the unusual nature of the Akhtyrka Mother of God's image, which did not conform to traditional canonic standards and evinced Western Renaissance influences.

Fortunately for the military servitors and their families served by the grace of the Akhtyrka Mother of God icon, the author of the Spiritual Regulation, Feofan Prokopovich, and other zealous bishops appointed by Peter I were no longer alive or in office by the time the results of the initial investigation were reported to the Holy Synod in 1744. In the case of the Shelbitsy icon of the Mother of God, Prokopovich had in 1731 questioned its authenticity as an Orthodox icon because of a Polish inscription on the icon and the portrayal of the Mother of God wearing a scapulary. The Holy Synod accordingly denounced this garment that certain Catholic orders wore to be "a Roman superstition that is completely contrary to the Eastern Greek confession of the church."[21] Earlier, Evfimii Chudovskii, an associate of Patriarch Ioakim (d. 1690), pointed to other problematic iconographic details on icons. He objected to depictions of the Mother of God and John the Baptist (Forerunner) in "rulers' clothing and crowns and wings, and the Holy Mother of God sometimes in dark red garments, sometimes as a bare-headed maiden, sometimes standing on the moon, sometimes ... having a white mantle on her head."[22] The description of Mary as standing on the moon and sometimes having a white mantle on her head or being bare-headed appears to refer to the depiction of the Immaculate Conception that had developed in seventeenth-century Spain and was becoming the standard way of depicting that notion in the West.[23] Had either Prokopovich or Chudovskii still been alive in 1744, they would assuredly have found the portrayal of the Akhtyrka Mother of God as an unveiled bare-headed maiden dressed in royal clothing and with her hands touching in prayer to have been too Catholic in nature.

Another factor came into play in the Akhtyrka icon's acceptance: the attention that the empress paid the icon. In fact, Elizaveta Petrovna became a patron of the icon, which attracted her attention as early as 1744. Another event associated with the Akhtyrka icon, in which the Virgin appeared to be a prophet, protector, and benefactor of the poverty-stricken on the local level, touched her. According to eye-witness testimonies, on 2 May 1748 twenty-seven-year-old Baroness Elizaveta, daughter of the Belgorod vice-governor and wife of a Roman Catholic general, beseeched the Akhtyrka Mother of God to help cure her of a life-threatening illness. In a vision that the ill woman had of Mary, the Mother of God told her to give her gold and silver to churches and the poor. When Elizaveta responded that if she did so she would not have anything left to clothe her children, Mary reportedly told her that her children would no longer be her responsibility as she, Elizaveta, would be going to her eternal rest within five days. The Mother of God reassured her that she, Mary, would provide for the two daughters. Here Mary may be viewed "as a human being, as a subject with agency." Elizaveta followed the Virgin's instructions and died within five days, as Mary had predicted.[24] When she was informed of the miracle, the empress took the deceased woman's daughters under her wing at court.[25] In 1753 she also commissioned the famous Italian architect Francesco Bartolomeo Rastrelli to build a stone cathedral in honor of the Pokrov Mother of God on the very spot where the Akhtyrka icon had miraculously appeared.[26]

THE AKHTYRKA ICON AS PATRONESS ON THE LOCAL AND
NATIONAL LEVELS

The naming of the new church in honor of the Pokrov Mother of God, which emphasized Mary's veil or mantle and hence her role as protectress, was not accidental. After all, "in the Orthodox tradition, uniquely, churches are often created and named in honor of specific icons."[27] Retaining the name of the wooden church in which the Akhtyrka Mother of God icon had initially been placed represented a mutual understanding between local Ukrainian patrons and the empress. As Serhii Plokhy has pointed out, Left-Bank Ukraine's Hetmanate Cossacks had in the late seventeenth and first half of the eighteenth century developed a cult of the Pokrov icon of the Mother of God and viewed her as a special patron of Ukraine. Their Pokrov icons depicting prominent Cossacks and the imperial double eagle validated the

Ukrainian/Little Russian–Russian Orthodox alliance against Catholic Poland.[28] Even though the Akhtyrka icon supposedly appeared out of nowhere and was thus supposedly not man-made (and could not be improved upon by an icon painter), it too included the double-headed eagle at its bottom edge. The empress, who had a special interest in Sloboda Ukraine—northeastern Ukrainian frontier lands, populated by Cossack settlements, which were exempt from serfdom and initially taxes—extended her patronage to this loyal region through her championing of the Akhtyrka Mother of God icon. Unlike the Hetmanate, this section of Ukraine had not enjoyed political autonomy. Its Cossacks were extremely important in defending the empire from Ottoman incursions. The image of the Akhtyrka Mother of God as protectress stuck. As late as 1844, Innokentii, archbishop of Kherson and Tavrida, referred to her as a "general protectress of our country."[29]

The miracle tales also express Sloboda Ukraine's loyalty to the crown through references to a rival miracle-working icon in the nearby small Hetmanate town of Kaplunovka/Kaplunivka. This image—a copy of the famous Kazan Mother of God icon—was initially reported to have appeared in a penitent's dream in 1689 and was carried onto the field in the victorious 1709 Battle of Poltava against the Swedes and Ukrainian forces led by Hetman Ivan Mazepa.[30] Clearly, residents of Sloboda Ukraine needed their own Mother of God icon to protect their community against quotidian misfortunes and to differentiate themselves from the Cossack traitors. Some of the recipients of cures that they attributed to the Akhtyrka Mother of God's help had visited both the Kaplunovka and Akhtyrka icons, but identified the newer Akhtyrka icon as being stronger.[31] Some may have hoped to increase the chances of their being healed of their afflictions if they paid their respects to more than one miracle-working image.[32] However, most narratives suggested that the two Mother of God images competed with each other. Suffering from "the black illness," Emelian Kramorenko of the town of Sumy fulfilled his vow to kneel before the Akhtyrka Mother of God. From there he decided to go to Kaplunovka, where he dreamed that a man dispatched from Akhtyrka hit him hard on the cheek. Feeling much better upon awaking, Kramorenko once again set off for Akhtyrka to venerate that town's Mother of God icon in thanks for his recovery.[33] Others in Kaplunovka learned of the existence of the more powerful Akhtyrka icon. Maksim Daniilov Nakeskoi, a resident of a Poltava regimental town within the Hetmanate, reported in 1746 to have been beset by devilish thoughts, which did not abate when he vowed to travel to Kaplunovka. He attributed what he believed to be his miraculous release from confusion to the fact that he set out for Akhtyrka after hearing stories about the existence of the miracle-working icon there.[34]

The two icons' rivalry within the miracle narratives also presents itself in the type of illnesses supplicants believed they cured. The foundational story firmly links the Akhtyrka icon to the healing of fever. Yet an examination of the miracle stories demonstrates that in 1743, the first year of the icon's numerous miracles, only 11 percent of the 109 recipients of cures suffered from fever, whereas more than half of them (58 percent) had eye ailments, temporary blindness, and near blindness. In the second year, an even greater imbalance takes place, with fever occurring in only two of a total of seventy-seven cured people and blindness or near blindness in forty-seven of them Ironically, the Kazan Mother of God icon (of which the Kaplunovka was a copy) was known for healing blindness.[35] It is possible that the populations of both Akhtyrka and Kaplunovka had in these two years suffered from the residual effects of smallpox epidemics, which would explain why vision problems became far less common in the miracle stories of subsequent years.[36] Eventually, believers credited the Akhtyrka icon with healing a broad range of ailments: painful toothaches, gripe, epilepsy, alcoholism, smallpox, postpartum illnesses, ear problems, demonic possession, barrenness, rheumatism, consumption, heart disease, back pain, poisoning, and even a crooked face (presumably the effects of stroke). And they came from far and wide to benefit from the Akhtyrka Mother of God's intercession on their behalf.

THE ICON'S VISUAL FEATURES

In its visual attributes lies the importance of the new prototype of the Akhtyrka icon. These elements stress her roles as intercessor and link to Christ, supplementing the popular image of Mary as protectress. The viewer sees an Italian Renaissance image of the Virgin with her head uncovered, her robes red and bejeweled, and her hands in prayer as she contemplates a miniature of her son's crucifixion on Golgotha. She is not, however, kneeling but is depicted from the waist up. The instruments of the Passion as well as Adam's skull (signifying the ancient myth about Adam's burial on Golgotha) are part of the crucifixion scene. Mary's prophetic vision of her son's suffering on the cross was literally—rather than figuratively—portrayed. As such, the Akhtyrka icon represents a radical reworking of the traditional iconographic portrayal of the Mother of God with the Christ child, in which Mary's sorrowful gaze, tilted head, and the gesture of her free hand all convey the future sacrifice that Jesus will make on behalf of all humanity. It also departs from Byzantine iconographic prototypes, which paired the Virgin and Child and the Crucifixion (with a lamenting older

Mary and John the Theologian, and sometimes other figures at the foot of the cross) as separate images on diptychs.[37]

Nonetheless, the new prototype's juxtaposition of the maiden Virgin against the Crucifixion fits Orthodox teaching. It symbolizes her foreknowledge and acceptance of her son's sacrifice for the sake of human redemption (Luke 1:38). It "highlight[s] her involvement in the central action of salvation,"[38] that is, the "incarnation of God through the agency of a human woman."[39] In the vespers service for the Sunday of the Publican and Pharisee (the week during which the Akhtyrka icon stayed with the iconographer), worshipers directly address the "most precious Virgin," asking for her intercession: "Since you possess maternal boldness before Him, all-praised lady / Pray unceasingly that our souls may be saved!"[40]

How did the inclusion of the Virgin and the Passion within a single frame of an icon of the Mother of God come about? Several Western and Eastern influences came together to create the distinctive Akhtyrka prototype. It was so unusual, in fact, that as late as 1841, Smaragd (Kryzhanovskii), archbishop of Kharkov and Akhtyrka (as the diocese was then called) referred to it as being very different from other accepted Orthodox Mother of God images when he presented a copy of it to the archbishop of Riazan.[41] A 1758 order for copies of both the Kaplunovka (which depicted Mary with a crown) and Akhtyrka Mother of God icons asked for the use of fine Venetian paints, confirming an Orthodox East Slavic awareness of Venetian iconography. The latter served both an Orthodox and Catholic marketplace with a combination of Byzantine and Renaissance styles, which in turn influenced Orthodox icon painting throughout the Russian Empire.[42]

In addition to Venetian influence, the depiction of a young Mary as the central figure juxtaposed with the Passion came about because of heightened interest in Christ's Passion and resurrection by the mid-seventeenth century in Orthodox Ukraine and Russia.[43] Isolde Thyrêt notes that these themes were already emphasized in Patriarch Nikon's conception of his New Jerusalem Monastery (built in 1656 on the River Istra, about forty kilometers outside Moscow) and his commissioning a life-giving cross of Christ for a monastic church on the island of Kii in the same year.[44] The 1667 Nikonian reforms even indicated a preference for having the Crucifixion (instead of God as the Lord of Sabaoth) portrayed on the supplicatory row or Deisis of the iconostasis, based on the fact that scenes of the Passion had been common in Eastern churches in Kiev and elsewhere since antiquity.[45] Mary had been and continued to be rendered on the Deisis in full figure as an intercessor to the left of Christ (on Christ's right) with John the Baptist, the other intercessor, to the right. Published stories about Christ's suffering—many of them adopted from Catholic sources—also became common in seventeenth-century Ukraine, Belarus, and Russia.[46] Consequently, scenes and symbols of the Passion proliferated on crosses and church vessels. The cross, lance, and sponge also appeared on the increasingly popular icon of the suffering Virgin of the Passion (Strastnaia) holding a young Christ.[47]

In addition to a growing emphasis on Christ's death and resurrection in print literature, iconography, and on religious objects, numerous legends about the Mother of God as intercessor abounded in Belarus, Ukraine, and Russia in the second half of the seventeenth century. These included the highly popular *Nebo novoe* (New Heaven) and the *Zvezda presvetlaia* (The most brilliant Star) which also evinced post-Reformation influences (discussed in Boeck's chapter) and were, in turn, given iconographic forms. The Most Brilliant Star icon of Mary illuminated a crowned, unveiled, and full-figured Mother of God holding the infant Jesus with a fifteen-paneled star depicting various events in her life, including the Crucifixion.[48]

Finally, various manuscripts, which the Church deemed unacceptable, frequently described, among other subjects, apocryphal or non-biblical tales about Mary's life. The Orthodox Slavic lands had inherited them from Byzantium, and they had become popular within the oral traditions of the early modern period. The apocryphal "Dream of the Mother of God," like the later Akhtyrka Mother of God icon, relates how Mary foresaw her son's crucifixion. In a dialogue with his grieving mother, Christ explains her significance, foretelling her dormition and glorification on icons. By representing how Mary lives on earth through her icon, the tale imparted to believers the notion that she wandered the earth to console them. Penitents kept text amulets of the "Dream" and ascribed to Mary the ability to save people from storms, fire, injustice, life-threatening illnesses, difficult births, demonic hallucinations, and other scourges.[49]

Western and Eastern fascination with Christ's sacrifice heightened interest in Mary as both a universal and more local, immediate figure, and such apocryphal stories thus created fertile ground for a new prototype for a Mother of God icon. New depictions as opposed to variations of traditional models also reflected believers' hopes for "protection and justice in a changing world."[50]

## BELIEVERS' RECEPTION OF AND FORMS OF PIETY ASSOCIATED WITH THE ICON

Is it possible to discern how the Akhtyrka Mary appeared to eighteenth-century believers? Were they cognizant of her role as intercessor with Christ and did they refer to the Crucifixion? Did miracles they ascribed to the icon occur most often in the Lenten and Easter periods of the year? Unfortunately, answers to these questions are dependent upon highly redacted miracle stories; clerical scribes did not include full eyewitness testimonies. After all, the purpose of the written record was to describe the miracles. Periodically, especially for the initial years between 1743 and mid-1749, the narratives do contain richer descriptions that provide insights into popular piety.

Surprisingly, given the popularity of the Passion stories and the emphases on Mary as intercessor and protector, few miracle tales mention Christ at all or focus on the Akhtyrka Mother of God's roles. Those that do articulate these themes suggest that believers understood the iconography's symbolism. Many of the above stories refer to how Mary appeared to them in dreams. Witnesses often describe her as a young, beautiful woman wearing clothes of the colors depicted in the icon or, less frequently, in the more universal (Western) white. Most penitents ask for the Mother of God's mercy or help, with an unnamed woman in one instance directly referring to the Mother of God as "my holiest protector."[51] Mary's role as intercessor comes through clearly in two miracle tales. A Sumy resident reported that she had dreamed of "a young woman in white clothing," who informed her: "Woman, when someone prays to the Mother of God and she [the Mother of God] becomes her patron saint, the Mother of God prays to her son for those individuals in particular." Without mistaking Mary for a saint, Mariia Taranuzhina Iakovicheva was on firmer theological ground when she attributed her restored health to "the almighty God" "through the powerful petitioning of the Mother of God."[52] Tatiana Kramarka, whose disobedient son Moisei suffered from memory loss, was one of two believers who paid tribute to both "Christ the Lord and his Mother." The other, Nikita Toranenkov, was more specific in identifying Christ as having been crucified.[53] Two tales about alcoholics also mention the Crucifixion. In the more unusual of the two, Vasilei Ivanov Khilchenko of the Kharkov regimental town of Tarakanovka had out of desperation shouted in church after a priest was unable to lead him in prayer, "God the Father, God the Son, God the Holy Spirit, have mercy on me; most holy virgin Mother of God save me; Archangel Michael, have mercy on me." He claimed that Archangel Michael subsequently explained to him that he, the archangel, "had informed the Mother of God of the Akhtyrka miracle-working icon" about Khilchenko's situation, whereupon Khilchenko understood intuitively, without having seen the icon, that it was "marked by a maternal image and crucified Christ."[54] Clearly, the Akhtyrka icon delivered the powerful messages to its venerators that Mary represented an integral part of the salvation story and that through her sorrows as a mother she could help others.

The most unusual narrative outlining Mary's central role in his healing and an implicit understanding of Christ's suffering came from the testimony of Archdeacon Naftonail Grigorev Voloshin of Kharkov's Transfiguration Monastery. In the course of his memory loss and mental confusion, the archdeacon had several visions of Mary in dreams and in real time. At one point he dreamt of "a woman with the most wonderful and most illustrious face in military dress." In recalling a vision that he had of Mary in a church at the end of his forty days of sickness (in remembrance of Christ's fasting on the Mount of Temptation and the Saturday of Easter Week) the archdeacon poetically referred to her as "the wondrous mother." In this instance she was wearing a monastic mantle. The monk noted that after asking after his health, she proceeded to tell him that "you will return to your Kharkov monastery healthy and you will learn to seek spiritual purity, chastity, a non-hypocritical demeanor; [maintain] an attentive vigil in moments of suffering, [and] misfortune and be grateful for scowling looks, hatred and vexation without challenging them and grumbling." Finally, she ordered him to "maintain magnanimity until the end and fulfill the promise that [he] made." The archdeacon's promise, it turns out, had been to take the schema, the highest monastic degree in the Orthodox church, which involved a heightened regimen of fasting, prayers, and silence. Undoubtedly he would have interpreted his forty-day illness as the supreme test for a higher spiritual life. Archdeacon Naftonail would also have understood that a schemamonk's vows involved a second renunciation of the world through symbolic crucifixion (the first renunciation having been conducted upon his initial tonsure) and that the schemamonk's special garment (*analav*) was adorned with the instruments of the Passion. His spiritual healing was thus directly connected to the story of the Crucifixion and to Mary's intercession. The monk's experience is, nonetheless, unique within the miracle cycle.[55]

Although the archdeacon's healing occurred on the Saturday after Easter, the timing of all the reported miracles does not evince a significant correlation with either the Lenten or Easter seasons. In other words, penitents did not understand the Akhtyrka Mother of God's curative powers to be limited to the stories of the Passion and the Resurrection. Almost 18 percent of the cures took place in May, which generally fell during Easter season.[56] Some of these were associated with mid-Pentecost. Just 7 and 7.7 percent of reported miracles occurred in March and April respectively, with a surge of 20.7 percent in June and then almost 10 percent in July, followed by 9.4 percent each in August and September. The spike in the summer months can be explained by the fact that pilgrims could travel more easily at that time, and with pilgrims came diseases that could be passed from one community to another.[57] August and early September also involved celebrations of various feast days of the Mother of God and included the two-week fast of the Dormition. Suppliants understood these special occasions in Mary's life as propitious times to venerate the Akhtyrka icon.[58]

Regardless of their timing, what comes through in many of the stories is the awe and fear that believers felt before the Akhtyrka Mother of God icon. Witnesses had expressed these emotions in the epiphanic icon's foundational legend when they described what they understood to be extraordinary encounters with divine power. As Marcus Levitt reminds us, "the power of icons works in both directions: ... not only [do] the viewer-supplicants ... seek entry to otherworldly glory, but also ... a power ... emanates from icons ... that can give life, overcome evil, or vanquish disease."[59] Two more lay experiences illuminate further the powerful emotions the Akhtyrka icon provoked. As soon as Grigorii Topkonogov, a resident of the town Sumy who had been blind for six months, touched Mary's face on the icon he regained his sight. "At that very moment," he recalled, "he saw a flame on her face, and out of fear fell to the ground, and as he raised his eyes upward, he saw the light, and with that mercy of the Mother of God he went home." In the same year of 1744, the barren Praskovia Voskoboinnuka, who sought Mary's help in dispelling her irrational devilish thoughts, also described seeing a flame emanating from the icon as she stood before the royal doors in front of the high altar. Frightened, "she fell to the ground and made full-body prostrations." She thereafter regained her sanity.[60] Believers perceived divine grace to be extraordinary, powerful, and life transforming.

Although almost all perceived encounters with divine authority emanating from the Akhtyrka Mother of God involved healings (with the exception of Mary's prediction of the death of the baroness), a few miracle tales also described divine retribution for sinful behavior. These narratives served an important didactic function, reminding believers that even repentant sinners could ultimately be saved through Mary's mercy and intercession. At the same time, the tales might have dissuaded some from committing egregious sins. In one case, Semen Kozyrenko Krovets attributed his son's sudden blindness at the end of 1744 to the Akhtyrka Mother of God's displeasure with the fact that Semen labored the week before the celebration of Christ's birth. "Recognizing his sin, he [Semen] came to the church with his son Manuil and prayed to the Mother of God and promised that he would not work on those days until his death." His son's eyes were healed on that 1 January 1745, which Krovets attributed to the Mother of God's response to his supplication. However, in the miracle narratives, the Akhtyrka Virgin's divine wrath fell hardest on clerics and their relatives who had not taken their spiritual responsibilities seriously.

The priest Vasilii of the regimental village Razbishevka, who in October 1744 blamed alcohol for his "devilish" thoughts and inability to carry out his clerical duties, had come to Akhtyrka to venerate the icon. When he informed Father Daniil of his problems, Father Daniil ordered him to stand all night at the altar and to prepare himself for performing the liturgy the next day. That night, according to Father Vasilii, there was such a dreadful wind that he found it impossible to stand before the icon. As the flame from the icon's votive lamp went out, he thought he heard a voice emanating from the icon. Rubbing his eyes with the icon's lamp oil, he understood that the Mother of God was ordering him not to defile the church and telling him that he stunk (*smerdish*)! He reported that the incident instilled such fear in him that he barely survived. Nonetheless, he was able to serve the liturgy the next day, during which he informed believers of this miracle and vowed never to touch spirits again. A cleric's wife similarly believed herself to have been the object of divine retribution. She thought that the Akhtyrka Mother of God made her ill on several occasions to punish her for not fulfilling her repeated vows to visit and venerate the Akhtyrka icon after three family members ascribed their healings to the holy image.[61] Within the Orthodox belief system, the woman's broken vows had both personal and community repercussions. By failing to publicly venerate the icon in thanksgiving, she denied others the knowledge of the Virgin's help and participation in communal prayers.[62]

In addition to shedding some light on worshipers' personal understandings of what they believed were encounters with divine authority, the miracle stories illuminate the ways in which the laity venerated icons. The tales refer to believers ordering special prayer services before the Akhtyrka icon, saying prayers and making genuflections before it, and giving tokens of appreciation and love. Finally, in the event of a healing that they associated with the icon, they ordered another service in the icon's honor and reported the nature of the miracle to the officiating cleric. A few believers even promised to visit the Akhtyrka Mother of God icon annually as part of their ritual of thanksgiving.[63]

An icon offering could include a humble object of no monetary value connected to the person's illness or alternatively a coin, a cross, a small silver plaque, or votive in the shape of the affected body part either as a way of strengthening requests to the Mother of God for a cure or in thanks for a healing.[64] As a memento of his thanks to the Akhtyrka Mother of God for restoring his health and reminding him of his vows to take up the schema, Archdeacon Naftonail left the simple rope that the cleric had used to tie him up in the Pokrov Church (so that the archdeacon would not endanger himself) and which he, the archdeacon, believed had been cut by the Mother of God herself.[65] The laity's offerings to the Akhtyrka icon were sometimes more substantial in nature. The widow Sofiia Ivanova Bunchukovskaia of the town of Sorochintsy attributed the lessening of her fever and the dreadful noise in her head to the vow that she had made "to donate a small silver plate" for the icon prior to traveling to Akhtyrka. Once at the site her ailment disappeared entirely.[66] In another testimony of two alleged miraculous cures—of a tooth ailment and near-death experience after childbirth—a husband and his wife left a silver tooth and a gold coin as gifts to the Akhtyrka icon.[67] Other miracle stories also mention votive offerings in the shape of a foot, a silver tablet imprinted with a face (the sufferer had experienced horrible pain in her eyes, ears, and face), and a gold and silver cross.[68] Providing gifts to what were believed to be miracle-working icons in anticipation of cures and as testament to healings was widespread in the Orthodox areas of the empire, although votives in the form of body parts appear to have been a Ukrainian practice.[69]

The Spiritual Regulation of 1721 frowned upon the "superstitious" hanging of baubles and votives on icons, no doubt because of concerns about baneful Catholic influences. Defending the practice in a 1771–1772 investigation of offerings before the Mother of God icon in the Lubensk Church of the Nativity of the Mother of God (also in Left-Bank Ukraine), Governor-General Ivan Bogdanovich noted that parishioners hung offerings merely as decorations "only out of pride in and reverence for the name of the Mother of God, in whose name this very church ... is consecrated."[70] Interestingly, Archdeacon Naftonail in his dramatic narrative about taking the schema voiced what he believed to be the Akhtyrka Mother of God's opinion on the sensitive matter of votives. According to the archdeacon's recollections from a dream he had in spring 1747 (well after Father Daniil had been relieved of his duties), she noted that these tokens of thanks were on the one hand pleasing to her. On the other hand, she pointed out, "I do not need to be thanked with silver or gold or other votives." Instead, worshipers should concentrate on "correct[ing] depraved lives, pleas[ing] her with good deeds and ... the saving of souls."[71] The archdeacon was thus trying to steer penitents toward their Christian duties without, however, banning material donations. His dream must have confirmed in his mind that the latter were not evidence of superstition.

Personal thanksgivings to the Akhtyrka Mother of God appear much less frequently than the offerings in the miracle tales, but reflect the love the laity felt for Mary. Ivan Timchanko, the son of Andrei, from the town Aposhenska left a tender thanksgiving to her for curing him of paralysis of his limbs: "Thank you Most Holy Virgin for your great mercy, for you great mother, you are my hope, you are my helper, you are my healer." Timchanko noted that all the witnesses to his cure from the Akhtyrka icon responded with tearful gratitude to the Mother of God, glorifying her as they did so. Similarly, Dorosh Turlo of the town of Liutenka described the moving reactions of the eyewitnesses in the Pokrov Church. After his five-year-old son Grigorii recovered his sight and was able to reach toward the votive lamp before the icon, "his father took him into the middle of the church [and] began to make prostrations with tears [in his eyes]; all of the people standing in the church, having seen that miracle, were touched by [it] and with tears glorified the Mother of God."[72] Beholding the occurrence of miracles, of course, translated into the broadcasting of the icon's supplicatory powers and efficacy of praying to it to a much larger audience as witnesses spread word about the cures. Their testimonies also became critical in the investigatory commissions inquiring into the Akhtyrka icon cult.


CONCLUSION

The eighteenth-century foundational story of the Akhtyrka Mother of God icon and subsequent miracle tales provide a glimpse into the perception of Ukrainian and Russian believers of the Birthgiver of God as a stern, awe-inspiring protector who, through her intercession with God, aided individuals and families in distress both physically and spiritually. Believers certainly could not take her help for granted. Making vows to venerate her by making the effort to visit one of her icons and sharing with other believers special prayers were Christian duties not to be taken lightly. Once at the holy site, recipients of cures might also become witnesses to what they perceived to be other manifestations of God's grace upon the Belgorod diocese and Left-Bank Ukraine, which became truly integral parts of Orthodox Russia through the official recognition of the Akhtyrka icon.

The Holy Synod's acceptance in the mid-eighteenth century of a new prototype of the Mother of God icon, with Mary depicted as a maiden foreseeing the Passion, demonstrated that this body was able to acquiesce to the need of local believers for new avenues of access to divine authority that it most likely would have rejected just a few decades earlier as superstitious and too Catholic. The Western influences flowing into the ethnically Ukrainian and Belarusian areas of the empire from Poland could no better be halted than those that percolated within Moscow, St. Petersburg, and Murom. The formal acceptance of the radical Akhtyrka prototype—departing as it did from traditional iconographic models of the Mother of God—seemed to suggest that some of the Petrine religious reforms may have been too extreme in nature. Iconographic styles were changing in the eighteenth century to

FIGURE 2.2 A late eighteenth-century copy of the Akhtyrka icon of the Mother of God, which presents Mary in a traditional Byzantine mantle covering all her hair, but keeping the Western Renaissance style of portraying Mary's hands in prayer. Courtesy of Jackson's International Auctioneers and Appraisers.

reflect a number of Western influences and believers' needs, but that subject is far outside this paper's scope.

The story of the Akhtyrka icon did not end in the eighteenth century. The icon grew in prominence as it regularly appeared in nineteenth-century collections of stories attributed to famous "miracle-working" Russian Orthodox icons of Mary, on composite icons depicting all of those icons of

Mary in miniature, and in copies around the empire that were believed to be miracle-working themselves.[73] Although some of the copies of the Akhtyrka icon preferred a traditional Byzantine image of Mary (see fig. 2.2), the Akhtyrka's more modern Italian Renaissance image did not deter the Holy Synod in 1844 from sanctioning an annual procession of the original icon to occur on 31 May from the Pokrov Cathedral to Akhtyrka's Holy Trinity Monastery, which had been founded in the icon's honor.[74]

## NOTES

1. Research for this paper was conducted with the support of the National Endowment of the Humanities, the University of Helsinki's Aleksanteri Institute, and Northern Illinois University. I am grateful to Amy Singleton Adams, Steven A. Grant, Wendy Salmond, Vera Shevzov, Susan N. Smith, and the Library of Congress Russian History Reading Group for their perceptive comments on earlier drafts. Any errors or misinterpretations of fact are mine alone.

2. Rossiiskii gosudarstvennyi arkhiv drevnikh aktov (RGADA), f. 357 (Rukopisnoe sobranie Sarovskoi pustyni), op. 1, d. 232 (Iavlenie ikony Matere Bozhiia Akhtyrskoi), ll. 124, 124 ob., 125.

3. Ibid., l. 125–125 ob., nos. 1–2. The Synodal decree was issued 21 February 1722. *Opisanie dokumentov i del, khraniashchikhsia v arkhive Sviateishego Pravitel'stvuiushchego Sinoda*, 50 vols. (St. Petersburg: Sinodal'naia tip., 1868–1916), vol. 2, part 1: 392–93, no. 243.

4. RGADA, f. 357, op. 1, d. 232, l. 126–126 ob., no. 3.

5. In the eyewitness testimonies of miracles attributed to the Akhtyrka icon, the first reference to the icon being in the Pokrov Church (29 February) does not appear until the twelfth miracle—the fourth one reported to have occurred that day. Father Daniil may have moved the icon to the church earlier than that date. Ibid., ll. 126 ob.–127 ob., nos. 4–12.

6. The foundational story of the icon's miraculous appearance and listing of the initial 220 miracles between 1743 and mid-1749 may be found in RGADA, f. 357, op. 1, d. 232. Those miracles are supplemented by 156 (not counting the four miracles that the two documents share) that reportedly occurred between mid-1749 and 1774. See "Prilozhenie XXII: Reestr kto imiany ot Akhtyrskiia chudotvornyia Presviatyia Bogomatere ikony boleznovavshiia poluchili istselenii znachit' po semu," in *Opisanie dokumentov*, vol. 32, 931–62. All calculations involving the miracles are mine.

7. Approximately 27 percent of all recipients of cures attributed to the Akhtyrka icon were children and adolescents.

8. Vera Shevzov, *Russian Orthodoxy on the Eve of Revolution* (New York: Oxford University Press, 2004), 174.

9. Eve Levin, "False Miracles and Unattested Dead Bodies: Investigations into Popular Cults in Early Modern Russia," in *Religion and the Early Modern State: Views from China, Russia and the West*, ed. James D. Tracy and Marguerite Ragnow (Cambridge: Cambridge University Press, 2004), 264, 269–70; and note 2 above.

10. Marcus C. Levitt, *The Visual Dominant in Eighteenth-Century Russia* (DeKalb: Northern Illinois University Press, 2011), 199–200.

11. Out of thousands of icon cults, the Holy Synod investigated a total of sixty-eight, including copies of famous and already accepted miracle-working icons of the Mother of God. The concerns here had to do with fraudulent mechanisms making icons weep, clerical graft, made-up miracles, and poor quality images. *Polnoe sobranie postanovlenii i rasporiazhenii po vedomstvu pravoslavnago izpovedaniia Rossiiskoi Imperii* (hereafter as *PSPR*), 50 vols. (St. Petersburg: Sinodal'naia tip., 1869–1915), ser. 1, vol. 1, no. 225, 243; vol. 2, no. 906, 622; vol. 5, 23; vol. 7, no. 2492, 362–67; vol. 7, no. 2568, 474; Levin, "False Miracles," 264; Gregory L. Freeze, "Institutionalizing Piety: The Church and Popular

Religion, 1750–1850," in *Imperial Russia: New Histories for the Empire*, ed. Jane Burbank and David L. Ransel (Bloomington: Indiana University Press, 1998), 229; and Levitt, *Visual Dominant*, 200–201.

12. For discussions of formal ecclesiastical investigations of newly manifested miracle-working icons in the nineteenth century and the tensions that sometimes resulted with the laity, see Shevzov, *Russian Orthodoxy*, chap. 5.

13. Anatolii Zalavs'kyi, "Vykradennia Okhtyrs'koi chudotvornoi ikony Bozhoi Materi," Okhtyrka.net, 16 October 2006, www.okhtyrka.net/content/view/1865/106/. Zalavs'kyi lists himself as a local expert and pedagogue. His use of the available primary sources is exemplary.

14. *PSPR*, ser. 2, vol. 2, no. 774, 274; and Aleksandr Kiselev, *Chudotvornye ikony Bozhiei Materi v russkoi istorii* (Moscow: Russkaia kniga, 1992), 131.

15. Zalavs'kyi, "Vykradennia" and O. Galkin, "Khramy Okhtirshchyny," rada.okhtryka.com/hramy-ohtyrschyny, accessed 20 April 2015. The empress did visit Kiev in 1744, so a trip to Akhtyrka was certainly possible. See Akhmed Akhmedovich Iskenderov, *The Emperors and Empresses of Russia: Rediscovering the Romanovs*, ed. Donald J. Raleigh (Armonk, NY: ME Sharpe, 1996), 89.

16. Zalavs'kyi, "Vykradennia."

17. *PSPR*, ser. 2, vol. 3, no. 1229, 375–76.

18. Zalavs'kyi, "Vykradennia" and Galkin, "Khramy."

19. *PSPR*, ser. 2, vol. 3, no. 1229, 375–76. The second of July also celebrates Constantinople patriarch Gennadios I's placing of the Mother of God's robe in the Church of St. Mary of Blachernae in 458. See "Chudotvornaia Akhtyrskaia ikona," OrthodoxSumy, http://www.orthodoxsumy.narod.ru/relics/ahtyrskaya.htm.

20. Zalavs'kyi, "Vykradennia" and Galkin, "Khramy."

21. *PSPR*, ser. 1, vol. 7, no. 2568, 474. For a fuller discussion of the investigation of the Shelbitsy icon, see Levin, "False Miracles," 269–70, 281.

22. Evfimii Chudovskii, "Voprosy i otvety po russkoi ikonopisi," in *Filosofiia russkogo religioznogo iskusstva XVI–XX vv.: Antologiia*, ed. N. K. Gavriushin (Moscow: Progress-Kul'tura, 1993), 52. Red signified the Passion, whereas a blue mantle stressed Mary's virginity. Two 1729 icons (one of the Presentation of Christ into the Temple and the other the Nativity) from the iconostasis of Kievan Caves Lavra's Dormition Cathedral depict a young Mary with a white cap and hair visible. Anatolii Mel'nyk, *Ukrains'kyi ikonopys XII–XIX st. z kolektsii NkhMU* (Khmelnytskyi, Ukraine: Galereia, 2005), no. 51, 93; no. 54, 96.

23. The author is grateful to Vera Shevzov for pointing out this connection.

24. The baroness was buried in Akhtyrka's Church of the Dormition. RGADA, f. 357, op. 1, d. 232, ll. 187 ob.–188 ob., no. 217. The quotation is from Jeannine Hill Fletcher, "Review of *Mary, Mother of God*, ed. by Carl E. Braaten and Robert W. Jensen" *Ars Disputandi* 6 (2006), paragraph 10, Taylor & Francis Online (6 May 2014), http://www.tandfonline.com/doi/pdf/10.1080/15665399.2006.10819916. Various sources have identified the baroness as Major-General Rodion Kondratevich von Weidel's spouse and her daughters as Anna (1744–1830) and Mariia (d. 1774). Anna later married Count Zakhar Grigorevich Chernyshev (1722–1784) and Mariia—Count Petr Ivanovich Panin (1721–1789). These sources, however, contain some discrepancies in names and dates. According to von Weidel's family tree, Rodion Kondratevich was married not to an Elizaveta but rather to Anastasiia Bogdanova (née von Passek), who died not in 1748, when the miracle was dated, but in 1754 ("Rodion Kondrat'evich fon Vedel'," Rodovid, http://ru.rodovid.org/wk/Запись:337948). Tatiana Petrovna Passek's memoir confirms that her ancestors Anna Rodionovna and Elizaveta (*sic*) Rodionovna were known as "the Mother of God's daughters" and that Anna frequently visited Akhtyrka, where she commissioned the building of the Church of the Nativity with living quarters for herself. Both sisters and Count Panin were benefactors of the new Pokrov Cathedral. On her deathbed in 1830, Anna bequeathed jewels to adorn the gold cover for the Akhtyrka icon. "Bogoroditsa Akhtyrskaia: V posramlenie eresei i raskolov," Odna rodyna, http://odnarodyna.org/content/bogorodica-ahtyrskaya-v-posramlenie-eresey-i-raskolov; Tat'iana Petrovna Passek, *Iz dal'nikh let: Vospominaniia T. P. Passek*, 2nd ed., 2 vols. (St. Petersburg: A. F. Marks, 1906), 2:269; and Nikita Petrovich Panin, *Materialy dlia zhizneopisaniia grafa Nikity Petrovicha Panina (1770–1837)* (St. Petersburg: A. Brikner, 1888), 1, 4.

25. "Akhtyrskaia ikona Bozhiei Materi," Drevo-info.ru, http://drevo-info.ru/articles/6725.html.

26. The church was dedicated on 2 July 1768.

27. Levitt, *Visual Dominant*, 211.

28. Serhii Plokhy, *Tsars and Cossacks: A Study in Iconography* (Cambridge, MA: Harvard University Press, 2002), 22; and Serhii Plokhy, *Ukraine and Russia: Representations of the Past* (Toronto: University of Toronto Press, 2008), 72.

29. Innokentii, *Sochineniia Innokentiia, Arkhiepiskopa Khersonskago i Tavricheskago*, 12 vols. (St. Petersburg: M. O. Vol'f, 1871–1874), 3:114.

30. *Blagodeianiia Bogomateri rodu, khristianskomu chrez ee sviatye ikony*, 2nd ed. (St. Petersburg: I. L. Tuzov, 1905), 329–31. After the Battle of Poltava Peter commissioned a silver and gold icon cover with precious stones and case for the Kaplunovka icon. "Izvestiia i zametki," *Listok dlia Khar'kovskoi eparkhii*, no. 18, 30 September 1893, 448–49.

31. Other stories in the Akhtyrka miracle cycle in which a cured supplicant also went to Kaplunovka include RGADA, f. 357, op. 1, d. 232, l. 156a, no. 157; ll. 156a–157 ob., no. 165; ll. 164 ob.–165 ob., no. 182. Agafia Petrusska reported that her sight returned after she fulfilled her vow to venerate the Akhtyrka icon, which she had announced publicly before another Mother of God icon in her parish church in Kaplunovka. Ibid., ll. 131 ob.–132, no. 36. Only one narrative in which a penitent attributed his cure to the Akhtyrka Mother of God mentions another pilgrimage destination, in this case the ancient city of Kiev. Ibid., l. 163, no. 178.

32. In two instances in 1748, mothers who applied oil from the votive lamps of both miracle-working icons to their little girls' smallpox-wracked bodies reported miraculous benefits. Ibid., l. 186, no. 213; ll. 186 ob.–187, no. 214.

33. Ibid., ll. 150 ob.–151, no. 132. Unfortunately, the tale does not describe the symptoms of the "black illness." In early modern Russia the "black disease" had a variety of psychological and physical symptoms including falling to the ground, convulsions, mental confusion (sometimes including references to demons), lack of consciousness, and sometimes inability to use one or more limbs. The symptoms varied with the individual. Many thanks to Professor Levin for generously sharing her insights with me in an e-mail exchange as well as her discussion of the black disease in her "Identifying Disease in Pre-Modern Russia," *Russian History* 35, nos. 3–4 (2008): 329.

34. RGADA, f. 357, op. 1, d. 232, l. 177–177 ob., no. 198.

35. On the Kazan Mother of God icon's reported ability to cure blindness, see Natal'ia Budur, *Russkie ikony* (Moscow: Olma-Press, 2002), 77.

36. After 1744, the number of miracles per year falls off dramatically to between one and twenty-six, and there are only five references to blindness or eye ailments and five specifically to fever between 1745 and 1774. According to Donald R. Hopkins, smallpox was "responsible for more than a third of all the blindness in Europe." See his *The Greatest Killer: Smallpox in History* (Chicago: University of Chicago Press, 2002), 75. Parasites as well as deficiencies in vitamins A and B were also responsible for eye ailments and poor vision in preindustrial societies. See Kenneth F. Kiple, *The Caribbean Slave: A Biological History* (Cambridge: Cambridge University Press, 1984), 29; and Andrew Pettegree, *Reformation and the Culture of Persuasion* (Cambridge: Cambridge University Press, 2005), 108. Finally, cataracts also caused inadequate vision.

37. In medieval Byzantium the Virgin Hodegetria and child icon, which celebrated the Incarnation, was paired with the Crucifixion, with the latter appearing on the reverse side as in a diptych or processional icon. Bissera V. Pentcheva, *Icons and Power: The Mother of God in Byzantium* (University Park: Pennsylvania State University Press, 2006); and Cleo McNelly Kearns, *The Virgin Mary, Monotheism, and Sacrifice* (Cambridge: Cambridge University Press, 2008), 271–75.

38. Donna Spivey Ellington, "Review of Mother of God: A History of the Virgin Mary by Miri Rubin" (review no. 820), October 2009, https://www.history.ac.uk/reviews/review/820.

39. Helen C. Evans, ed., *Byzantium: Faith and Power (1261–1557)* (New York: Metropolitan Museum of Art, 2004), 184.

40. Part of tone five of the Apostikha (of the Resurrection), The Orthodox Page, www.ocf.org/OrthodoxPage/prayers/ triodion/pubnphar.

41. "Pis'ma Smaragda, arkhiepiskopa Riazanskago, k Gavriilu, arkhiepiskopu Riazanskomu zhe," *Chteniia v Imperatorskom obshchestve istorii i drevnostei rossiiskikh* (July–September 1873), 173.

42. The document is reprinted in A. S. Lebedev, "Votchinnyi byt monastyrei: Kurskago Znamenskago i Belogorodskago Nikolaevskago (po arkhivnym dokumentam)," *Sbornik Khar'kovskago istoriko-filologicheskago obshchestva*, no. 4 (1892), 177. On the importance of post-Byzantine art and culture on Crete, which came under Venetian rule from the Fourth Crusade onward, see Angeliki Lymberopoulou, "The Painter Angelos and Post-Byzantine Art," in *Locating Renaissance Art*, ed. Carol M. Richardson (New Haven, CT: Yale University Press, 2007), 175–212; and Svetlana Rakić, "The Representations of the Virgin on Cretan Icons in Serbian Churches in Bosnia-Herzegovina," *Serbian Studies* 20, no. 1 (2006): 57–93.

43. While the Akhtyrka Mother of God icon was not the first Orthodox icon to depict Mary with her hair down and bareheaded, it may have been the first to juxtapose her as a maiden against a miniature crucifixion. Definitive claims about late seventeenth- and early eighteenth-century icons are, however, difficult to make as those associated with Mazepa's Hetmanate may have been "deliberately destroyed, as a matter of policy, throughout the nineteenth century." Plokhy, *Tsars and Cossacks*, 31n1. The Bolshevik Revolution led to the destruction, sale, and loss of icons everywhere in the former empire. The Samara Mother of God icon, which disappeared after 1929 and was supposedly a copy of the original Akhtyrka image (although it portrays the Mother of God in the Byzantine maphorion rather than bareheaded), may have predated it. The Samara icon became known for miracles attributed to it as early as 1736 (at some unknown location), three years before the appearance of the Akhtyrka icon. In 1770 the Samara icon was transferred to a Zaporozhian Cossack church in what today is either the village Pokrovske or Kapulivka (not to be confused with Kaplunivka) in the Dnipropetrovsk region. "Ikona Bozhiei Materi 'Samarskaia,'" *Russkoe pravoslavie*, http://ortho-rus.ksproject.org/cgi-bin/or_file.cgi?8_5005.

44. Isolde Thyrêt, "The Cult of the True Cross in Muscovy and Its Reception in the Center and the Regions," in *Die Geschichte Russlands im 16. und 17. Jahrhundert aus der Perspektive seiner Regionen*, ed. Andreas Kappeler (Wiesbaden: Harrassowitz, 2004), 248, 245.

45. That reform was reprinted in the Holy Synod's 12 April 1722 ruling on iconography. *PSPR*, ser. 1, no. 534, art. 46, vol. 2:179.

46. D. A. Rovinskii, *Russkie narodnye kartinki*, ed. A. F. Nekrylova (St. Petersburg: Tropa Troianova, 2002), 164.

47. The Virgin of the Passion appeared in Greek iconography by the mid-fifteenth century and in Nizhnii Novgorod in the first half of the seventeenth century. L. A. Shitova, *Russkie ikony v dragotsennykh okladakh konets XVII–nachalo XX veka* (Sergiev Posad: Sviato-Troitskaia Sergieva Lavra, Sergievo-Posadskii gosudarstvennyi istoriko-khudozhestvennyi musei-zapovednik, Prodiuserskii dom Aidis, 2005), 231; Irina Dovgal, "The Icon of the Virgin of Passion in Post-Byzantine and Russian Art," Icon-network.org, http://www.icon-network.org/Approaches-to-Conservation.html; and Alfredo Tradigo, *Icons and Saints of the Eastern Orthodox Church*, trans. Stephen Sartarelli (Los Angeles: J. Paul Getty Museum, 2004), 188.

48. An example of a *Zvezda presvetlaia* icon, painted (c. 1690) by Aleksandr Kazantsev (b. 1658) of Murom's Annunciation Monastery, which art historians have identified as evincing influences of the Western European Madonna del Rosario, may be found in O. A. Sukhova et al., eds., *Ikony Muroma* (Moscow: Severnyi palomnik, 2004), 284–87.

49. G. P. Fedotov, *Stikhi dukhovnye (Russkaia narodnaia vera po dukhovnym stikham)* (Paris: YMCA-Press, 1935), 48, 49, 52, 53; W. F. Ryan, *The Bathhouse at Midnight: An Historical Survey of Magic and Divination in Russia* (University Park: Pennsylvania State University Press, 1999), 298–99; and Rovinskii, *Russkie narodnye kartinki*, 166.

50. Peter Robert Lamont Brown, *The Cult of Saints: Its Rise and Function in Latin Christianity* (Chicago: University of Chicago Press, 1981), 22; also quoted in Cherie Woodworth, "The Venerated Image among the Faithful: Icons for Historians," *Kritika* 8, no. 2 (2007): 400.

51. RGADA, f. 357, op. 1, d. 232, l. 173, no. 196.

52. Ibid., ll. 133 ob.–134, no. 52; and l. 169 ob., no. 189.

53. Ibid., l. 139, no. 76; and l. 159, no. 167.

54. Ibid., l. 180–180 ob., no. 202; l. 185–185 ob., no. 211.

55. Ibid., l. 173–173 ob., 174 ob., 175 ob.–176 ob., no. 197 (quotation on l. 176 ob.); Scott M. Kenworthy, *The Heart of Russia: Trinity-Sergius, Monasticism, and Society after 1825* (New York: Oxford University Press, 2010), 114–15; "Vows of the Tonsure to the Great Schema," *Orthodox Monk* (blog), 14 May 2007, www.orthodoxmonk.blogspot.com/2005/10/vows-of-tonsure-to-great-schema.html. Many thanks to Professor Kenworthy for his help with this part of the tale. It is unclear whether the reference to a woman in military dress was Mary but, as Vera Shevzov points out in her chapter in this volume, Mary "was liturgically praised as a 'victorious leader'" for aiding Byzantine armies.

56. Between 1743 and 1774, the years when miracles attributed to the Akhtyrka icon were recorded, Easter fell between 22 March and 22 April, and Pentecost between 10 May and 10 June.

57. In the eighteenth century pilgrims and other migrants carried such infectious diseases as smallpox, influenza, and the plague. The plague struck Ukraine in 1738–1739 (1739 was the year of the icon's epiphanic appearance) and between 1770 and 1773, but the Akhtyrka miracle stories do not mention it. Although they do not refer to influenza either (it was not a disease that non-medical people identified at the time), some of the individuals who reported cures might have suffered from the ailment. See Arcadius Kahan, *The Plow, the Hammer, and the Knout: An Economic History of Eighteenth-Century Russia* (Chicago: University of Chicago Press, 1985), 15, table 1.11. The Bogoliubskii icon of the Mother of God was connected to Moscow's 1771 plague riot. See Levitt, *Visual Dominant*, chap. 7.

58. Similarly, donations to the Kaplunovka Mother of God icon reached their peak during the major feast days in honor of Mary. O. O. Romanova, "Ochikuvannia 'chuda' iak osnova narodnoi pobozhnosti (Kyevs'ka Mytropoliia, XVIII st.)," *Ukrainskyi istorychnyi zhurnal*, no. 1 (2010): 23n65.

59. Levitt, *Visual Dominant*, 211.

60. RGADA, f. 357, op. 1, d. 232, l. 149, no. 124; and ll. 164 ob.–165 ob., no. 182.

61. Ibid., l. 161, no. 172; ll. 159 ob.–160 ob., no. 170; ll. 167–168 ob., no. 187.

62. Shevzov, *Russian Orthodoxy*, 242.

63. RGADA, f. 357, op. 1, d. 232, l. 97, no. 142; l. 142 ob., no. 100; ll. 145 ob.–146, no. 109.

64. Antonina Kizlova, "Viddzerkalennia ochikuvan' bogomol'tsiv u ikhnikh darakh do sviatyn' Kyeva (kinets XVIII–kinets XIX st.)," *Proseminarii, Mediievistyka, Istoriia tserkvy, nauky i kul'tury* 7 (2008), 307.

65. RGADA, f. 357, op. 1, d. 232, l. 176, no. 197.

66. "Prilozhenie XXII," 951–52.

67. RGADA, f. 357, op. 1, d. 232, ll. 170 ob.–171, no. 190.

68. Ibid., l. 144 ob., no. 106; ll. 178 ob.–179, no. 201; l. 151 ob., no. 135.

69. Kizlova, "Viddzerkalennia," 299–307; and Sophia Senyk, "For the Beauty of God's House: Notes on Icon Vestments and Decorations in the Ruthenian Church," in *Letters from Heaven: Popular Religion in Russia and Ukraine*, ed. John-Paul Himka and Andriy Zayarnyuk (Toronto: University of Toronto Press, 2006), 220.

70. Quoted in Romanova, "Ochikuvannia 'chuda," 87.

71. RGADA, f. 357, op. 1, d. 232, ll. 176 ob.–177, no. 197.

72. Ibid., ll. 155–57, no. 158 (quotation on l. 157); and ll. 134–35, no. 56 (quotation on l. 135).

73. Copies of the Akhtyrka Mother of God icon were eventually housed in churches throughout Kharkov diocese, Orel's Akhtyrsk Cathedral, Moscow's Church of St. Nicholas and the Church of the Resurrection on the Arbat, Samara's Pustynno-Nikolaevskii Monastery, the Church of the Ascension in Kozel, Saratov's Akhtyrka Mother of God Icon Women's Monastery, and the Church of the Dormition in Varzuga on the Kola Peninsula. "Akhtyrskaia ikona" and D. B. Kochetov, "Akhtyrskoi ikony Bozhiei Materi zhenskii monastyr," in *Pravoslavnaia entsiklopediia*, www.pravenc.ru/text/77220.html. Many thanks to Elena Kahla for telling me about an Akhtyrka icon in Varzuga.

74. Savva, "Khronika moei zhizni: Avtobiograficheskiia zapiski Vysokopreosviashchennago Savvy, Arkhiepiskopa Tverskago i Kashinskago," *Bogoslovskii vestnik* (December 1902), 138.

# 3

## Pushkin Framing Mary
### Blasphemy, Beauty, and National Identity

SARAH PRATT[1]

Пушкин—наше всё . . .

Аполлон Григорьев

Pushkin is our everything . . .

Apollon Grigorev

THERE ARE TWO ULTIMATE ANSWERS to any question about Russian culture. One answer is "Russian Orthodoxy." The other answer is "Pushkin." Past, present, and future—all lead into, or out of, Russian Orthodoxy or Pushkin. The shared investigation of *Framing Mary. The Mother of God in Modern, Revolutionary, and Post-Soviet Russian Culture* leads naturally to an examination of Russian Orthodoxy. But it is also possible to ask how Mary is framed within the context of *both* driving forces of Russian culture, Russian Orthodoxy *and* Pushkin. What is the relation between Pushkin the poet and Mary the Mother of God as they frame and are framed by modern Russian culture and each other?

Within the context of this question, it is worth taking another look at Apollon Grigorev's famous statement, "Pushkin—nashe vse" ("Pushkin is our everything"). Grigorev introduces the notion that Pushkin functions as a point of contact with other cultures, an intake valve of sorts, and by means of this function he somehow becomes a distillation of all that is Russian: "But Pushkin is our everything: Pushkin is the representative of our whole spiritual existence, of our uniqueness, of that which remains our own unique spiritual existence after all our encounters with others alien to us, with other worlds."[2] In this acknowledgment of Pushkin's relation to other cultures, Grigorev prefigures the concept of Pushkin's "universal responsiveness" (*vsemirnaia otzyvchivost'*) combined with "national spirit" put forward by Fyodor Dostoevsky in his Pushkin speech of 1880. Dostoevsky argues that the Russian people and Pushkin share a capacity to fuse the essence of an alien culture with one's native culture, and that this is what makes Pushkin the Russian national poet.[3] The paradox of Pushkin's role in Russian culture, then, is that he functions as a cultural conduit from Europe to Russia, infusing Russian culture with the thought and writings of Évariste de Parny, George Gordon (Lord) Byron, Friedrich Schiller, and many others through the power of his own works. At the same time, he comes to represent everything Russian, *nashe vse*.

A curious aspect of this function becomes evident in Pushkin's relation to the Mother of God, specifically in two poems that span the greater part of Pushkin's career and personal life as an adult. Odd as it may seem, Pushkin's relation to the figure of Mary provides a finely calibrated measure of his relation to the world. The first poem is the scabrous mock epic "Gavriiliada" or "The Lay of Gabriel" from 1821, and the second is the much more seemly poem "Madona" or "Madonna" from 1830. This focus on Mary by Russia's national poet supports the claim made by Vera Shevzov in her essay in this volume (further bolstered by Wendy Salmond's essay) that "Russia's Marian culture is dynamic and fluid and can accommodate changing circumstances." Shevzov notes that "stories associated with Mary and her icons can be easily modified. . . . Hence, Mary and her icons can potentially add great authoritative weight to any message that Orthodox clergy or laity wish to communicate."[4]

Pushkin, of course, represented laity to the point of occasionally being labeled a freethinker. Precisely because of the combination of fluidity and weight noted by Shevzov, the juxtaposition of the poems provides a telling perspective on the Pushkin myth put forward by Grigorev, Dostoevsky, and in more simplistic form by countless textbooks, calendars, greeting cards, and even candy wrappers and perfumes.[5] The myth casts Pushkin as a courtly gentleman inclined to liberal politics, and perhaps inclined also to certain libertine ways typical for young men of his social class. With few exceptions, the bad behavior and "frat boy" humor are quickly covered over by the notion of literary genius, at least as far as the myth is concerned, and are rarely integrated into our understanding of the poet's lifetime literary project. That project was to breathe in the culture of the world, and exhale a purified, rarified Russian air that would nourish the Russian spirit for millennia.[6] The examination of "Gavriiliada" and "Madona" leads us not so much away from the Pushkin myth, as toward a more holistic understanding of Pushkin's function in Russian culture. He becomes more thoroughly grounded and his contribution becomes even richer.

Pushkin was baptized, married, and buried with the rites of the Russian Orthodox Church.[7] He had the usual cultural exposure to Russian Orthodoxy, its rituals, and its icons. At the same time, of course, he was an impious young scapegrace who chafed at the strictures of Orthodox dogma and expectations of reverence. This is particularly evident in his first major attempt at framing Mary, "Gavriiliada," a boisterously irreverent retelling of the Annunciation written in 1821 and not published until well after Pushkin's death (and well beyond Russia's borders) in England in 1861.[8]

The work depicts Mary as a naïve, yet sexually curious teenager. "The young Jewess" (*molodaia evreika*), as Pushkin calls her, is marked by "the bouncy movement of two virginal hills beneath the fabric of her robe" (dvukh devstvennykh kholmov / Pod polotnom uprugoe dvizhen'e).[9] She is betrothed to a "gray-haired old man"—Joseph is not even named until much later in the text. We know only that he is old, busy with his work as a less than skillful carpenter and that, as a "lazy husband," he lives with Mary "like a father" and does not use his "old watering can to water the secret flower" that is his by right of betrothal. In this down-to-earth and even risqué description of the beginning of the Holy Family, "Gavriiliada" is reminiscent of the long tradition of Nativity plays, miracle plays, and pageants, in which the sphere of the divine is not remote or fearsome, but integrated into quotidian human experience. (As one scholar pointedly notes, "the Virgin often swears in miracle plays."[10])

The jolly tone of the work is supported by bubbling, irreverent rhymes such as the liturgical phrase used at the beginning of readings from the Gospel, "*vo vremia ono*," set against the Church Slavonic and Russian word *lono*, meaning bosom or womb, in a description of God's "affable gaze" as he looks down on his lovely creation: "No, s pravednykh nebes vo vremia ono / Vsevyshnii Bog sklonil privetnyi vzor / Na stroinyi stan, na devstvennoe lono" (But at that time from the righteous heavens, God on High cast his affable gaze upon the shapely figure, upon the virginal bosom) (121). Predictably, Joseph's neglect of his wife leads to drastic consequences. As Mary slumbers, God comes to her in a dream set in heaven. Despite the fact that Mary is already married to Joseph, God uses the subtext of the story of the wise virgins in the Gospel of Matthew to announce, "the bridegroom cometh, cometh to his handmaiden" (Zhenikh griadet, griadet k svoei rabyne).

What is interesting here, and what will become more relevant in the later poem "Madona," is Pushkin's use of apparent ekphrasis in the style of Western religious art rather than the style of Russian religious icons. First there is the fact that God the Father appears at all, which in theory is not allowed in Russian icons and frescos, although the convention is occasionally disregarded. In addition, the portrayal of heaven itself is marked not so much by majesty as by hubbub. Crowds of angels "bob and boil," countless seraphim fly around, and cherubim strum harps. The focal point is the throne of the Eternal One, which is covered with bright clouds. When the lusty Lord God appears, the harps fall silent and he addresses Mary directly: "Beauty of my beloved earthly daughters, the young hope of Israel! I call you, burning with love, be a communicant of my glory" (Krasa zemnykh liubeznykh docherei, / Izrailia nadezhda molodaia! Zovu tebia, liuboviiu pylaia, / Prichastnitsa ty slavy bud' moei). Having essentially propositioned Mary, God leaves, the throne is covered in clouds, a legion of winged spirits appears, and the sound of harps resounds again (121–22). There is no known specific model for this apparent ekphrasis. But the portrayal of heaven as a place of hubbub ruled by a human-like, fatherly God relates far more closely to Western traditions of religious art than to traditional Russian and Byzantine icons—to paintings like Anton Raphael Mengs's *Annunciation*, which Pushkin might have seen because it was acquired by Catherine the Great for the Hermitage in the 1780s, or Raphael's *Disputation of the Sacrament* in the Vatican, which might have been available to Pushkin in the form of lithographs or painted copies.[11]

Following God's announcement "the bridegroom cometh," Mary is seduced three times in the course of a single day—first by the Devil, then by the Angel Gabriel, and finally by the Holy Spirit in the form of a dove. The devil tells Mary stories, with daring speech and liberal illustrations (*smelyi slog, vol'nye kartiny*) and his wily words lead her to a vision of a young and handsome fellow, a version of himself, who enchants her with his flashing eyes and seduces her. Throughout this process, Mary remains silent—a fact that will turn out to be important later on.

> Она молчит; но вдруг не стало мочи,
> Едва дыша, закрыла томны очи,
> К лукавому склонив на грудь главу,
> Вскричала: ах! . . . и пала на траву . . . (129)

[She remains silent; but suddenly she had no more strength, barely breathing, she shut her languid eyes, resting her head on the sly devil's chest, she cried: ah! . . . and fell to the ground . . .]

After this, not wasting any time, the Angel Gabriel and the Holy Spirit take their turns in quick succession "on the rumpled sheet" (*na smiatoi prostyne*) of Mary's bed. Mary, understandably exhausted, nonetheless remarks to herself with a certain pride, "I must say, I held up pretty well: I've had Satan, an archangel, and God all in one day" (133).

For obvious reasons, Pushkin initially denied authorship of "Gavriiliada" when interviewed by Emperor Nicholas I. But textual analysis by scholars as well as Pushkin's own letters and history of irreverent poetry—the poems "Monakh" (The monk, 1813) and "Ten' Barkova" (The shade of Barkov, 1814–1815), among others distinguished by "extreme indecency of content and shocking crudity of expression"—ultimately identify the work as his.[12] There can be no doubt that the point of these poems is to have a good time and cause a scandal. If the young Pushkin were alive today, he would surely be a rapper, flaunting his ability to create brilliant and obscene rhymes against a driving backup track.

Some scholars justify the irreverence by linking it to Pushkin's propensity for parody. Vladislav Khodasevich, for example, in an essay on Pushkin entitled "Koshchunstva," or "Blasphemies," argues that the vast majority of Pushkin's "blaspheming" poems should be considered parodies. They should be viewed as the product of Pushkin's enlightenment links to writers like Voltaire and Parny, rather than as efforts at outright religious rebellion. Ultimately, Khodasevich maintains, "the atheism of 'Gavriiliada' is too jolly, open and light to be dangerous."[13] More recent scholars tend to follow Khodasevich's lead, arguing that the work focuses merely on foibles, human and divine, and should not be considered either truly obscene or a genuine attack on religion.[14]

Khodasevich and others are right that the roots of "Gavriiliada" are Western, but they reach back to periods well before the Enlightenment. The imagery of heaven suggests Renaissance European painting far more than Russian icons or church frescos, and the characters behave like stock characters in Western medieval mystery plays, including Nativity plays, which evolved from and alongside liturgical performances primarily, though not solely, in the West.[15]

Three years before he wrote "Gavriiliada," Pushkin portrayed Mary as he adapted the French tradition of the Christmas tale to his own satirical purposes in his poem "Skazki: Noël" (Tales: Noël). Here, Mary, already a mother, sings a lullaby to the crying Christ child. The lullaby portrays a bogeyman who is supposed to scare the crying child into silence. This, it turns out, is none other than the Russian tsar, who walks in and commands the people to rejoice because he is well-fed, healthy, and plump (*O raduisia, narod: ia syt, zdorov i tuchen*)—and because he plans to give the people laws in place of the *Ober-politseimeister* (Chief of Police) Ivan Savvich Gorgoli, a genuine historical figure. The tsar's beneficent plans are undercut, however, by the silliness of the bouncy meter and the notion that he is just telling tales (*skazki*) and not the truth—with the word *skazki* appearing both in the poem's title and as its final word. If this piece could be taken seriously enough to be perceived as framing Mary, we would have to say that it portrays Mary as a simple yet savvy person, apparently uncowed by the pompous pronouncements of the tsar. In this, she prefigures the younger Mary portrayed in "Gavriiliada," who remains unawed by the powerful figures she encounters, from God to the Devil to the Holy Spirit.

"Skazki: Noël" raises another interesting issue as well. From the start, Pushkin tends to avoid the standard Orthodox way of naming Mary as *Bogomater'* (Mother of God) or *Bogoroditsa* (Theotokos or God-Bearer). In this early poem, she is called simply *Mariia* and *mat'* (the mother), while in "Gavriiliada" she is likewise called *Mariia*, as well as by the epithets *evreika molodaia* (young Jewess) and *nevinnaia evreika* (innocent Jewess). It is only in 1826 in a poem entitled "K ***" (To ***), with the first line "Ty bogomater', net somnen'ia" (You are the mother of god, there is no doubt), that Pushkin uses the term *bogomater'*. He also uses the term *bogoroditsa moia* (my Theotokos) as the concluding words of the same poem. However, he is punning on these terms, transforming their meaning from the Orthodox Mother of God, to a lesser meaning, "the mother of *a* god"—in this case, the mother of Cupid, the god of love. The poem as a whole is a sacrilegious and witty compliment to an unidentified woman. The first quatrain of the poem echoes the tenor of "Gavriiliada," for as soon as the poet labels his beloved *bogomater'*, he remarks that she is *not* the one who enchanted only the Holy Spirit—she charms all and sundry; and she is certainly *not* the one who gave birth to Christ without even consulting her spouse (Khrista / Rodila, ne sprosias' supruga). The rest of the poem turns serious with a focus on the meaning of beauty, a theme to be addressed later on. The poet concludes by stating that the god of love and beauty looks just like his beloved, that she is the mother of Cupid, and therefore, in his eyes, a god-bearer: "On ves' v tebia—ty mat' Amura, / Ty bogoroditsa moia!"[16]

The young Pushkin seems to use Mary primarily as a vehicle for his own high spirits and mild bouts of rebellion against church and state. He glances off the Orthodox vision of Mary in her maternal role without engaging it in serious fashion. In "Skazki: Noël," the Mother of God merely serves as a reference point that allows the poet to consider the idiocy of the tsar in the context of a French Christmas poetic tradition; in "Ty bogomater', net somnen'ia," the Mother of God serves as the basis for a pun.

The figure of Mary that most interests Pushkin, the figure with which he engages and to which he devotes his full poetic energy, is a different type— Mary marked by beauty and sexual potential. This is the thread that links

"Gavriiliada" to the poem "Madona," and a poem that serves as a point of transition, "Net, ia ne dorozhu miatezhnym naslazhdeniem" (No, I do not cherish the stormy pleasuring). Like "Madona," "Net, ia ne dorozhu" was written in 1830 and is assumed to be addressed to Natalia Goncharova, who was finally Pushkin's fiancée after a tortuous courtship. With this frank and even graphic poem, Pushkin seems to be foreswearing his former bachelor ways and reassuring Goncharova that he prefers her—or at least his vision of her—to more active seductresses.

In the first stanza, the poet describes the stormy, serpent-like embrace of a "young Bacchante," who hurries the moment of the last sexual tremors—which, the poet protests, he does not cherish. In the second stanza, he describes the kind of sex that he does cherish—sex with his "meek one" who, "abashed and frigid," only involuntarily comes to "share [his] flame" at the end of the poem.

> Нет, я не дорожу мятежным наслажденьем,
> Восторгом чувственным, безумством, исступленьем,
> Стенаньем, криками вакханки молодой,
> Когда, виясь в моих объятиях змией,
> Порывом пылких ласк и язвою лобзаний
> Она торопит миг последних содроганий!
>
> О, как милее ты, смиренница моя!
> О, как мучительно тобою счастлив я,
> Когда, склоняяся на долгие моленья,
> Ты предаешься мне нежна без упоенья,
> Стыдливо-холодна, восторгу моему
> Едва ответствуешь, не внемлешь ничему
> И оживляешься потом все боле, боле—
> И делишь наконец мой пламень поневоле![17]

[No, I do not cherish the stormy pleasuring, the sensual ecstasy, the madness, the frenzy, the moans and shrieks of a young bacchante, when, writhing like a serpent in my embrace, with a burst of ardent caresses and festering kisses, she hastens the moment of final tremors.

O, how much sweeter you are, my meek one! O, how happy and tormented I am when, bending to my long supplications, you give yourself to me tenderly without rapture, abashed and frigid, you hardly respond to my ecstasy, you do not heed anything (around you), and then you are aroused more, more—and finally you involuntarily share my flame!]

This is not the place for an extended analysis of the poem, but it is worth noting that the form conveys a large part of the message. Pushkin's use of the six-foot iambic line is striking. The single sentence of the first stanza mimics the pushy, pulsing, slithering, serpent-like approach of the Bacchante. Then in a totally different fashion within the same meter, the second stanza seems to be almost static as the beloved "barely responds" (*edva otvetstvuesh'*) until the sudden rush of the final two lines when she "shares his flame." In addition, the rhyme phrases tell the whole story almost by themselves. In the first stanza:

> *naslazhden'em / istuplen'em* (pleasuring / frenzy)
> *vakkhanki molodoi / zmeei* (young Bacchante / like a serpent)
> *iazvoiu lobzanii / poslednikh sodroganii* (festering kisses/ final tremors)

And in the second stanza:

> *smirennitsa moia / schastliv ia* (my meek one / happy I am)
> *dolgie molen'ia / bez upoen'ia* (long supplications / without rapture)
> *vostorgu moemu / ne vnemlesh' nichemu* (my ecstasy / don't heed anything)
> *bole, bole / plamen' ponevole* (more, more /involuntarily [share] my flame)

In addition to the telling rhymes, Pushkin uses a type of poetic and sexual mimicry. There is the repeated O-sound of the interjection "*O*" in the first two lines of the second stanza, suggesting groans of sexual pleasure as the poet begins his description and seduction of his initially unresponsive beloved and then again same O-sound as the poet describes his sexual triumph—"bole, bole ... ponevole." And then there is the whole issue of sexual control. By using a fourteen-line structure (one might say a cousin of the tightly constructed sonnet), Pushkin demonstrates his own exquisite poetic control and mimics the type of sexual control favored by his poet-persona in the slowly building second stanza with the climax at the end.

In the context of "Gavriiliada," it is tempting to assume that the lusty, sixteen-year-old Mary is more akin to the Bacchante of the first stanza above than to the "meek one" of the second stanza of "Net, ia ne dorozhu." But this is not the case. When the Devil seduces Mary in the earlier poem, Mary does not lose herself in "ardent caresses and festering kisses" like the Bacchante. Rather, she remains silent (*ona molchit*). It is only when she can resist no longer that she succumbs, cries "Ah!" and tumbles to the ground. Likewise, when the Angel Gabriel begins to kiss her, Mary reacts with silence, blushes, and tries to push him away before she finally succumbs to his blandishments (132). Like the "meek one" in the second stanza of "Net, ia ne dorozhu," Mary's participation in the sex act is restrained and at first involuntary, though ultimately fulfilling.

It is the Devil, the incarnation of active lust, who parallels the Bacchante. And it is perhaps no accident that the Devil first appears to Mary as a serpent in "Gavriiliada," while the Bacchante who writhes in the poet's embrace in "Net, ia ne dorozhu" is described as being "like a serpent."

As part of the transition from "Gavriiliada" to Pushkin's poem "Madona," it is worth considering Pushkin's own transformation from the talented and insolent young whippersnapper of 1821 to the mature, increasingly harassed poet and determined fiancé of 1830. How had Pushkin's life and writing changed in the meantime? He had written most of *Evgenii Onegin*. He had seen Onegin transformed from the flippant dandy of the early cantos to the darker, more complex and confused figure of the ending. Like Onegin, Pushkin had traveled across a wide swath of Russia. He had lived in exile. He had, at a distance, experienced the Decembrist Revolt and its consequences. He had met and courted Natalia Goncharova and was about to marry her. And, odd as this may seem, he had been reading the Bible. Perhaps inspired partly by the activities of the Bible Society in Russia in the 1820s, Pushkin wrote to a friend from Odessa in April 1824 that he was reading the Bible, and in November the same year he wrote to his brother Lev, requesting that he send him, and this is in Pushkin's own words with two exclamation points, "a Bible, a Bible! and without fail the French one!"[18] The nuance of political subversion created after the elimination of the Russian Bible Society in 1826 most likely piqued Pushkin's interest still further. Whatever the case, he had multiple copies of the New Testament and the Bible in various languages in his library and, perhaps not so surprising now in hindsight, his works contain more allusions to the Bible than to any other work.[19]

What does all of this boil down to in terms of poetry, in terms of Pushkin's relation to Mary? It boils down to the poem "Madona" (Madonna) from 1830. The poem is a far cry from "Gavriiliada" in many ways. As opposed to the boisterous tone, five-foot lines, and irregular stanzas of the earlier work, this is a rigorously constructed sonnet in stately six-foot lines. Within the interlocking rhyme scheme AbbA AbAb CCd EdE, the rhymes reinforce the message of the poem. *Zritel'* (viewer) rhymes with *Spasitel'* (Savior), signaling the ekphrastic nature of the poem, as well as the ambiguous relationship between the viewer and subject of the painting, between the lyric voice and the subject of the poem itself; *Siona* (Zion) rhymes with *Madona* (Madonna), both foreign words signaling the non-Russian setting of the painting and the poet's own vision; and *Tvorets* (Creator) rhymes with *chisteishii obrazets* (purest model), suggesting the "divine" nature projected by the poet upon his beloved.

The opening of "Madona" sends two kinds of signals. One set has to do with Western culture, specifically Western artistic and religious culture. The other reflects the persona's gentle rebellion against social conventions. The title, which in some editions is spelled with one *n* and in others with two, is clearly not Russian, but Italian. Here again, Pushkin eschews the use of the Slavonic terms *Bogomater'* and *Bogoroditsa*. The sonnet form of the poem (in some editions emphasized by the subtitle "*sonet*") points to a Western poetic form. And once the poem gets underway, it becomes clear that the persona is musing about Western art, specifically the Old Masters.

Мадона

Не множеством картин старинных мастеров
Украсить я всегда желал свою обитель,
Чтоб суеверно им дивился посетитель,
Внимая важному сужденью знатоков. (296)

[Not with a plethora of pictures by Old Masters would I ever wish to decorate my cloister, so that a visitor, heeding the pompous judgments of connoisseurs, would be impressed on the basis of prejudgment.]

The second and third stanzas, a quatrain and a tercet, respectively, continue the theme of almost antisocial humility and provide a counter example to the plethora of Old Masters rejected by the persona.

В простом углу моем, средь медленных трудов,
Одной картины я желал быть вечно зритель,
Одной: чтоб на меня с холста, как с облаков,
Пречистая и наш божественный спаситель —

Она с величием, он с разумом в очах —
Взирали, кроткие, во славе и в лучах,
Одни, без ангелов, под пальмою Сиона.

[In my simple corner amidst my lengthy labors, I would wish eternally to be a viewer of one picture, only one: so that from the canvas, as if from the clouds, the Most Pure One and Our Divine Savior—

She with majesty, he with intelligence in his eyes, the meek ones, would gaze down on me in glory and rays of light, all alone, without angels, under a palm of Zion.]

While the plethora of paintings by the Old Masters was dismissed in a single stanza without any attempt at description, the ekphrastic portrayal of the one painting desired by the persona stretches tortuously over two stanzas.

After the colon when the persona asserts that he wants just *one* painting, readers run into all kinds of tangled syntax. The clause starts with a series of prepositional phrases related to something that will come later: "so that upon me from the canvas, as if from the clouds." It then continues with the dual subject, "the Most Pure One and Our Divine Savior," only to bump into the end of the stanza. The syntactic suspense created by the cross-stanza enjambment intensifies the focus on the figures of the Most Pure One and Our Divine Savior, a focus still further heightened by another phrase set off by dashes, "—She with majesty, he with intelligence in his eyes—." Only at this point do readers finally come to the verb they have been waiting for, *vzirali* (would gaze). The common root of the verb *vzirat'* (to gaze) and the noun with which the persona describes himself, *zritel'* (viewer, gazer) underscores the paradoxical fact that the poet wants the figures in the painting to look at him while he is looking at them. In this relationship, it is impossible to know for certain who is the subject and who is the object.

In the final tercet, which is woven back into the preceding text through rhymes, the persona finally gets what he wants. He makes this clear with a short, blunt opening sentence that interrupts the stateliness of the six-foot line: "Ispolnilis' moi zhelaniia" (My desires have been fulfilled). This is followed by the sudden introduction of the second person addressee of the poem, presumably Goncharova, in an alliterative enjambment *Tvorets / Tebia* (the Creator/ You) that emphasizes the "divine" nature of the poet's personal "Madonna." The repeated placement of first and second person forms next to each other in the penultimate line (*Tebia mne … tebia, moia*) further strengthens the bond between the poet and his beloved.

> Исполнились мои желания. Творец
> Тебя мне ниспослал, тебя, моя Мадона,
> Чистейшей прелести чистейший образец.

> [My desires have been fulfilled. The Creator has sent you down to me, you, my Madonna, the purest model of the purest delight.]

It is only in this penultimate line, when the poet turns directly to his beloved, that the whole point is revealed: the poet is in love with the painting because what he really wants is his beloved, "the purest model of the purest delight."

Pushkin is rehearsing themes that will come into their own in his late poetry, especially his reflective poem from 1834, "Pora, moi drug, pora! Pokoia serdtse prosit" (It's time, my friend, it's time! My heart seeks peace). The later poem was also presumably written to Natalia, by then his wife, and written in a six-food iambic line. It emphasizes weariness and a desire to find to a peaceful place of contemplation, labor, and bliss with the closing lines, "Davno, ustalyi rab, zamyslil ia pobeg / V obitel' dal'nuiu trudov i chistykh neg" (A weary slave, I long ago imagined escape to a distant cloister of labor and pure bliss.)[20] "Madona" partakes less of weariness and ends on a note of elation, to be sure, but like "Pora moi drug, pora," it is based on a parallel notion of escape from society's norms, and underscores this sense of separation from the world through the use of the same word *obitel'*, "cloister" or "abode." In each case the poet seeks a life of labor (*trud*) linked somehow to purity expressed in the adjective *chistyi* and a noun denoting delight or bliss (*prelest'* or *nega*).

But back to Pushkin's courtship of Natalia Goncharova: in the summer of 1830, the poet wrote to Natalia from Petersburg as follows: "The ladies ask to see your portrait, and do not pardon me for not having it. I console myself by spending hours in front of a blonde Madonna who is as much like you as two drops of water, and whom I would have bought, if she did not cost forty thousand rubles."[21] Clearly, this is a reference to a work of art displayed for sale. Although the exact identity of the piece will probably never be known, Pushkin's recent biographer, T. J. Binyon, believes that the "blonde Madonna" was a Virgin and Child, attributed to Raphael on exhibit at Slenin's bookshop on Nevsky Prospect.[22] Pushkin had apparently seen a resemblance between Natalia and the typical Renaissance Madonna from the beginning, teasingly calling his nearsighted fiancée a "red-haired Madonna with a squint."[23] And he was not the only one who saw divine beauty in Natalia. The wife of the Austrian ambassador to Russia, who snidely found Natalia "far from witty," nonetheless writes of "Mme Pushkina, whom we call the poetic, not so much because of her husband as because of her celestial and incomparable beauty." The ambassador's wife continues in a manner reminiscent of Pushkin's statement about staring at the portrait in the shop, "She has a face before which one could stay for hours, as before a perfect work of the creator."[24] Addressing the effect of such profound, otherworldly beauty, the Pushkin scholars David Bethea and Sergei Davydov note that "if Pushkin believed in anything, it was in the transfiguring power of beauty, whether the physical charm of Venus or the spiritual calm of the Virgin, and for him, 'Nathalie,' perhaps unknown to her, was the embodiment of both."[25]

Over the years there have been various hypotheses as to the identity of the work described in the poem "Madona," as well as the one so admired by Pushkin on Nevsky Prospect, which may or may not have been the same. Some scholars and memoirists assert that Pushkin had a Madonna by Perugino in mind, while others assert that it was a Raphael.[26] Certainly the educated classes of Russia were smitten with Raphael throughout much of the nineteenth century, starting with Vasilii Zhukovskii's article, "Raphael's *Madonna*," based on his visit to the Dresden Gallery where the *Sistine Madonna* was on exhibit. "This is not a picture, but a vision," wrote Zhukovskii. "The longer you look, the more deeply you become convinced that something supernatural is taking place before you." Zhukovskii claimed, moreover, that one of the cherubs looking up from beneath the clouds represented Raphael himself, who was contemplating the Madonna as "a genius of pure beauty."[27] This is the phrase *genii chistoi krasoty* that Zhukovskii used in his poem of 1824, "Ia muzu iunuiu, byvalo" (The young muse I used to . . . ), and that Pushkin most famously used in *his* poem, "K*** (Ia pomniu chudnoe mgnovenie)" (To *** [I remember the wondrous moment]) of 1825. Less famously adding fuel to the same fire, Vilgelm Kiukhelbeker also wrote an article on the *Sistine Madonna* in 1824, calling it "the holy of holies."[28]

Pushkin never saw the *Sistine Madonna* itself, but engravings were widely available, and it is said that painted copies of it hung in the Academy of Arts and the empress's reception room.[29] His knowledge of the work is suggested in a poem from 1828 about Anna Olenina, his beloved at that time, entitled "Ee glaza" (Her eyes). Scholars hypothesize that "Raphael's angel" in the poem could be one of the cherubs looking upwards toward Mary in the *Sistine Madonna*. The poem concludes: "and if she raises [her eyes]—thus Raphael's angel contemplates the divinity" (Podnimet—angel Rafaelia / Tak sozertsaet bozhestvo.)[30]

But Pushkin's poetry suggests a broader knowledge Raphael's works as well. In the poem "Kto znaet krai, gde nebo bleshchet . . ." (Who knows the land, where the sky sparkles . . .) from 1828, based loosely on Goethe's "Kennst du das Land, wo die Zitronen blühn" (Do you know the land where the lemon trees bloom), Pushkin develops the popular theme of Italy as the seat of warmth and culture "where Raphael painted." In the second stanza, he mentions a lovely baker girl, *La Fornarina*, usually attributed to Raphael, as well as an unspecified Madonna by Raphael, thought by scholars to be the *Madonna della seggiola* (Madonna with a chair). But in addition to contributing to the standard Romantic portrayal of Italy, the poem had another goal. It was an attempt by Pushkin to curry favor with Mariia Musina-Pushkina (not a close relation), who had recently returned from a trip to Italy, and whom he characterizes in the poem as "another Mary."[31] There is no known image of Mariia Musina-Pushkina, but there is a substitute in the form of Pushkin's attestation of her beauty. He declares that she is even more entrancing than Raphael's paintings of La Fornarina and a "young Madonna":

В молчанье смотрит ли она
На образ нежный Форнарины

Или Мадонны молодой,
Она задумчивой красой
Очаровательней картины.[32]

[And whether she gazes at the image of the tender *Fornarina* in silence or at the young *Madonna*, she, with her pensive beauty, is more entrancing than the picture.]

Here again, the divine beauty of the beloved is linked to silence, even pensiveness, and linked to echoes from Pushkin's "Ia pomniu chudnoe mgnoven'e: Ee nebesnye cherty" here repeats "Tvoi nebesnye cherty" from the earlier poem, and the rhyming phrase "Bogini vechnoi krasoty" echoes the earlier phrase "genii chistoi krasoty." In the poem's conclusion, Pushkin challenges "inspired Raphael, crowned by the graces," to "forget the young Jewess" (the epithet used earlier in "Gavriiliada") and "capture the otherworldly charm, capture the joy of the heavens, and paint a different Mary with a different infant in her arms"—which is to say, Mariia Musina-Pushkina, who had a young son.

In the end, Mary, for Pushkin, was not the Russian Mother of God, *Bogomater'* or *Bogoroditsa*. Mary's role as a mother plays out only incidentally in the course of jokes or witticisms, or to create parallels with a young lady Pushkin was trying to impress. Otherwise, Mary is portrayed either naturalized to her origins as the "young Jewess" or, most powerfully, in explicitly Western terms as a Raphael-like Madonna, a model of purity and beauty, typically associated with a woman Pushkin was wooing. But in the figures he engages seriously, the issue is not just beauty, but a particular attitude toward sex. Neither as a young Jewess, nor as a Madonna, is Pushkin's Mary sexually assertive. She is reserved and seemingly frigid. Her participation in sex is involuntary. But in the end, thanks to the exquisite skills of her lover, she "shares his flame." She represents what Marina Warner calls "Mary, Madonna, and idealized mistress."[33] Pushkin's Mary is a creature of heavenly beauty and a creature of paradox: she is both chaste and accessible, and, true to Pushkin's role in Russian culture, she is a Western model made quintessentially Russian.

## Notes

1. This essay is dedicated to the students in my seminar on Evgenii Onegin—Natalia Dame, Anna Krivoruchko, Bernardetta Palumbo, and Anastasia Vanyakina—who helped me understand part of the "everything" that is Pushkin. I am grateful to Natalie Dame for research support, to the readers of the manuscript for excellent suggestions, and to the hosts and organizers of the conference,

especially Amy Singleton Adams and Vera Shevzov, for setting this multifaceted and extremely productive scholarly endeavor in motion.

2. Apollon Grigor'ev, "Vzgliad na russkuiu literature so smerti Pushkina," in *Sochineniia* (St. Petersburg: Obshchestvennaia pol'za, 1876), 238, cited in T. J. Binyon, *Pushkin: A Biography* (New York: Vintage, 2002), xxv. See also Vadim Serov, ed., *Entsiklopedicheskii slovar' krylatykh slov i vyrazhenii*, accessed 1 January 2011, http://www.bibliotekar.ru/encSlov/15/275.htm; and Apollon Grigor'ev, *Sochineniia v dvukh tomakh*, vol. 2 (Moscow: Khudozhestvennaia literatura, 1990).

3. F. M. Dostoevskii, "Pushkin (Ocherk)," *Polnoe sobranie sochinenii*, ed. V. G. Bazanov (Leningrad: Nauka, 1984), 26:146–47. See further discussion in David L. Cooper, "Vasilii Zhukovskii as a Translator and the Protean Russian Nation," *The Russian Review* 66, no. 2 (2007): 201–3.

4. See Vera Shevzov, "On the Field of Battle: The Marian Face of Contemporary Russia," and Wendy Salmond, "Kuzma Petrov-Vodkin's *1918 in Petrograd* (*The Petrograd Madonna*) and the Meanings of Mary in 1920" in the present volume.

5. See Stephanie Sandler, *Commemorating Pushkin: Russia's Myth of a National Poet* (Stanford, CA: Stanford University Press, 2004); Boris Gasparov, "Obraz Pushkina v istorii russkoi kul'tury," in *Poeticheskii iazyk Pushkina* (St. Petersburg: Akademicheskii proekt, 1999), 14–20; Marcus C. Levitt, *Russian Literary Politics and the Pushkin Celebration of 1880* (Ithaca, NY: Cornell University Press, 1989); Catharine Theimer Nepomnyashchy, introduction to *Strolls with Pushkin*, by Abram Tertz (Andrei Sinyavsky), trans. Catherine Theimer Nepomnyashchy and Slava I. Yastremski (New Haven, CT: Yale University Press, 1995), 30–41.

6. William Mills Todd's integration of the ribald aspect of Pushkin's personality into a larger context is especially valuable. See *The Familiar Letter as a Literary Genre in the Age of Pushkin* (Princeton, NJ: Princeton University Press, 1976). Daniel Rancour-Laferriere's articles on Pushkin's *Mednii vsadnik* (*The Bronze Horseman*) and Tatiana's dream in *Evgenii Onegin* treat some of the same impulses specifically in a psychoanalytic framework. See Daniel Rancour-Laferriere, "The Couvade of Peter the Great: A Psychoanalytic Aspect of *The Bronze Horseman*," in *Puškin Today*, ed. David M. Bethea (Bloomington: Indiana University Press, 1993), 73–85; and "Pushkin's Still Unravished Bride: A Psychoanalytic Study of Tat'iana's Dream," in *Russian Literature* 25, no. 2 (1989): 215–58.

7. Binyon, *Pushkin*, 4, 345, 609–10.

8. Ibid., 135; N. P. Ogarev, ed., *Russkaia potaennaia literatura XIX veka* (London: Tribner, 1861), cited in Susanne Fusso, "Maidens in Childbirth: The Sistine Madonna in Dostoevskii's Devils," *Slavic Review* 54, no. 2 (1995): 265; Maria Rubins, "Puškin's Gavriiliada: A Study of the Genre and Beyond," *Slavic and East European Journal* 40, no. 4 (Winter 1996): 623–31; see also M. P. Alekseev, "Zametki o Gavriiliade," in *Pushkin*, ed. M. P. Alekseev (Leningrad: Nauka, 1972), 281–325; William Harkins, "Pushkin as Comic Poet," in *Three Comic Poems*, by Alexander Pushkin (Ann Arbor, MI: Ardis, 1977), 9–22; Greta N. Slobin, "Appropriating the Irreverent Pushkin," in *Cultural Mythologies of Russian Modernism: From the Golden Age to the Silver Age*, ed. Boris Gasparov, Robert Hughes, and Irina Paperno (Berkeley: University of California Press, 1992), 214–30; Robert Sorenson, "Pushkin's Gavriiliada: From Style to Meaning," *Russian Language Journal* 35 (1981): 59–73; Boris Tomashevskii, "Gavriiliada, Istoriia sozdaniia, Postroenie poemy," in *Pushkin* (Moscow: Izd-vo Akademii nauk, 1956), 425–35; L. Vol'pert, "O literaturnykh istokakh Gavriiliady," *Russkaia literatura* 3 (1966): 95–103.

9. A. S. Pushkin, *Gavriiliada: Poema*, in *Sobranie sochinenii v 10 tomakh* (Moscow: Gosudarstvennoe izd-vo khudozhestvennoi literatury, 1960), 3:120–35. All subsequent quotations of Pushkin's works are from this edition. Page numbers for *Gavriiliada* from this edition will be cited in parentheses in the text.

10. Marina Warner, *Alone of All Her Sex: The Myth and the Cult of the Virgin* Mary (New York: Alfred A. Knopf, 1976), 156; Frederick T. Wood, "The Comic Elements in the English Mystery Plays," *Neophilologus* 25, no. 1 (1940): 194–206; Eleanor Prosser, *Drama and Religion in the English Mystery Plays: A Re-evaluation* (Stanford, CA: Stanford University Press, 1961); Jaroslav Pelikan, *Mary through the Centuries: Her Place in the History of Culture* (New Haven, CT: Yale University Press, 1996).

11. Fusso, "Maidens in Childbirth"; Irene Pearson, "Raphael as Seen by Russian Writers from Zhukovsky to Turgenev," *The Slavonic and East European Review* 59, no. 3 (1981): 351–52.

12. I. A. Pil'shchikov and M. I. Shapir, eds., *Pushkin: Ten' Barkova; Teksty, kommentarii, ekskursy* (Moscow: Iazyki slavianskoi kul'tury, 2002), 7. The author wishes to thank Marcus Levitt for this reference and much wisdom about Pushkin in Russian culture. Binyon, *Pushkin*, 134–35; A. D. P. Briggs, *Alexander Pushkin: A Critical Study* (London: Bristol Classical Press, 1991), 138–39. See also Andrew Kahn, *Pushkin's Lyric Intelligence* (Oxford: Oxford University Press, 2008), 170–71, 278–338.

13. V. F. Khodasevich, "Koshchunstva Pushkina v ego kn.," in *O Pushkine* (Berlin: Petropolis, 1937), 112–15. See also Fusso, "Maidens in Childbirth," 266, 273–74, and Alekseev, "Zametki."

14. Binyon, *Pushkin*, 135; Briggs, *Alexander Pushkin*.

15. See note 9 above. A Byzantine source is explored in Egon Wellesz, "The Nativity Drama of the Byzantine Church," *The Journal of Roman Studies* 37, nos. 1–2 (1947): 145–51.

16. Pushkin, *Sobranie sochinenii*, 161.

17. Pushkin, *Ibid.*, 347.

18. Letter to L. S. Pushkin, November 1824, cited in Thomas Shaw, "Puškin's 'The Stationmaster' and the New Testament Parable," *Slavic and East European Journal* 21, no. 1 (1977): 24n13. See also Gabriella Safran, "Love Songs between the Sacred and the Vernacular: Pushkin's 'Podrazhaniia' in the Context of Bible Translation," *The Slavic and East European Journal* 39, no. 2 (1995): 167.

19. Safran, "Love Songs"; Shaw, "Stationmaster," 6 and 24nn12–13; David M. Bethea and Sergei Davydov, "Pushkin's Life," in *The Cambridge Companion to Pushkin*, ed. Andrew Kahn (Cambridge: Cambridge University Press, 2006), 17.

20. Pushkin, *Sobranie sochinenii*, 387.

21. Cited in Binyon, *Pushkin*, 323. See also Pearson, "Raphael."

22. Binyon, *Pushkin*, 323.

23. Ibid., 323, 361.

24. Countess Dolly Ficquelmont cited in Binyon, *Pushkin*, 368.

25. Bethea and Davydov, "Pushkin's Life," 20.

26. Pearson, "Raphael," 351–52. See G. M. Koka, "Pushkin pered madonnoi Rafaelia," *Vremennik Pushkinskoi komissii* (1964): 38–43; Thomas J. Shaw, ed. and trans., *The Letters of Alexander Pushkin* (Madison: University of Wisconsin Press, 1967), 2:466; cited in Kenneth H. Ober and Warren U. Ober, "'Scorn not the sonnet': Pushkin and Wordsworth," *Germano-Slavica* 15 (2005): 109–15.

27. See Fusso, "Maidens in Childbirth"; Pearson, "Raphael," 348–50. The piece was originally part of a letter written in 1821, and was published in *The Polar Star* (Poliarnaia zvezda) in 1824.

28. Pearson, "Raphael," 248–350.

29. Ibid.

30. Pushkin, *Sobranie sochinenii*, 212, 702. Pearson, "Raphael," 351.

31. At first he calls Mariia Musina-Pushkina "Liudmila," presumably to emphasize her Russian origins, but later switches to "another Mariia."

32. Pushkin, *Sobranie sochinenii*, 202, 700.

33. Warner, *Alone of All Her Sex*, back flap of the cover; see also 134–56, 192, 225–26, 235.

# 4

## The Mother of God and the Lives of Orthodox Female Religious in Late Imperial Russia

WILLIAM G. WAGNER

FOR ORTHODOX FEMALE RELIGIOUS (WOMEN who had entered monastic communities) in late Imperial Russia, the Mother of God constituted a ubiquitous presence. Her image adorned the spaces they inhabited and she figured prominently in their daily liturgical devotions. They regularly venerated the Mother of God, prayed or rendered thanks for her help in their communal and personal lives, and sang hymns in her honor. Annual festivals celebrating the key moments in Mary's life and role in the Christian story of salvation helped delineate time for their community, and in many cases the community itself was dedicated to her. These multiple encounters with Mary were experienced both collectively and individually, often in both dimensions simultaneously. For Russian Orthodox female religious, they thus represented a means of integrating collective devotion and communal identity with personal beliefs and piety.[1] In a similar way, as the examples of the Nizhnii Novgorod Convent of the Exaltation of the Cross and of Abbess Taisiia of the Leushino Saint John the Forerunner Convent in Novgorod diocese demonstrate, such encounters with Mary provided Orthodox female religious with a powerful medium for the construction, reinforcement, understanding, and representation of relationships of authority and community.

Discussing Marian imagery in American Catholicism, historian Robert Orsi argues that such "devotional images are media of presence [that] are used to act upon the world, upon others, and upon oneself. Such media ... are believed to hold the power of the holy figure [represented] ... and to make it present ... [Hence] they serve as points of encounter—between humans ... and between humans and sacred figures."[2] In Orthodoxy, icons are similarly understood as media of presence, providing a channel for the direct personal interaction between humans and the sacred figures represented.[3] With regard particularly to reputedly miracle-working icons of Mary, historian Vera Shevzov notes that for Orthodox believers in late Imperial Russia they reflected "the community's perception of Mary's ongoing presence within it."[4] For Russian Orthodox female religious, the pervasive presence of Marian imagery within the sacred space of the convent therefore meant the constant encounter with Mary herself. According to Orsi, such ongoing encounters with sacred figures through their images foster in believers a deeply felt personal relationship with these figures that in turn helps shape an individual's perceptions, behavior, and relationships with others.[5] The influence of such a perceived relationship with the sacred figure of Mary can be seen clearly in both the communal life of the Nizhnii Novgorod Convent of the Exaltation of the Cross and the personal life of Abbess Taisiia.

COMMUNAL ENCOUNTERS WITH MARY: THE NIZHNII NOVGOROD
CONVENT OF THE EXALTATION OF THE CROSS

The Nizhnii Novgorod Convent of the Exaltation of the Cross offers an example of the type of environment in which encounters between Orthodox female religious and Mary occurred in late Imperial Russia. The experience of the convent demonstrates how, on the communal level, such encounters helped to structure authority and to shape relationships and identity not only within a monastic community, but also in relation to the world outside its walls. Located in the city of Nizhnii Novgorod and formed in the wake of Catherine II's monastic reforms of 1764 by the merger of two older convents, during the nineteenth and early twentieth centuries the Convent of the Exaltation of the Cross grew to become one of the wealthiest and most prominent monastic institutions in Nizhnii Novgorod diocese. In the process, the convent exhibited the trends characteristic of the rapid expansion of female Orthodox monasticism during this period: the size of the community increased substantially; the social and demographic background of new members shifted from mainly urban women of privilege to women largely from less privileged social estates and the peasantry and from predominantly older women—especially widows—to overwhelmingly much younger unmarried women; the convent was reorganized on a communal basis; and it engaged more systematically in educational and social welfare activities.[6]

Not unusually for a Russian Orthodox convent, Marian imagery, symbolism, and devotion were prominent at the Convent of the Exaltation of the Cross. Inventories compiled during the last third of the eighteenth century, for example, list ninety-six icons in the convent's church and refectory. Of these, thirty-six (38 percent) were of the Mother of God (including at least fourteen different images); nineteen (20 percent) were of Christ, with those of John the Forerunner being a distant third at five (5 percent). There were only six icons of other female saints, including two of Mary's mother Anne.[7] Nearly one hundred years later, the predominance of Marian imagery and symbolism at the convent had increased. Of the thirty-two "notable" icons listed in the Convent's annual inventory and other descriptions of its now four churches, seventeen (53 percent) were of the Mother of God; five (16 percent) were of Christ, with Saint Nicholas, at two (6 percent), being third. Three of the convent's churches were consecrated to Mary (one jointly): the Churches of the Iveron Mother of God, the Kazan Mother of God, and the Mother of God named Joy of All Who Sorrow. Five of the seven altars in the four churches also were consecrated to Mary (two jointly). Of the one hundred and one icons listed in the convent's other spaces, including private and work spaces, thirty-seven (37 percent) were of the Mother of God, with at least twenty-seven different images; thirty-three (33 percent) were of Christ, with Saint Nicholas again a distant third with four (4 percent). Only two icons were of other female saints, Saint Anne and Saint Dorofeia, the name taken by the abbess who in the early nineteenth century had reorganized, expanded, and rebuilt the convent. The icon of the Iveron Mother of God, moreover, stood over the entryway on the external side of the Holy Gates of the convent and over the entryway on the internal side of the west gates, two of the most important locations for an icon in an Orthodox monastic community.[8] Liturgically, in addition to the prayers to and readings and hymns relating to the Mother of God prescribed for all services, the daily rule at the convent included a special canon and prayers to Mary introduced by Abbess Dorofeia and prayer before the icon the Mother of God named Joy of All Who Sorrow, and on Saturdays an akathist in honor of Mary was sung. Following the normal Orthodox festival calendar, six of the twelve major feasts celebrated annually at the convent were devoted to the Mother of God or to events in which she played a prominent role, four of the convent's ten local festivals also were dedicated to her, and throughout the year several individual Marian icons were celebrated. Finally, both annual processions that directly involved the convent similarly celebrated Marian icons.[9]

Clearly, Mary pervaded the daily lives and the visual, aural, and devotional world of the women living at the Convent of the Exaltation of the Cross. At least in the nineteenth century, the predominance of Marian imagery and symbolism was encountered not only in the convent's liturgical and public spaces, but also in its private spaces. Through multiple media, then, a Marian ideal—however it was understood by contemporaries—was constantly being projected and inculcated at the convent. Marian imagery, moreover, constituted virtually the only female imagery represented.

Unfortunately, due largely to the absence of a tradition of spiritual and autobiographical writing by Russian Orthodox female religious, written expressions of the meaning and significance of Marian imagery and devotion at the Convent of the Exaltation of the Cross for individual members of the community are lacking.[10] Communally, however, the extensive Marian imagery, symbolism, and devotion at the convent played a central role in shaping the internal life and the identity of the community as well as its relationships with the outside world. Visually, wherever one turned one encountered the Mother of God. As a result, members of the community were constantly reminded of what they perceived as Mary's perpetual and ubiquitous presence in their midst and the fact that their actions consequently were constantly under her gaze. Whatever effects on individuals such perception of constant Marian presence may have had, this presence formed a central component of the shared complex of symbols and experiences that helped define the community and bind it together.[11] The Marian imagery at the convent, moreover, was imbued with particular meanings. As Shevzov has shown through her study of celebrations of the Kazan Mother of God icon in late Imperial Russia, particular Marian icons were associated with specific historical narratives and stories that shaped the visual experience of looking upon them. Through the meanings and understandings conveyed by such associations, the Marian iconography at the Convent of the Exaltation of the Cross invested the community as a whole with meaning for its members and helped to place it—and each member individually—both in Russia's Orthodox culture and in sacred history.[12]

The visual imagery at the convent operated in tandem with its ritual life. Observing that Eastern Christianity places primary emphasis on "the experience of God," religious scholar John Binns notes that within Orthodoxy both doctrinally and experientially "the Church is created, sustained and visibly present" through collective participation in liturgical worship.[13] Discussing the influences of ritual on religious experience and beliefs in general, sociologist Meredith McGuire similarly argues that "simply participating in ritual practices structure[s] people's emotional and social experiences, giving them meaning by practice."[14] With regard specifically to Marian devotion, art historian Robert Maniura likewise contends that regular performance of the rituals used to invoke Mary's presence and to form a relationship with her exerts a formative influence on the being and consciousness of devotees.[15] As noted above, Marian devotion figured prominently in the daily, seasonal, and annual ritual life of the Convent of the Exaltation of the Cross. In addition to collectively offering prayers and singing hymns to Mary in the daily liturgy and other services, all members of the convent began each day with the communal performance of a special canon and prayers to the Mother of God, the week ended with an akathist performed collectively in her honor, the community frequently celebrated particular Marian icons, and it demarcated times of the year with festivals either dedicated to Mary or in which she was a central figure.[16] Shared participation in these ritual practices helped demarcate the convent community for its members, bind them together, and give meaning to their communal life. Because, moreover, many of the liturgical services, rituals, and festivals at the convent were open to the lay community, shared participation in these rituals by members of the wider community served similarly to connect them with the convent community and contributed to the creation and perpetuation of a commonly experienced Orthodox identity in which in turn the convent occupied a respected place.[17]

Icon processions played an important role in these processes of demarcation, integration, and identity formation, and in this regard the Convent of the Exaltation of the Cross figured prominently in the most important of these processions in the yearly religious life for Orthodox in the city of Nizhnii Novgorod: the annual arrival of the Oranki Mother of God icon from the Mother of God Monastery in Oranki. The most venerated icon in the Nizhnii Novgorod region, the Oranki Mother of God icon was a copy of the revered Vladimir Mother of God icon in the Assumption Cathedral in the Moscow Kremlin that had been made in 1629 for the military servitor Petr Andreevich Gliadkov. In 1634, reputedly directed by Mary, Gliadkov built a church at an isolated forest site in Mordvinian territory in the Nizhnii Novgorod region to house the icon and established a small monastic community there to venerate it. According to its history, the icon began almost at once to demonstrate its miraculous powers, providing for believers a medium through which Mary was seen to effect numerous healings and repeatedly to protect the monastic community from brigands and hostile bands of pagan Mordvinians. The icon was first brought to the city of Nizhnii Novgorod in 1771, for the purpose of seeking relief from a severe outbreak of the plague that was afflicting the city. Credited with having secured Mary's intercession to end the epidemic, the icon each year thereafter was brought again to Nizhnii Novgorod, both in gratitude and as a prophylactic against future misfortune.[18] After the relocation of the Convent of the Exaltation of the Cross to the outskirts of the city and the establishment of the Nizhnii Novgorod trade fair in the early nineteenth century, on its arrival in Nizhnii Novgorod the icon would spend a day and night at the convent before being taken on to the main cathedral of the city and then to the fairgrounds, where it would remain for several months. On its return journey to Oranki, the icon again would pass the night at the Convent of the Exaltation of the Cross.[19]

The association of the convent with the Oranki Mother of God icon had several effects. First, association with the most venerated icon in the region extended its sacred power to the Convent of the Exaltation of the Cross, thereby elevating the convent's status, visibility, and authority within the spiritual economy of the city and region. This elevation of status and authority brought both spiritual and material benefits. Spiritually, the presence of such a highly venerated miracle-working icon—understood by believers as the presence of Mary herself[20]—emphasized the role of the convent as a sacred and intercessory space for the Orthodox community. While the convent always represented a site where members of the community could seek help from the Mother of God and other sacred figures with their personal cares, problems, and maladies, the services celebrated during the icon's stay demonstrated this role particularly publicly, encouraging the faithful to seek help or offer thanks not only during the icon's presence but at other times as well.[21] Materially, higher visibility and spiritual status led to increased donations, income from the sale of candles and other religious items, and payments for religious services, especially but not only during the periods of the icon's presence. According to press reports, for example, the arrival of the icon each year regularly drew "thousands" of pilgrims to the convent.[22]

Second, shared participation in the icon procession and in the attendant liturgies and rituals helped to connect and define the Orthodox population of the city within a multi-confessional context and to integrate the convent community into this wider Orthodox community. Each spring, a large number of residents from Nizhnii Novgorod and nearby villages would gather at the Oranki Monastery several days in advance of the two-day procession from Oranki to the Convent of the Exaltation of the Cross. Accompanied by this crowd of Orthodox faithful, which grew along the way, and by five hundred men bearing religious banners, the icon was carried to the convent by clergy and laymen. Awaiting its arrival in the field in front of the convent were a group of ecclesiastical, civil, and military dignitaries, the abbess and sisters of the convent, a multitude of believers, and several rows of troops. As the procession approached, a military choir sang the hymn "How Glorious Our Lord in Zion," followed by a hymn to Mary sung by the sisters of the convent. The diocesan bishop, assisted by clergy from the convent and other churches in the city, then began the celebration of a prayer service in honor of Mary that continued in the convent's packed cathedral and was followed by an all-night prayer vigil. In the morning the procession began again, bearing the icon through the streets of Nizhnii Novgorod and stopping at several churches before reaching the city's main cathedral, where the bishop again performed a prayer service and liturgy.[23] The movement of the Oranki Mother of God icon to and through the city of Nizhnii Novgorod thus wove Orthodox believers of all social groups from the city and surrounding region, the convent community, and multiple sacred spaces together into a shared encounter with Mary and celebration of her active involvement both in their region's past and in their lives in the present.

Finally, at least as they had evolved during the nineteenth century, the ceremonies welcoming the Oranki Mother of God icon to the city of Nizhnii Novgorod not only demonstrated and reinforced the interconnections between structures of ecclesiastical and state authority, but also situated the convent within these structures. Greeting the icon were the diocesan and the vicar bishops and the senior clergy of Nizhnii Novgorod, the abbess and clergy of the Convent of the Exaltation of the Cross, the provincial governor and vice governor, the provincial and sometimes several district marshals of the nobility, the mayor of Nizhnii Novgorod, and the commander of the provincial military garrison, arranged to reflect and publicly represent their relative status and authority, both within their respective spheres and in their interrelations with one another, with Mary's presence through her icon seeming to extend legitimacy and protection to these structures of authority. Within this symbolic representation of interrelated hierarchies of authority, the abbess of the Convent of the Exaltation of the Cross occupied a prominent though subordinate position as the head of a large, wealthy, and socially engaged community of women.[24]

The Iveron Mother of God icon provides a similar example of the ways in which Marian imagery and symbolism shaped the internal life and the social role of the Convent of the Exaltation of the Cross during the late imperial period. According to its life history, the original Iveron Mother of God icon had been spared from destruction during the iconoclast conflicts in Byzantium through Mary's intercession and then miraculously appeared in a pillar of fire off the coast of Mount Athos near the Iveron Monastery at the end of the tenth century. Resisting efforts by the monks to place her icon in their main church, Mary instructed one of them in a vision to place the icon above the entryway of the monastery's Holy Gates, promising to protect the monastery in the future as long as the icon remained there.[25] The icon first appeared in Russia in the seventeenth century when, fulfilling a promise, the superior of the Iveron Monastery sent a copy to Tsar Aleksei Mikhailovich, one of whose daughters allegedly later was healed through its intercession. By the early nineteenth century, several reputedly miracle-working copies of the icon existed in various parts of Russia.[26]

The Iveron Mother of God icon first appeared at the Convent of the Exaltation of the Cross in the early nineteenth century and is closely associated with the efforts of its abbess at the time, Dorofeia, to reorganize the convent on a communal basis and to elevate its status and role as a symbol of piety and a place of pilgrimage for the Orthodox community. As part of these efforts, early in her tenure Dorofeia petitioned the Holy Synod to rename the convent the New Iveron Mother of God Convent. Although Dorofeia's petition was denied, when a few years later the convent was rebuilt on a new site on the city's outskirts, the Iveron Mother of God icon was placed above the entryways of its Holy and west gates, and the chapel—later church—under the main cathedral that was intended for the private use of the community was consecrated to the Iveron Mother of God icon.[27] The icon therefore clearly had special meaning for Dorofeia and for the leadership of the community during her tenure as abbess, and through their efforts, for the community as a whole, although unfortunately there are no explicit statements of what that meaning was. From the context, however, at least three possible meanings suggest themselves, relating to the role and authority of the abbess and other leaders of the community, to the organizational and interpersonal character of the community, and to the convent's relationship with the wider community.

The reorganization of the Convent of the Exaltation of the Cross on a communal basis undertaken by Abbess Dorofeia (not without resistance from several older sisters) entailed a significant strengthening of the authority of the abbess and other convent leaders, especially through their enhanced control over the members and resources of the convent. All property now was shared for the benefit of the community as a whole, and both its use and the activities of the members of the community were determined by the convent's leadership. The converse side of the increased authority and control of the leadership was the expectation of and greater ability to enforce full obedience on the part of the other members of the community.[28] Among the most frequent metaphors invoked to represent, legitimize, and reinforce these relationships of authority, control, and obedience was that of the family, with the role of the abbess compared to that of a mother with respect to her children. Just as a mother's authority was perceived as deriving from her love for and responsibility to care for, nurture, educate, and protect her children, so too the authority of an abbess was held to derive in part from her parallel responsibilities as the "spiritual mother" of the members of her monastic community. In a very insightful paper on this theme, Marlyn Miller rightly cautions against making any direct causal connections between images and understandings of Mary and the invocation of the metaphor of mother to represent and reinforce an abbess's authority.[29] But suggestively, at the Convent of the Exaltation of the Cross, beginning with Dorofeia, at their death abbesses were buried in the Iveron Mother of God Church, in front of the altar that had the Iveron Mother of God icon as its central image. This positioning clearly was intentional, and it does not seem unreasonable to conclude that it was meant symbolically to represent both the relationship between the Mother of God present through her icon and the convent's abbesses and the abbess's relationship to the community as spiritual mother.

The prominence that Dorofeia gave to the Iveron Mother of God icon at the convent and her desire to rename the convent in its honor coincided with her efforts to reorganize the convent on a communal basis and to enhance its identity both as an exemplar of Orthodox piety and a destination for Orthodox pilgrims. This coincidence in timing could, of course, have been nothing more than that. The positioning of the Iveron Mother of God icon over the convent's Holy Gates, however, replicating the placement of the icon at the original Iveron Monastery, suggests strongly an intention to associate the Convent of the Exaltation of the Cross with the Iveron Monastery on Mount Athos. Dorofeia's efforts to reorganize the convent derived from and formed part of a movement for monastic reform and revival in Imperial Russia in the late eighteenth and early nineteenth centuries that was inspired in part by ideas, ideals, and examples associated with the monastic communities on Mount Athos.[30] It therefore seems likely that the introduction of and prominence given to the Iveron Mother of God icon at the Convent of the Exaltation of the Cross at this time was intended symbolically to identify the reorganized, reconstructed, and reconsecrated convent with the monastic ideals associated with the communities on Mount Athos. If so, then this particular Marian imagery would have represented both an important symbol of the convent's character as a community based on communalism and eldership and a legitimizing agent for Dorofeia's efforts.

Finally, by establishing a small hospital and an almshouse for elderly women at the reconstructed convent, Dorofeia introduced a form of engagement with the wider community that would grow under her successors. Though supported by some advocates of monastic reform, this social engagement by monastic communities more often at this time was discouraged as being contrary to the contemplative life reformers idealized. Dorofeia's introduction of a social role for the convent, even on such a modest scale, therefore was innovative and exceptional for her time. Her motivation lay in part in a recognition of the difficulties and hardships faced especially by elderly widows and unmarried women in Russian society.[31] But her actions may also have been at least partly inspired and validated by the example of Mary's perceived action in the world, through the medium of her icons, in support of the weak and suffering.[32] In this regard, the Iveron Mother of God icon would have been only one of many Marian images at the convent whose life histories provided Dorofeia with a model for female social engagement. After all, according to the icon's life story, Mary had exercised her worldly power to save her image from iconoclast destruction, deliver it to the Iveron Monastery, determine its location, and through it protect the monastery from assault by Turkish and other marauders, heal the sick, and perform numerous other miracles—hardly an image of female passivity and disengagement from the world.[33]

This last possibility indicates the complex and contextualized ways in which Marian imagery and symbolism operated in shaping the individual and collective lives of Russian Orthodox female religious. Prior to the nineteenth century, in a context where the organized provision of education for girls and of public welfare for elderly and needy women was extremely limited, abbesses of the Convent of the Exaltation of the Cross and its predecessors had not been moved to engage their communities in such activities, despite inhabiting an environment rich in iconic symbols and liturgical recognition of Mary's active involvement in the world and, in the eighteenth century, being pressured by the state to undertake these types of activities. Indeed, in the eighteenth century, women at the convent appear to have been more the recipients than the dispensers of charity. But in the nineteenth century, as women helped to develop and expand organized educational, charitable, and social welfare activities and as ideals of monasticism changed, the image of Mary as actively engaged in the world that was projected through her iconography, proclaimed liturgically in prayers and hymns, and promoted by popular beliefs could serve for Dorofeia and her successors as a source of inspiration for and validation of their own activities as religious women.[34] This ideal of Mary's worldly engagement was expressed clearly in the prayer to the Mother of God introduced by Dorofeia at the Convent of the Exaltation of the Cross and repeated collectively by members of the community every morning:

We bow to You, Most Holy Birthgiver of God, who by Your Birth showed us
the true Light, Queen of Heaven and earth, Hope to the hopeless, Helper of
the weak and Intercessor for all who have sinned; cloak and protect us from
all spiritual and bodily misfortunes and needs and through Your all-powerful
prayers be our Protector.[35]

Just as the women at the convent asked daily for Mary's help and protection,
so too they could imagine themselves through their community following her
example in similarly providing assistance to needy women and orphaned girls.


PERSONAL ENCOUNTERS WITH MARY: ABBESS TAISIIA

The experiences of Abbess Taisiia, as recounted in her autobiography,
demonstrate how ongoing encounters with Mary also shaped the personal
lives and perceptions of Orthodox female religious in the late imperial period,
in ways similar to those for communities as a whole.[36] Born into a hereditary
noble landowning family in Novgorod province, Taisiia (1842–1915), née
Mariia Solopova, combined deep spirituality and keen intelligence with
exceptional practical capability. Developing a strong religious sensibility
from an early age, and feeling both uncomfortable with and constrained
by the social conventions and expectations for young noblewomen of her
generation, she entered the Tikhvin Convent of the Entry of the Mother of
God into the Temple in Novgorod diocese in 1860, a year after completing
the Pavlovsky Institute for Young Noblewomen in St. Petersburg. Hence for
Taisiia the choice of a monastic vocation represented the opportunity for
a personally more self-defining and satisfying as well as a spiritually more
fulfilling life. She became abbess of the Leushino convent—at the time an
unofficial women's religious community—in 1881, a position she held until
her death.[37] The community prospered under Taisiia's leadership, becoming
particularly noted for its educational activities. A composer of spiritual poetry
and hymns throughout her monastic life, Taisiia wrote her autobiography—
covering the first fifty years of her life—at the urging of the elder Feodosii of
the Kievan Caves Lavra.[38] Though expressing the conventional modesty with
regard to her autobiography, Taisiia clearly meant it to be a guide to spiritual
life for others as well as a profession of her own life in faith.

Although Taisiia presents her life as having been shaped and guided
profoundly by personal encounters with a number of sacred figures, Mary
was foremost among them. Taisiia suggests that her relationship with Mary
in fact had preceded her birth. Despairing after losing her first two children

shortly after their birth, Taisiia's mother undertook numerous pilgrimages to churches consecrated to the Mother of God in order to pray before her reputedly miraculous icons. According to Taisiia, in these encounters with Mary her mother "poured out [her] tearful entreaties, daringly reminding Her that She too was a Mother and could therefore sympathize with the sorrows of earthly mothers, who, though sinful and unworthy of Her help, have Her as their sole, steadfast hope."[39] Taisiia's birth appeared to answer these prayers and entreaties, in gratitude for which the new infant was christened Mariia. The circumstances of her birth, Taisiia seems to be saying, both prefigured her future relationship with Mary and demonstrate how through the medium of her icons the Mother of God responds to the prayers and direct personal appeals of the sincerely faithful for worldly assistance.

Taisiia's relationship with Mary continued throughout her life, being normally experienced through her prayers, devotions, liturgical observances, and pilgrimages to venerated Marian icons but at particularly critical moments taking the form of appearances by Mary in her dreams. Taisiia describes nineteen dreams in her autobiography, seven or, most likely, eight of which involve Mary.[40] Hence, although Mary was only one of several sacred figures whom Taisiia recounts as encountering in her dreams, she was Taisiia's most frequent sacred visitor and—apart from the appearance of an icon of Saint Paraskeva—the only female, attesting both to the prominence of the Mother of God in Orthodox Christianity and her importance for Taisiia personally. In nearly every instance, the dreams occurred while Taisiia was confronting a particularly difficult and challenging situation or decision. Always characterized by Taisiia as providing emotional comfort and spiritual fortification at these moments, through a rich array of symbols her dreams in most cases reassured her about the path she had chosen, though in some cases they guided her to a particular decision.

During her novitiate, for example, at a moment when Taisiia seriously doubted her ability to bear the difficulties and deprivations of monastic life, she dreamt one night that she was struggling up a narrow, rugged road covered in snow drifts. Along the way she was constantly encountering obstacles that hindered her progress. Contemplating abandoning her journey, she turned to measure the distance back. Looking forward again, she discovered the road had become smooth, and in the distance Mary beckoned her from an open door filled with brilliant light, saying to her, "Keep going, keep going! I am the Gatekeeper!" Thus reassured by Mary's apparent assurance of the rightness of her choice of a monastic life and the promise of Mary's assistance if she persevered, Taisiia recounts that she awakened "in great joy [and] renewed in spirit" and resolved to remain in the convent whatever the challenges.[41]

Taisiia describes seven, and quite likely eight, such encounters with the Mother of God, who appeared in either bodily or disembodied form, through her icons, or in multiple forms. These encounters occurred in the midst of a conflict with her mother over her desire to undertake a monastic life, as she struggled to adapt to the difficulties of that life, just prior to and at the moment she faced the daunting prospect of leading the Leushino community, and as she confronted several especially challenging moments in that community's life.[42] Considered together, Taisiia's accounts of these perceived encounters with Mary demonstrate how they could shape personal behavior and relationships in complex and contradictory ways, both reinforcing and subverting relations of authority and fostering obedience, submission, resignation, empowerment, and strength.

Taisiia's negotiation of the tense and emotionally difficult relations between her and her mother provoked by her desire to enter a convent, for example, reveals particularly clearly how perceived Marian presence could structure and mediate relations of authority. Though desperately eager to undertake a monastic life, Taisiia hesitated to disobey her mother, who adamantly opposed this step. While supporting Taisiia's wish to pursue a monastic vocation, her spiritual confessor and guide, Archimandrite Lavrentii of the nearby Iveron Mother of God Monastery, at the same time also cautioned her not to defy her mother's authority. The impasse was resolved through a sequence of dreams and interactions between Taisiia, her mother, and Lavrentii in which Marian presence figured prominently. The invocation of Mary's superior authority as the Mother of God in effect enabled Taisiia to circumvent her mother's familial authority without appearing to be disobedient, thus leaving the latter authority intact.[43]

The sequence began when the Mother of God appeared to both Taisiia and her mother in separate dreams on the same night. Taisiia understood Mary in her dream to be assuring her that her desire to take monastic vows would be fulfilled, thereby strengthening her resolve. In the dream, Taisiia sought to join a combined earthly and celestial procession bearing the Tikhvin Mother of God icon heavenward. Barring Taisiia from joining the procession, her mother directed her to pray before a copy of the Kazan Mother of God icon, the icon with which the mother had been blessed at her wedding. Doing so, Taisiia was miraculously transported into the midst of the procession, where speaking from above the throng Mary welcomed her, saying "and now you too are with Me."[44] For her part, Taisiia's mother understood Mary in her dream to be admonishing her to allow her daughter to enter a convent, an interpretation of the dream endorsed by Lavrentii, who directed her to pray for guidance before the same Tikhvin Mother of God icon that had appeared in Taisiia's dream. After doing so, Taisiia's mother relented, believing that the Mother of God herself was calling Taisiia to a monastic vocation.[45] In effect, by acknowledging the superior authority of the Mother of God, Taisiia's mother could accede to Taisiia's desire without impairing her own maternal authority. The transfer of authority over Taisiia from her mother to the Mother of God (and terrestrially, to the mother superior of the Tikhvin Convent) was symbolically affirmed by a series of blessings of Taisiia by her mother and Lavrentii with various Marian icons, but was acknowledged particularly dramatically by Taisiia's mother on her deathbed.[46] Blessing her younger daughter with a copy of the Tikhvin Mother of God icon sent to her by Taisiia, who after praying for guidance before the original had rejected her mother's request that she abandon her monastic life and return home, Taisiia's mother declined to bless Taisiia, saying, "I blessed her long ago; let God's blessing dwell in her ... the Queen of Heaven has chosen her for Herself."[47]

Similarly, Taisiia relates how, in a later pair of dreams, Mary affirmed her own assumption of authority as mother superior of the Leushino community. Just prior to being asked to become abbess of the community, Taisiia dreamt that while she was attempting to cross a progressively deeper expanse of water, an abbess's staff fell from the sky into her right hand, enabling her to reach the far shore. Emerging from the water, the sisters from a nearby convent greeted her, singing the hymn "Meet It Is...," and escorted her into the convent.[48] Believing that she had been called to the position, Taisiia accepted the appointment as abbess. Shortly after assuming the position, however, she had resolved to resign, doubting her ability to overcome the many challenges confronting the community, including the resistance of some members to her authority. She then had a second dream in which a conflagration threatened to engulf the Leushino convent. Frightened, Taisiia was uncertain what to do. But then Mary—in the form of her icon "Quick to Hear"—and Saint John the Forerunner together appeared to her, with Mary reassuring her that "We will always preserve our community! Do not fear!" and encouraging her to "have more faith." Believing her authority to have been reaffirmed and with her confidence strengthened by Mary's promise of support, Taisiia decided to remain as abbess.[49]

If Marian presence through her dreams in some instances served to strengthen and empower Taisiia, though, in others it promoted submission and obedience. When, as described above, Taisiia encountered the difficulties and deprivations of monastic life for the first time, and later when she experienced what she considered to be unjust treatment by an abbess, Marian visitations reminded her of her obligations of obedience, submission, and acceptance of monastic asceticism and labor. While these visitations helped mediate Taisiia's subordination to monastic rigor, obedience, and superior authority, however, in the process affirming the structure of authority within the convent, they also provided Taisiia with strength to endure.[50] Later, at several moments when the Leushino community confronted particularly daunting challenges, Taisiia similarly drew strength from dreams in which Mary reassured her both of her ability to lead the community through the difficulties and of Mary's support and appreciation of her efforts.[51] Repeatedly after such encounters with Mary Taisiia describes herself as "renewed and receiving new strength to continue my work" and "completely fortified in spirit and body for further labors."[52]

Although Taisiia is vague with regard to the ontological questions raised by her encounters with the Mother of God and other sacred figures in her dreams, for her these encounters clearly were real and in her mind Mary and the other figures were genuinely present. This popularly shared and doctrinally affirmed belief in the possibility of personal encounters with sacred figures, especially Mary, provided Taisiia with a powerful language and set of images through which she understood and represented her experiences and justified as well as shaped her behavior and her relations with others. In this regard, the power and persuasiveness of Taisiia's visions, both for her and for others, appear to have derived in part from the fact that they were informed by images and understandings of the Mother of God and by religious tropes and practices drawn from the cultural fund available to Taisiia and her contemporaries. Taisiia's dream experienced during her conflict with her mother, for example, wove together images of the popular religious practices of collective icon processions and individual prayer before icons with those of two of the most venerated icons of the Mother of God in Russia and with belief in the power of Mary to be present and act through her icons to affirm—to Taisiia, her mother, Lavrentii, and later to her readers—Taisiia's choice of a monastic life.[53] In this regard, given official doctrinal teachings and prevailing popular practices and beliefs regarding Mary, the multiple meanings ascribed to and the practical effects of Taisiia's encounters with Mary through her dreams would have been the same whatever the ontological status of these encounters.

THE MANY MEANINGS OF MARY

The experiences of Abbess Taisiia individually and of the Nizhnii Novgorod Convent of the Exaltation of the Cross as a collective community both demonstrate the complexity of the roles played by Marian imagery, symbolism, and devotion in the lives of Orthodox female religious in late Imperial Russia and suggest a mutually formative interaction between these two dimensions of experience. One must be cautious about drawing conclusions from only these two examples, of course, not least because Taisiia's monastic life was spent in communities other than, albeit very similar to, the Convent of the Exaltation of the Cross. But both for Taisiia personally and for the community of women living at the Convent of the Exaltation of the Cross Mary provided an important medium for constructing, mediating, comprehending, and representing relationships of authority, subordination, and obedience and for both empowerment and disempowerment. Mary similarly represented an important medium through which Taisiia individually and the convent community collectively encountered and experienced what they understood as sacred presence, practiced and demonstrated their Orthodox and monastic identities, invested their lives with meaning, and effected communal integration. Mary's perceived action in the world through the medium of her icons offered a model and validation for similar action by Taisiia as abbess of the Leushino community and by the leadership and members of the Convent of the Exaltation of the Cross, even while the invocation of Mary's example of obedience and of her sacred authority helped to legitimize the hierarchies and institutions to which female religious—including powerful abbesses—were subordinate and which constrained their field of activity.

The capacity of Marian imagery, symbolism, and devotion to play these diverse and contradictory roles derived from and depended on the meanings of this imagery and symbolism and the understandings of Mary generally available culturally at the time.[54] In this regard, with apologies to Catholic theologian George Tavard, Mary had "a thousand faces"—Birthgiver of God, loving Mother of the Merciful God, Fountain of Tenderness, Ever-Virgin, Second Eve, Handmaid of the Lord, Bride of Christ, Queen of Heaven, living Temple of God, New Jerusalem, all-powerful Intercessor for and Protectress of humanity, a woman who suffered in her humanity but is the ideal of heavenly perfection and is "more honorable than the Cherubim, and more glorious beyond compare than the Seraphim"—which reflected and gave rise to multiple, often competing Marian ideals for emulation.[55] Surveying Orthodox devotional literature in late Imperial Russia, for example, Shevzov discerns two broad representations of Mary, focusing respectively on her life before and after Christ's resurrection. While the qualities of humility, meekness, modesty, obedience, respect for elders, self-denying service to others, mercifulness, and forgiveness associated with the preresurrectional Mary often were invoked in support of the established order and ecclesiastical authority, postresurrectional Mary was presented as "a distinct and active agent in sacred history ... [who] along with Christ was continually watching the flow of human history, responding to it according to the measure of human faith and belief, and

guiding the body of 'faithful ones.'"[56] Iconographically, "Marian icons tended
to involve believers mostly with the preresurrectional Mary by portraying the
face of an exemplary life. Yet through their stories, specially revered Marian
icons also involved believers with the postresurrectional Mary who openly
and authoritatively took her place at the helm of the economy of salvation."[57]
Church doctrine, liturgy, and festival celebrations likewise reflected and
celebrated the qualities embodied in both the pre- and the postresurrectional
Mary. Hence Russian Orthodox female religious encountered Mary through a
wide range and rich variety of images and ideals that could be combined and
recombined in multiple ways.

At the same time, though inflecting the meanings found in these images
and ideals in their own way in response to their particular circumstances,
through their actions, practices, and representations Taisiia and the
community of female religious at the Convent of the Exaltation of the Cross
helped to maintain, disseminate, and transgenerationally transmit them.
Taisiia did so individually through her writings as well as her actions as
abbess of the Leushino convent. Both her religious community and the
Nizhnii Novgorod Convent of the Exaltation of the Cross did so collectively
both through their intracommunal devotional and ritual practices and
through such shared experiences with lay believers as liturgical services,
icon processions, and festival celebrations. Russian Orthodox convents
at this time regularly practiced both types of activities. Thus, although
particular, the encounters and experiences of Taisiia individually and of the
members of the Convent of the Exaltation of the Cross collectively with the
Mother of God were not unique for Orthodox female religious during the
late imperial period.

Nor in many ways were they uncommon for male monastics, whose
encounters with Mary through imagery, liturgical worship, devotional
practices, and rituals would have been similar to those of the members of the
Convent of the Exaltation of the Cross. Marian imagery was common in any
Russian Orthodox monastic institution, Church liturgies and festivals were
largely though not entirely prescribed, and male as well as female monastic
communities organized and participated in processions celebrating revered
Marian icons. The Oranki Mother of God icon, for example, was possessed
by the Oranki Mother of God Monastery, which organized several annual
processions with the icon, including the one to Nizhnii Novgorod. Hence the
Mother of God was a prominent presence in male as much as female monastic
communities and Mary was represented to both male and female monastics as
an exemplar, an intercessor, and a protectress, through whose icons help could
be sought and a personal relationship with her formed.

Despite sharing much in common with respect to Mary, Russian Orthodox female and male monastics nonetheless encountered the Mother of God in a religious and broader cultural context that defined the nature and calling of and treated women and men differently. Mirroring the generally subordinate position of women in late Imperial Russian society, within the Russian Orthodox Church women were subordinated to a male hierarchy, priesthood, and administrative and academic elite and excluded from certain roles in Church life and even areas of a church accessible only to men. Symbolically, the Trinity and archangels were male or male-gendered and the overwhelming majority of recognized saints were male. In this otherwise predominantly masculine pantheon, Mary stood out as an exceptional female presence and feminine symbol. While according to Church doctrine human and not divine, she was held to have been raised to heaven, where she was exalted above all others, and was perceived as playing a vital and ongoing role in sacred and human history. With regard to earthly women, reflecting developments in the secular world, ideals of womanhood became increasingly contested in Russian Orthodox writings and sermons in the late imperial period. Nonetheless, authors and churchmen generally stressed motherhood as the natural and divine calling of women, maintained that the qualities they associated with this role—nurturing, tenderness, compassion, selflessness, modesty, humility, patience, tolerance, piety, and obedience—composed the innate character of women, and argued that women consequently should confine themselves either to the home or to occupations considered to be consistent with their allegedly natural qualities. Disagreement tended to focus on the degree of autonomy to be accorded women as individuals and which occupations and roles outside the home and within the Church were appropriate for them.[58] In this religious, cultural, and social context, the Mother of God presented female and male monastics alike with a commonly venerated but complex and multivalent image that it seems likely they perceived, interpreted, and responded to based on their personal experiences as women and men as well as Orthodox believers and monastics.[59]

From this perspective, Taisiia's advice to women contemplating or beginning a monastic life, first published in 1900, is revealing. While accepting the prevailing notion that women are by nature weaker than men, at least physically, Taisiia asserted that they are equally capable as men of performing exceptional ascetic feats, practicing strict self-denial, leading a deeply contemplative life, and striving for spiritual perfection, and she maintained that women were as responsible as men for the introduction and development of the Christian monastic way of life.[60] Although citing several early female as well as male Christian ascetics as exemplars, she urged women at the point of taking their vows to hold Mary in their mind as the ideal for emulation. Mary, she advised, offered the quintessential model of a humble woman of faith who consciously and voluntarily submitted herself to God's will and suffered hardship in order to play an active and vital role in the divine plan for human salvation.[61] As a woman aspiring to a contemplative spiritual life yet also overseeing both a monastic community and extensive educational activities, Taisiia could see herself in that image.

## NOTES

1. On the interactions between collective and individual beliefs and practices in Orthodoxy, see Nikos Kokosalakis, "Icons and Non-Verbal Religion in the Orthodox Tradition," *Social Compass* 42, no. 4 (1995): 433–49; Jill Dubisch, "Pilgrimage and Popular Religion at a Greek Holy Shrine," in *Religious Orthodoxy and Popular Faith in European Society*, ed. Ellen Badone (Princeton, NJ: Princeton University Press, 1990), 128–32; Vera Shevzov, *Russian Orthodoxy on the Eve of Revolution* (New York: Oxford University Press, 2004), 194–95, 235–36, and "Scripting the Gaze: Liturgy, Homilies and the Kazan Icon of the Mother of God in Late Imperial Russia," in *Sacred Stories: Religion and Spirituality in Modern Russia*, ed. Mark D. Steinberg and Heather J. Coleman (Bloomington: Indiana University Press, 2007), 61–92.

2. Robert A. Orsi, *Between Heaven and Earth: The Religious Worlds People Make and the Scholars Who Study Them* (Princeton, NJ: Princeton University Press, 2005), 49.

3. See Léonid Ouspensky, *Theology of the Icon* (Crestwood, NY: St. Vladimir's Seminary Press, 1978), 191; John Binns, *An Introduction to the Christian Orthodox Churches* (Cambridge: Cambridge University Press, 2002), 97–106; Shevzov, *Russian Orthodoxy*, 190–95, 222–26; Scott M. Kenworthy, *The Heart of Russia: Trinity-Sergius, Monasticism, and Society after 1825* (New York: Oxford University Press, 2010), 196, 205–8; and Kokosalakis, "Icons and Non-Verbal Religion," 443. On how saints' relics similarly operated as media of presence for Orthodox faithful in late Imperial and early Soviet Russia, see Robert Greene, *Bodies Like Bright Stars: Saints and Relics in Orthodox Russia* (DeKalb: Northern Illinois University Press, 2010).

4. Shevzov, *Russian Orthodoxy*, 223.

5. Orsi, *Between Heaven and Earth*, 48–72.

6. See the following by William G. Wagner: "Female Orthodox Monasticism in Eighteenth-Century Imperial Russia: The Experience of Nizhnii Novgorod," in *Women in Russian Culture and Society, 1700–1825*, ed. Wendy Rosslyn and Alessandra Tosi (London: Palgrave Macmillan, 2007), 191–218; "Fashioning Ideals of Monasticism and Womanhood: The Nizhnii Novgorod Convent of the Exaltation of the Cross, 1802–1857," in *Everyday Life in Russian History: Quotidian Studies in Honor of Daniel Kaiser*, ed. Gary Marker, Joan Neuberger, Marshall Poe, and Susan Rupp (Bloomington, IN: Slavica Publishers, 2010), 85–102; "Paradoxes of Piety: The Nizhegorod Convent of the Exaltation of the Cross, 1807–1935," in *Orthodox Russia: Belief and Practice under the Tsars*, ed. Valerie A. Kivelson and Robert H. Greene (University Park: Pennsylvania State University Press, 2003), 211–38; "The Transformation of Female Orthodox Monasticism in Nizhnii Novgorod Diocese, 1764–1929, in Comparative Perspective," *The Journal of Modern History* 78, no. 4 (2006): 793–845. See also Petr Al'bitskii and Nikolai Mamontov, *Krestovozdvizhenskii pervoklassnyi zhenskii monastyr' v gorode Nizhnego Novgoroda: Stoletie ego sushchestvovaniia (1813–1913 g.g.); Istoriko-statisticheskii ocherk* (Nizhnii Novgorod: Tipografiia Gubernskago Pravleniia, 1913). On the growth of Orthodox female monasticism in general in late Imperial Russia, see O. V. Kirichenko, *Zhenskoe pravoslavnoe podvizhnichestvo v Rossii, XIX–seredina XX veka* (Moscow: Aleksievskaia pustyn', 2010); and E. V. Beliakova, N. A. Beliakova, and E. B. Emchenko, *Zhenshchina v pravoslavii: Tserkovnoe pravo i rossiiskaia praktika* (Moscow: Kuchkovo pole, 2011), 174–299.

7. Tsentral'nyi Arkhiv Nizhegorodskoi Oblasti (hereafter abbreviated TsANO), f. 570, op. 555 za 1796 g., d. 39 (inventories for 1775, 1784, 1796). The other female saints represented were Paraskeva, Blessed Elena, and Evdokiia (two icons).

8. TsANO, f. 582, op. 1, dd. 42, 249; N. Khramtsovskii, *Istoriia i opisanie Nizhnego Novgoroda* (Nizhnii Novgorod: Nizhegorodskaia Iarmarka, 1998), 331–51; and I. Solov'ev, "Nizhegorodskii Krestovozdvizhenskii pervoklassnyi zhenskii monastyr," *Nizhegorodskiia eparkhial'nyia vedomosti* (hereafter abbreviated *NEV*), 1887, *chast' neofitsial'naia* (hereafter *ch. neof.*), 759–72; no. 16, *ch. neof.*, 839–65; and no. 17, *ch. neof.*, 898–913. The inventories and other sources do not include personally owned icons. The increase in Marian imagery and devotion at the Convent of the Exaltation of the Cross during the nineteenth and early twentieth centuries conforms to general European patterns. See Barbara Corrado Pope, "Immaculate and Powerful: The Marian Revival in the Nineteenth Century," in *Immaculate and Powerful: The Female in Sacred Image and Social Reality*, ed. Clarrisa W. Atkinson, Constance H. Buchanan, and Margaret R. Miles (Boston, MA: Beacon Press, 1985), 173–200.

9. See reference to Khramtsovskii, *Istoriia*, in note 8. See also Al'bitskii and Mamontov, *Krestovozdvizhenskii pervoklassnyi zhenskii monastyr'*, 12–13, 86–90; A. Snezhnitskii, *Adres-Kalendar' Nizhegorodskoi eparkhii, v pamiat' ispolnivshagosia v 1888 godu 900-letiia kresheniia Rusi* (Nizhnii Novgorod: Tip. Gubernskago pravleniia, 1888), 39–91; N. N. Dranitsyn, *Adres-Kalendar' Nizhegorodskoi eparkhii na 1904 g.* (Nizhnii Novgorod, 1904), 2–25; Alexander Schmemann, *The Virgin Mary: The Celebration of Faith; Sermons, Volume 3* (Crestwood, NY: St. Vladimir's Seminary Press, 1995), 61–62, 86–93; Hugh Wybrew, *Orthodox Feasts of Jesus Christ and the Virgin Mary: Liturgical Texts with Commentary* (Crestwood, NY: St. Vladimir's Seminary Press, 2000); *Divine Liturgy*, 2nd ed. (South Canaan, PA: St. Tikhon's Seminary Press, 1977); *Service Book of the Holy Orthodox-Catholic Apostolic Church*, ed. and trans. Isabel Florence Hapgood, 7th ed. (Englewood, NJ: Antiochian Orthodox Christian Archdiocese of North America, 1996); and Johanna Manley, comp. and ed., *The Bible and the Holy Fathers for Orthodox: Daily Scripture Readings and Commentary for Orthodox Christians* (Crestwood, NY: St. Vladimir's Seminary Press, 1984).

10. Orthodox female religious typically expressed their spirituality and religiosity through other media, particularly action, liturgical practices, and artistic works. See Isolde Thyrét, "Women and the Orthodox Faith in Muscovite Russia: Spiritual Experience and Practice," in Kivelson and Greene, *Orthodox Russia*, 160–66, 174.

11. On the role of shared imagery, devotions, and rituals in shaping and providing an identity for monastic communities, see Patricia Wittberg, *Creating a Future for Religious Life: A Sociological Perspective* (New York: Paulist Press, 1991), 11–35, and *The Rise and Fall of Catholic Religious Orders: A Social Movement Perspective* (Albany: The State University of New York Press, 1994), 142–51. See also George A. Hillery, Jr., "Love and the Monastic Community," in *Monastic Life in the Christian and Hindu Traditions: A Comparative Study*, ed. Austin B. Creel and Vasudha Narayanan (Lewiston,NY: The Edwin Mellen Press, 1990), 361–91.

12. Shevzov, "Scripting the Gaze."

13. Binns, *An Introduction*, 107, 40, and 39–43.

14. Meredith B. McGuire, *Lived Religion: Faith and Practice in Everyday Life* (New York: Oxford University Press, 2008), 31.

15. Robert Maniura, "Persuading the Absent Saint: Image and Performance in Marian Devotion," in *Saints: Faith without Borders*, ed. Françoise Meltzer and Jaś Elsner (Chicago: University of Chicago Press, 2011), 253–78.

16. See note 9 above.

17. On the role of shared participation in religious activities in creating a common Orthodox identity in late Imperial Russia, see Shevzov, *Russian Orthodoxy*, 131–213; and Wagner, "The Transformation of Female Orthodox Monasticism," 823–26. In general, see note 11 above.

18. *Blagodeianiia Bogomateri rodu khristianskomu chrez eia sv. ikony* (St. Petersburg: M. P. Frolovoi, 1905; Moscow: Pravoslavnyi Palomnik, 1997), 156–79; *Skazanie o chudotvornykh ikonakh Bogomateri i o eia milostiakh rodu chelovecheskomu* (Kolomna: Sviato-Troitskii Novo-Golutvin zhenskii monastyr', 1993), 290–310; "Iz istorii Oranskoi pustyni," *NEV*, 1866, no. 12, *ch. neof.*, 479–89;

no. 13, *ch. neof.*, 537–50, and no. 21, *ch. neof.*, 802–3; and Gavriil, *Opisanie Oranskago Bogoroditskago pervoklassnago monastyria: S prilozheniem skazaniia o chudesakh, byvshikh ot chudotvornoi ikony Vladimirskiia, nakhodiashcheisia v onom monastyre, s vidom monastyria i snimok s ikony Vladimirskiia Bozhiei Materi* (Nizhnii Novgorod: Tip. P. A. Kosareva, 1871). See also "Zhurnal Komissii po uporiadocheniiu khodov s sv. ikonami, iznosimymi iz monastyrei v uezdakh Nizhegorodskoi eparkhii," *Nizhegorodskii tserkovno-obshchestvennyi vestnik* (hereafter abbreviated *NTsOV*), 1912, no. 40, 973–76.

19. Solov'ev, "Nizhegorodskii Krestovozdvizhenskii pervoklassnyi zhenskii monastyr'," no. 17, *ch. neof.*, 912–13; *NEV*, 1895, no. 8, *ch. neof.*, 185–87; "Vstrecha Oranskoi ikony Bozhiei Materi," *NTsOV*, 1907, nos. 17–18, 452; *NTsOV*, 1912, no. 26, 634; "Vstrecha Oranskoi ikony Bozhiei Materi," *NTsOV*, 1913, no. 17, 445; *NTsOV*, 1916, no. 16, 326; and TsANO, *fond* M. P. Dmitriev, photographs 699, 708, 718.

20. Shevzov, *Russian Orthodoxy*, 223.

21. See note 19 above.

22. See note 19 above and A. V_skii, "Nechto ob Oranskom monastyre," in *Nizhegorodskaia starina: Sbornik statei kasaiushchikhsia Nizhegorodskogo kraia*, comp. N. I. Drazhitsyn, vol. 1 (n.p., n.d.).

23. "Vstrecha Oranskoi ikony Bozhiei Materi," *NTsOV*, 1907, nos. 17–18, 452; V_skii, "Nechto ob Oranskom monastyre"; "Vstrecha Oranskoi ikony Bozhiei Materi," *NTsOV*, 1913, no. 17, 445; and *NTsOV*, 1916, no. 16, 326. On the religious complexion of the city and region, see B. I. Gudkov, E. V. Kuznetsov, and V. V. Sarychev, "Religioznaia obstanovka v Nizhegorodskoi gubernii v kontse XIX veka," *Voprosy istorii i istorii kul'tury Nizhegorodskogo Povolzh'ia (Mezhvuzovskii sbornik)* (Gorky, 1985), 78–99.

24. See notes 19 and 23 above.

25. *Blagodeianiia Bogomateri*, 460–65, and Graham Speake, *Mount Athos: Renewal in Paradise* (New Haven, CT: Yale University Press, 2002), 21, 130.

26. Speake, *Mount Athos*, 130; Vera Georgievna Chentsova, *Ikona Iverskoi Bogomateri: Ocherki istorii otnoshenii Grecheskoi tserkvi s Rossiei v seredine XVII v. po dokumentam RGADA* (Moscow: Indrik, 2010); *Blagodeianiia Bogomateri*, 465–86; and *Skazanie o chudotvornykh ikonakh*, 211–21.

27. Wagner, "Fashioning Ideals of Monasticism," 87–90.

28. Ibid., 86–93; TsANO, f. 582, op. 1, dd. 86, 250, 335; Rossiiskii Gosudarstvennyi Istoricheskii Arkhiv (hereafter abbreviated RGIA), f. 796, op. 88, d. 951; op. 89, d. 788; f. 793, op. 98, d. 301; and Al'bitskii and Mamontov, *Krestovozdvizhenskii pervoklassnyi zhenskii monastyr'*, 53–58.

29. Marlyn Miller, "Spiritual Mothers: Female Leadership, Mary, and the Idea of Motherhood in Nineteenth-Century Russian Monasticism" (paper presented at the Fortieth National Convention, American Association for the Advancement of Slavic Studies, Washington, DC, 16–19 November 2008).

30. On this movement, see Oleg Kirichenko, *Dvorianskoe blagochestie XVIII v.* (Moscow: Palomnik, 2002), 301–85; Olga A. Tsapina, "Secularization and Opposition in the Time of Catherine the Great," in *Religion and Politics in Enlightenment Europe*, ed. James E. Bradley and Dale K. Van Kley (Notre Dame, IN: University of Notre Dame Press, 2001), 334–89; N. N. Lisovoi, "Vosemnadtsatyi vek v istorii russkogo monashestva," in *Monashestvo i monastyri v Rossii XI–XX veka: Istoricheskie ocherki*, ed. N. V. Sinitsyna (Moscow: Nauka, 2002), 186–222 (especially 202–17); Brenda Meehan-Waters, "Metropolitan Filaret (Drozdov) and the Reform of Russian Women's Monastic Communities," *Russian Review* 50, no. 3 (1991): 310–23; and Irina Paert, *Spiritual Elders: Charisma and Tradition in Russian Orthodoxy* (DeKalb: Northern Illinois University Press, 2010), especially 41–102.

31. TsANO, f. 582, op. 1, d. 86, l. 6; Wagner, "Fashioning Ideals of Monasticism," 93–97; and "Paradoxes of Piety," 214–17. In general, see Brenda Meehan-Waters, "From Contemplative Practice to Charitable Activity: Russian Women's Communities and the Development of Charitable Work, 1861–1917," in *Lady Bountiful Revisited: Women, Philanthropy, and Power*, ed. Kathleen D. McCarthy (New Brunswick, NJ: Rutgers University Press, 1990), 142–56; Kirichenko, *Zhenskoe pravoslavnoe podvizhnichestvo*, 229–64; and Beliakova et al., *Zhenshchina v Pravoslavii*, 252–99.

32. On this point, see Shevzov, *Russian Orthodoxy*, 214–57.

33. See note 25 above.

34. On social engagement by the Convent of the Exaltation of the Cross and its predecessors, see the following by Wagner: "Female Orthodox Monasticism," 209–10; "Fashioning Ideals of Monasticism," 93–97, 99–102; "The Transformation of Female Orthodox Monasticism," 823–26. On changing conceptions of the social role of women in Orthodox writing in general in the nineteenth century, see Wagner, "'Orthodox Domesticity': Creating a Social Role for Women," in *Sacred Stories: Religion and Spirituality in Modern Russia*, ed. Mark D. Steinberg and Heather J. Coleman (Bloomington: Indiana University Press, 2007), 119–45; and Beliakova et al., *Zhenshchina v Pravoslavii*, 9–25, 348–66. On Mary in Orthodox doctrine, see Schmemann, *The Virgin Mary*; for liturgies, see *Divine Liturgy*; *Service Book*; and *The Bible and the Holy Fathers*; and on popular beliefs, see Shevzov, *Russian Orthodoxy*, 217–22.

35. Al'bitskii and Mamontov, *Krestovozdvizhenskii pervoklassnyi zhenskii monastyr'*, 88.

36. Although completed in 1892, Taisiia's autobiography was not published until 1916, a year after her death. *Sochineniia igumenii Taisii (Solopovoi)*, ed. O. P. Moskvina (Moscow: Izdatel'skii tsentr Ventana-Graf, 2006), 11–134 (available in English: *Abbess Thaisia of Leushino: The Autobiography of a Spiritual Daughter of St. John of Kronstadt* [Platina, CA: St. Herman of Alaska Brotherhood Press, 1989]). On Taisiia, see Brenda Meehan, *Holy Women of Russia: The Lives of Five Orthodox Women Offer Spiritual Guidance for Today* (San Francisco, CA: HarperSanFrancisco, 1993), 95–141; and Scott Kenworthy, "Abbess Taisiia of Leushino and the Reform of Women's Monasticism in Early 20th-Century Russia," in *Culture and Identity in Eastern Christian History: Papers of the First Biennial Conference of the Association for the Study of Eastern Christian History and Culture*, ed. Russell E. Martin and Jennifer B. Spock, *Ohio Slavic Papers 9, Eastern Christian Studies 1* (Columbus, OH: Ohio State University, Department of Slavic and East European Languages and Literatures, 2009), 83–102. See also Taisiia's published conversations with and letters to the charismatic priest and now saint John of Kronstadt, with whom she became closely associated, in *Sochineniia igumenii Taisii*, 135–84; and *Abbess Thaisia of Leushino*, 243–306.

37. On women's religious communities in Imperial Russia, see Brenda Meehan-Waters, "Popular Piety, Local Initiative, and the Founding of Women's Religious Communities in Russia, 1764–1907," *St. Vladimir's Theological Quarterly* 30, no. 2 (1986): 117–41, and "To Save Oneself: Russian Peasant Women and the Development of Women's Religious Communities in Prerevolutionary Russia," in *Russian Peasant Women*, ed. Beatrice Farnsworth and Lynn Viola (New York: Oxford University Press, 1992), 121–33; and Kirichenko, *Zhenskoe pravoslavnoe podvizhnichestvo*.

38. For examples of Taisiia's poetry, see *Abbess Thaisia of Leushino*, 311–31. She also wrote a popular and frequently republished guide for women contemplating or beginning a monastic life that clearly reflects her personal experiences; *Sochineniia igumenii Taisii*, 185–234 (also available in English: *Letters to a Beginner: On Giving One's Life to God* [Wildwood, CA: St. Xenia Skete Press, 1993]).

39. *Sochineniia igumenii Taisii*, 16.

40. Ibid., 20, 20–24, 51–52, 61, 62, 66–67, 73–74, 90–91, 92, 95–97, 98–99, 99–100, 103–4, 104, 109–10, 112, 113–15, 116, 117, 118–19. Among the other sacred figures encountered by Taisiia in her dreams were the following: Christ (four times), Saint John the Forerunner, Saint Matthew the Evangelist, Saint Michael the Archangel, Saint Nicholas, Saint Paraskeva, Saint Symeon the God-Receiver, and Simeon the Fool for Christ.

41. Ibid., 61.

42. Ibid., 51–52, 61, 90–91, 103–4, 113–15, 116, 117. Although Mary does not appear directly in Taisiia's dream prophesying her appointment as abbess, in the dream (described in the text below) Taisiia is greeted by the sisters at the convent to which she is being drawn with the singing of the hymn "Meet It Is…," which appears to be a reference to the Marian icon of that name that appeared in another of Taisiia's dreams and to which the convent's compound in Cherepovets later was consecrated. Ibid., 99–100, 114; and *Abbess Thaisia of Leushino*, 223–24.

43. *Sochineniia igumenii Taisii*, 51–52, 56, 57, 61–63, 68–70, 117–18.

44. Ibid., 51.

45. Ibid., 51–52, 70, 117–18.

46. Ibid., 52, 56, 68–70.

47. Ibid., 70.

48. Ibid., 99–100. The hymn appears to be a reference to the Marian icon "Meet It Is. . ." See also p. 114.

49. Ibid., 103–4.

50. Ibid., 61, 99–100.

51. Ibid., 113–15, 116, 117. The first of these concerned raising the funds to build a new church at the convent, the Church of the Laudation of the Mother of God, which eventually was constructed on the site indicated by Mary to Taisiia in her dream.

52. Ibid., 116, 117.

53. On popular religious practices and beliefs in the late imperial period, see Shevzov, *Russian Orthodoxy*; Greene, *Bodies Like Bright Stars*; Chris J. Chulos, *Converging Worlds: Religion and Community in Peasant Russia, 1861–1917* (DeKalb: Northern Illinois University Press, 2003); M. M. Gromyko, "O edinstve pravoslaviia v Tserkvi i v narodnoi zhizni," *Traditsii i sovremennost': Nauchnyi pravoslavnyi zhurnal* 1, no. 1 (2002): 3–31; M. M. Gromyko and A. V. Buganov, eds., *O vozzreniiakh russkogo naroda* (Moscow: Palomnik, 2000); and T. A. Listova, ed., *Pravoslavnaia zhizn' russkikh krest'ian XIX–XX vekov* (Moscow: Nauka, 2001).

54. On the relationship between the perception of "presence" in images, their power and meanings, and their cultural context, see Robert Maniura and Rupert Shepherd, introduction to *Presence: The Inherence of the Prototype within Images and Other Objects*, ed. Robert Maniura and Rupert Shepherd (Burlington, VT: Ashgate, 2006), 1–30. On understandings of Mary and the meanings of Marian imagery and devotion in the cultural context of late Imperial Russia, see—in addition to the relevant essays in this volume—especially the work of Vera Shevzov: *Russian Orthodoxy*, 214–57; "Scripting the Gaze"; "Poeticizing Piety: The Icon of Mary in Russian Akathistoi Hymns," *St. Vladimir's Theological Quarterly* 44, nos. 3–4 (2000): 343–74; "Between 'Popular' and 'Official': *Akafisty* Hymns and Marian Icons in Late Imperial Russia," in *Letters from Heaven: Popular Religion in Russia and Ukraine*, ed. John-Paul Himka and Andriy Zayarnyuk (Toronto: University of Toronto Press, 2006), 251–77; and "Mary and Women in Late Imperial Russian Orthodoxy," in *Women in Nineteenth-Century Russia: Lives and Culture*, ed. Wendy Rosslyn and Alessandra Tosi (Cambridge: Open Book Publishers, 2012), 63–90.

55. George H. Tavard, *The Thousand Faces of the Virgin Mary* (Collegeville, MN: The Liturgical Press, 1996). The quoted phrase occurs frequently in the liturgy, for example *Divine Liturgy*, 68. This multiplicity of images and ideals is characteristic of Christian Mariology generally. For good broad surveys, see Jaroslav Pelikan, *Mary through the Centuries: Her Place in the History of Culture* (New Haven, CT: Yale University Press, 1996); Sally Cunneen, *In Search of Mary: The Woman and the Symbol* (New York: Ballantine Books, 1996); and Miri Rubin, *Mother of God: A History of the Virgin Mary* (New Haven, CT: Yale University Press, 2009). The seemingly endless variety of Marian images, the complexity of their meanings and impact, and the consistency and pervasiveness of their presence and influence across time and cultural space give rise to the question of why Marian imagery and the idea of Mary are so generative of meanings.

56. Shevzov, *Russian Orthodoxy*, 221 and 217–26, and "Mary and Women." On Orthodox Mariology in general, see Schmemann, *The Virgin Mary*.

57. Shevzov, *Russian Orthodoxy*, 222.

58. On these debates, see Wagner, "'Orthodox Domesticity'"; Shevzov, "Mary and Women"; and Beliakova et al., *Zhenshchina v Pravoslavii*, 9–25. Interestingly, the image of Mary was invoked only occasionally in the debates. For an example, see Wagner, "'Orthodox Domesticity,'" 131–32. On the position of women generally in late Imperial Russian society and on movements for reform at this time, see Barbara Alpern Engel, *Women in Russia, 1700–2000* (Cambridge: Cambridge University Press, 2004); Richard Stites, *The Women's Liberation Movement in Russia: Feminism, Nihilism, and Bolshevism* (Princeton, NJ: Princeton University Press, 1978); and Rochelle Goldberg Ruthchild, *Equality and Revolution: Women's Rights in the Russian Empire, 1905–1917* (Pittsburgh, PA: University of Pittsburgh Press, 2010).

59. This question merits further study, although ultimately it may not be possible to answer satisfactorily. But Carolyn Walker Bynum's analysis of maternal imagery in the writings of twelfth-century Cistercian monks is suggestive. See her essay "Jesus as Mother and Abbot as Mother: Some Themes in Twelfth-Century Cistercian Writing," in her collection *Jesus as Mother: Studies in the Spirituality of the High Middle Ages* (Berkeley: University of California Press, 1982), 110–69. Similarly, Nadieszda Kizenko notes differences based on gender (as well as social and educational background) in confessional letters written to the charismatic priest John of Kronstadt and in the appeal both of his cult as a saint and of that of Kseniia of St. Petersburg. See the following by Nadieszda Kizenko: *A Prodigal Saint: Father John of Kronstadt and the Russian People* (University Park: Pennsylvania State University Press, 2000), 59, 97–150; "Written Confessions and the Construction of Sacred Narrative," in *Sacred Stories: Religion and Spirituality in Modern Russia*, ed. Mark D. Steinberg and Heather J. Coleman (Bloomington: Indiana University Press, 2007), 96–97, 110–12; "Protectors of Women and the Lower Orders: Constructing Sainthood in Modern Russia," in *Orthodox Russia: Belief and Practice under the Tsars*, ed. Valerie A. Kivelson and Robert H. Greene (University Park: Pennsylvania State University Press, 2003), 105–24. In *Bodies Like Bright Stars*, 80, Robert Greene observes that women responded differently than men to the cult of Anna of Kashinsk. For similar differences in an earlier period, see Isolde Thyrêt, "Muscovite Miracle Stories as Sources for Gender-Specific Religious Experience," in *Religion and Culture in Early Modern Russia and Ukraine*, ed. Samuel H. Baron and Nancy Shields Kollmann (DeKalb: Northern Illinois University Press, 1997), 115–31. But see also Christine D. Worobec, "Miraculous Healings," in *Sacred Stories: Religion and Spirituality in Modern Russia*, ed. Mark D. Steinberg and Heather J. Coleman (Bloomington: Indiana University Press, 2007), 30.

60. *Sochineniia igumenii Taisii*, 192–94. Taisiia cites as her source a study by Petr Kazanskii, a professor at the Moscow Theological Academy, that appeared in 1854 and has recently been republished: P. S. Kazanskii, *Istoriia pravoslavnogo monashestva na vostoke* (Moscow: Pravoslavnyi palomnik, 2000), vol. 1, especially 59–90, 398–460.

61. *Sochineniia igumenii Taisii*, 192–93, 231, and 230–34. See also Meehan, *Holy Women of Russia*, 139–41.

# 5

## The Woman at the Window

### Gorky's Revolutionary Madonna

AMY SINGLETON ADAMS

A revolution is fruitful and able to renew life only when it happens first spiritually, in the minds of people, and only then physically on the streets and barricades. ... [Otherwise,] it cannot change our life but will only increase brutality and evil.

Maxim Gorky, 7 April 1918

DURING A JUNE 2009 CONVERSATION backstage at Moscow's Vakhtangov Theater, actress Dar'ia Maksimovna Peshkova expressed surprise that Western scholars were again researching Maxim Gorky; no one, she said, had asked her about her grandfather in twenty years.[1] By then, access to archival materials in the mid-1990s had already dispelled the stereotypical notion of Gorky as Lenin's uncritical supporter and the founder of Socialist Realism under Stalin.[2] Moreover, the early years of the twenty-first century would see a renewed interest in Gorky as an important writer and thinker of the Silver Age, whose intentions were those of a cultural preservationist rather than a political opportunist. Around the time of my meeting with Dar'ia Peshkova, scholars, writers, politicians, historians, and journalists were beginning to reevaluate the aesthetic merits of Gorky's work, focusing on his attempts to inject into early Soviet revolutionary philosophy and proletarian culture his own brand of collective humanism, or "God-building" (*Bogostroitel'stvo*).[3]

Following prevailing trends, the post-Soviet rediscovery of Gorky often highlights the same mytho-religious imagery and themes that Soviet era editors tried to eliminate.[4] Especially from the Russian side, contemporary descriptions of Gorky's writings take on a quasi-religious character of their own.[5] Pavel Basinskii's 2011 chronicle of Gorky's final days, for example, is imagined as a kind of passion play. In the 2008 film documentary *Gorky: A Living History* (Gor'kii: Zhivaia istoriia), award-winning Russian writer Dmitrii Bykov joins other post-Soviet interpreters in understanding Gorky's philosophy of God-building not as a spiritual form of Marxism but, rather, as a new kind of "Russian gospel."[6] Contextualizing Gorky in the fin-de-siècle atmosphere inspired by Nietzsche, Einstein, and the Bolsheviks, Bykov reexamines Gorky's notion of a "new heaven and new earth" (*novoe nebo i novaia zemlia*) inhabited by a new kind of person (*novyi chelovek*) who would differ fundamentally from the people who had lived before him.[7] The "reborn" person, as Gorky describes in *Untimely Thoughts* (Nesvoevremennye mysli, 1917–1918), would be remade morally, intellectually, and spiritually; works like *A Confession* (Ispoved', 1908) and *Mother* (Mat', 1906) call on familiar religious archetypes—at one time anathema to Soviet editors—to convey in rich but simple terms this vision of salvation.[8]

As tempting as it may be to claim revisionist thinking on the part of Gorky's contemporary readers, one has only to recall Lenin's vehement and methodical opposition to the writer's Capri School (1909–1913) and the notion of God-building itself to realize the value of such characterizations.[9] In the years surrounding the Russian Revolution, religious thought played an enormously important role in the struggle between the iconoclastic Bolsheviks and socialist intellectuals like Gorky who believed, as Richard Stites writes, "that bread and politics alone were not enough, that life had to be enriched by emotion, that communism itself was a kind of religious commitment, and that many people needed a unified set of rituals and symbols to bind their feelings to the goals of the regime."[10] Indeed, in her compelling study of political iconography during the early years of Soviet power, Victoria Bonnell shows how the Bolsheviks' concerns in 1917 were "not merely the seizure of power but [also] the seizure of meaning."[11] Soviet political posters, Bonnell continues,

> were the new icons—standardized images that depicted heroes (saints) and enemies (the devil and his accomplices) according to a fixed pattern (the so-called *podlinnik* in church art). The icons of Soviet political art did not reflect the social institutions and relations of the society. Rather, they were part of a system of signs imposed by the authorities in an effort to transform mass consciousness. Like other "invented traditions," the iconographic images

were consistent and incessantly repeated, and they resonated strongly with mythologies from the Russian past.[12]

As highly symbolic visual texts, early Soviet political posters functioned like the sacred icons Russians traditionally deciphered through a similar system of signs, or semiotics.[13] However, the field of symbols that comprised these iconographic images could also became a field of battle as various political and cultural forces often envisioned the "sacred" values of the revolution in conflicting ways.[14]

In his writings and literary works, Gorky's descriptions of the Mother of God icons and of characters that imitate that icon type in their appearance or pose provide the central metaphor of his God-building philosophy—the human and (mostly female) face of cultural and spiritual rebirth—and of his vision of what fellow writer Isaac Babel called a "good" revolution.[15] Gorky's metaphor is enhanced by the semiotic nature of the icon and by the Russian treatment of the sacred image as a sacramental sign (in which the line between the image and the thing itself is blurred), giving rise to the ekphrastic motif of the revolutionary Madonna.[16] In literary works such as "Twenty-Six and One" ("Dvadtsat' shest' i odna," 1899), *Mother* (Mat'), and *A Confession*, and in his later journalistic essays, Gorky draws ironic and non-ironic comparisons between female characters and Mother of God icons. Doing so, he demonstrates firstly his knowledge of the formal conventions of icon painting (the *podlinniki* to which Bonnell refers) that he acquired as a young apprentice in a Nizhnii Novgorod icon workshop, an experience he describes in the second part of his autobiographical trilogy, *In the World* (V liudiakh, 1916).[17] In this account, he expresses a clear preference for the Mother of God icon types he lists, although he finds something sterile and stiff about the images that the workshop's painters produce. "From my grandmother's stories," he writes, "I imagined the *bogoroditsa* as young, pretty, and kind, like the paintings in magazines. But their icons portrayed her as old and stern, with a long, crooked nose and wooden hands."[18] Throughout this episode, Gorky repeatedly draws attention to the eyes and other facial features of the Mother of God icons, further underscoring his fascination with the face by describing his extreme discomfort at the sight of the unfinished, faceless icons that line the walls of the workshop. Gorky's early writing often describes women's faces with the recognizable attributes and symbolism of the Orthodox icon—a face with large, lachrymose eyes often foregrounded against rays of sun, birds, and other prescribed symbols. Gorky also provides some kind of frame for these women. For example, he depicts them in doorways, windows, lying prone in wagons, and ringed by workers to create an icon-like composition.[19]

These "frames" function iconographically, establishing a boundary between two worlds: sacred and profane, "heaven" and "hell," revolutionary and prerevolutionary.

But, most importantly, these frames and the literary icons they define signify points in the narratives that develop Gorky's vision of a spiritual revolution in which women as sacred mothers play a central role. It is not surprising that, in *Untimely Thoughts*, Gorky lists the qualities of a "good" revolution as qualities mainly thought to be possessed by women: love, compassion, and warmth of feeling toward humanity.[20] Within the context of his God-building philosophy, Gorky's heroines—as living literary icons—embody and reflect the universal and collective energy of the people, breathing new life into exhausted forms of culture and faith.[21] In actual practice, the power of the icon is believed to be refreshed by repainting or by replacing the decorative overlay (*oklad*).[22] Imitating such practices symbolically, Gorky often "reframes" his literary icons to challenge the authenticity of revolutionary ideals and to demonstrate the collective power of his revolutionary Madonnas. Ultimately, reading through this motif gives shape to Gorky's attempts to influence the moral character of the revolution and provides a better understanding about why Lenin aggressively prevented the God-building movement from taking shape and flourishing.

## GORKY IN THE CONTEXT OF SILVER AGE THOUGHT

Although marked by political and social upheaval, the Silver Age in Russia (1890s to the early 1920s) was a period of tremendous creativity and innovation in the Russian arts. For Gorky and other Silver Age writers like Isaac Babel, Alexander Blok, Andrei Bely, and Evgenii Zamiatin, philosophical and religious themes and symbolism were especially potent ways to describe the promise of cultural and spiritual renewal that seemed almost palpable in the revolutionary climate. However, while his contemporaries appreciated Gorky as an artist, Edward Brown rightly notes that he did not "properly fit any of the classifications so far established in the world of Russian writing."[23] But Gorky did fit—at that moment in Russian history and by virtue of his somewhat legendary biography—the image of the "new" Russian writer.[24] And, in this role, Gorky occupied the center of literary discussion and production, from the *Sreda* circle (named for its Wednesday meetings) and its *Znanie* (Knowledge) publishing house, to the later House of the Arts and the World Literature project, as well as organizations designed to provide material support and pleas for release from imprisonment (or even execution) to scholars, artists, and writers.[25] Famously dubbed the "Noah of the Russian Intelligentsia," Gorky nurtured both the writers and their work.[26] "His role in shaping the newborn Soviet literature of the twenties," Konstantin Fedin writes, "was a tremendous one and his interest in the fate of a writer often determined the entire further development of a talented person and brightened the path of many a young writer."[27]

The giants of the Silver Age were the Symbolists, among them Valerii Briusov, Alexander Blok, Andrei Bely, and Fedor Sologub. As a group, the Symbolists of the early twentieth century were influenced primarily by the mystically transcendent worldview of Vladimir Solov'ev, whose vision of absolute unity among people and ideas, as Natalia Ermolaev's essay shows, was particularly appealing in such turbulent times. Fittingly, and almost by definition, Solov'ev's philosophy also represented a rejection of past social conventions and a protest against the limitations of ordinary language to express real meaning. Especially in the early revolutionary period, Solov'ev's ideas strongly influenced the Russian liberal intelligentsia, whose "God-seeking" (Bogoiskatel'stvo) movement was considered a renewed form of Christianity that opposed the old Orthodox faith and was marked by an anxious search and spiritual craving for meaning.[28] The modernist urge to transform or even transfigure faith and the world through art, however, still relied on the revival of older Orthodox forms to manifest its ideas. Thus, throughout Symbolist poetry and prose, complex images of Christ, Blok's Beautiful Lady (Prekrasnaia dama), and Sophia (the incarnation of Divine Wisdom) represent Symbolist ideas about spiritual unity, Sophiology, and Godmanhood.[29]

Gorky read and admired Solov'ev's work, even expressing regret in a 1912 letter to Vasilii Rozanov that—as with other "heretics" of the revolution—Solov'ev's "servitude to God" would go the way of the Khazars.[30] But in the case of the God-seekers, Gorky has strong words. The presumptive founder of the God-seeking movement Dmitrii Merezhkovskii is a "swindler and a clever little beast" who deserves "two or three good slaps in the face," while his followers are "little people who have taken to searching for God out of shame for the emptiness of their lives."[31] Despite these characterizations, Gorky does invoke what Barry Scherr calls the "impulses" of God-seeking in the novel A Confession, especially in those episodes from the peripatetic Matvei's life that also echo the "seeking" genres of the saint's life, bildungsroman, adventure novel, or the confession.[32] But, like Dostoevsky before him, Gorky modifies the conventions of religious autobiography to redirect spiritual self-discovery toward others and collective salvation.[33]

This push toward the realization of the collective self ultimately overshadows and undermines the elements of God-seeking in A Confession (and, as

Gary Rosenshield shows in the case of Dostoevsky, the genre of confession itself), offering instead an interpretation of Gorky's political philosophy of God-building. Doing so, Gorky is careful to portray not only the essential humanism of his philosophy, but also the "miraculous power" of the collective itself. "In my new novella," he writes to his wife in February of 1908, "I have tried to illuminate the path towards a merger with the whole; it is in this merger, and nowhere else, that happiness and the source of the highest spiritual pleasures are to be found."[34] This "merger" of the individual with the collective is capable, Gorky shows, even of earthly "miracles"—healings, resurrections, and salvation—usually associated, as Christine Worobec shows, with church-sanctioned icons and God himself.[35] But Gorky's vision of spiritual unity is based in the *human* collective. "Every individual, if he is a spiritually sound being, ought to be striving towards the world and not away from it— that's the thesis of my novella," he writes.[36] In *A Confession* and other works, it is often a female figure, one of Gorky's "living" miracle-working icons, that focuses the energy of the collective and demonstrates the possibility of collective salvation. Doing so, she transcends her own individuality, embodying the humane at the heart of the collective experience. "Everything personal is amazingly insignificant," Gorky continues in his description of *A Confession*, "of this I am convinced. It is not that I'm recommending a renunciation of the self, not at all. I am just talking about the need to find, to comprehend, and to cultivate the humane within one's self. There is little of the humane in the personal."[37] For Gorky, the ideal image of the collective self looked very much like the Mother of God icon.

REFRAMING THE WOMAN AT THE WINDOW: IDOLS AND ICONS

For Gorky, all women are mothers, either actual or—with the Mother of God as a model—symbolic. "A woman in my view," he writes in one of his 1918 essays for the daily newspaper *New Life* (Novaia zhizn') "is first and foremost a mother, though physically she may be a virgin; she is a mother in her feelings not only toward her children but also toward her husband, lover, and in general toward humanity."[38] Russian women, Gorky writes, have a "great cultural role." He envisions them as the "spiritual mothers" whose "creative powers" and maternal joy, although challenged by the "chaos of revolutionary days," will give birth to a "new" person. "You howl like beasts at the moment of birth and you smile the happy smile of the Virgin, pressing the newborn to your breast," he writes, "And I wish with all my heart, with all my soul that you should soon smile the smile of the Madonna, pressing to your breast the newborn people of

Russia!"[39] Gorky urges Russian "mothers" to remain true to what he calls their "psychophysiology"—the urge to give life rather than destroy it—by nurturing the spiritual elements of the revolution. "Physical mothers of the human world," he writes, "you could be its spiritual mothers as well."[40] Women need to introduce "something bright and good" into the revolution, he urges, and become representatives of the "revolutionary" values of "love," "compassion," "softness," "warmth," and "tenderness."[41] "Russia will not perish," he writes, "if you mothers will sacrificially pour everything beautiful, everything tender which is in your souls into the bloody and filthy chaos of these times."[42] Culturally and spiritually significant, the role of mothers in revolutionary Russia was of historical importance as well. God-building understood collective faith as energy to be tapped into through certain individuals; for Gorky, safeguarding the humane qualities of the revolution as a mother would protect her child serves an important historical and social function.[43]

Throughout human history, the role of women has largely been defined by their ability or inability to move freely from the domestic realm to public spaces. In this sense, the Russian icon of the Mother of God in Gorky's work can be considered a recasting of the ancient and powerful image of the "woman at the window," whose frame defines her cultural and historical function. In her study of this particular motif, Nehama Aschkenasy examines two sometimes contradictory aspects of the image. In ancient art, biblical narrative, and in examples of modern literature, the woman at the window (or doorway) can be associated with cults of fertility or with sexual availability, but also sometimes with danger and even death.[44] The motif, in these cases, Aschkenasy explains, "is linked to female deities who possessed omnipotent power and often used that power to taunt or punish men, adding a sense of awe to the image."[45] Other traditions convey a much different meaning, that of a woman "hemmed in, even locked" inside the domestic realm, unable to participate in the public sphere. In these instances, as Suzanne Delehanty notes, the window itself "expresses longings for worlds other than those confining, unhappy places of the present."[46] This interpretation reflects an everyday reality; until quite recently, women worldwide spent most of their lives indoors. "Yet," Aschkenasy writes, "they probably spent much time at the window, joining public life vicariously, as spectators rather than active participants."[47] Indeed, a woman's enclosure within the window frame emphasizes her confinement but also highlights her "removal from history."[48]

In visual art, the interpretation of the woman at the window depends largely on point of view. Regarded from the front, the image can be suggestive. But viewed from behind, from an interior space, the image emphasizes the woman's narrowed horizons and often her chastity. The icon, which does not function as a work of art per se, offers an exception; although Gorky's descriptions place the reader in front of his literary icons, the image remains chaste.[49] Only when Gorky "reframes" the woman does the significance of her role change. For example, in a May 1917 *New Life* piece entitled "A Nightmare" ("Koshmar"), Gorky describes his gradual realization about a young woman's perniciousness using this reframing technique. At first, seated before a window, she is a Madonna, backlit by the morning sun.

> Small, slender, and elegantly dressed, she came to me in the morning when the sun was looking into the window of my room; she came and sat so that the rays of the sun embraced her neck and shoulders and made her fair hair seem golden. . . . The rays of the sun tinted her ear the color of coral. All of her was so spring-like, festive.[50]

This portrait recalls the impromptu prayers of Gorky's grandmother to the Mother of God as "Golden Sun" (*solnyshko zolotoe*) that he chronicles in the autobiographical *Childhood* (Detstvo, 1913–1914) and mentions again in *In the World* as a defining characteristic.[51] Biblical descriptions such as the "woman clothed in the sun" (Rev. 12:1) and the woman who "appears like the dawn . . . bright as the sun" (Song of Sol. 6:10) would also be familiar to Gorky.

When Gorky's visitor reveals herself as a tsarist informant and offers to become the author's mistress in exchange for social "salvation," however, the sun "seemed wrong for her." Instead, Gorky sees her as a "poisonous flower" and, when he rejects her request for help, he does so as she is stopped in the doorway rather than framed in the light of the window.[52] The biblical sources of the motif of the woman in the doorway suggest the dual role of womanhood. "Like the earth that she represents," Aschkenasy writes, "the woman has power to bring forth life, but she can also entrap and devour, turning from shelter into grave."[53] In Gorky's "Nightmare" episode a pattern similar to the one Aschkenasy describes emerges. Initially Gorky assumes that the woman has come to bring him something creative—a "poem or a story"—and he admits to a "dark, convulsive desire." But when her treachery is exposed, she is threatening. She becomes the deadly flower; "her pretty little head resembled a pistil in the black petals of the lace of her [low-cut] blouse."[54] Now casting only a "black shadow" on Gorky's soul, the implied icon she earlier embodied is exposed as dangerously false.

Gorky describes the unmasking of a "renewed" icon as a fake in *A Confession*, but he did not support the actual Bolshevik practice of exposing miracles and religious fraud.[55] The destruction of meaningful rituals without replacing them with new rituals seemed inhumane to him. In his fiction, though, in addition to indicating the questionable moral character of its subject, the idea of the false "icon" can also reveal the weaknesses inherent in its own worship. In Gorky's early story "Twenty-Six and One" ("Dvadtsat' shest' i odna"), a group of overworked pretzel makers idolizes the sixteen-year-old housemaid, Tania, who devastates them when she unwittingly (but happily) fails their test of her purity. In the story, Gorky introduces the dynamic of reframing that he uses in the later *New Life* entry. In "Twenty-Six and One," however, the exposure of the false "icon" does not so much reflect on the girl's virtue but on the misguided efforts of the men to create their own object of worship in order to alleviate the misery of their existence.[56]

A series of shifting frames trace the changing significance of the men's interaction with Tania. She is first introduced into the story at the basement window; her flattened face against the glass (recalling Gorky's childhood ideal of the young *Bogoroditsa*) suggests what Boris Uspensky calls the "deformation" of the icon's perspective.[57]

> Every morning a little, rosy face with cheerful blue eyes would press against the little window cut into the door leading from the hall into the workshop and a clear, tender voice would call out to us.... We would all turn to that clear sound and would joyfully and good-naturedly look at that pure, girlish face, gloriously smiling at us. We liked seeing the nose and the small, white teeth—sparkling behind the pink lips, open in a smile—flattened up against the glass.[58]

For the men virtually imprisoned in a dank, dark basement kitchen, Tania takes the place of the sun (*zameniavshee nam solntse*), a description that anticipates the imagery of Gorky's 1917 "Nightmare" entry in *Untimely Thoughts*. They seem not to notice how her cheerful yet quite genderless sensuousness (the narrator's descriptions of her "pure, girlish" face studiously avoid feminine modifiers) makes an unlikely model for the *Bogoroditsa*.[59] The illusory nature of their worship is underscored when Tania steps into the doorway and becomes more of an idol than a living icon (a dynamic that recalls Aschkenasy's discussion about the framing of female deities).[60] While she stands on the raised threshold, the men seated below give her pretzels as "a daily offering to an idol" (*ezhednevnaia zhertva idolu*) while they pronounce "special words" (*osobye slova*) like an incantation. When they realize that they have deceived themselves by treating her as an object of worship, these words become insulting and obscene. They angrily surround her—thus creating a final frame—but she breaks away, her "flashing" eyes full of indignant pride. Having destroyed their own "icon," the men are left with nothing. "After that we silently went back into our damp, stone hole. As before, the sun never looked in through the window at us, and Tania never visited us again!"[61]

## LIVING ICONS AND THE POWER OF THE COLLECTIVE

You can't become a saint by staring at the icon.

Maxim Gorky, *Mother*

The crux of "Twenty-Six and One" is the men's inexplicable desire to test to failure the same "idol" ("nam strashno khotelos' isprobovat' krepost' nashego bozhka") they hope will satiate their hunger for something pure and life-affirming. Almost twenty years later in *A Confession*, Gorky is able to resolve this contradiction with a more explicit articulation of God-building and its philosophy of collective salvation. The hero Matvei's quest for spiritual meaning is paralleled in a way by his search for a "true" icon. His story begins with an all-night vigil in front of an icon of the Mother of God. His subsequent journey (which he compares to those of Lot and Noah) is fraught with tragedy and false starts and results in a progressive loss of faith in the institutional church, which is signified by encounters with various icons that fail to inspire in him belief and the "joy of prayer" (*radost' molitvy*).[62] Matvei only experiences true spirituality when he encounters "living" icons. In one instance, his own reflection in a mirror—a portrait of despair—prevents him from killing himself and launches him on his pilgrimage.

The novella culminates with a living version of the icon—a lame girl who is cured by the collective energy of a pilgrimage crowd. This scene plays out the essential link between Gorky's literary icons and the spiritual collective as the girl transcends her own frame to establish for Gorky the "church" (*khram*) of God-building in the hearts of the people (*narod*). Matvei encounters the girl at a monastery near Kazan, where a large crowd waits for the ceremonial return of a miracle-working icon of the Mother of God and in which the girl's father has apparently lost hope.[63] The girl is lying in the back of her parents' wagon. Her stillness, the waxen whiteness of her face, and Matvei's focus on her melancholy eyes depict a different, but initially almost lifeless, "icon." Indeed, the hopeless words of the girl's father seem more like a requiem than a prayer for the living.

> At the monastery, people waited for miracles: in a smallish wagon a young girl lay motionless; her face was frozen, like white wax, her gray eyes were half open, the only sign of life seemed concentrated in her long, trembling eye lashes. . . . It was evident that her father had been carting his daughter to monasteries for a long time and had already lost hope for her recovery. He sang out the same words, but from him they sounded dead. People listened to his pleas and, sighing, crossed themselves, while the eye lashes on the girl trembled, covering her melancholy eyes.[64]

But in this final scene, suffused with rays of sun and the emblematic birds, feathers, and flight found frequently in Mother of God icons, the collective prayers of the people offer the girl new life and hope where none before seemed possible. Furthermore, the sacramental nature of Gorky's living icon locates the real power to heal among the pilgrims and within the girl herself. The promise of a miracle cure originates in the girl's own gaze, which in turn inspires the crowd and Matvei to concentrate the power of their prayers on her. The people join in this mutual gaze with the girl as they would to venerate the miracle-working icon they came see. It unites them in a new faith community of "world-wide God-building" (*vsemirnoe bogostroitel'stvo*), which Matvei experiences as that "other thing" he cannot quite describe, and injects the previously inert scene with life and movement.[65] The semantic nuances of lifting up and calling out (*vozbuzhdenie, vyzvannykh, vosstavshei*) combine with the powerful gaze of the people to effect a true transcendence of the self that allows a collective and universal force to sweep up the girl and Matvei— "like feathers in the fire's flame"—in her miraculous rebirth.

> There was great excitement [*vozbuzhdenie*]: people were pushing against the wagon. The head of the girl feebly and weakly rocked back and forth and her eyes looked at them in fear. Dozens of eyes bathed the sick girl with rays of light, concentrating on her weakened body a great force, called to life [*vyzvannykh k zhizni*] by the overpowering desire to see the sick girl rise up out of the wagon [*vosstavshei s orda*]. And I too looked into the depth of her gaze, and inexplicably desired together with the others that she stand up—not for my sake or for hers, but for the sake of some other thing, before which she and I were just like feathers in the fire's flames.[66]

In this interpolated "miracle tale," the girl is both the pilgrim in search of a cure and the source of the cure itself, a dynamic that demonstrates Gorky's use of "sacramental" metaphors and that contrasts sharply with the false icons and idols in his earlier work. Again, the comparison between the young woman and a Mother of God icon—in this case a miracle-working icon—is central to Gorky's articulation of his God-building philosophy. In *A Confession*, the girl's "miracle" cure offers the people an alternative to the actual miracle-working icon they have come to the monastery to venerate as well as the fraudulent icon that Savelka tries to pass off at the beginning of the tale. By shifting spiritual authority from the institutional church to the people, Gorky's God-building icons also become antiauthoritarian in their function.[67]

Reversing the nature of the human "frame" found in "Twenty-Six and One" and the imagery of "A Nightmare," Gorky has the crowd surround the girl not to test her as a living icon but to revive her instead. The pilgrims embody the "miraculous power" (*chudotvornaia sila*) of the people with their "belief in their own power to effect miracles" (*vera vo vlast' svoiu tvorit' chudesa*).[68] True faith in their own power, not the worship of false idols, restores the girl to life. In the freshness of her rebirth, she is like a fledgling bird or a small child, learning to fly or walk for the first time.

> Rosy shadows began to glow on her dead face and her astonished and joyous eyes widened even further. Slowly moving her shoulders, she meekly lifted her trembling hands and obediently stretched them out before her—her mouth was open and she looked like a fledgling bird, flying out of its nest for the first time.[69]

Trusting in the people, whose unseen power supports her, the once paralyzed girl actually walks, smiling and white all over, "like a flower" in the dusty crowd—a reverse of the dark "petal" of lace worn by the woman in "A Nightmare." In *A Confession*, the repeated phrase "she walks" (*idet*) and the mention of her hands reaching out in front of her (*vpered*) echo the refrain of the Russian icon procession that the icons are coming or "the gods are walking" (*bogi idut* or *bogi idut vpered*), although here Gorky radically changes the meaning of the ancient phrasing.[70]

> She stopped, gave a lurch—and was walking [*idet*]. It was as if she were walking [*idet*] on a knife that cut her toes. But she was walking [*idet*], afraid and laughing, like a small child. The people around her were also joyful and affectionate, as if toward a child. She was afraid and her body was shaking, but she raised her hands in front of her [*vpered*], supporting herself with them in the air that was permeated with the power of the people. From all around hundreds of rays of light held her up.[71]

For Gorky, such frameless, living icons reify the tenets of God-building that meld spiritual and material worlds. While symbolizing the moral characteristics of Gorky's "good" revolution, they also represent its liberating effects. Like this young girl released from her physical confinement, the subject of Gorky's living icons can transcend social and political frames as well. Most notably, in his 1906 novel *Mother*—the work, as Mark Steinberg notes, through which the Soviet government shifted the author's own historical role from "conscience of the revolution" to "father of Soviet socialist literature"—Gorky uses apocryphal narrative and iconographic frames to trace the trajectory of his heroine Nilovna's growing revolutionary awareness and activity.

## THE EARTHLY LIFE OF GORKY'S MADONNA

Gorky's "God-building people," as he calls them in *A Confession*, represent not just spiritual and creative energy, but a social and political force as well. Indeed, any individual "that is elevated by this collective energy and embodies it most fully," writes Irene Maryniak in her study on the revival of God-building in Soviet literature of the late 1980s, "is charged with a historical function."[72] In his novel *Mother*, Gorky uses the imagined and apocryphal stories about the earthly life of the Mother of God to chronicle the liberation of a young revolutionary's mother from the confines of the "old" faith of the institutional church. In his comparison between Nilovna and Mary, he also shows how his heroine overcomes her own political powerlessness and social obscurity to become a revolutionary herself.

Gorky's familiarity with and use of such tales was part of an upsurge of interest in Marian apocryphal literature at the turn of the twentieth century in Russia that played an important role in the discourse on early women's movements.[73] In his own library on various religious topics, Gorky owned several works on New Testament apocrypha, even one specifically devoted to the life of Mary.[74] But it is more likely that his own grandmother fed his early imagination with folkish (*narodnyi*) stories about Mary's life and her continued concern with the everyday struggles of earthly life. According to Akulina Ivanovna Peshkova, Mary herself put flowers on earth to ease human suffering.[75]

Evident in the generic structure of Gorky's *Mother* is *The Earthly Life of the Most Holy Birthgiver* (Zemnaia zhizn' presviatoi Bogoroditsy), the most popular nineteenth-century form of the apocryphal biography of Mary, which focuses on Mary's own experience of the Passion and on her active role in her son's ministry.[76] In her study of published versions of the *Life* at the turn of the twentieth century, Vera Shevzov explains how, like encounters with the ubiquitous iconographical images of Mary, the act of imagining and imitating the details that fill out the canonical lacunae of her life became a form of devotion. Some examples of the *Life* seem to follow other agendas as well, showing how Mary emerges from the "anonymity of motherhood" to take a part in her son's ministry during his lifetime and after his death.[77] Mary is the carrier of the "word" in both senses—Christ as God's Word incarnate and also her son's teachings. As such, she represents ideas about the role of women as purveyors of "history and culture" who, following the example of Mary's life, move from the confines of marriage and motherhood to what can only be understood in early revolutionary Russia as the political realm.[78]

As with Mary in the *Life*, Gorky emphasizes Nilovna's real and symbolic role as widowed and working mother to her son and to the other young revolutionaries.[79] But her true act of imitation of Mary's life is her progressive movement out of a series of frames that define and confine her. This movement is accompanied by her newfound mobility as well as a growing association with the written and spoken revolutionary word. Forming the core of Gorky's novel, Nilovna's trajectory echoes the same kind of concern as its apocryphal subtext, while also considering the political and historical implications of the frame itself. Nilovna begins as a traditional "woman at the window," subject to social restriction and unable to participate in political and history-making events that take place in the free and mobile male sphere. "The woman at the window," Aschkenasy writes, "as reflective of the prototypical female position postulates the subordination of the element of time to the element of space in the woman's existence. At the same time, the encasement within the window highlights not only the woman's removal from history, but her spatial constriction as well."[80] There are biblical tales, she continues, where women find a way around these limits and join the "chronological-historical mode," usually through the clever use of language and ingenuity or by having the tale shift focus in a way that moves the woman to the center of the canvas. In *Mother*, Gorky indicates the historical role of his heroine through a process of increasing freedom of movement and speech.

In *Mother*, Gorky portrays Nilovna first as an individual woman with a personal biography and, gradually, as a more collective entity, a "mother of all." This trajectory begins as Nilovna develops affection for her son Pavel's fellow revolutionaries and later culminates as she is conflated with the revolutionary cause itself and becomes the "spiritual mother" of the group.[81] Thus, the story of her life takes on "the significance of a symbol," and suggests that, as in the later *A Confession*, the roots of Gorky's novel lie in religious biography.[82] Indeed, much of Gorky's book focuses on Nilovna's emotional state and burgeoning consciousness, rather than on her son, whose political development is complete early in the book. "It must be good and terrible to have such a son," one revolutionary woman says to Nilovna, suggesting her role as the *Mater Dolorosa* (*skorbiashchaia mat'*).[83] In *Mother*, as narrative attention shifts from son to mother, the story traces Nilovna's growing ease with language and literacy, as well as her active role in the revolutionary cause. At certain points in Nilovna's development—the May Day parade, the distribution of leaflets, the death of the revolutionary Egor, and her final moments of freedom at the train station—Gorky pauses narration with an icon-like pose that allows the readers/viewers to share the mother's understanding of the revolution as the new source of spiritual renewal. In one example that demonstrates the dynamics of Gorky's image-icons, the revolutionary Nikolai's stories "evoked in the mother's soul a feeling similar to that with which she used to stand before an icon."[84] While imitating the relationship between the icon and the worshipper, however, Gorky shifts the meaning of the icon itself. Indeed, the image-icon that Nikolai's stories create represent for Nilovna the "great truth" of the revolution, rather than of the established church. For her, this truth is one that "raises humanity from the dead, welcomes all equally, and promises all alike freedom from greed, wickedness, and falsehood"—the tenets of Gorky's God-building.[85] Instead of allying the image with the established church or state power, Gorky makes it clear that his Mother of God actually challenges existing hierarchies of power. Thus his revolutionary Madonna urges the viewer to consider both spiritual renewal and social protest.

At first, the windows that provide Gorky the "frame" for his image-icons are perceived as a fragile boundary between the world outside and the relative safety of Nilovna's home, the center of early revolutionary activity in the novel. Suspicious residents of the settlement peer through the window and, at the same window, the neighbor Maria Korsunova warns of an impending raid on the house. Later, a "hostile darkness" clings to the window as if to express Nilovna's initial fear and uncertainty about her son's political activities.[86] But as she better understands the revolutionaries, the nature of the "frame" changes—a rap on the window is no longer something she fears. "There was a knock at the window. Then another. She was used to such a knock; they did not frighten her, but this time she gave a little start of joy. Vague hopes lifted her quickly to her feet."[87] Gradually, Gorky moves the mother from the interior of her home (she often sits behind a partition) to the window itself. As she grows more active in the revolutionary cause, as on the night before she secretly distributes leaflets at the factory, she is repositioned in the window frame. And, on the morning of the May Day parade—a pivotal scene that liberates her from her former life and integrates her into the active life of the revolutionary world—she "sat down at the window, holding one hand to her face as if she had a toothache ... She was filled with a strange calmness."[88] She sits briefly, but long enough to allow the reader/viewer to witness Nilovna's realization of the day's significance. In a transformation that parallels that of her son, she finds her own voice. Echoing the tradition of the "Stabat Mater" that depicts Mary at the foot of Christ's cross, she addresses the crowd, explaining her son's mission as her own.[89]

The death of the revolutionary Egor marks the next stage of the mother's revolutionary commitment and creates a new image-icon. Egor's death inspires in her a "great pity for humanity" but also a "somber but courageous force goading her from within."[90] This force seems to coalesce as Nilovna stands with two of Egor's comrades at the hospital window.

> Liudmila got up and went to open the window. Presently they were all standing there close together, staring into the dark face of autumn night. . . . Through the silence came the weary night sounds of the city. . . . Out in the corridor they could hear smothered, frightened sounds—groans, whispers, and a shuffling of feet. But the three of them stood silent and motionless at the window, staring into the night.[91]

The scene suggests a Lamentation (Ne Rydai Mene, Mati) type icon, with its focus on the Mother of God, the disciple John and Mary Magdalene. Egor's body lies on the bed behind the mother, Liudmila, and the doctor, who stand at the window and are lit from behind against the dark night. Gorky is careful to avoid describing movement after Liudmila moves to the window. The mother and the doctor simply appear at the window and the three remain silent and motionless amid the bustle of the hospital and the city. Nilovna's new, intense period of involvement that follows Egor's death is characterized not only by symbolic acts of motherhood, but also by scenes in which Nilovna witnesses violence and bloodshed. In Nilovna's mind blood is connected with Christ's truth and resurrection. When her own clothes are soaked in the blood of a wounded revolutionary, it seems to prefigure her beating at the train station. There, finally captured, she famously proclaims, "Not even an ocean of blood can drown the truth!"[92]

In the final scene, the mother stops in a doorway at the train station where she is distributing revolutionary literature. Sensing her imminent arrest, she flings the copies of Pavel's speech into the crowd. In several ways, the scene echoes the familiar composition of the miracle-working Bogoliubovo Mother of God icon, with her raised hand, scroll, and attentive crowd whom the image protects and preserves. Nilovna captivates the crowd that rings her primarily through her words and with her iconographic expression. "The people were irresistibly drawn to the grey-haired woman with the large candid eyes in a kindly face," Gorky writes. "Isolated in life, torn away from each other, they now found themselves together here, listening with deep feeling to the flaming words which perhaps many of these hearts, hurt by life's injustice, had long been searching for."[93] Even when her body succumbed to a beating, "her eyes did not lose their shine. And they met other eyes, all of them burning with the bright fire she knew and loved so well."[94]

Even more so than in the other icon-like poses in *Mother*, however, Gorky emphasizes here the gaze of the mother and the corresponding gaze of the viewer within the novel and without—as in the case of the readers themselves. As Pavel Florenskii explains, the Russian icon is not a work of art, but "a work of witness"; the act of visually contemplating the icon can be spiritually—or for Gorky, politically—transformative.[95] Indeed, the complex nature of Gorky's image-icons is captured in the illustrations the collective artistic group "Kukryniksy" produced for the 1950 edition of Gorky's *Mother*.[96] Combining elements of the twelfth-century Bogoliubovo icon and Iraklii Moisevitch Toidze's famous 1941 war poster "Your Motherland Needs You" ("Rodina-Mat' Zovet!"), the Kukryniksy visually capture the culmination of Nilovna's transformation into the kind of social and spiritual activist typical of the Earthly Life tale.

In this sense, the portrayal of the mother as "living icon" and her life story as a religious biography raises certain questions about Gorky's symbolic and generic "frames." Gorky's "woman at the window" is not confined by the frame, but rather invited into the chronological-historical world of language, change, and movement. His "living icons" of women are not only key images in Gorky's revolutionary vision, but also key players. The transformative power of Gorky's revolutionary Madonna is not a catalyst for religious epiphany, but a realization of social and spiritual truths associated with the revolution and an inspiration for revolutionary activity as well. But Gorky's Madonna is a sacramental image that represents a spiritual union among people rather than the hierarchy of state or church power with which *Bogoroditsa* icons have long been associated.[97] In *Mother* and especially in *A Confession*, Gorky is careful to undermine the relationship between his "living icons" and the hierarchies of power. In some ways, Gorky's use of iconic imagery reformulates the relationship, imagining the more horizontal structure of God-building, wherein man is God to man. Although Gorky's revolutionary Madonna was short-lived—Lenin perceived the whole God-building movement as a threat to his own political power—she may reverberate somehow through the modern and postmodern Madonnas, whose relationship with their frames may define them, but cannot confine them.

## Notes

1. The performance was *The Last Moons* (Poslednie Luny) (based on Furio Bordon's *Le Ultime Lune*), directed by Rimas Tuminas.

2. Starting in the 1990s, access to archival materials allowed researchers to question assumptions about Gorky's friendship with Stalin. See, in particular, Lidiia Spiridonova, "Gorky and Stalin (According to New Materials from A. M. Gorky's Archive)," *The Russian Review* 54, no. 3 (July 1995): 413–23. Other sources that reconsider the relationship include Andrew Barrat and Barry P. Scherr, *Maksim Gorky: Selected Letters* (Oxford: Clarendon Press, 1997) and Tovah Yeldin, *Maxim Gorky: A Political Biography* (Westport, CT: Praeger, 1999).

3. The most recent sources to consider Gorky's work in the realm of culture, literature, and the arts include Stuart Finkel, "Purging the Public Intellectual: The 1922 Expulsions from Soviet Russia," *Russian Review* 62, no. 4 (October 2003): 589–613 and Martha Weitzel Hickey, *The Writer in Petrograd and the House of the Arts* (Evanston, IL: Northwestern University Press, 2009).

4. A history of Gorky's reworking of *Mother* to weaken the role of religious imagery in the novel can be found in S. V. Kastorskii, *Povest' M. Gor'kogo "Mat'": Ee obshchestvenno-politicheskoe i literaturnoe znachenie* (Leningrad: Gosudarstvennoe uchebno-pedagogicheskoe izd-vo, 1954), 60–69, 70–104. By the 1980s, *Mother* was widely accepted by Soviet critics as a work of pure Socialist Realism. See D. M. Stepaniuk, "Ob otnoshenii M. Gor'kogo k antireligioznoi teme v literature," *Voprosy russkoi literatury* 2, no. 24 (1974): 26–32 and Andrei Siniavskii, "Roman M. Gor'kogo *Mat'*—kak ranii obrazets sotsialisticheskogo realizma," *Cahiers du Monde russe et soviétique* 29, no. 1 (1988): 33–40.

5. Pavel V. Basinskii, *Strasti po Maksimu: Gor'kii: Deviat' dnei posle smerti* (Moscow: Astrel', 2011); Aleksandr Zaretskii, Eleonora Livshchits, and David Roitberg, *Gor'kii: Zhivaia istoriia*, 4 x 44 minutes, 2008, video.

6. Dmitrii Bykov, *Literatura Sovetskaia: Kratkii kurs* (Moscow: PROZAik, 2012), 23–25. See also Viktor Petelin, *Zhizn' Maksima Gor'kogo: "Ia—kotorzhnik, kotoryi vsiu zhizn' robotal na drugikh"* (Moscow: Tsentrpoligraf, 2007).

7. Bykov, *Literatura Sovetskaia*, 14–15.

8. *Maxim Gorky, Untimely Thoughts: Essays on Revolution, Culture, and the Bolsheviks, 1917–1918*, trans. Herman Ermolaev (New Haven, CT: Yale University Press, 1995), 118.

9. From 1906 to 1913, Gorky lived on the island of Capri, where he promoted cultural thought that would dovetail with his understanding of the Bolshevik cause. Together with Anatolii Lunacharskii—the first Soviet commissar of enlightenment—he began to articulate the philosophy of "God-building," a kind of religious humanism that would imbue the revolution with creativity, morality, compassion, and joy. Lenin was adamantly opposed to the idea of "God-building," but Gorky continued to believe that cultural values were crucial to the success of the revolution. Correspondence between Gorky and Lenin on God-building, Luncharskii, and the school on Capri can be found in *Vladimir Lenin and Maxim Gorky, Letters, Reminiscences, Articles*, trans. Bernard Isaacs (Moscow: Progress Publishers, 1973), 17–57.

10. Richard Stites, *Revolutionary Dreams: Utopian Vision and Experimental Life in the Russian Revolution* (Oxford: Oxford University Press, 1989), 120.

11. Victoria E. Bonnell, *Iconography of Power: Soviet Political Posters under Lenin and Stalin* (Berkeley: University of California Press, 1997), 1.

12. Bonnell, *Iconography of Power*, 7–8.

13. Boris Uspensky, *The Semiotics of the Russian Icon* (Lisse, Belgium: Peter De Ridder Press, 1976), 7–30.

14. Like church icons, political iconography conveyed important ideas about the nature and location of the sacred. This idea is discussed in Bonnell, *Iconography of Power*, 8.

15. Babel owed his literary career to Gorky's mentoring and shared with him a belief in the "good" revolution, one that Babel articulated most clearly in the *Red Cavalry* story "Gedali" (1924), in *Sobranie sochinenii v chetyrekh tomakh* (Moscow: Vremia, 2006), 142–47.

16. In *The Semiotics of the Russian Icon*, Uspensky explains how the basic sign system ("semiotics") of the icon becomes the "manifestation of the idea in the sensible" (21–22n17) and is thus essentially sacramental in nature. Indeed, summarizing Pavel Florenskii, he notes how the icon becomes the thing it represents. In other words, the icon is a "sacramental sign" of a sacred mystery, rather than a metaphoric representation. See also Amy Singleton Adams, "'Not by Bread Alone': Maxim Gorky's Sacramental Metaphors," in *A Convenient Territory: Russian Literature at the Edge of Modernity; Essays in Honor of Barry Scherr*, ed. John M. Kopper and Michael A. Wachtel (Bloomington, IN: Slavica Publishers, 2015), 245–58.

17. Gorky chronicles the entire episode of this two-year apprenticeship (1881–1883) in chapters 12 through 15 of *In the World* (V liudiakh). Maksim Gor'kii, *Sobranie sochinenii v vosemnadtsati tomakh* (Moscow: Gosudarstvennoe isdatel'stvo khudozhestvennoi literatury, 1962), 9:312–61. A

catalog of Gorky's library also lists a work on icon painting: *Ikonopisnyi sbornik* (St. Petersburg: R. Golike i A. Vil'borg, 1906).

18. Gorky, *In the World*, 313.

19. See Uspensky, *Semiotics*, 46n41 on how windows, archways, and doors can function as frames.

20. Gorky, *Untimely Thoughts*, 207–12.

21. During this apprenticeship Gorky was struck by the rigidity and doctrinaire quality of both icon painting and the faith that icons supposedly expressed. Gerhard Habermann notes, too, how Gorky saw in their veneration "the Oriental passivity of people whose faith was spiritually petrified by the fetters of prejudice and dogma." *Maksim Gorki* (New York: Frederick Ungar Publishing Company, 1971), 20. In chapter four of *In the World*, Gorky describes his encounter with the Oranki Mother of God icon—the same icon considered in William Wagner's essay—as an unintentional testing of Orthodox devotional conformity. Unprepared for the "visitor's" (Mary's) arrival, the young Gorky worries that he will offend Mary by touching her icon with dirty fingers and, as numerous icon-related miracle tales suggest, whether his hands would shrivel as punishment. Inspired by his grandmother's characterization of the Mother of God as gentle, loving, and kind, the young Gorky spontaneously kisses Mary's lips instead of her hands, eliciting shock from bystanders and testing the limits of their devotion and sincerity. Many thanks to Vera Shevzov for pointing out this example.

22. See Uspensky, *Semiotics*, 8, 16, about how replacing the *oklad* changes conventions and, similarly, how repainting the same image over old icons can invest them with "fresh power."

23. Edward J. Brown, "The Symbolist Contamination of Gor'kii's 'Realistic' Style," *Slavic Review* 47, no. 2 (Summer 1988), 234.

24. For a contemporary discussion on Gorky's prominent place in the literary world of his day, see Boris Eikhenbaum, "Pisatel'skii oblik Gor'kogo," in *Moi Vremennik: Marshrut v bessmertie* (Moscow: Agraf, 2001), 114–22.

25. On Gorky's advocacy and care for other writers and artists, see the following sources: Mary Louise Loe, "Maksim Gor'kii and the *Sreda* Circle: 1899–1905," *Slavic Review* 44, no. 1 (Spring 1985): 49–66; Nicholas Luker, ed. and trans., *An Anthology of Russian Neo-Realism: The "Znanie" School of Maxim Gorky* (Ann Arbor, MI: Ardis, 1982); Finkel, "Purging the Public Intellectual." Also, see Martha Hickey, "Maksim Gor'kii in the House of the Arts (Gor'kii and the Petrograd Literary Intelligentsia)," *Soviet and Post-Soviet Review* 22, no. 1 (1995): 40–64 and Barry Scherr, "Notes on Literary Life in Petrograd, 1918–1922: A Tale of Three Houses," *Slavic Review* 36, no. 2 (June 1977): 256–67.

26. Victor B. Shklovskii, *Gamburgskii shchet: Stat'i-vospominaniia-esse (1914–1933)* (Moscow: Sovetskii pisatel', 1990), 161.

27. Konstantin Fedin, *Gor'ki sredi nas: Kartiny literaturnoi zhizni* (Moscow: Molodaia Gvardiia, 1967), 3. See also Hickey, *The Writer in Petrograd*.

28. The God-seekers of this era developed out of the Religious-Philosophical Meetings (1901–1903) led by Dmitrii Merezhkovskii, his wife Zinaida Gippius, and Vasilii Rozanov. The religious and political philosopher Nikolai Berdiaev, however, regarded "God-seeking" as an organic trait of Russian culture and literature that reaches back to Petr Chaadaev and is embodied in the work of Gogol and Dostoevsky. "A great pining, an incessant *God-seeking* is lodged within the Russian soul, and it was expressed over the expanse of an entire century. The God-seekers reflected our spirit, rebellious and hostile to every philistinism. Almost the whole of Russian literature, the Russian great literature, is a living document, witnessing to this God-seeking, to an unquenchable spiritual thirst," he writes in his 1907 essay "Russian God-Seekers" ("Russkie Bogoiskateli"), originally published in *Moskovskii ezhenedel'nik* 29 (1907): 18–28.

29. Irene Masing-Delic provides a substantial overview of Silver Age thought in *Abolishing Death: A Salvation Myth in Russian Twentieth-Century Literature* (Stanford, CA: Stanford University Press, 1992). On Blok in particular, see Martha M. F. Kelly, "Aleksandr Blok's Other Body," *Russian Review* 70, no 1 (January 2011): 118–36. For a more extensive treatment of Solov'ev, the Divine Sophia, and Godmanhood, see Judith D. Kornblatt, *Divine Sophia: The Wisdom Writings of Vladimir Solovyov* (Ithaca, NY: Cornell University Press, 2009).

30. Barrat and Scherr, *Maksim Gorky*. See letters to Anton Pavlovich Chekhov, between 1 and 7 October 1900 (60), Vasilii Vasilievich Rozanov, about 10 April 1912 (167) and Vladislav Felitsianovich Khodasevich, 8 November 1923 (241).

31. Letter to V. S. Miroliubov, December 1901, in Barrat and Scherr, *Maksim Gorky*, 65–67.

32. Barry Scherr, "God-Building or God-Seeking? Gorky's *Confession* as Confession," *Slavic and East European Journal* 44, no. 3 (2000): 448–69.

33. Gary Rosenshield, "The Realization of the Collective Self: The Rebirth of Religious Autobiography in Dostoevsky's *Zapiski iz Mertvogo doma*," *Slavic Review* 50, no. 2 (Summer 1991): 317–27. Gorky owned several sets of Dostoevsky's collected works, including a volume containing *Zapiski*.

34. Barrat and Scherr, *Maksim Gorky*, 131.

35. See Christine Worobec's essay, "The Akhtyrka Icon of the Mother of God: A Glimpse into Eighteenth-Century Orthodox Piety on a Southwestern Frontier," in this volume (58–81).

36. Barrat and Scherr, *Maksim Gorky*, 131.

37. Ibid.

38. Gorky, *Untimely Thoughts*, 207.

39. Ibid., 209.

40. Ibid., 213.

41. Ibid., 210, 212.

42. Ibid.

43. Irena Maryniak, "The 'New God-Builders,'" in *Ideology in Russian Literature*, ed. Richard Freeborn and Jane Grayson (London: Macmillan, 1990), 191.

44. Nehama Aschkenasy, *Woman at the Window: Biblical Tales of Oppression and Escape* (Detroit, MI: Wayne State University Press, 1998), 14. In nineteenth-century Russian literature, for example, the suggestiveness of the "woman at the window" can be seen most notably in Alexander Pushkin's "Queen of Spades" ("Pikovaia dama," 1834) and in Mikhail Lermontov's "Princess Mary" chapter in *A Hero of Our Time* (Geroi nashego vremeni, 1840).

45. Aschkenasy, *Woman at the Window*, 14.

46. Suzanne Delehanty, ed., *The Window in Twentieth-Century Art* (Purchase, NY: Neuberger Museum, State University of New York, 1986), 13.

47. Aschkenasy, *Woman at the Window*, 14.

48. Ibid., 17–18.

49. On the essential difference between the icon and visual art, see Pavel Florenskii, *Iconostasis* (Crestwood, NY: Saint Vladimir's Seminary Press, 1996), 134. On the difference between the icon and other works of art in Russian literature, see Jefferson J. A. Gatrall, "Between Iconoclasm and Silence: Representing the Divine in Holbein and Dostoevsky," *Comparative Literature* 53, no. 3 (Summer 2001): 214–32.

50. Gorky, *Untimely Thoughts* 26–27. "The Sun and the Moon" (Electa ut Sol, pulchra ut Luna) is one of the texts of the Canticles applied to Mary. Also, some interpretations of Rev. 12:1–6 understand the woman "clothed with the sun, having the moon under her feet, and on her head a crown of twelve stars" as Mary as well.

51. Maksim Gor'kii, *Detstvo* (*Childhood*), in *Sobranie sochinenii*, 9:168.

52. Gorky, *Untimely Thoughts*, 28.

53. Nehama Aschkenasy, "Biblical Females in a Joycean Episode: The 'Strange Woman' Scene in James Joyce's *A Portrait of the Artist as a Young Man*," *Modern Language Studies* 15, no. 4 (Autumn 1985): 29. The primary biblical source for this study is the story of Jael and Sisera in Jgs. 4:17–22 New Revised Standard Version.

54. Gorky, *Untimely Thoughts*, 30.

55. On this Bolshevik practice, see Stites, *Revolutionary Dreams*, 108. Renewed icons referred to those icons which, because of age, had darkened to the point where their image was unrecognizable and then were claimed to have "miraculously" lightened on their own. In *A Confession*, Savelka uses a phosphorescent substance to create this effect on a Burning Bush (Neopalimaia kupina) type of Mother of God icon.

56. George Gutsche reads the story as an early, artistic expression of Gorky's ideas on God-building, but does not consider the poignant tension between that nascent philosophy and the problems Gorky perceived in God-seeking. See Gutsche's article, "The Role of the 'One' in Gor'kij's 'Twenty-Six and One,'" in *Studies in Honor of Xenia Gasiorowska*, ed. Lauren G. Leighton (Columbus, OH: Slavica Publishers, 1983), 145–54. On the complexities of Gorky's position in the debate between God-building and God-seeking, see Scherr, "God-Building or God-Seeking?"

57. Uspensky, *Semiotics*, 33–35. Tania's pose seems to echo the Virgin of Tenderness of Evil Hearts, the 1915 painting by Kuzma Petrov-Vodkin, whose freedom Gorky negotiated after the artist was arrested in 1919. For Petrov-Vodkin, the compression of perspective also seems temporal, as the painting combines three stages of the *Bogoroditsa*'s life—her youth, the birth of Christ, and his crucifixion. The painting is displayed on the cover of the present volume.

58. Gor'kii, *Sobranie sochinenii*, 2:405.

59. Indeed, in the original Russian, one can see how the physical descriptions of Tania only refer to her in the masculine and neuter gender, as well as in the plural, thus avoiding any feminine attributes.

> Каждое утро к стеклу окошечка прорезанного в двери из сеней к нам в мастерскую,— прислонялось маленькое, розовое личико с голубыми, весёлыми глазами и звонкий, ласковый голос кричал нам.... Мы все оборачивались на этот ясный звук и радостно, добродушно смотрели на чистое девичье лицо, славно улыбавшееся нам. Нам было приятно видеть приплюснутый к стеклу нос и мелкие, белые зубы, блестевшие из-под розовых губ, открытых улыбкой.

60. See note 45 above.

61. Gor'kii, *Sobranie sochinenii*, 2:414.

62. Gor'kii, *Ispoved'* (*A Confession*), in *Sobranie sochinenii*, 5:191.

63. Given the location and timing of this pilgrimage, the icon is likely to be the icon of the Mother of God of the Seven Lakes (Sedmiozernaia), a miracle-working icon of healing. This icon is celebrated in midsummer and is believed to have put an end to a plague that claimed nearly 50,000 lives around the city of Kazan in 1654.

64. Gor'kii, *Sobranie sochinenii*, 5:301.

65. Vera Shevzov discusses the significance of gazing upon an icon in "Scripting the Gaze: Liturgy, Homilies, and the Kazan Icon of the Mother of God in Late Imperial Russia," in *Sacred Stories: Religion and Spirituality in Modern Russia* (Bloomington: Indiana University Press, 2007), 61–62. "Looking upon an icon in Russian Orthodoxy," she writes, "was indeed a complex act. On the one hand, a believer's apprehension of an icon was deeply personal.... On the other hand, the act of the devotional gaze involved more than a single individual and a detached image. Icons and believers were also part of a broader faith community that provided a living environment in which icons were both produced and received ... the production and reception of an icon were not simply attributable to the iconographer and the individual believer, respectively, but involved religious, cultural, and even political processes."

66. Gor'kii, *Sobranie sochinenii*, 5:303.

67. On the promotion and control of miracles by the Russian Orthodox church in the late imperial era, see Christine Worobec, "Miraculous Healings," in *Sacred Stories: Religion and Spirituality in Modern Russia*, ed. Mark D. Steinberg and Heather J. Coleman (Bloomington: Indiana University Press, 2007), 22–43. Also, see her essay, "The Akhtyrka Icon of the Mother of God: A Glimpse into Eighteenth-Century Orthodox Piety on a Southwestern Frontier," in the present volume (58–81).

68. Gor'kii, *Sobranie sochinenii*, 5:303.

69. Ibid.

70. Uspensky, *Semiotics*, 21.

71. Gor'kii, *Sobranie sochinenii*, 5:304.

72. Maryniak, "The 'New God-Builders,'" 199, 191.

73. Vera Shevzov, "Mary and Women in Late Imperial Russian Orthodoxy," in *Women in Nineteenth-Century Russia: Lives and Culture*, ed. Wendy Rosslyn and Alessandra Tosi (Cambridge: Open Book Publishers, 2012), 69–70.

74. These works are the following: S. A. Zhebelev, *Evangeliia kanonicheskie i apokrificheskie* (Prague: Ogni, 1919); Vega (pseudonym of the group of researchers and translators of New Testament apocrypha led by archpriest Aleksandr Vasilevich Smirnov of Kazan around the time of the First World War), *Apokrif, skazaniia o Khriste*, vol. 2, *Kniga Marii Devy* (St. Petersburg: Pervaia zhen. Tip. Tvorchestva, 1912); P. A. Lavrov, *Apokrificheskie teksty* (St. Petersburg: Tipografiia Akademii nauk, 1899).

75. Gor'kii, *Detstvo*, 42–43.

76. On the conventions of this apocryphal genre, see Shevzov, "Mary and Women," 64–90.

77. Ibid., 74–78.

78. On the movement from the "small sphere" of domestic life to the "big sphere" of the political and public realm, see ibid., 84.

79. On Mary's movement from mother to public missionary, see ibid., 76–81.

80. Aschkenasy, *Woman at the Window*, 17–18.

81. Gor'kii, *Sobranie sochinenii*, 4:177.

82. Gor'kii,, *Sobranie sochinenii*, 4:217. On the convention of the genre of religious biography, its invocation by a modern literary work and the idea of the resurrection of the collective self, see Rosenshield, "The Realization of the Collective Self."

83. According to Vera Shevzov, the *Life* is quick to point out the unique insight and suffering of Mary. Another popular apocryphal tale of Mary's life—the Russian Easter tale (*paskhal'nyi rasskaz*) also emphasizes Mary's maternal connection with Christ and her central role in the Passion. For sources of the Easter tale see, for example, N. M. Tupikov, *Strasti Khristovy v zapadno-russkom spiske XV v. Pamiatniki drevnei pis'mennosti* (St. Petersburg, n.p. 1901), vyp. 140; for its treatment as a literary genre, see V. N. Zakharov, "Paskhal'nyi rasskaz kak zhanr russkoi literatury," *Evangel'skii tekst v russkoi literature XVII-XX* vekov (Petrozavodsk: Izd-vo Petrozavodskogo universiteta, 1994), 249–64. Modern Russian literature tends to repeat similar phrases to invoke these genres. Anna Akhmatova, for example, introduces the same idea in "Requiem," when her own *Bogoroditsa* figure says, "You are my son and my horror" (Ty syn i uzhas moi).

84. Gor'kii, *Sobranie sochinenii*, 4:324.

85. Ibid.

86. Ibid., 26.

87. Ibid., 78.

88. Ibid., 161.

89. On the theme of transformation in this scene, see Alyssa W. Dinega, "Bearing the Standard: Transformative Ritual in Gorky's *Mother* and the Legacy of Tolstoy," *Slavic and East European Journal* 42, no. 1 (1998): 76–101.

90. Gor'kii, *Sobranie sochinenii*, 4:251.

91. Ibid., 250.

92. Ibid., 383.

93. Ibid., 381.

94. Ibid., 383.

95. Florenskii, *Iconostasis*, 134.

96. The Kykryniksy was an art collective formed by Mikhail Kupriianov, Porfirii Krylov, and Nikolai Sokolov. They were known mostly for their satirical political posters. Gorky encouraged the group's work beginning in the early 1930s when he first met them. This particular illustration of Nilovna at the train station can be viewed in Oleg Davydov's article, "Bolotnaia mat'," in the online journal *Peremeny* (http://www.peremeny.ru/column/view/1002/).

97. As Vera Shevzov discusses in *Russian Orthodoxy on the Eve of Revolution* (New York: Oxford University Press, 2004), 181–90, the power of the icon is often located in the collective human experience itself.

# 6

# Marina Tsvetaeva's Images of the Mother of God in the Context of Russian Cultural Developments in the 1910s–1920s

ALEXANDRA SMITH

THE EMPHASIS OF RUSSIAN MODERNISM on the power of human creativity and the elevation of art to the status of secular religion set the stage for a new approach to art and cultural identity through a reinterpretation of the medieval icon. The roots of such an approach can be traced to the Russian Silver Age. Among the tenets of Silver Age thought was the belief in the creative individual who would not only express through literature, poetry, music, and art Russia's experience of those turbulent times, but, through the transformative power of creativity, also give birth to a new consciousness and even a new kind of cultural spirituality. "The Silver Age," Galina Rylkova writes, "was created as a result of the collective appropriation of the historical experience that befell the Russian people in the first third of the twentieth century."[1] The popularity during the Russian Silver Age of Sarah Bernhardt's performances, Gordon Craig's productions, Marie Bashkirtseff's diary, Oscar Wilde's works, and Henrik Ibsen's plays shows that audiences were intrigued by new ideas and by challenges to traditional sex/gender ideology associated with Russian Orthodoxy and patriarchal values.

The 1921 death of Symbolist poet Alexander Blok seemed to inspire a resurgence of Silver Age thought with its innovative and experimental qualities that encouraged both men and especially women to transgress the boundaries of traditional roles and profit from the trend toward professionalization in Russia. For the first time in Russian history, many women became known as prominent and highly successful writers, performers, artists, and political figures. The immensity of the achievements of women in Silver Age literature, art, and theatre was due to a unique opportunity that enabled writers, performers, and artists to invent themselves as modern subjects embracing the cosmopolitan aspects of urban life. However, the institution of authorship, shaped by the Orthodox Christian culture of the Russian Church, continued to be influenced by the myth of the martyred author and by the veneration of icons during the first three decades of the twentieth century, despite the fact that striking changes in the perception of the secular and the sacred took place. Commenting on Russian modernist culture, Gregory Freidin writes: "Unlike medieval Russia, where the icon dominated, if not monopolized, pictorial representation, modern Russia gave free play to both the Eastern and Western order of visual representation, thereby offering a legitimate perspective on the icon as a 'work of art.'"[2]

The rediscovery of Russian medieval icons at the beginning of the twentieth century inspired private collectors to reconsider icons as artifacts, thus treating them more like collectible art than as objects of devotion. By 1909 Stepan Riabushinskii and Ilia Ostroukhov had already opened their private museum of ancient icons; in 1913 they presented many valuable medieval icons from their collection at the exhibition celebrating the 300th anniversary of the Romanov dynasty.[3] In his essay, "What can be learnt from the ancient icons?" (Chemu uchat ikony?), which describes this exhibition, Maximilian Voloshin suggests that the archaeological discoveries of ancient Russian icons—with their reverse perspective, clarity of composition, and sense of spiritual purity—and their restoration had a revolutionizing effect on the contemporary viewers.[4] In Voloshin's view, the exhibition struck a positive chord among the Russian audience partly as a response to the chaos and disparate cultural trends of the time. The ancient icon, argues Voloshin, should be treated as "a lesson of harmonious balance between tradition and innovation, method and intention, line and color."[5] The widespread debates about the medieval icon in the 1910s also led to discussions of Russian national identity and the specific qualities of a Russian artistic tradition. In his 1915 article on the fifteenth-century icon painter Andrei Rublev, the art critic Nikolai Punin observes how the Russian icon imbeds cultural identity within its traditions. "The path of our art is stony and the crown of our artistic genius is a crown of thorns. If we have not been mindful of our treasures, if we have lost and forgotten them, even so we remember the valleys where once, divinely great, we were in possession of them. We must look for our lost greatness, for no art can live without traditions. Where are our traditions?"[6]

In his 1913 article published in the prestigious Symbolist journal *Apollo* (Apollon), Punin expressed his belief in the positive influence the Russian medieval icon had on contemporary art, saying that "icons, in their magnificence and living beauty, will help contemporary art accomplish achievements which differ from those that have been influencing European art for the last few years."[7] In response to such calls to forge a new, distinctly Russian tradition, many prominent Russian avant-garde artists were eager to draw analogies between Russian medieval iconic painting and Cubism. It is not coincidental that Anatolii Lunacharskii, Bolshevik commissar for enlightenment in the 1920s and an established playwright and critic himself, highlighted Kazimir Malevich's indebtedness to the iconic tradition. He noted how Malevich, influenced by French Cubists, began his career by imitating icons. Subsequently, Malevich developed a personal mode of painting in which he combined elements taken from Russian medieval icons, Russian folklore, and popular primitive prints (*lubok*).[8] Alexander Benois, an influential artist associated with the World of Art movement, even suggested that Russian medieval icons might be seen as useful interpretative tools for European and Russian contemporary art. "Not only can any fourteenth-century Nicholas the Miracle Worker or Nativity of the Mother of God help us understand Matisse, Picasso, Le Fauconnier and Goncharova," Benois wrote, "but through Matisse, Picasso, Le Fauconnier and Goncharova . . . we feel greatly the beauty of these Byzantine pictures much better."[9]

WOMEN'S INTUITION: THE AVANT-GARDE ICON IN ART AND LITERATURE

> You will rule, you will grieve
> Take the crown,
> Oh, my firstborn!
>
> Marina Tsvetaeva, 1916

Although lauded by Benois for her experimentation, avant-garde artist Natalia Goncharova (1881–1962) was subjected to severe criticism by Russian conservative critics who scorned her imitation of Russian icons and the transgressive qualities of her paintings. The public response was based in part on Goncharova's life studies of the female nude, which (ironically in the case of a female artist) were deemed to be criminally sexed. According to Jane

Sharp, who writes about the ensuing trial in 1910, Goncharova was the only Russian artist ever tried for pornography in high art for the nude life study.[10] Later, in March 1914, Goncharova's paintings were again subjected to public scrutiny for what was perceived as a blasphemous depiction of Christian iconography. One critic—who seems to have been as bothered as much by Goncharova's gender as he was by her reworking of iconographic images and themes—expressed his concern in the article "Futurism and Blasphemy" (Futirizm i koshchunstvo) that the female artist's gaze actually interfered with the reception of sacred objects. Sharp explains that the anonymous author of "Futurism and Blasphemy" states his case boldly, suggesting that women should not be allowed to take part in the revival of religious art and epic painting in Russia. "Goncharova's difference in gender," Sharp writes, "heightened his concern that avant-garde (here, futurist) artists, both male and female, were engaged successfully in the process of introducing non-canonical forms of representation into canonical Christian iconography."[11] The unnamed critic concluded his angry attack on what he regarded as Goncharova's subversion of patriarchal authority with these words: "Let the [female] futurist [futuristka] exhibit as many women's portraits, cats and other things resembling cabinets and rubbish as she likes; but let her not touch with her dirty hands the subjects of religious devotion belonging to the whole Russian people."[12]

Goncharova's religiously themed paintings were also scrutinized by Russian ecclesiastical authorities and government censors: the religious content of some exhibitions to which Goncharova contributed prompted the Holy Synod to get involved on behalf of the state.[13] Goncharova's first retrospective held in St. Petersburg in March–April 1914, Sharp writes, "became a test case for avant-garde art, with some twenty-two religious paintings, which had initially passed the typographic censor, formally banned by the Spiritual Censorship Committee of the Holy Synod. Later the ban was removed and the paintings readmitted to the exhibition. ... Prior to the opening of the 'Donkey's Tail' exhibition, paintings with religious subject matter were removed (including those later banned in 1914), and, in addition, the city governor insisted that the name of the exhibition be abbreviated or changed."[14] According to Sharp, the typographic censor first approved a number of paintings with religious subject matter, excluding only the *Evangelists* (Evangalisty, 1911) and the *Coronation of the Virgin* (Venchanie Bogomateri, 1910).[15] The scandal surrounding the exhibition as well as public performances of Russian Futurists attracted the attention of many journalists and critics. As Sharp rightly points out, many of the public spectacles organized by Mikhail Larionov, Goncharova, and Vladimir Mayakovsky enabled Russian Futurists to mold themselves into the image of public spokespersons. "Seen as a form of speech and model of agency," writes Sharp, "avant-garde *épatisme* made the process of self-representation explicit to such a degree that it could be appropriated, reclaimed by their audiences both female and male. It is this model of appropriated authority, drawn from the artist-provocateur of the debate forum and the streets, more than any narrowly defined formal innovation or 'way out of Cubism,' that led to the extension of avant-garde projects to street and factory following the revolution."[16] However, the process of appropriating authority would be seen by many artists and writers as subversive. The act of transgressing existing conventions presented considerable problems for the women artists and authors wishing to deviate from the religious norms imposed upon them.

The vision of women as the embodiment of the divine archetype was challenged by many female poets and artists of the late nineteenth and early twentieth century; according to Olga Matich, the anxieties and spiritual hopes of modernist authors were often filtered "through an apocalyptic lens."[17] In her work, Russian poet Marina Tsvetaeva (1892–1941) represents these *fin de siècle* concerns through references to icons. In her poems, she often creates her own descriptive images of the Mother of God based on the images found in famous icons. Tsvetaeva's poetic veneration of Russian icons is inseparable from the myth of the martyred author that she cultivated throughout her creative career, a myth that sought to problematize the identity of the female creator in modern times. Most of her poems featuring the Mother of God were written during World War I and the Civil War years (1917–1922). They are often concerned with Tsvetaeva's self-fashioning both as a spokesperson for other female believers and a spiritual truth seeker. One of the striking examples of Tsvetaeva's own controversial treatment of several icons featuring the Mother of God can be found in her 1916 cycle of poems "Poems about Moscow" (Stikhi o Moskve), which includes Tsvetaeva's poems dedicated to her daughter and to Osip Mandelstam, the young Acmeist poet from Petrograd with whom Tsvetaeva was infatuated as she worked on the cycle. His interest in combining medieval traditions with modern ones is similar to Tsvetaeva's search for a new mode of expression. Mandelstam's 1911 essay "The Morning of Acmeism" (Utro akmeizma) calls for the formation of a new world culture with the help of some references to Russian medieval art.

The lyric persona of the first poem of the cycle "Poems about Moscow" characterizes her firstborn daughter as a rightful heiress of traditional Russian culture epitomized by Moscow's religious architecture. Here, the lyric persona instructs her daughter to undertake a kind of cultural pilgrimage through the city. She impels her to revere the cathedrals and churches in Moscow, making sure that she would visit all of them by foot: "Walk everywhere–tirelessly!" (Iskhodi peshkom—molodym shazhkom!). Tsvetaeva expects her daughter to examine all sacred places despite their far-flung location among the seven hills of Moscow (*sem' kholmov Moskvy*).[18] In the second poem of the cycle, the poet talks to a male friend. She addresses her interlocutor as a stranger who needs to discover for himself the spiritual beauty and the power of the city's "forty times forty" churches.

In "Clouds are everywhere" (Oblaka vokrug), the poet describes the churches of Moscow as three-dimensional objects of veneration, even invoking principles of icon painting. She asks her daughter to observe all the rituals, including Lenten practices, and, in due course, to pass on the holy urban space to her *own* daughter after the lyric persona has been buried in the Moscow's Vagankov Cemetery, itself located on one of Moscow's seven hills. Here, the image of Holy Moscow is associated in the poem with a description of the beautiful chiming of bells, allusions to miracles, and the sense of both freedom and authority. The poet predicts that her daughter will be happy in Moscow for many years to come—"It will be joyful for you to rule here" (Budet radostno tsarevat' tebe)—as long as she continues to observe all the religious rituals associated with the veneration of Russian icons and the veneration of Russian saints. The poem states: "And venerate all the forty times forty churches" (I vse sorok chti sorokov tserkvei).[19] Tsvetaeva's neologism *semikholmie* (seven-hilled) in the phrase "all this vast space located on seven hills" (*vse privol'noe semikholmie*) is highlighted by the inner rhyme between the adjective *privol'noe* (vast and free) and the word *semikholmie* (the space located on seven hills). It imitates the open-ended narratives of Russian medieval icons, which utilize the principle of reverse perspective since it brings together the enclosed and open spaces. The use of the iconographical principle that collapses temporal and geographical space (two distinct events or locations can coexist simultaneously) enables Tsvetaeva to point to the existence of transcendental truths with a view to encourage both her daughter and the reader to search for them actively.

In other words, Tsvetaeva presents Moscow not as an enclosed space but a space that opens up a new spatial dimension imbued with divine truth. The latter was often perceived by Russian artists and thinkers in theosophical terms as a fourth dimension. It was discussed both in Charles Hinton's influential 1904 work *The Fourth Dimension* and in Petr Ouspensky's seminal work *Tertium organum: A Key to the Enigmas of the World* (Tertium Oeganum: Kliuch k zagadkam mira), published in St. Petersburg in 1911.[20] As Anthony Parton points out, Ouspensky's ideas derive from Hinton's notion of the four-dimensional self. "Hinton argued," writes Parton, "that we must be four-dimensional beings; otherwise we would be unable to conceive of a fourth dimension. However, our consciousness is trapped within three dimensions, so that we can perceive only a three-dimensional section of our four-dimensional selves, and the three-dimensional world becomes one of appearances alone."[21] In Parton's view, Larionov's and Goncharova's mode of expression—rayism—was largely inspired by theories of the fourth dimension, especially because rayism was presented by them as a special kind of painting that points to the existence of immaterial objects and intangible forms in the space beyond the painting and the objects it depicts in abstraction. Tsvetaeva's vision of Moscow as sacred space is even more richly received through the prism of these theories about the fourth dimension. Indeed, the manifestations in Russian modern art—as in the work of Larionov and Goncharova—is reflected in her poetic interpretation of the Russian medieval icon.[22]

Tsvetaeva explores the idea of four-dimensional space in "Poems about Moscow" not only by imagining Moscow as an open pictorial space but also by envisioning *movement* through that space. While invoking the notion of the pilgrim in search of spiritual truth, Tsvetaeva also indicates that it is the mission of the artist to seek a truer form of aesthetic experience and expression through movement. Again, these goals are achieved through implicit references to iconography. The lyric persona of "Clouds are everywhere," for example, addresses her daughter in a way that suggests she holds a key to the enigma of Moscow and its palimpsest-like qualities; she shies away from the fixed point of view and implies that the image of the holy city should be observed from a different perspective. In other words, the reader of the poem is expected to look at Tsvetaeva's process of painting with words from the point of view of a person versed in icon-viewing and admire it simultaneously as a sacred and aesthetic object. Such a process of creating verbal reproductions of icons implies the existence of the reverse perspective explained in detail in Pavel Florenskii's 1919 essay "Reverse Perspective" (Obratnaia perspektiva).[23] It also presents the lyric persona as an artist who, like the medieval icon painter, is empowered with special vision. "The artist," Ouspensky writes in *Tertium Organum*, "must be a clairvoyant: he must see that which others do not see; he must be a magician: must possess the power to make others see that which they themselves do not see, but which he does see."[24]

According to Florenskii, the organization of the icon's space presupposes the representation of various surfaces of the same object that cannot be viewed simultaneously from a fixed position. This is especially true in the depiction of architectural space in icons. Viewed in this light, Tsvetaeva's image of Moscow as a space with seven hills (*semikholmie*) might be perceived as an iconic image, which is strengthened in her portrayal of simultaneous walking and viewing, which collapses both time and space. The imaginary walk she describes in the poem as a prerequisite for understanding the sacred nature of Moscow derives from the widespread discussion about reverse perspective in Russian medieval icons that was at play among the Russian intelligentsia in the 1910s. The "simultaneous representation of different planes of the same image on the picture surface" implies, at the same time, a simultaneous existence of different planes (described in Florenskii's work as "supplementary planes"). And so, as Clemena Antonova maintains, the image created in the mind of the beholder of the icon is viewed from the perspective of God—who sees all time and space at once.[25] Similarly, Tsvetaeva's poem demonstrates the author's awareness of the existence of these supplementary planes as the essential feature of the organization of space in the medieval icon. As Antonova points out, at the heart of a religious worldview lies the belief that "a timelessly eternal God to whom all moments in time exist simultaneously should be able to see all points in space simultaneously as well."[26] Given the popularity of such a belief in the 1910s, it is not surprising to see Tsvetaeva's attempt to instill in the mind of her readers the same ability to see everything at once, appealing thereby to their visual imagination, in hope that imaginary and real walks in Moscow would enable them to comprehend the city located on seven hills as a sacred space protected by the Mother of God.

In addition to positing the Mother of God as the protectress of holy Moscow, Tsvetaeva connects the city's sacred spaces and architecture with women and the woman poet. As Sibelan Forrester rightly notes, Tsvetaeva establishes this connection between Moscow and women in the early poem "Houses of Old Moscow" (Domiki staroi Moskvy) from her 1912 collection of poetry *The Magic Lantern* (Volshebnyi fonar'). Tsvetaeva continues to forge her identity as the poetic voice of Moscow in her works of the revolutionary and Civil War period by comparing the city itself to important historical women.[27] By suggesting Moscow as an "element of her poetic identity" through these associations with powerful maternal figures, Forrester continues, Tsvetaeva is able to challenge Moscow's role as the seat of ancient patriarchal power. "Even the Moscow Kremlin, grammatically masculine and symbolic of patriarchal authority in Muscovite Russia, was transformed by Tsvetaeva's focus on the 'feminine' churches at its heart and by its geographical and poetic proximity to the 'doubly feminine' Moskva-reka [Moscow River]"[28] Indeed, Tsvetaeva does not suggest herself as the alter ego of a traditional Moscow—the stodgy city of Alexander Pushkin's *Eugene Onegin*. The lyric heroine of her poems written in the 1910s sees Moscow as a city that evolves. She hopes that her native city would be able to reimagine itself through the refreshed forms of its own traditions. "A close reading of poems from 1916," Forrester writes, "shows that Tsvetaeva rejected the denigration of Moscow as a poetic and historical backwater as she elaborated instead her own version of her native city and its traditions."[29] The cultural authority that this comparison allowed Tsvetaeva extended to her anxiety about the preeminence of the Petrograd (St. Petersburg until 1914) poets; by claiming Moscow as her double, she was able to approach the northern school as an equal.[30] Tsvetaeva's concerns in this matter are especially valuable for the present discussion since they clearly demonstrate that Tsvetaeva was aware of the link between icon-painting methods and Cubism and its potential power to help her reinvent the traditional image of Moscow.

FIGURE 6.1 Icon of the Mother of God named Unexpected Joy. Courtesy of the Museum of Russian Icons, Clinton, MA.

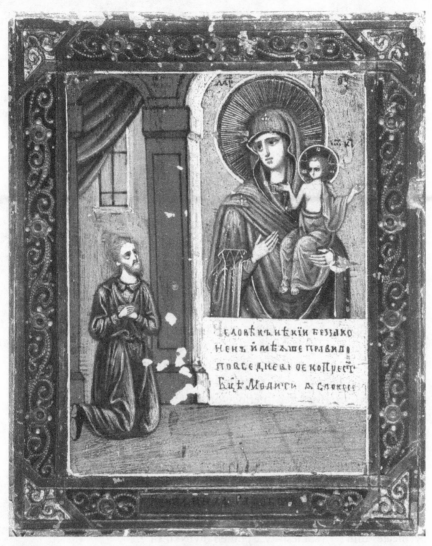

FIGURE 6.2 Icon of the Mother of God named Unexpected Joy. Courtesy of the Master, Fellows and Scholars of the College of Saint Peter le Bailey at the University of Oxford.

Tsvetaeva's friendship with Mandelstam influenced her thoughts about Moscow as reinvented sacred, aesthetic, and historical space. Tsvetaeva's reworking of the traditional image of Moscow is evidenced in the second poem of the cycle "Poems about Moscow"—"From my hands . . ." (Iz ruk moikh . . .). In this poem, Tsvetaeva continues her poetic portrayal of her native city in the style of Russian medieval icons. Calling her poetic Moscow "a city not made by human hands" (*nerukotvornyi grad*), Tsvetaeva suggests a link with the icon of "the Savior Not-Made-By-Human Hands" (Nerukotvornyi Spas), which depicts the face of Christ and is believed to have miraculously appeared on cloth.[31] She offers this verbal icon as a token of friendship: "My strange, my marvelous brother, / Take from out of my hands this city, not-made-by-human hands" (Iz ruk moikh—nerukotvornyi grad / Primi, moi strannyi, moi prekrasnyi brat).[32] The poet leads her "brother" to another icon, the Mother of God named Unexpected Joy (Nechaiannaia radost'; see figs. 6.1 and 6.2), which, according to Elena Korkina's note about this poem, was located in 1916 in the Church of the Annunciation on the Zhitnyi Courtyard in the Tainitskii Garden, which was part of the Moscow Kremlin.[33] Other sources report that this icon was much loved in the prerevolutionary period and was well known for its miracle-working qualities.[34] Treating the icon as a living woman and not merely an image, Tsvetaeva is more easily able to unite herself as lyric persona with the Mother of God in the miraculous act of protecting her beloved "brother"—purportedly Mandelstam himself. While she alludes to an icon depicting a sinner pleading for mercy, it is difficult to tell what "evil" Tsvetaeva's interlocutor is shielded from. Yet the symbolic resurrection and transformation through the sights and sounds of Moscow's churches is implied in the poem in the style of the icon featuring a sinner and the Mother of God that the lyric heroine and her interlocutor viewed together. The lyric persona featured in Tsvetaeva's poem (inspired by her walks and conversations with Mandelstam) promises her interlocutor a miracle; she states that her friend will see the bright cupolas of cathedrals and will hear the thunder-like sounds of bells that are always ready to ring ("chervonnye vozbleshchut kupola, / Bessonnye vzgremiat kolokola"). Following this visual spectacle, the Mother of God will send her mantle (*pokrov*) from the crimson-red clouds to protect the shoulders of her friend from evil forces ("I na tebia s bagrianykh oblakov / Uronit Bogoroditsa pokrov").[35] The lyric persona promises her friend that he will symbolically rise from the dead, invigorated by the wondrous force that permeates him ("I vstanesh' ty, ispolnen divnykh sil").

With its suggestion that the lyric persona is herself a miracle worker, Tsvetaeva's poem establishes a non-traditional link with the Mother of God; the poet does not represent herself as a mother, but as a miracle worker and object of her interlocutor's love. Indeed, the poem ends unexpectedly, saying: "You will not regret the fact that you used to love me" (Ty ne raskaesh'sia, chto ty menia liubil). The notions of female authorship and female spectatorship become entwined in this poem—as they did in the controversy surrounding Goncharova's own contemplation of sacred images—presenting the act of contemplation of the icon in terms of seduction and enchantment. While presenting her friend with the verbal (that is, not made by hands) icon, the female poet also states her intention to create herself as well; for Tsvetaeva, the veneration of the Mother of God icon links the act of writing to a sacred act. Tsvetaeva's vaguely blasphemous equation of the female poet with the Mother of God echoes, too, certain religious tenets of Goncharova's art. In 1916 Tsvetaeva was a friend of Tikhon Churilin whose books were illustrated by Goncharova, and so was familiar with her art and ideas. For Tsvetaeva, who wrote an essay on the artist in 1929, the power of Goncharova's work was its ability to combine both a feminine and masculine presence, thus embodying female poetic virility as "a kind of artistic bisexuality," embarking on "a flight away from the fragile and beautiful heroine-poetess with her seductive disguises designed by sympathetic male artists."[36] In "From my hands . . .," Tsvetaeva presents her "wonderful brother" as a second double, thereby offering *two* poetic voices, male and female. Given that the poem, like Goncharova's work, might be also seen as a reevaluation of the cultural stigma of female logic associated with an excessively emotional, irrational, and anarchic female identity.

Because of Tsvetaeva's friendship with Mandelstam, it is possible to see the poem as a response to Mandelstam's 1912 poem "Hagia Sophia" (Aiia Sofiia), in which the poet describes the Byzantine Hagia Sophia Church in Constantinople (converted into the Aya Sofya Mosque in 1453 by Mehmed II). Viewed in this context, the poem appears to be alluding to the male poet who is a stranger: he is discovering for the first time the beauty of Moscow and the spiritual wonders of Russian medieval culture associated with the city. It is also implied that he is a sinner since he depicted the mosque as a "marvelous cathedral floating in the world" (*prekrasnyi khram, kupaiushchiisia v mire*).[37] In contrast with Mandelstam's two-dimensional depiction of the world, Tsvetaeva offers a different vision both of sacred space and of the self depicted in the style of the above-mentioned notion of four-dimensional individuals. Such individuals have the potential to create their selves through the cultivation of a clairvoyant-like ability to see through things and contemplate invisible objects. That is why the icon of the Mother of God named Unexpected Joy in Tsvetaeva's poem has a double narrative: it presents an image of the Mother of God with the young Jesus Christ in her left arm and it also features a sinner kneeling in front of the icon. The poem implies that the strange and foreign-looking poet from Petrograd has done something sinful and needs the Mother of God's protection and intercession. Given the fact that Mandelstam was interested in world culture and European models worthy of imitation, it could be argued that Tsvetaeva was eager to share with him her knowledge of Moscow's sacred images and their powerful influence on the viewer, thereby inviting her fellow poet to study Russian medieval traditions in new contexts.

Like many of her contemporaries (including Anna Akhmatova and Alexander Blok), Tsvetaeva invoked religious themes and biblical images in her work throughout her creative career. On 12 May 1918 Tsvetaeva wrote a poem in which the lyric heroine presents herself again as an embodiment of an image of the Mother of God. This time the poem refers to the representation of the Seven Swords (Semistrel'naia) or Softener of Evil Hearts (Umiagchenie zlykh serdets) icon of the Mother of God:

> Семь мечей пронзали сердце
> Богородицы над Сыном.
> Семь мечей пронзили сердце,
> А моё—семижды семь.
> Я не знаю, жив ли, нет ли
> Тот, кто мне дороже сердца,
> Тот, кто мне дороже Сына ...
> Этой песней—утешаюсь.
> Если встретится—скажи.

> [Seven swords were stabbing the heart
> Of the Holy Virgin above Her Son.
> Seven swords have stabbed Her heart,
> Mine—was stabbed seven times seven.
> I do not know if he is dead or alive.
> He, who's more precious to me than the heart,
> He, who's more precious to me than the Son ...
> This song—cheers me up.
> If you happen to meet him—let me know.][38]

In an unusual manner, Tsvetaeva's poem weaves folk tradition and religious imagery in its use of impersonal statements that consitute an authoritive discourse. They are presented as stylized utterances (*skaz*). Repetitive structure and the use of the expression "seven times seven" resemble a folk poem intended for performance and chanting. The poem "Seven swords ..." might be defined as a stylized verbal construction that combines elements of psalmic and folkloric texts. The performance of grief expressed in Tsvetaeva's poem mingles narrative voices found in various genres, making her text sound impersonal. It might be seen as an example of fragmentary speech as described in Maurice Blanchot's works as a mode of artistic expression that threatens the dissolution of the subject. The use of fragmentary speech presents the world as a source of infinite interpretations and conveys the experience of consciousness without subjectivity. As Blanchot points out, it is "neither prophetic, nor eschatological," but it expresses a sense of discontinuity, remaining outside the dialectic of difference and identity.[39]

The aforementioned experimental attempt to render Russian sacred images and visual representations of the Mother of God is evident in other works penned by Tsvetaeva in the 1910s and 1920s. It might be linked to her desire to transgress geographical and temporal boundaries in search of a new mode of Russianness that has no need of definition by ethnicity and political traditions. Sarah Ossipow Cheang observes that during this period Tsvetaeva often mixes different modes of representation. This blending also enables Tsvetaeva to transgress the generic boundaries of various traditions that rely on fixed gender identities. Cheang focuses on Tsvetaeva's use of folk lament and lament psalm: "The main difference between these two different types of lamentation is that the former is closely linked with the ritual and ideology of the Judeo-Christian religion, while the second is rooted in folk culture, which in Russia mixes Christian belief with paganism. . . . Another significant difference between lament psalm and folk lament lies in the fact that the former is overridingly presented as a masculine genre, while the second is reserved to women. . . . [B]y modulating on these two types of lament at the same time, Tsvetaeva makes the gender differentiation of these two genres obsolete and implicitly demonstrates its artificiality."[40] Viewed in this light, Tsvetaeva's "Seven swords . . ." might be interpreted as a text that exemplifies well Solov'ev's teaching on the androgynous nature of the transfigured self and invokes his vision of the collective sanctified self (*sobornost'*). "The Church is not just a gathering together . . . of people," writes Solov'ev, "but mainly *that which gathers them together* . . . , i.e., the essential form of union given to people from above by means of which they can participate . . . in Divinity."[41] Tsvetaeva's poem reinforces Solov'ev's belief in the idea that the Church does not just grant salvation to individual people but leads to the salvation of the world. The icon described in Tsvetaeva's text is also known as the image of the Mother of God that is meant to soften evil hearts. It is closely linked to the tradition of the representations of the Seven Sorrows of the Virgin Mary found in European medieval culture. Thus in the context of the ending of the World War I and the beginning of the Civil War in Russia, it might be seen as a manifestation of Tsvetaeva's commitment to the presentation of the Russian icon as a symbol of unity with a view to remind Russians and Europeans of the necessity to retain a peaceful policy based on the notion of Christian love and brotherhood.

In order to understand the significance of the above-described sacred image for Tsvetaeva's articulation of personal and collective suffering, it would be useful to highlight the link between this icon and the symbolic representation of the Passion. Carol Schuler links the representation of the seven sorrows (signified by seven swords) to the tradition of symbolic Passion imagery and points out that it became popular in late medieval European art as an expression of common piety.[42] The image of seven sorrows entwined with the Passion motif can be often found in apocryphal texts. Schuler states that representations of the seven sorrows take several forms and that the simplest of them express Mary's multiple sorrows through seven swords piercing her breast, or radiating around her. Schuler writes: "The sword—a symbol employed by artists from the mid-thirteenth century onwards—derives from the high priest Simeon's prophecy to Mary during Christ's Presentation in the temple... Referred to as the sword of sorrow (*gladius doloris*), Symeon's sword (*gladius Simeonis*), or the sword of compassion (*gladius compassionis*), this motif was interpreted by medieval commentators variously as a symbol of Mary's pain at the Passion, as the counterpart of the lance used to pierce Christ's side, and as the embodiment of Christ's pain shared by his mother."[43] In sum, the symbolic meaning of the sword relates to an expression of compassion, alluding thereby to the Mother of God's ability to share her son's pain. On a personal level, "Seven swords ..." reveals Tsvetaeva's anxieties about the fate of her husband, who joined the White Army during the Civil War and went missing. The thematic motif associated with this sacred image enables Tsvetaeva to shift attention from Christ's sufferings to the Mother of God's grieving over her son's tragedies. By referring to the image of the Mother of God standing over her suffering son, Tsvetaeva's poem brings together Russian tradition and European medieval traditions with a view to preventing further destruction of spiritual and humanist values.

According to Schuler, the roots of seven sorrows devotion lie in late medieval piety, which is associated with a range of traditions including the movement of affective, meditative devotions in a monastic context and the popular movements that characterize late medieval Christianity. In several traditions a significant place was given to the Virgin as "exemplar and mediator of compassionate response."[44] Yet despite many textual and visual representations of the Mother of God's role in the events surrounding the Passion, there is no strong biblical evidence for her participation.[45] Tsvetaeva's poem, however, makes full use of popular belief. Given that Tsvetaeva studied and lived in Europe in her childhood and youth, it comes as no surprise to see her engagement with Western visual representations of the Mother of God as well. Her "Seven swords ..." resembles an anonymous medieval painting featuring the Virgin praying over her son's body called *Seven Sorrows of the Virgin* in the Paris Louvre (Cabinet de Rothschild) that would have been known to Tsvetaeva since she studied for several months at the Alliance Française at the age of sixteen.[46] More importantly, her engagement with Western artistic productions of the sorrowful image of the Mother of God enables Tsvetaeva to present herself as an exemplar and mediator of compassion. Tsvetaeva's employment of rhetorical strategy alludes to her own bond with the suffering figure of Jesus Christ.

This type of self-representation strategy can be also found in Tsvetaeva's 1923 cycle of poems "Magdalene" (Magdalina) in which her sanctified poetic self stems from the popular association of Saint Mary Magdalene and Saint Mary of Egypt with fallen women despite their religious status as exalted saints. According to Lisa Knapp's insightful analysis of Tsvetaeva's cycle of poems dedicated to Mary Magdalene included in Tsvetaeva's 1923 collection *After Russia* (Posle Rossii), this cycle has special significance for Tsvetaeva's creative career, especially because it presents her vision both of the essence of Christianity and of her poetic craft. Knapp explains that "Tsvetaeva's poetic treatment of Mary Magdalene becomes, then, part religious vision and part artistic credo" to the extent that by depicting Jesus Christ himself as a person who "pays a loving homage to Mary Magdalene (and gives her so much credit), Tsvetaeva gives her vision a certain authority."[47] Knapp sees Tsvetaeva's attempt to challenge the long-standing tradition that ascribes Mary Magdalene a lesser role in the life and afterlife of Jesus Christ as a manifestation of radical theology. One of the most radical and non-canonical features of Tsvetaeva's cycle is her appropriation of the voice of Jesus who addresses Mary after the resurrection as "dear" ("milaia") and suggests that she is his true disciple. In Knapp's words, it is a vivid example of Tsvetaeva's "profoundly feminist re-writing of Jesus's life and passion."[48]

In conclusion, it is important to point out that Tsvetaeva's engagement with the Russian Orthodox and European representation of the Mother of God and Mary Magdalene enabled her to forge her own identity as a female poet who is both a visionary and an active participant in modern life as well as in cultural developments. Her poems featuring Russian icons and sacred images aim to free Christianity and secular culture from philistine tendencies. It can be argued that Tsvetaeva's reinvention of religious themes and sacred images was triggered by her poetic dialogue with her friend Sophia Parnok, with whom she had an affair in 1915–1916, prior to her meeting with Mandelstam. In Parnok's view, the atmosphere of an Orthodox Christian Church deadens women. According to Knapp's interpretation of Parnok's poem "Again they peer with unseeing eyes" (Smotriat snova glazami nezriachimi), Parnok portrays the Mother of God in negative terms, suggesting that her eyes were unable to see the suffering of those who worship her. Knapp goes as far as to suggest that Parnok's poem evokes "the vision of the alternative (and feminine) church based on the name 'Marina.'"[49] Viewed in the light of Parnok's longing for an alternative church, Tsvetaeva's poems related to the Marian paradigm might be seen as an embodiment of the Solov'evean model of active involvement in the salvation of the world through contemplation of Russian medieval icons.

## NOTES

1. Galina Rylkova, *The Archaeology of Anxiety: The Russian Silver Age and Its Legacy* (Pittsburgh, PA: Pittsburgh University Press, 2007), 7.

2. Gregory Freidin, "By the Walls of Church and State: Literature's Authority in Russia's Modern Tradition," *The Russian Review* 52, no. 2 (April 1993): 149–65, 163.

3. In 1913 the Moscow Institute of Archaeology organized the exhibit where Ostroukhov and Riabushinskii's icons were shown. In the same year, they were exhibited at the grand Second All-Russian Folk Art Exhibition in St. Petersburg. On the tremendous effect of these exhibitions of modernist artists such as David and Wladimir Burliuk, Goncharova, Larionov, Malevich, and others, see John E. Bowlt, "Neoprimitivism and Russian Painting," *Russian Art, 1875–1975: A Collection of Essays* (New York: MSS Information Corporation, 1976), 94–111, 104.

4. On the conventions of the icon, see Boris Uspensky, *The Semiotics of the Russian Icon* (Lisse, Belgium: Peter de Ridder Press, 1976).

5. Maksimilian Voloshin, "Chemu uchat ikony?," in *Liki tvorchestva* (Leningrad: Nauka, 1988), 291–95, 295.

6. Nikolai I. Punin, *Andrei Rublev*, 2nd ed. (Petrograd: Apollon, 1916), 23. Quoted in Lindsey Hughes, "Inventing Andrei: Soviet and Post-Soviet Views of Andrei Rublev and His Trinity Icon," *Slavonica* 9, no. 2 (November 2003), 83–90, 85.

7. Nikolai Punin, "Puti sovremennogo iskusstva i russkaia natsional'naia ikonopis'," *Apollon* 10 (1913): 234. Quoted in English in Andrew Spira, *The Avant-Garde Icon: Russian Avant-Garde Art and the Icon Painting Tradition* (Aldershot, UK: Lund Humphies, 2008), 81.

8. Anatolii Lunacharskii, "Russkie khudozhniki v Berline," *Ogonek*, No.30, 1927; reprinted in: A.V. Lunacharskii, *Ob iskusstve* (Moscow: Direkt-Mediia, 2014), 2:253–56, 252–3.

9. Aleksandr Benua, "Khudozhestvennye pis'ma: Ikony i novoe iskusstvo," *Rech'* 93, 5 April 1913, 4. Quoted in English in Spira, *The Avant-Garde Icon*, 120.

10. Jane Sharp, "Redrawing the Margins of Russian Vanguard Art: Natalia Goncharova's Trial for Pornography in 1910," in *Sexuality and the Body in Russian Culture*, ed. Jane T. Costlow, Stephanie Sandler, and Judith Vowles (Stanford, CA: Stanford University Press, 1993), 97–123, 98.

11. Ibid., 122–23.

12. Dubl'-ve, "Futurizm i koshchunstvo," *Peterburgskii listok* 73, 16 March 1914. Quoted in Jane Sharp, "Redrawing the Margins," 97–123.

13. Jane Sharp, "The Russian Avant-Garde and Its Audience: Moscow, 1913," *Modernism/Modernity* 6, no. 3 (1999), 91–116, 100.

14. Sharp, "The Russian Avant-Garde," 91–116, 100. The "Donkey's Tail" (Oslinii khvost) was a group of artists—including Mikhail Larionov, Kazimir Malevich, and Marc Chagall—influenced by the Cubo-Futurist movement. This was their only exhibit.

15. Ibid., 116.

16. Ibid., 107.

17. Olga Matich, *Erotic Utopia: The Decadent Imagination in Russia's Fin de Siècle* (Madison: University of Wisconsin Press, 2005), 3.

18. Tsvetaeva's references to the seven hills of Moscow, of course, remind readers of the city's spiritual claims as the "Third Rome," the city most well known for its seven hills.

19. Marina Tsvetaeva, *Stikhi o Moskve*, in *Stikhotvoreniia i poemy*, ed. E. B. Korkina (Leningrad: Sovetskii pisatel', 1990), 99–104, 99.

20. Petr Uspenskii, *Tertium organum: Kliuch k zagadkam mira* (St. Petersburg: Trud, 1911).

21. Anthony Parton, "Russian 'Rayism,' the Work and Theory of Mikhail Larionov and Natalia Goncharova, 1912–1914: Ouspensky's Fourth-Dimensional Super Race?," *Leonardo* 16, no. 4 (1983): 298–305, 298.

22. It is also likely that Tsvetaeva was aware of the important observations on the influence of the Russian and Byzantine medieval icons on the representation of space in Russian and Cubo-Futurist paintings in Aleksei Grishchenko's book *On the Connection between Russian Painting and Byzantium and the West, 13th–20th Centuries: The Artist's Thoughts* (O sviaziakh russkoi zhivopisi s Vizantiei i Zapadom XIII–XX vv.: Mysli zhivopistsa) (Moscow: A. A. Levenson, 1913).

23. Pavel Florensky's essay was written in 1919. It was delivered as a lecture in 1919 and 1920. The full version of this essay is available in: Pavel Florenskii, "Obratnaia perspektiva," in *Sobranie sochinenii v chetyrekh tomakh* (Moscow: Mysl', 1999), 3:46–98; Pavel Florensky "Reverse Perspective," *Beyond Vision: Essays on the Perception of Art*, ed. Nicoletta Misler, tr. Wendy Salmon (London: Reaktion Books Ltd, 2002), 197–274.

24. Petr D. Ouspensky, *Tertium Organum: The Third Canon of Thought; A Key to the Enigmas of the World*, trans. N. Bessaraboff and C. Bragdon, 2nd ed. (London: Kegan Paul, Trench Trubner, 1922), 145.

25. Clemena Antonova, "Seeing the World with the Eyes of God: An Alternative Explanation of the 'Reverse Perspective,'" in *Space, Time, and Presence in the Icon: Seeing the World with the Eyes of God* (Burlington, VT: Ashgate, 2010), 103–52, 108.

26. Ibid., 110.

27. Sibelan Forrester, "Bells and Cupolas: The Formative Role of the Female Body in Marina Tsvetaeva's Poetry," *Slavic Review* 51, no. 2 (Summer 1992), 232–46, 233.

28. Ibid., 234.

29. Ibid.

30. Ibid.

31. In keeping with Tsvetaeva's challenge to the historical power of Moscow's tsars and patriarchs, this reference also recalls Alexander Pushkin's poem "I am erecting a monument to myself, not made by human hands" (1836), which touts the eternal power of poetry to overcome the tyranny of earthly rulers.

32. Tsvetaeva, *Stikhotvoreniia i poemy*, 99.

33. Ibid., 706.

34. Russian Tsar Nicholas II wrote about this icon in his diary with special affection during his visit to the Kremlin with his family in 1903. See Ol'ga Lashkova, "Nechaiannaia Radost' v Moskve," Damian.ru, http://damian.ru/Cerkov_i_sovremennost/lashkova/n_radost.html (16 September 2012).

35. Tsvetaeva, *Stikhotvoreniia i poemy*, 100.

36. Svetlana Boym, "Loving in Bad Taste: Eroticism and Literary Excess in Marina Tsvetaeva's 'The Tale of Sonechka,'" in *Sexuality and the Body in Russian Culture*, ed. Jane T. Costlow, Stephanie Sandler, and Judith Vowles (Stanford, CA: Stanford University Press, 1993), 167.

37. Osip Mandel'shtam, "Aiia-Sofiia," in *Stikhotvoreniia* (Leningrad: Sovetskii pisatel', 1973), 74.

38. Tsvetaeva, *Stikhotvoreniia i poemy*, 169. (Translation is mine. —A.S.).

39. Maurice Blanchot, *The Infinite Conversation*, trans. Susan Hanson (Minneapolis: University of Minnesota Press, 1993).

40. Sarah Cheang Ossipow, "The Generic Intertext of Psalms in the Poetry of Marina Tsvetaeva (1892–1941)" (PhD diss., University of Nottingham, 2008), 297.

41. Quoted in Richard F. Gustafson, "Solovjev's Doctrine of Salvation," in *Russian Religious Thought*, ed. Judith Deutsch Kornblatt and Richard F. Gustafson (Madison: University of Wisconsin Press, 1996), 42.

42. Carol M. Schuler, "The Seven Sorrows of the Virgin: Popular Culture and Cultic Imagery in Pre-Reformation Europe," *Simiolus: Netherlands Quarterly for the History of Art* 21, nos. 1–2 (1992), 5–28, 5.

43. Ibid., 6.

44. Ibid., 7.

45. Ibid.

46. Simon Karlinsky, *Marina Tsvetaeva: The Woman, Her World, and Her Poetry* (Cambridge: Cambridge University Press, 1985), 28.

47. Lisa Knapp, "Tsvetaeva's Marine Mary Magdalene," *The Slavic and East European Journal* 43, no. 4 (Winter 1999): 597–620, 597.

48. Ibid., 602.

49. Ibid., 605.

# 7

# Kuzma Petrov-Vodkin's *1918 in Petrograd* (*The Petrograd Madonna*) and the Meaning of Mary in 1920

WENDY SALMOND

A YOUNG WOMAN HOLDING A sleeping child sits in the shallow space of an upper-floor balcony framed by two plain white pilasters. The child lies in the crook of her arm, cheek on fist, while she clutches his right hand to her chest in a gesture both protective and wary. The smooth oval of her face is framed by a white kerchief tied at the nape of her neck, and a red shawl threatens to slip off her left shoulder. Her eyes, swollen from weeping, sleeplessness, or privation, meet ours uncertainly. Behind her, separated by a low railing, are the semicircular arches of an arcade painted sky blue, the panes of its first-floor windows shattered. Under the leftmost arch three women with baskets draw a motley assortment of customers, at first in ones and twos, then in a more organized mob converging from the right. In the wide square behind them a few more people congregate in desultory groups, ignoring the tattered posters and proclamations pasted on the corners of the apartment buildings that surround them. The frame of the balcony limits our vision to this man-made world: neither sky nor nature relieves the claustrophobic space. The painting seems eerily still and quiet, stabilized by the woman's grave presence, but this impression of calm is shaken by the slight torque of the balcony rail and pilasters, and is further disturbed as the buildings tilt up and away. Her body is set slightly off-center and angled to the viewer's left, as if sheltering the child from some barely perceptible yet persistent force.

This haunting painting, Kuzma Petrov-Vodkin's *1918 in Petrograd* (*The Petrograd Madonna*) (1918 god v Petrograde, 1920), was one of the very last public images of Mary to be created in Soviet Russia for other than anti-religious purposes (see fig. 7.1).[1] Petrov-Vodkin painted it in 1920, at a moment when the relationship between religion and revolution could still be openly debated. As the title makes clear, it evokes the memory of a particular place and time: the northern capital in the aftermath of the October Revolution, a time of hunger, chaos, and terror. It is thus a kind of history painting, looking back on a year in which uncertainty and privation were mixed with hopes for a transformed world.[2] Yet it is also a visionary painting, for the young mother instantly and intentionally evokes the Mother of God, miraculously made manifest amidst human suffering and despair. The bracketed subtitle (*Petrograd Madonna* [Petrogradskaia Madonna]) appears to have attached itself to the painting almost immediately, confirming both the artist's and the public's recognition of

FIGURE 7.1 Kuzma Petrov-Vodkin, *1918 in Petrograd* (*The Petrograd Madonna*), 1920, oil on canvas. Courtesy of the State Tretiakov Gallery, Moscow.

this resemblance and bringing the image within the orbit of a still vital and expanding iconography of the Mother of God.[3]

This essay explores what Petrov-Vodkin might have intended this image of motherhood to communicate to his contemporaries in the Soviet Russia of 1920. With its dizzying disjunctions of scale and space and its frank homage to medieval icons and Quattrocento frescoes, *1918 in Petrograd* reflected the artist's crusade to teach the mass audience a "science of seeing" and so reveal the universal sources of energy available to "the human apparatus" in his dealings with the phenomenal world. For Petrov-Vodkin, motherhood was a state richly endowed with this cosmic electric spark and throughout his life he returned repeatedly to its depiction. Yet of all the mothers he painted, *The Petrograd Madonna* was unique for the particular way it organized familiar signs of sacred and secular, eternal and temporal into a dynamic relationship that promised hope in the midst of catastrophe. The result was a new icon—or more precisely icon-painting—of the spiritual revolution for which so many members of the Russian intelligentsia yearned after February 1917.

## IN SEARCH OF THE "ICON-PAINTING"

No one exploring the trajectory of Petrov-Vodkin's career, from his childhood in the Volga town of Khlynovsk to his status as a lion of Socialist Realism in the 1930s, can ignore the deep imprint that icons made upon his work. Growing up in a largely Old Believer community, he was as familiar with the production of icons as he was with their daily veneration. His first contact with art materials took place in the workshop of a local icon painter and his first boyhood effort at painting was an icon of the Mother of God with Sleeping Child.[4]

In the world to which the young Petrov-Vodkin belonged, recognizing the distinction between an icon and a painting was a fundamental tenet of faith, and the Orthodox audience was ever alert to that boundary beyond which an icon lost its canonical and sacred bearings and became merely a religious painting. Viktor Vasnetsov's decoration of St. Vladimir's Cathedral in Kiev (1885–1895) had inspired hopes for an icon-painting renaissance that would bridge this divide by integrating the humanist traditions of easel painting into the Byzantine canon. But this compromise did not begin to address what Petrov-Vodkin and other painters of his generation came to regard as the bankruptcy of post-Renaissance painting, delimited as it was by Euclidean space and Albertian perspective.[5] Nor did it provide ways to capture his personal intuition of universal, cosmic forces at work in the everyday world, what he called *planetarnost'*. This planetary sensation was first revealed to him as a child when, accidentally falling down on the rolling banks along the Volga, he felt that he was flying high above the earth and could clearly see its curvature. When some years later, in 1906, he witnessed the eruption of Vesuvius during his first trip to Italy, the seeds of "cosmism" and "catastrophism" took firm root in his worldview and in his painting.[6]

While still a student at the Moscow School of Painting, Sculpture, and Architecture, Petrov-Vodkin secured a commission that would launch him

FIGURE 7.2 Kuzma Petrov-Vodkin. Mother of God icon, 1905, majolica. Façade of the Orthopedic Clinic, Aleksandrovskii Park, St. Petersburg. Photo by Elena Volkova.

on a decade of lucrative church decoration projects, each one of them an opportunity to test the expressive limits of the Orthodox canon.[7] In 1903 he was hired to design an icon of the Mother of God for the façade of a new Orthopedic Clinic, sponsored by the empress and situated in St. Petersburg's Aleksandrovskii Park.[8] In a monumental cartoon for the icon, the artist brought a contemporary but reverential eye to the canonical Kazan icon of the Mother of God, endowing Mary with the features of a personal feminine ideal and the child with luxuriant copper curls.[9] Beneath her bright red maphorion, a white wimple replaced the Byzantine coif (*kerkyrphalos*), imparting a distinct Italianate flavor. In its final form (1905), translated into majolica at the Royal Doulton works in London, the icon eluded any specific iconographic type, yet remained close enough to the solemn Kazan or Hodegetria that a viewer could respond without difficulty to the familiar rhythms and contours that evoked a state of prayer (see fig. 7.2). Her hands protectively encircling the child's body injected a more intimate and human note in tune with the new icons made fashionable by Vasnetsov and Mikhail Nesterov. The final palette of dove gray, pale green, and lilac suited the contemporary taste for soothing pastels, while the ornamental elements gave the icon an air of fin-de-siècle chic in harmony with Silver Age aesthetic sensibilities.

After a brief infatuation with obscure Symbolist themes inspired by the dramas of Maurice Maeterlinck and several years in Paris, around 1911 Petrov-Vodkin embarked on his own path of reconciling the still largely segregated worlds of Russian icons and European easel painting. Simultaneously engaged in commissions to decorate the walls of churches and in painting canvases for exhibition, his formal language underwent a series of carefully calibrated adjustments and a personal lexicon began to emerge. The turning point was *Playing Boys* (Igraiushchie mal'chiki, 1911), a transposition into easel painting of his fresco *Cain and Abel*, painted for the restored twelfth-century church of Vasilii Zlatoverskii at Ovruch (1910).[10] In both fresco and painting the space is divided into two zones (heaven and earth), the figures brought up close to the foreground, and the palette reduced to red, green, and blue. The resemblance to Henri Matisse's *The Dance* (1908) in the Shchukin collection is unmistakable,[11] but *Playing Boys* also reveals a search for a universal language of archetypes, what the artist referred to as *tipazh*. The Annunciation fresco for the Naval Cathedral at Kronstadt (1913) similarly had its painterly twin in his most icon-like painting, the *Mother of God Softener of Evil Hearts* (Bogomater' umilenie zlykh serdets, 1914–1915), which drew on several iconographic variants, yet was clearly intended to maintain its identity as an easel painting for exhibition.[12] And though not directly related to a church commission, in both coloration and theme his *Bathing the Red Horse* (Kupanie krasnogo konia), which hung above the entrance to the 1912 "World of Art" exhibition, acknowledged his generation's rapturous embrace of Novgorod icons.

In these early icon-paintings, as Petrov-Vodkin called them, a conundrum emerged that would perplex viewers of all his subsequent work. Was he using icons as a stepping-stone to a new painterly language, as a number of his more "avant-garde" contemporaries were doing at this time? Or was he creating paintings capable of conveying the icon's spiritual power and cosmic intimations, free of the restrictions of the Orthodox canon? In later years, he would describe these early works as a personal search for an alternative to both the tired formulae of academic painting and the production-line templates of commercial icon painting. This "search for a vision dimly seen," plotted between the two poles of secular painting and sacred icon without settling in either, would become the defining feature of his painting.

For Petrov-Vodkin's contemporaries—and for the artist himself—this search yielded its first viable results in a series of paintings created in 1915–1917, depicting peasant women and children bathing by the Volga.[13] The expressive rhythmic possibilities of multiple figures set against flattened, gently curving spaces echoed the musical paintings of Viktor Borisov-Musatov and the Blue Rose painters with whom Petrov-Vodkin had been intimately associated a decade before. The legacy of medieval Russian frescoes and icons was also very much on his mind at this time, reflected in facial types, monumental gestures, and broad color planes. Yet whereas his earlier Symbolist figures lived outside any specific place and time, these were firmly rooted in the familiar reality of Russian peasant life in a way that led Igor Grabar to later congratulate him for "throwing out a bridge to the viewer."[14] The artist himself described *Girls on the Volga* (Devushki na Volge, 1915) as an "expansion of the auditorium," that is, a conscious effort to communicate his sensation of universal truths to a broad public.

The problems inherent in creating a synthetic icon-painting were more complicated when he tackled the theme of the single mother and child. It was here, in the visual and emotional correspondence between human mothers and the Mother of God, that the boundary between sacred and secular was especially permeable and fluid. Petrov-Vodkin's first experiment with this theme depicted a young peasant woman sitting amidst the rolling hills of a broad Volga landscape and nursing her child (*Mother* [Mat'], two versions, 1913). With its strong resemblance to Aleksei Venetsianov's bucolic peasant paintings of the 1830s, the picture transformed the ethnographic signs of peasant life into a more lyrical and universal theme, that of the peasant mother as an enduring trope of Mother Russia.[15] Though the woman conforms to a recognized Marian type (the Mlekopitatel'nitsa or Nursing Mother of God), her earthbound nature is accentuated in the soles of her bare feet (a pair of shoes in the second variant), the busy repeat pattern of her calico headscarf, and the nursing child so touchingly vulnerable with his little shirt and bare bottom.

Returning to the theme in 1915 in the *Mother* (Mat'), now in the State Russian Museum, Petrov-Vodkin reorganized the lyrical genre scene into an unmistakable visual dialogue with icons (see fig. 7.3). The same young mother is now brought inside a peasant home and positioned between two frames— on the viewer's right the window looking out on a village scene, on the left

**FIGURE 7.3** Kuzma Petrov-Vodkin, *Mother*, 1915. Oil on canvas. Courtesy of the State Russian Museum, St. Petersburg.

the *kiot* or icon case.[16] The *kiot* is not quite empty—a few small brownish icons, their subjects illegible, languish in dusty disarray alongside an inkpot and some bits of paper—but the overall impression is of something absent.[17] The whole composition encourages us to see the young woman as abundantly filling that absence. Though her bright blue-white blouse and scarf convey a sense of frontal stability, her body is in fact twisted so that she projects out diagonally from the icon corner across the space of the room,[18] her head turned back over her right shoulder to gaze dreamily past us. This mother invites thoughts about the presence of otherworldly forces in everyday life, and how a painting might generate such intimations without actually having to be an icon. In this game of resemblances Petrov-Vodkin never suggests that this robust young peasant madonna is *the* Madonna, the Mother of God, yet the viewer is continually reminded of the devotional sensations her image evokes. Even the crisp points of her headscarf suggest the cruciform inscribed within the halo of icons of Christ. Nor is it coincidental that the picture is reoriented from the horizontal to the vertical format of the portrait and the icon. As for the space surrounding her, the artist uses the linear markers of the log walls and the window frame to create the sensation of a world tilted off axis and picking up momentum as our gaze moves away from the icon corner toward the window and the world visible beyond it.

The extent to which icons—and above all Mother of God icons—were on the artist's mind throughout the war years is evident in a recently discovered painting called *Vasia* (1916).[19] The refined features of the tow-haired peasant boy with sunburned nose reflect Petrov-Vodkin's admiration for Dionisii's frescoes at the Ferapontov Monastery, which he had sketched in May of that year on his way home to Khlynovsk to report for active duty. Like the nursing mother, the boy directs his solemn unseeing gaze past the viewer's left shoulder, but the almost empty *kiot* is now replaced by a large icon of the Vladimir Mother of God on a wooden ledge, standing protectively by the boy's right shoulder and on a level with his head, as though whispering in his ear.[20] Icon and boy inhabit a space that is made more intimate and closed to the everyday world by the blank log wall to the right (the artist painted over a window that would have increased the resemblance to the earlier *Mother*); their proximity fosters a similar meditation on the infiltration of the human and phenomenal sphere by the cosmic and spiritual.

Just how earnestly Petrov-Vodkin was seeking to express a correspondence between these spheres is brought home by a third variant on this theme, a drawing published in the journal *Plamia* (The flame) in 1919 (see fig. 7.4). The compositional and symbolic possibilities attempted in *Mother* and *Vasia* are here reorganized in an evocation of the artist's childhood memories of

FIGURE 7.4 Kuzma Petrov-Vodkin, drawing of the interior of a peasant hut with icon corner, 1919. Pen and ink on paper. Reproduced in *Plamia* [The flame], 51 (1 May 1919).

village Russia. A table is set before the icon corner in a peasant hut, where a woman and two children begin a simple meal. The kerchiefed head of the mother in her calico print blouse is framed by the icon behind her, literally taking its place, while a smaller Mother of God icon watches over the family scene and the world spins by outside the window. This literal displacement of the Mother of God by the archetypal peasant mother might be mistaken for a simple statement of the artist's embrace of overtly secular themes after the revolution, if the grouping of the three figures, their downcast eyes, and solemn gestures did not so clearly endow this genre scene with sacramental dignity, calling up another iconic theme of importance to the artist, the Old Testament Trinity.[21]

Above all, this sequence of images seems pointedly, even didactically expressive of motherhood's intercessory role in connecting human experience to cosmic forces, grounding this awareness, tinged with planetary sensation, in experiences and types accessible to all. That he intended this kind of momentous message is amply confirmed by *Midday. Summer* (Polden'. Leto, 1917), a painting inspired by the death of his father the previous year. Dotted across an idyllic Russian countryside, tiny figures are absorbed in the rhythms of human life, from birth to death. The viewer gazes down through the branch of an apple tree on an expansive landscape not unlike the landscapes of Pieter Bruegel and Joachim Patinir that render God's view of the world. Not one but two images of motherhood anchor the picture on the curved vertical axis that pulls magnetically toward the upper right. In the upper register, tranquilly observing the funeral procession that passes along the midline of the painting is the nursing mother that Petrov-Vodkin painted in 1913 and 1915. On our side of the coffin a second mother advances toward us, holding out her child as if trying to catch our attention. Her prototypes are clear: she is a synthesis of Raphael's Sistine Madonna and Viktor Vasnetsov's famous Mother of God in the apse of St. Vladimir's Cathedral, one of the most popular new icons of the late imperial period. She alone connects directly with the viewer, both a spark of energy animating the lives of human beings and a point of contact with worlds beyond the pull of earth's gravity.

## VOLFILA, SPIRITUAL REVOLUTION, AND "THE SCIENCE OF SEEING"

With its expansive planetary vision and celebration of primordial peasant life, *Midday. Summer* was a grand summation of themes, types, and formal devices painstakingly developed during the years of the war to express the place of humans in the cosmic order of things. It definitively affirmed that, in the Russian village at least, people had not yet lost touch with nature, the stars and the planets, the life force itself. When the February Revolution occurred, this personal intuition of cosmic forces at work in the lives of men seemed vindicated. Whatever his private reservations about the Bolsheviks' rise to power,[22] Petrov-Vodkin fully embraced the revolution as a necessary, even longed-for cataclysm, seeing in it the unleashing of vast reserves of elemental energy from which humankind might emerge reborn. It was this vision of new beginnings and spiritual transformations that drew him into the orbit of the Scythians, a community of poets and critics whose roots lay in the Symbolist philosophy of Vladimir Solov'ev, but whose politics drew them to embrace political revolution as the necessary prelude to a social and finally a spiritual revolution. Politically, their sympathies were with the Left Socialist Revolutionaries and their theoretician was the writer Razumnik Ivanov-Razumnik, who most vigorously articulated their ideal of socialism rooted in a "new Christianity" with a messianic role for Russia. [23] Appearing in the group's first almanac, *Scythians*, published by Ivanov-Razumnik in mid-1917, were Andrei Bely, Sergei Esenin, Valerii Briusov, Nikolai Kliuev, Aleksei Remizov, Mikhail Prishvin, and Lev Shestov. Though his work appeared in neither of the group's two anthologies, Alexander Blok's poems "The Twelve" (Dvenadtsat', 1918) and "The Scythians" (Skify, 1918) epitomized its members' hopes and fears.

Responding to the revolutions of 1917, the Scythians drew on the imagery of Christianity to express their anticipation of a third "spiritual revolution." In this epoch of grand dualities, only such transcendent images, with their themes of sacrifice, renunciation, and resurrection, had the power to evoke the magnitude of the transformations taking place. "Ahead of us is the difficult Way of the Cross of the great Russian revolution," Ivanov-Razumnik wrote in April 1917. [24] In his poem "To the Motherland" (Rodine, August 1917), Bely invoked Russia as "Messiah of the coming age," and in "Christ Is Risen" of the following year as both "the woman clothed in the sun" and "Godbearer [*bogonositsa*] defeating the dragon." In the most celebrated Christian image of the revolution, Blok ended his long poem "The Twelve," written in January 1918, with a vision of Christ emerging from the blizzard of the revolution in a wreath of white roses, leading his twelve violent "apostles" toward a new world.

For the Scythians, particularly Blok, Bely, and Ivanov-Razumnik, Petrov-Vodkin was a kindred spirit, an artist whose planetary consciousness matched their own. It was him they chose to design the cover and half-titles for the two issues of *Scythians*. [25] And it was him Blok invited to create a cover for "The Twelve," thereby acknowledging a sense of mutual understanding of the revolution and the intelligentsia's responsibilities toward the people. Petrov-Vodkin's refusal (because, as he said, Blok's image of Christ "in a wreath of white roses" "grated on the ear") suggests a dissonance between the artist and the poet in their conception of the spiritual revolution to come, but not in their acceptance of its inevitability or its Christian roots. [26]

These personal connections and intellectual kinships brought Petrov-Vodkin into the very center of the small group that met in Petrograd in September 1918 to organize what would become the Free Philosophical Association (Volfila). [27] The core members of Volfila have been described as "loners who represented separate islands in the sea of Bolshevik Russia." [28] What brought them together was a shared belief in the efficacy of "practical idealism" (the intertwining of Christian truth and Marxist sociology) and "spiritual maximalism" (affirming ideas through one's individual behavior and social position). Conceived as an informal academy of learning, Volfila hosted lectures and discussions from 1919 to 1924 by the intellectual luminaries of Petrograd, often drawing audiences of a thousand or more.[29] The inaugural lecture, in November 1919, was Blok's "Collapse of Humanism" (Krushenie gumanizma) followed in 1920 by a lecture series on "the crisis in culture seen as a culture in revolution." There were evenings devoted to Tommaso Campanella's *City of the Sun*, to Alexander Herzen, Petr Lavrov, and the Decembrists, to Lev Tolstoy and Fyodor Dostoevsky, and the philosophy of Vladimir Solov'ev and Friedrich Nietzsche. As Ivanov-Razumnik put it, "In Volfila we are striving not to let the flame of eternal Revolution, of that final spiritual Revolution wherein lies the only path towards a hoped for Transformation, die out in our generation."[30]

It was in these early years at the center of Volfila that Petrov-Vodkin staked out most clearly his own philosophical position on the need to teach people to see the world anew and regain their lost connection with the universe. Throughout 1920 he delivered a series of public lectures, inspired by his faith that "a work of art that can inflame the popular masses is possible."[31] His most important treatise, delivered twice at Volfila in early 1920 and again in April 1921, was titled "The Science of Seeing" (Nauka videt'). As the blueprint for an entirely new system of art education, the lecture advocated an active art that would engender in the viewer "not an impression but a sensation from object-phenomena."[32] For all those blind to the life force linking humans to the planet, he prescribed "the reeducating of our dulled perceptions through sharpening [*obostrenie*] the eye."[33]

In other lectures given in 1920, Petrov-Vodkin elaborated on his vision of human beings endowed with the potential for transformation through art, yet becalmed in a static world of phenomena. "People know the earth is round, rotates on its axis, and circles around the Sun, but they have absolutely no sensation of this: their eyes do not see, their ears do not hear his planet."[34] Art was a universal language, "a means for all," and when properly deployed could convey the planetary sensation of the Earth and its rhythms that modern people had lost. "Art ... is the human capacity for apprehending the phenomena of the world on the level of sensation, by means of expressing them as a sign."[35] That this vision of human potential had for the artist an intrinsic religious component is made clear in his lecture, "Aleksandr Ivanov and the Paths of the Russian Icon's Development," in which he posited the formula "Art = the Science of Seeing and religious awareness."[36]

In his paintings, drawings, and graphic works of the Civil War years, the artist turned to the same Christian iconography of sacrifice and transformation that marked the imagery of the poets and writers most closely associated with Volfila.[37] The image of the Crucified Christ and the Mother of God became a recurring motif, their sorrowfully bowed heads and downcast gaze so alike and so icon-like that the line between them blurs.[38] Also symptomatic of his Volfila affiliations was a project to depict twenty-eight scenes from the Gospel according to St. John. Only three were published, as illustrations to a story in *Plamia* (1919): *On the Cross* (Na kreste), *The Kiss of Judas* (Potselui Iudy) and *The Denial of Peter* (Otrechenie Petra).[39] These scenes of betrayal and sacrifice echoed Ivanov-Razumnik's condemnation of the intelligentsia for failing to support the revolution and his depiction of "the Russian people and their revolution as a Christ going to be crucified by the Old World."[40] A careful reading and annotation of the New Testament in May 1920 further stimulated Petrov-Vodkin's interest in Christ's sacrifice.[41]

These activities suggest that throughout 1920 the artist was in the grip of an almost apostolic urge to speak to all those who had lost the capacity to hear the breathing of the cosmos and feel the world energy that animated the phenomenal world about them. More than any other of his paintings, *1918 in Petrograd* reflected this mixed sensation of despair and hope, of witnessing diminished human capacities while believing in each person's potential for transformation.

## THE PETROGRAD MADONNA

The most striking element of *1918 in Petrograd*, as many have pointed out, is the resemblance of the young mother at the painting's center to an icon of the Mother of God.[42] Not since his commission for the Orthopedic Clinic had the icon's presence come so powerfully to the fore in Petrov-Vodkin's work. In response to Volfila's call for spiritual maximalism and practical idealism, he created a painting in which the exquisite balance between sacred and secular that he had cultivated in his prerevolutionary paintings was momentarily disturbed, in hopes that the Mother of God's "electric spark" might galvanize his audience into spiritual awareness. Like many of his contemporaries seeking to reconcile religion and revolution, Petrov-Vodkin's interest in icons at this period was no mere aesthetic curiosity. Rather, it spoke to an evangelical desire to address a mass audience hungry for spiritual as well as physical food.[43] The spectacle of a starving population scouring the streets for food in *1918 in Petrograd* thus had a distinct metaphorical dimension.

As an artist committed to figuration, Petrov-Vodkin assigned distinct roles to subject matter (*siuzhet*, sign) and form (sensation) in both his pedagogical theory and his paintings. In a note written in August 1920 he described *siuzhet* as "the state of the artist's spirit. A story in objects," while the formal elements of painting were "a language common to all. Teaching people through color, perspective."[44] In *1918 in Petrograd* Petrov-Vodkin deployed both in a heartfelt effort to reach the widest possible audience.

Central to the legibility of his grand message was the young woman's clothing, each element painstakingly organized to elicit two contradictory associations.[45] Like the women in his prerevolutionary paintings, beginning with 1913's *Mother*, she wears her headscarf tied at the nape of the neck, a long-established sign of peasant origins. But in the new Soviet world order, how a woman covered her head quickly acquired ideological significance and the *kosynka* (headscarf) became as much an emblem of the New Woman as the cloth cap was for the New Man. This new revolutionary signage is visible in the urban background of *1918 in Petrograd*, where red and white scarves, some tied in front, others in back, jostle a smattering of hats marking out women of the bourgeoisie.

It is not at all surprising that Soviet-era commentators seized eagerly on the white sphere of the young woman's headscarf to tell a simple new narrative—that of a new proletarian (perhaps a factory worker) installed in an apartment recently vacated by a fleeing bourgeois family.[46] Yet visibly contradicting this everyday meaning is her archaic green gown, the fabric of its neckline pleated into sharp folds that recall countless icons of the Mother of God. Complicating her identity further is the mantle or maphorion that has slipped off her head and clings in a red line to her hunched left shoulder and arm, a vibrant visual barrier against the hungry mob advancing in the street below. This red thread reads as a sign of literal revelation unique in Petrov-Vodkin's painting, as portentous and jarring as Blok's Christ with his "crown of white roses."

The young mother's relocation from the Volga countryside to the paved canyons of Petrograd also inflected a familiar motif with new meanings. This was Petrov-Vodkin's first urban scene, a quintessentially Petersburgian cityscape. The thick-walled arcade references the Gostinnyi Dvor on Nevsky Prospect or more likely the Andreevskii Market on Vasilevskii Island, not far from Petrov-Vodkin's apartment.[47] Banished from contact with the natural world and its rhythms, above all isolated from the vault of the heavens, like insects the inhabitants of Petrograd single-mindedly pursue their daily search for survival, as oblivious to the constant movement of the planet as they are to the source of new life in their midst. Seeking ways to communicate his awareness of cosmic forces made manifest in everyday life—and of human blindness to them—Petrov-Vodkin found inspiration in those Florentine Quattrocento frescoes that so impressed him on his first trip to Italy. The frescoes by Masolino and Masaccio in the Brancacci Chapel (1425–1427) especially come to mind. In their wide city squares lined with arcades and houses rendered in careful perspective, saints in classical draperies pass as though in a dream among doll-like figures in contemporary dress.

In other ways, too, *1918 in Petrograd* showed the lasting impression made on the artist by his first visit to Italy in 1905–1906. Of special importance to him was Giovanni Bellini's *Brera Madonna* (1510). The expressive gravity of the central figure and the dramatic shift between majestic foreground and miniscule background figures offered an entire language of storytelling and spatial disjunction that resonated deeply with the artist (a photograph of the painting was one of his cherished souvenirs). In his Petrograd Madonna Petrov-Vodkin caught some of the hallucinatory presence of this Venetian prototype. In observing that the "half length and iconic austerity, physical and psychological" of Bellini's Madonnas signify the artist's "intentional evocation of the venerable models of Byzantium," Rona Goffin offers a possible explanation for why this artist should have affected Petrov-Vodkin's developing visual lexicon of motherhood.[48] Goffen notes too that "the lack of spatial continuity [between foreground and background] functions with the Madonna and Child types and their positions to enhance the viewer's impression that the image is extraordinary, beyond empirical definition, and apart from any environment."[49] This sense of the extraordinary revealed to an oblivious, untransformed world lies at the heart of Petrov-Vodkin's vision of Mary in revolutionary Petrograd.

Petrov-Vodkin later described his state of mind in the early months of 1920 as one suffused with "new sensations of loneliness in the world. Being cut off from nature ... despite passionate experiences with friends and loved ones it just became more clear-cut how isolated human *apparati* [Petrov-Vodkin's term for individual human beings - WS] were from each other."[50] This somber comment accords with Tamara Machmut-Jhashi's reading of the painting as expressing not "the hopes and dreams for a new proletarian life that Soviet writers have often claimed," but "the disintegration of old dreams and the unwelcome erosion of the traditional way of life," and his "evolving attitude toward the Revolution, while supporting the claims of the Revolutionaries for democratic ideals and social equality."[51] Yet Petrov-Vodkin's abiding faith in a forthcoming spiritual revolution and the "planetary consciousness" he shared with so many Volfila members in 1920 invite a less pessimistic reading. In *1918 in Petrograd*, the winter of "The Twelve" has given way to spring or summer. The broken windows are witnesses to the recent violence and a solitary bourgeois lady (perhaps inspired by a similar figure in Blok's poem) creeps along under the arcade, marked out by her class uniform of hat and coat. Hunger and privation are still a constant that draws people irresistibly toward the traders beneath the arcade, turning their backs on the strong planetary pull that even the buildings obey. Yet the presence of the sleeping child, shielded within the triangle of his mother's arms like a modern-day icon of the Sign, offers the viewer a fragile but definite sense of hope. The continuities with *Midday. Summer* are unmistakable. While human beings are no longer grounded in the natural world and are reduced to the animal level of physical survival, the mother with her child is now just inches away, on the spectator's side of the balcony, insisting that her mute message of spiritual renewal be heard.

In 1926 Petrov-Vodkin wrote of the period 1920–1921 in which he created the Petrograd Madonna: "If all of my attention had not been concentrated on the problems of space ... the same thing would have happened to me as happened to Blok. Blok understood my [illegible] and wandering as just an intuitive surrendering to nature, and not as working on nature, and that is why he was unable to extricate himself from the torpor of the human atmosphere."[52] One might take this to mean that, in his ability to rise above the confines of the horizon where modern people had become trapped, to make contact with higher cosmic spheres and potentialities through art (the "electric spark" passing through the Mother of God, the dynamic sensation of planetary movement), the artist saw a source of both self-protection and self-actualization that eluded Blok, for whom the revolution would become a source of massive disillusionment. Speaking at an evening organized by Volfila to commemorate Blok, who died in August 1921, Andrei Bely described the poet's work, beginning with his poems to the Beautiful Lady, as "the organic development of an entire line of searching, of spiritual maximalism, of the aspiration to bring the dream to life, to show that this dream is not a dream, but our reality."[53] Petrov-Vodkin would undoubtedly have been present to hear these words about his friend and fellow seeker, and to reflect on their mutual efforts to "bring the dream to life" in images of Christ and the Mother of God, twin symbols of an entire revolution in consciousness.

## PETROV-VODKIN'S SOVIET MADONNAS

As late as the year of Blok's death the powerful collective imagery of Christianity and the icon was common coin for all those in search of spiritual revolution. But despite the Bolsheviks' claim that "the very fact of Volfila's existence shows how tolerant the existing regime is,"[54] the Bolsheviks' growing intolerance of opposition and its determination to break the authority of the

Orthodox Church made alternative visions of the future increasingly suspect. It was inevitable that, in such a climate, *1918 in Petrograd* would be Petrov-Vodkin's last public icon-painting.

Though the image of the Mother of God lived on in his work, it could only do so in a private realm. After sixteen childless years of marriage, a great void in his personal life was finally filled in October 1922 with the birth of his daughter Lena. It was in anticipation of this event, at once traumatic and transformative, that he painted the first of several icon-paintings of the Mother of God, so personal and intimate that they rarely surface in discussions of the artist, despite their link to his famous "mothers" and above all to the Petrograd Madonna, to which they bear a strong family resemblance. Petrov-Vodkin called it the *Awakening Mother of God* (Bogomater' Probuzhdaiushchaia) and he brought it to his wife in the hospital to comfort her during her long and difficult labor.[55] In it the Mother of God of the 1910s (the Annunciation fresco, the Softener of Evil Hearts) reemerges, with her fluted white veil and bright red maphorion once again covering her head. Her cheek tenderly grazes the head of the sleeping child, suffused with the emotional warmth of the *Umilenie* or Tenderness type and perhaps too with the father-to-be's feeling of exclusion from the mysteries of motherhood.[56] An Adoration in the Mead Museum at Amherst College conveys a similar sense of wonder before the newborn child. The ineffable other world is made visible not just in the color blue, but in the cherubim that recall both the Sistine Madonna and the paintings of his close friend Pavel Kuznetsov, whose mystical fountain studies circa 1905–1907 resembled "icons exalting the mysteries of birth and motherhood."[57] In a third image, from 1923 (Gordeev collection, Moscow) the Mother of God's sorrowful gaze and ravaged face preserve the somber mood of the Petrograd Madonna and her hand cradles the fragile child with a similar defensive gesture. The image is inscribed on the back: "Annunc. Holy Saturday," perhaps indicating that the artist took it to church to be blessed and thus established its active identity as a devotional icon.

Two more icon-paintings of the early 1920s are set, like the Petrograd Madonna, against a cityscape. *The Mother of God against a Besieged City* is something of a mystery.[58] Tucked into the top right edge in a sea of green is the tiny white cube of the Spas Nereditsa Church near Novgorod, but this emblem of Holy Rus' is dwarfed by the crenellated city in the middle ground, whose ramparts teeming with tiny figures are more like the Sienna of brothers Pietro and Ambrogio Lorenzetti than any Russian city. Like the earlier *Mother* of 1915, the Mother of God stares vacantly off into the distance, momentarily forgetful of her meek child. She wears the red maphorion wrapped tight about her shoulders like a shawl, but the white veil proclaims her sacred identity, as do the flat gold haloes framing the two heads, a feature not seen in his Madonnas since the first majolica icon of 1904–1905. (A curious detail is the stratification of the lower portion, as if to simulate an icon emerging from multiple layers of paint during restoration.)

The last of Petrov-Vodkin's Soviet Madonnas was painted during his final trip to Paris in 1924–1925, an official assignment from the Petrograd Academy of Arts to study the French system of art education. With the Cathedral of Notre Dame behind her (Vladimir Kostin called the painting the Madonna of Paris),[59] she is cropped at the shoulders in the manner of the Kazan Mother of God and brought very close to the viewer, with all the intimacy of a Netherlandish devotional image. The marks of suffering are smoothed away from her face and the child, now fully awake, is absorbed in playing with her hands. Both are restored to life and internal equilibrium, some crisis averted. Like the Petrograd Madonna she timidly acknowledges the viewer's presence, rather than gazing past or through us (the visionary, otherworldly gaze).

It seems deeply incongruous that this Madonna of Paris should have been created in the same year that Petrov-Vodkin was commissioned to paint his first "icon" of Lenin, who died in January 1924. In *Lenin in His Coffin* (V. I. Lenin v grobu), the disjunctions of scale and the rapid shift from foreground to background visually align the painting with *1918 in Petrograd*. Just what role the artist assigned Lenin in his worldview is unclear, but it is striking that when in 1934 he painted a portrait of Lenin at his desk, he imagined the dead revolutionary leader with his arms positioned in just such a triangular pose as the Petrograd Madonna, his eyes meeting ours with hypnotic intensity.

In September 1924 Volfila was closed down and "those heady post-Revolutionary years, in which a marriage was thought to be possible between communism and Christ, were now over."[60] For Petrov-Vodkin there could be no more Madonnas after this, but instead a new breed of Soviet mothers, radiant with health and physical well-being. In 1925 he painted *Motherhood* (Materinstvo), in which a mother nurses a swaddled infant while a woman looks on.[61] Other variations on the theme followed, earnest expressions of Soviet ideology or happy scenes of domestic tranquility. By 1936, the author of Petrov-Vodkin's first monograph could report that "the dry, ascetic image of the woman-Madonna has softened and acquired features more alive and closer to us."[62] The artist seemed to confirm this, writing: "During this time [the 1920s] I painted mothers where the *Mother* of 1915 no longer exists—now she is something different. Women here in Russia are different [*inye*]."[63]

In *House-Warming: Working Petrograd* (Novosel'e: Rabochii Petrograd, 1937), Petrov-Vodkin brought together his key themes and archetypes for one last bow. The setting is apt: the richly appointed dining room of a bourgeois

Petrograd apartment in 1922 (the artist was quite specific), newly occupied by a proletarian family and their friends. The young mother of 1918 has moved from the balcony to the warmth and comfort of the interior, where she holds court in the center of the crowded room. Enthroned in a comfortable armchair she nurses her baby. She has completed the Marxist-Leninist journey from country to city and her bare head and modern dress mark this evolution.[64] Yet despite the artist's political credentials and earnest efforts to strike the right ideological note, the painting was ignominiously removed from the exhibition "Industry of Socialism" (Industriia sotsialisma, 1938) and consigned to the Tretiakov Gallery's storerooms. After his death the following year, Petrov-Vodkin joined the ranks of all those whose vision of the revolution had not, after all, kept pace with reality.

In 1933 the critic Abram Efros put his finger on the problem with Petrov-Vodkin as a Soviet artist. "There is no essential difference between such extreme points as *Motherhood* and *The Death of a Commissar* (Smert' komissara): both are essentially icon-like ... where the mother and child are more like the Mother of God than a woman, the dying commissar is a holy martyr rather than a Bolshevik. Petrov-Vodkin never progressed beyond this understanding of the revolution, nor could he."[65]

CONCLUSION: *THE PETROGRAD MADONNA* AFTER 1924

Petrov-Vodkin's *1918 in Petrograd* (*The Petrograd Madonna*) was admitted to the canon of Soviet painting in the 1960s, after a quarter century of oblivion. This was only possible with the sort of obligatory cultural and historical amnesia that applied to icons as a whole, reframing them as ideologically neutral works of art. The presence of Mary in this image was tolerable and tolerated only if she could be seen as giving way triumphantly to the new proletarian mother. Soviet scholars could not ignore the painting's obvious iconic references, but they took pains to see it as a transitional work in which the butterfly of new Soviet womanhood had yet to emerge fully from the dry chrysalis of a defunct world order.

Post-Soviet admirers have rediscovered the Mother of God in Petrov-Vodkin's works, along with the Pietà, the Crucifixion, and the Old Testament Trinity.[66] It has become almost axiomatic to see in the Petrograd Madonna "not a simple worker, but the symbol of the Christian world with the sorrowful and searching gaze of the Vladimir Mother of God and the Sistine Madonna."[67] And yet, as Anatolii Mazaev suggests, the full aesthetic and spiritual essence of Petrov-Vodkin's work continues to elude us.[68] Mazaev places him squarely

among the followers of "aesthetic Christianity," pursuing a vision that passed
from Dostoevsky's "beauty will save the world" through Vladimir Solov'ev and
the "second-generation Symbolists" to culminate in the "third spiritual revolution" of Volfila. Arguably, *1918 in Petrograd* is the most complete visual manifestation of this tradition in Russian philosophical thought. It also marks the
summit of Petrov-Vodkin's own spiritual journey, a moment of synthesis and
revelation briefly attained and soon of necessity abandoned. Avril Pyman's
characterization of Blok's "The Twelve" as "the culmination of a lifetime of
work, thought and experience" can equally be applied to *1918 in Petrograd*.[69]
Indeed, it seems likely that the painting was to some degree an intentional
response to the poem whose cover he had declined to create two years before.
In recent years several writers have noted the resemblance between the
appearance of Christ at the end of "The Twelve" and the Petrograd Madonna
on her balcony, offset against the chaos and famine that followed that first
revolutionary winter.[70] As Petrov-Vodkin's philosophical worldview becomes
more fully understood, it is in this dialogue between word and image that his
icon-painting may find its fullest explication.

## Notes

1. In the 1920s icons of the Mother of God became fodder for official atheist propaganda in
magazines like *Bezbozhnik* [The Atheist] (1922–1941) and *Bezbozhnik u stanka* [The Atheist at the
Workbench] (1923–1931). Elizabeth Waters also notes the didactic value of invoking Mother of God
imagery: "In the posters on mothering produced after October 1917 there were some echoes, suitably
secularized, of the composition and style of the Orthodox Bogomater' and the Catholic Madonna:
women held their babies close to their bodies or sat them on their laps; often mother and child were
positioned against a blank or ornamental background, or isolated by distance from society" ("The
Modernisation of Russian Motherhood, 1917–1937," *Soviet Studies* 44, no. 1 [1992]: 131).

2. Petrov-Vodkin made a number of "memory paintings" of the Civil War period, including *The
First Demonstration (A Worker's Family on the First Anniversary of October)* (Pervaia demonstratsiia
[Sem'ia rabochego v pervuiu godovshchinu Oktiabria], 1927), *Death of a Commissar* (1928), *1919 The
Alarm* (1919 Trevoga, 1934), and *The Housewarming: Working Petrograd* (1937).

3. The name was already in use in June 1921, when the painting was included in an exhibition
of new acquisitions at the Tretiakov Gallery. The artist wrote to his wife: "The Petrograd Madonna is so
meek and has so much depth that her success in Moscow is quite easy to understand" (E. N. Selizarova,
*K. S. Petrov-Vodkin: Pis'ma, stat'i, vystupleniia, dokumenty* [Moscow: Sovetskii khudozhnik, 1991],
212). On the continuing emergence of new miracle-working icons in the late imperial period, see Vera
Shevzov, *Russian Orthodoxy on the Eve of Revolution* (New York: Oxford University Press, 2004), chap. 6.

4. In his autobiography Petrov-Vodkin recalled the refusal of the priest at the Khlynovsk
Cathedral to bless this first crude icon. See Kuz'ma Sergeevich Petrov-Vodkin, *Khlynovsk, Prostranstvo
Evklida, Samarkandiia*, comp. Iu. A. Rusakov (Moscow: Iskusstvo, 1982), 272–75.

5. For a wider discussion of Petrov-Vodkin's work in this context, see Tamara Machmut-Jhashi,
"The Art of Kuzma Petrov-Vodkin (1878–1939)" (PhD diss., Indiana University, 1995).

6. On Russian "cosmism," see *Russkii kosmizm: Antologiia filosofskoi mysli*, comp. S. G. Semenova
and A. G. Gacheva (Moscow: Pedagogika Press, 1993); also Svetlana Kulakova, "Religiozno-filosofskie
vzgliady K. S. Petrova-Vodkina," in *K. S. Petrov-Vodkin i XXI vek: K 130-letiiu so dnia rozhdeniia*, ed. V.
I. Borodina and L. V. Pashkova (Saratov: SGChM, 2008), 15–25.

7. In the Soviet-era literature these later commissions are overshadowed by the artist's first ill-fated commission to paint frescoes in Saratov's Kazan Cathedral, together with Pavel Kuznetsov and Petr Utkin. The frescoes' destruction by the local clergy has been narrowly interpreted as evidence of the Orthodox Church's hostility toward aesthetic innovation in icon and fresco painting.

8. Petrov-Vodkin also agreed to paint the icons for the iconostasis for free. See E. E. Pondina, "Pokrovitel' i drug: R. F. Mel'tser i K. S. Petrov-Vodkin," in *Petrov-Vodkin i XXI vek*, 129.

9. The cartoon is now in the collection of Petr Aven.

10. Petrov-Vodkin owed this commission to the architect Aleksei Shchusev, who was charged with restoring the ruined twelfth-century church. His frescoes (*Cain Killing Abel* and *The Sacrifice of Abel*) were located in one of the towers. See O. A. Tarasenko, "Znachenie ovruchskikh rospisei v tvorcheskom samoopredelenii K. S. Petrova-Vodkina," in *Panorama iskusstv 5* (Moscow: Sovetskii khudozhnik, 1982), 217–20.

11. "It's possible that Matisse inspired my *Playing Boys* in a comradely sort of way" is how the artist phrased it. Cited in *Kuz'ma Petrov-Vodkin: Zhivopis', Grafika, Teatral'no-dekorativnoe iskusstvo*, ed. Iu. A. Rusakov (Leningrad: Avrora, 1986), 58.

12. On the Annunciation fresco, see V. Borodina, "Blagoveshchenie K. S. Petrova-Vodkina iz Morskogo sobora v Kronshtadte (Novye nakhodki)," *Novosti Radishchevskogo muzeia*, 2 November 2012, http://radmuseumart.ru/projects/169/639/. Svetlana Stepanova writes of the *Mother of God Softener of Evil Hearts*, pictured on the cover of the present volume: "Her upraised hands recall both the image of the Orante, the Pokrov, and the Sporitel'nitsa khlebov [Grower of Crops] without repeating any specific prototype." Svetlana Stepanova, "Russkaia Madonna Petrova-Vodkina," *Religiia i iskusstvo* 3 (2012), http://andredevoted.livejournal.com/72065.html.

13. Efim Vodonos explores this process as it played out in the "girls on the Volga" motif. See E. Vodonos, "Poiski lichnogo monumental'nogo stilia: O gruppe kartin K. S. Petrova-Vodkina, sviazannykh obshchim motivom," in *K. S. Petrov-Vodkin i XXI vek*, 61–68.

14. Ibid., 63.

15. For a richly nuanced discussion of this and other themes in the painting, see Machmut-Jhashi, "The Art of Kuzma Petrov-Vodkin," 86–96.

16. N. V. Gavrilova points out the importance childhood memories of the icon corner held for Petrov-Vodkin, citing his memoirs: "how before dinner 'we crossed ourselves before the kiot,' drank tea 'in the corner before the icons,' and 'the sackcloth runner [that] led as much to the icon case as to the table.'" ("Ikona v Saratovskom povolzh'e XIX–nachala XX vekov 'Prostranstvo Evklid,'" *Materialy VII Bogoliubskikh chtenii*, 11–14 April 2000, http://ogis.sgu.ru/ogis/bogo/mat7/mat7-11.html.)

17. Tamara Machmut-Jhashi sees in the empty kiot "a lack of faith in a world where such a war [WWI] could be waged." See Machmut-Jhashi, "The Art of Kuzma Petrov-Vodkin," 99.

18. The treatment of the corner here parallels Vladimir Tatlin's corner reliefs and the hanging of Kazimir Malevich's *Black Square* (Chernyi kvadrat) at the "0.10" exhibition, both of which made their appearance at precisely this time.

19. The painting was auctioned at Christie's London in 2010.

20. Valentina Borodina, director of the Petrov-Vodkin Museum in Khlynovsk, describes his face as "a kind of metaphor of stoicism and the Russian person's devotion to faith from an early age." V. I. Borodina, "Naideno neizvestnoe polotno K. S. Petrova-Vodkina," in *Novosti Radishchevskogo muzeia*, 5 June 2010, http://www.museum.ru/N40487.

21. Underlying this image is an earlier 1915 commission for a stained-glass window of the Old Testament Trinity commissioned by sugar baron Pavel Kharitonenko for a church in the town of Sumy.

22. Together with Blok, Petrov-Vodkin played a leading role in encouraging the intelligentsia to work with the Bolshevik Party, while maintaining their autonomy. But despite his willingness to negotiate with them, it was evidently for strategic reasons only. As Ivanov-Razumnik noted, "Organizers of Volfila such as the artist Petrov-Vodkin responded to the Bolsheviks with fierce intransigence" (V. Ivanov-Razumnik, *Tiurmy i ssylki* [New York: Izd-vo im. Chekhova, 1953], 40). According to Aaron Shteinberg, the artist's violent opposition to the Bolsheviks was tinged with anti-Semitism (A. Shteinberg, *Druz'ia moikh rannikh let [1911–1928]* [Paris: Izd-vo Sintaksis, 1991], 32).

23. On Ivanov-Razumnik's political views, see Peter J. S. Duncan, "Ivanov-Razumnik and the Russian Revolution: From Scythianism to Suffocation," *Canadian Slavonic Papers* 21, no. 1 (March 1979): 15–27.

24. Cited in Duncan, "Ivanov-Razumnik," 17.

25. See V. I. Borodina, "K. S. Petrov-Vodkin: Cherez Afriku k 'skifstvu'," *Novosti Radishchevskogo muzeia*, 29 April 2009, http://radmuseumart.ru/projects/169/6451/.

26. On 25 February 1918 Blok visited Petrov-Vodkin to discuss the cover. One interpretation of his refusal was that "striving to represent a harmonious reality, the artist found Blok's 'disintegrated,' chaotic world alien" (A. M. Gordin and M. A. Gordin, *Aleksandr Blok i russkie khudozhniki* [Leningrad: Khudozhnik RSFSR, 1986], 290). Petrov-Vodkin recommended the artist Viktor Zamirailo (Aleksandr Blok, *Zapisnye knizhki* [Moscow: Khudozhestvennaia literatura, 1965], 390, 391), but the poem was ultimately illustrated by Iurii Annenkov, who depicted Christ as "a void [*pustota*], a white patch of blizzard" (ibid., 306).

27. He was a member of the association's four-man council, with Blok, Ivanov-Razumnik, and critic Boris Kushner. A gathering of founding members in January 1919 included Bely, Petrov-Vodkin, Konstantin Erberg, and Aaron Shteinberg, but in February the group, including Petrov-Vodkin and Blok, was briefly arrested in connection with the suppression of the Left Socialist Revolutionariess, and the official opening did not take place until November 1919. On Volfila, see V. Belous, *Vol'fila ili Krizis kul'tury v zerkale obshchestvennogo samosoznaniia* (Moscow: Mir, 2007); also his *Vol'fila: Petrogradskaia Vol'naia Filosofskaia Assotsiatsia, 1919–1924*, 2 vols. (Moscow: Tri kvadrata, 2005).

28. Belous, *Vol'fila ili Krizis kul'tury*, 15.

29. Among the artists and art critics who spoke were Mikhail Matiushin ("An Artistic Experiment in New Space"), Kazimir Malevich ("The World as Objectlessness"), Lev Bruni ("On Tatlin's Monument"; "Time's Edge" [Against Art]"), and Nikolai Punin ("Khlebnikov and 'The Kingdom of Time'"). Belous, *Vol'fila: Petrogradskaia*, 210–11.

30. From Ivanov-Razumnik's recollections presented at an evening in memory of Blok at Volfila, 28 August 1921, Vehi.net, http://www.vehi.net/blok/PamBlock.html.

31. Cited in O. Tarasenko, "K. Petrov-Vodkin i traditsii drevnerusskoi zhivopisi," *Tvorchestvo* 11, no. 263 (1978): 9.

32. By impression he meant the surface of objects, whereas sensation involved an awareness of the object's position in space. See R. M. Gutina, ed., "K. S. Petrov-Vodkin, Nauka videt'," *Sovetskoe iskusstvoznanie 27* (1991): 452.

33. Gutina, "K. S. Petrov-Vodkin," 459.

34. Ibid., 452.

35. "On Beauty," cited in Kulakova, "Religiozno-filosofskie vzgliady," 23.

36. Ibid., 23.

37. See N. L. Adaskina, "'Pravo cheloveka byt' bozhestvennym...': Mesto i znachenie religioznykh motivov v tvorchestve K. Petrova-Vodkina," in *Bibliia v kul'ture i iskusstve: Materialy nauchnoi konferentsii Vipperovskie chteniia—1995. Vypusk* 28, ed. I. E. Danilova (Moscow: GMII, 1996), 251–71.

38. Elena Gribonosova-Grebneva makes this point in respect to the linocut *Head of A Woman* (Zhenskaia golova, 1921), which shares affinities with his images of the Crucified Christ. See E. V. Gribonosova-Grebneva, "Kollektsiia proizvedenii K. S. Petrova-Vodkina v sovremennom chastnom sobranii Moskvy," *Materialy XII Bogoliubskikh chtenii*, 2010, http://ogis.sgu.ru/ogis/bogo/mat12/mat12-30.html.

39. See S. M. Daniel', "O risunke K. Petrova-Vodkina 'Otrechenie Petra'," in *Bibliia v kul'ture i iskusstve*, 272–76; also V. Veidle, "Chetvertoe Evangelie Petrova-Vodkina i russkoe religioznoe iskusstvo," *Zveno* 4 (1 April 1928): 209–13.

40. R. Ivanov-Razumnik, "Dve Rossii," in *Skify* 2 (1918), cited in Duncan, "Ivanov-Razumnik," 20. Viktor Kutovoi notes that "it was no coincidence that in 1919 the artist, the first part of whose surname was the name of the supreme apostle, should create a drawing for the journal *Plamia* on the New Testament theme of the Denial of Peter" (Viktor Kutovoi, "Neuznannyi K. S. Petrov-Vodkin: K

130-letiiu so dnia rozhdeniia khudozhnika," Pravoslavie.ru, http://www.pravoslavie.ru/jurnal/28171.htm).

41. T. N. Stepanova, "'S Khristom otkrylos' nebo. . .': Zametki K. S. Petrova-Vodkina na Evangelii," in *K. S. Petrov-Vodkin i XXI vek*, 38–45; L. V. Mochalov, "Istoriia Khrista kak tematicheskii arkhetip v tvorchestve K. S. Petrova-Vodkina," in *K. S. Petrov-Vodkin i XXI vek*, 26–37.

42. See, for instance, Machmut-Jhashi, "The Art of Kuzma Petrov-Vodkin," 188; T. P. Khristoliubova, "Bibleiskie motivy v tvorchestve K. S. Petrova-Vodkina: Sakral'noe i obydennoe," *Mir nauki, kul'tury, obrazovaniia* 4, no. 29 (2011): 131.

43. In a 1924 interview the artist commented, "I don't regret that I suffered hunger—I was convinced that this was precisely the way for me to nourish my art and my thoughts." (Interview for *Nouvelle litteraire* in 1924, cited in K. V. Shilov, "Petrov-Vodkin i Anna Akhmatova," in *K. S. Petrov-Vodkin i XXI vek*, 92). See also this comment by a fellow Volfila member: "The more hunger gripped life, the stronger and more genuinely did the intelligentsia manifest a need for spiritual contact, so to speak, for a philosophical foundation for physical life" (N. I. Gagen-Torn, *Memoria: Vospominaniia, rasskazy* [Moscow: Vozvrashchenie, 1994], 26).

44. Selizarova, *Petrov-Vodkin,* 251.

45. See Christine Worobec's comments in the present volume (pp. 64–65) on the uncovered head of the Akhtyrka Mother of God icon.

46. A. S. Galushkina, *K. S. Petrov-Vodkin: 42 illiustratsii* (Moscow: Ogiz, 1936), 44; E. N. Selizarova, *Petrov-Vodkin v Peterburge—Petrograde—Leningrade* (St. Petersburg: Lenizdat, 1993), 142. This motif of the proletariat occupying bourgeois apartments reemerges in his last major painting, *The Housewarming: Working Petrograd* (1937), which is set in 1922.

47. Selizarova, *Petrov-Vodkin v Peterburge*, 142.

48. Rona Goffen, "Icon and Vision: Giovanni Bellini's Half-Length Madonnas," *The Art Bulletin* 57, no. 4 (December 1975): 487.

49. Ibid., 492. Also linking Petrov-Vodkin to Bellini is the motif of the sleeping child—his sleep prefiguring his death—that originated in Trecento Venice, but rarely figured in Russian icons.

50. E. K. Dunaeva, "Prikosnovenie k dushe," *Volga* 10 (1987): 169.

51. Machmut-Jhashi, "The Art of Kuzma Petrov-Vodkin," 188.

52. Dunaeva, "Prikosnovenie k dushe," 170.

53. From Andrei Bely's recollections presented at an evening in memory of Blok at Volfila, 28 August 1921, Vehi.net, http://www.vehi.net/blok/PamBlock.html.

54. A statement by Mikhail Kristi on the anniversary in 1918 of the "Voskresenie" group. See Gagen-Torn, *Memoria*, 9.

55. It is the only one of his Mother of God images painted on wood panel. The painting is now in the State Russian Museum (Inventory No. Ж-6572).

56. Petrov-Vodin stressed his wife's "inwardness" and self-absorption during her pregnancy, in a way that recalls Pavel Kuznetsov's preoccupation with the mysteries of childbirth. See Dunaeva, "Prikosnovenie k dushe," 163.

57. Peter Stupples, *Pavel Kuznetsov: His Life and Art* (Cambridge: Cambridge University Press, 1990), 58. This motif evoking otherworldly states such as poetic inspiration and memory recurs in his *Portrait of Anna Akhmatova*, his *Self-Portrait*, and *After the Battle*.

58. This painting was shown in 2007 in the exhibition "Kuzma Petrov-Vodkin and His Pupils" at the KGallery in St. Petersburg, together with other little-known paintings on religious themes from private collections, including *Christ the Sower* and *Head of Christ*, evidently a sketch for a Crucifixion. (*Katalog vystavki "Kuz'ma Petrov-Vodkin i ego ucheniki,"* comp. K. V. Bereozovskaia [St. Petersburg: KGallery, 2007].)

59. A preparatory drawing in the Dudakov collection shows her full length, standing to one side of the cathedral. The painting is in a private French collection and was shown in Russia for the first time at the Russian Museum's exhibition of works on loan from private collections, "A Time to Collect," in 2008.

60. Katerina Clark and Michael Holquist, *Mikhail Bakhtin* (Cambridge, MA: Harvard University Press, 1984), 131.

61. In his wide-ranging analysis of the painting Vasilii Uspenskii notes the survival of sacred references to icons and Renaissance works like the *Brera Madonna* and Leonardo da Vinci's *Madonna with Saint Anne*. See. V. Uspenskii, *Kuz'ma Sergeevich Petrov-Vodkin: Materinstvo* (St. Petersburg: Arka, 2010). Even so, the setting is unequivocally secular, in line with the new demands of Soviet reality.

62. Galushkina, *K. S. Petrov-Vodkin*, 50.

63. Selizarova, *Petrov-Vodkin*, 329.

64. For a suggestive reading of this painting as a disguised Last Supper, see Kutovoi, "Neuznannyi K. S. Petrov-Vodkin."

65. Cited in A. I. Mazaev, *Iskusstvo i bol'shevism, 1920–1930* (Moscow: URSS, 2007), 291.

66. Kutovoi, "Neuznannyi K. S. Petrov-Vodkin."

67. E. Medkova, "*1918 god v Petrograde* Petrova-Vodkina," *Iskusstvo* 13 (2006), http://art.1september.ru/article.php?ID=200601306. Tatiana Khristoliubova attributes this about-face to the "post-Soviet syndrome of rejecting intrusive propaganda." ("Analiz zritel'skoi interpretatsii khudozhestvennogo proizvedeniia na primere kartiny K. S. Petrova-Vodkina *1918 v Petrograde*," in *Informatsiia i obrazovanie: Granitsy kommunikatsii INFO'09; Sbornik nauchnykh trudov*, ed. A. A. Temerbekova [Gorno-Altaisk: RIO GAGU, 2009]), 190.

68. Mazaev, *Iskusstvo i bol'shevizm*, 292.

69. Avril Pyman, ed., *Alexander Blok: Selected Poems* (Oxford: Pergamon Press, 1972), 275.

70. See Medkova, "1918 god v Petrograde"; F. Shaposhnikova, "Petrogradskaia Madonna: O kartine Petrova-Vodkina 1918 god v Petrograd," *Iskusstvo* 9 (1975): 54. More broadly, Sergei Daniel' points out that "the 'synthetic' orientation of the late Blok has a very close analogy in the work of Kuzma Petrov-Vodkin. Like Blok, Petrov-Vodkin consciously strove toward the synthetic assimilation of culture, the organic merging of diverse artistic languages." Cited in Elena Gribonosova-Gribneva, "Tvorchestvo K. S. Petrova-Vodkina i zapadnoevropeiskie 'realizmy' 1920–1930-x gg" (PhD diss., Moscow State University, 2009).

# 8

## Our Mother of Paris
### The "Creative Renewal" of Orthodox Mariology in the Russian Emigration, 1920s–1930s

NATALIA ERMOLAEV

IN HER GROUNDBREAKING STUDY, *The Ministry of Women in the Church* (1991), the theologian Elisabeth Behr-Sigel dedicates a chapter to the topic of Mary in the Orthodox tradition.[1] She opens by reiterating the frequent observation that there is a paradox in the Eastern Church's veneration of the Mother of God. While Mary is ubiquitous in liturgical, iconographic, and popular culture, Orthodoxy is markedly reserved on the level of dogma, or even serious theological reflection, about the Mother of God. In contrast to the numerous Marian doctrines of Catholicism, the Eastern tradition relies on just two dogmatic statements: that Jesus Christ was "born of the Holy Spirit and the Virgin Mary" as stated by the Nicene creed, and that Mary is the *Theotokos*, or God-bearer, proclaimed by the Council of Ephesus in 431.

Behr-Sigel also mentions a development that tends to be overlooked in standard teachings about Orthodox Mariology—what she calls its "creative renewal" in the religious-philosophical circles of the Russian Silver Age (circa 1880–1920). This period of artistic, literary, and spiritual flourishing was marked by an enchantment with the "divine feminine," a trend initiated by the poet-philosopher Vladimir Solov'ev (1853–1900) and his vision of Sophia, the feminized representation of Divine Wisdom.[2] Solov'ev and his Sophia led many of the period's poets, artists, and thinkers to reconceive the interplay between divinity, humanity, and sexuality, and, in this context, gave rise to new articulations of Mary the Mother of God.[3]

While Russian Sophiology captivates the critical imagination to this day, the numerous studies on this topic have not provided a comprehensive picture of its impact on Mary in modern Orthodox thought. To help fill this gap, this essay uses Solov'ev and the Silver Age as a point of departure, and argues that the "creative renewal" of Mariology continued to develop in subsequent generations, most notably in the émigré circles of the "Paris School" of the 1920s and 1930s. Three thinkers in particular—the theologian Sergius Bulgakov (1871–1944), the religious philosopher Nikolai Berdiaev (1874–1948), and the social activist, poet, and nun Elizaveta Skobtsova (also known also by her monastic name "Mother Maria," 1881–1945)—framed and reframed the figure of Mary within the Mariological and Sophiological traditions, drawing on her both as a source of Orthodox values and as inspiration for fresh approaches to the faith in modern times.

The émigré-period Marian works by Bulgakov, Berdiaev, and Skobtsova—who are considered representative of the Paris School's progressive, world-affirming spiritual ethos—reveal some surprising continuities and divergences from both the Silver Age legacy and conventional Christianity. In addressing the topic of Mary they delve deeply into themes of maternity, virginity, corporeality, and authority, and set the stage for discussions about gender and sexuality that would emerge in Orthodox circles in the West in later decades.[4] In a broader context, the Mariologies of these three thinkers contribute a rich Eastern Christian perspective on the powerful, complex role that the Mother of God has played and continues to play in Christian culture.[5]

## SOPHIA AND MARY IN SILVER AGE RELIGIOUS THOUGHT

The Silver Age notion of Sophia notoriously eludes straightforward definition. While each poet and thinker formed a unique understanding of the "divine feminine," several shared features can be observed. At its core, Sophiological inquiry represents the encounter of the ancient faith with the realities of modern life. As the twentieth century turned, the fabric of Russian society was torn by tensions between tradition and progress, faith and reason, old and new values. Sophia was seen as a reconciling force; Solov'ev hailed her as the "principle of integration," the mediator between God and the world who would facilitate eschatological "total unity" (*vseedinstvo*) of all things. Russian intellectuals looked to Sophia to solve the problems brought about by the modern condition; she stood for wholeness (*tsel'nost'*) in a time of cultural crisis, imminent war, and revolution. Sophia, they believed, was the ephemeral force that could foster coherence between art and life, tradition and modernity, the transcendent and the everyday.

Sophiology also signaled the *anthropological* orientation of Silver Age religious inquiry, where conventional meditations on God's inner life gave way to explorations of the divine mysteries as expressed in human experience and the natural realm.[6] Pivotal for this development was Solov'ev's conceptualization of the dynamic interaction between God and the world, which he termed *Bogochelovechestvo* (translated either as "Godmanhood" or "Humanity of God"). Sophia is integral in the divine-human process: though she simultaneously exists in the eternal sphere, Solov'ev saw Sophia's distinct presence in the here-and-now as the "World Soul," "God's body," and the "principle of humanity."

For Solov'ev and his Silver Age scions, the line from Sophia to the Mother of God was easy enough to draw. Both are holy female entities who mediate between the transcendent and material realms and facilitate the integration of the two.[7] Moreover, Sophia and Mary had been linked in the Eastern Slavic imagination from early times, as evidenced by a rich iconographic, hymnographic, and liturgical tradition. The priest and philosopher Pavel Florenskii (1882–1937) noted that the Russian understanding of Holy Wisdom evolved in conjunction with its devotion to the Mother of God, giving rise to Russian Sophiology's distinctly Marian bent.[8]

It is not surprising that these anthropologically inclined Silver Age thinkers would turn their attention to the Mother of God. Even more so than an abstract concept of God's wisdom, Mary represents a flesh-and-blood example of God's immediate presence in the world. As the Church teaches, the Mother of God is the perfectly divinized human being, a person so holy that she became, as she is lauded in hymnody, "more honorable than the cherubim and beyond compare more glorious than the seraphim."[9] Florenskii adds that the Mariological and thus *personal* nature of Sophia was always a priority for the Russians. The philosophizing Greeks—who linked Sophia primarily with the Logos—approached Divine Wisdom as an "object of contemplation," but the Slavs moved beyond theological speculation and "came to love the purity and sanctity of an individual soul."[10] That is, Russian Christianity venerates Divine Wisdom in the *person* of Mary.

Consistent with its emphasis on the embodiment of divinity, Russian Sophiology initiated a new approach not only to humanity in general, but to *woman*kind specifically. Against the backdrop of society's reassessment of gender roles and the rise of the women's movement, the religious intellectuals of the Silver Age produced a variety of bold, idiosyncratic, and often contradictory philosophies of Eros, sex, and love in the Christian context. Sophia and Mary appear frequently as points of reference in attempts to understand "the feminine" and its ever-shifting position on the spectrum between divine and creaturely, ideal and real, transcendent and material.[11]

Solov'evean Sophiology greatly influenced the prerevolutionary work of Bulgakov, Berdiaev and Skobtsova, and continued to impact their thought as it evolved in emigration. As leading figures of the Paris School community, they kept the Silver Age faith that the "divine feminine" could help solve the main challenges facing their generation. They lived in increasingly cataclysmic times, and the ruptures caused by the revolution and exile made articulating a sense of unity ever more urgent. The émigré theologians believed they had been given both the opportunity and the task to revitalize staid Russian religious culture, to probe Orthodoxy's ancient roots but also to engage the faith with contemporary issues. For Bulgakov, the Mother of God was integral to his revision of Orthodox dogmatics. Berdiaev associated Mary with new Christian anthropology and ethics. Skobtsova saw Mary as the foundation for her program of Christian social work. While the Mother of God served as a gravitational center for all three, a close analysis of their writings—and especially their treatment of motherhood—reveals how they diverged on certain core beliefs about the relationship between God and the world.[12]

## GODMOTHERHOOD AND BULGAKOV'S SOPHIOLOGICAL DOGMATICS

In 1925, when Bulgakov arrived in Paris to become dean of the newly established Saint Sergius Theological Academy, his reputation preceded him. Born to a clerical family in the provincial town of Livny, Bulgakov rejected the faith of his youth, moved to Moscow, and made a name for himself as a Marxist political economist. When he returned to Christianity some years later, he did so under the sway of philosophical idealism and Solov'ev. Solov'ev's inspiration is evident in Bulgakov's main pre-emigration writings, such as *The Philosophy of Economy* (Filosofiia khoziaistva, 1912) and *Unfading Light* (Svet nevechernii, 1917), where he lays out a speculative theology with the notion of Sophia at its center.[13] Sophia, Bulgakov writes, is the dynamic force that brings the world to God by bridging the divide between earth and heaven, matter and spirit, body and soul. Like Solov'ev before him, Bulgakov forged his vision by integrating elements from the Neoplatonic, Gnostic, Kabbalistic, medieval Western, European Romantic, and native Russian traditions. He came dangerously close to establishing an entirely new theological system; his suggestion that Sophia is a fourth hypostasis of the Trinity caused scandal among his Orthodox readership.[14]

In the tumultuous years of the Bolshevik Revolution and Civil War, the direction of Bulgakov's thought began to shift. He was ordained to the priesthood in 1918, and three years later was sent into exile. In the two decades Father Sergius spent in France, he remained wholly committed to the core Sophiological project of exploring the link between divinity and the world. But he showed a concerted move away from the syncretic, speculative approach of his early years to a more standard theological framework. This dogmatic turn—the shift from religious philosophy to theology—is a distinctive feature of Bulgakov's émigré career.

In emigration, Bulgakov treated Sophia within the context of Orthodox dogmatics. As both the hypostatic love within the Godhead and the expression of God's love for creation, Divine Wisdom is at the core of Bulgakov's Trinitarian theology, and permeates his voluminous writings on Christology, Mariology, anthropology, ecclesiology, eschatology, and theology of culture. [15] As Paul Valliere has convincingly argued, Bulgakov's broad-ranging dogmatic writings made Solov'ev's abstract philosophy concrete, and thus revitalized Orthodox dogma so it was relevant to the modern believer and applicable to daily life.[16] Indeed, Bulgakov's creative engagement with the dogmatic tradition has made him one of the most highly regarded, but also controversial, Orthodox theologians of the twentieth century.[17]

The role of the Mother of God in Bulgakov's mature writings has received considerable scholarly attention only in recent years.[18] Though Mary had been linked with Sophia in his pre-emigration imagination (Mary even inspired some of his pivotal religious experiences), she did not figure prominently in his early texts. This changed as he strove to explain Sophia in more conventional Orthodox terms. For example, one of Bulgakov's first tasks after leaving Russia was to clarify his problematic "fourth hypostasis" claim. In the article "Hypostasis and Hypostaticity: Scholia to the *Unfading Light*" ("Ipostas' i ipostasnost'. Scholia k 'Svetu nevechernemu,'" 1925), Bulgakov goes to great lengths to prove the orthodoxy of his Sophiology, in part with a Marian defense.[19] Acutely aware that Russian Mariology must be better articulated, Father Sergius devoted one of his first full-length émigré works to the topic: *The Burning Bush: An Attempt at a Dogmatic Explanation of Some Aspects of the Orthodox Veneration of the Mother of God* (Kupina neopalimaia, Opyt dogmaticheskogo istolkovaniia nekotorykh chert v pravoslavnom pochitanii Bogomateri, 1927).[20] From that point forward, all of Bulgakov's major works contain extensive meditations on the Mother of God.

Bulgakov's treatment of Sophiology in conjunction with Mariology invigorated both traditions. The Mother of God, he argued, is "created wisdom" and the "personal manifestation" of Sophia. As the "special hypostatic center" of the world, Mary has the task to "raise up in herself, *elevate* humanity and all creatures" to God. Bulgakov called her the "Sophianic person" who demonstrates that the distance between Creator and creation can be overcome; Mary exemplifies that the material realm can dwell with God.[21]

These exuberant Marian writings highlight what is generally recognized as Bulgakov's special attention to "the feminine," both divine and real.[22] Like Solov'ev and others before him, Father Sergius describes a cooperative and complementary gender balance in the divine sphere.[23] The Godhead, he writes, contains both male and female principles, and this divine male-female unity is expressed in the world through Jesus Christ and the Mother of God (through grace by the Holy Spirit). Thus Christ and Mary are the true divine-human, male-female pair. This mystery is best expressed in the Church's iconographic tradition, Bulgakov writes, where icons of the Mother of God with the Child depict the unity and indivisibility of the Logos and the creature receiving Him.[24]

Bulgakov held firm that the divine male-female dynamic has a "correlation" in the human realm.[25] Christ and Mary sanctify all of humanity: Christ the men, Mary the women. Christ passes his glory on to all males, and Mary (through the grace of the Holy Spirit) to females, "so that not only the male but also the female nature is glorified and divinized (though *in a different way*)" (italics in the original).[26] Men and women are necessary complements—"the male is truth in beauty, the female is beauty in truth: truth and beauty are indivisible and of one essence"[27]—who together express the pre-eternal male-female unity of God.

The pride of place Bulgakov assigns to Mary's motherhood surpasses even conventional Russian Mariology's partiality to her maternal role. In analogy to Solov'ev's notion of *Bogochelovechestvo*, a nominalization of Christ's title *Bogochelovek*, Bulgakov builds on Mary's appellation *Bogomater'* (Slavonic for *Theotokos*) for the concept of *Bogomaterinstvo* (translated as "Godmotherhood," or "Motherhood of God"). With his focus on *Bogomaterinstvo*, Bulgakov raises the spiritual significance of Mary's motherhood and offers a corrective to Solov'ev's grand vision by suggesting that motherhood as *also* a key juncture in the divine-human dialogue. For Bulgakov, Mary is important not only because she was visited by the Holy Spirit and became the *Bogomater'*, but because her *Bogomaterinstvo* fundamentally altered the trajectory of divine-human history. In giving birth to Christ, Bulgakov writes, Mary became the "glory of the world, a world glorified in God and with God, having in itself and giving birth to God."[28] Her Godmotherhood was not hers alone—it extends to all creation. With Mary, he writes, the world has become the womb that bears God.

As he celebrated divine motherhood, Bulgakov also extolled maternal love among human women, who, he stressed, have an inherent connection to the Mother of God because of their shared femaleness. In *The Burning Bush*, Bulgakov reflects on the joy mothers experience by participating in the mystery of *Bogomaterinstvo*. Each pregnant woman carries in her womb that which God has created; she feels the "tangibleness of what is being begotten or already born and the joy over this begottenness."[29] As a special receptacle, a mother knows and loves her child as divine creation. This is the essence of maternity: "love for the one being conceived and still not born but already begotten." The immediate bond between mother and child is strengthened by the mother's willingness to sacrifice for that child, "a voluntary, loving surrender of the self, a going out from the self to the other, life simultaneously in the self and in the other."[30]

Ever the insightful pastor, Father Sergius delivered a touching paean to motherhood in his sermon, "Most Pure Motherhood: Dedicated to Russian Mothers," delivered the day after Christmas—the Synaxis of the Mother of God—in 1928.[31] He calls on women to meditate on the "true human motherhood" revealed to them by Mary at the Nativity.[32] Appealing to mothers and mothers-to-be, Bulgakov encourages them to fulfill their spiritual mission by partaking in the glory of Mary's motherhood.[33] Women have the Mother of God as their leader, he writes, which is why they are destined to share her joy and find in her comfort from their pain.[34]

While Bulgakov's Marian writings contain some of Orthodoxy's most tender expositions on the generative aspects of femininity, they also reveal the theologian's core ambiguities about gender, sexuality, and the body. Though Bulgakov can be commended for trying to elevate the status of women's spiritual experience, his theological anthropology nonetheless reveals an adherence to the patriarchal religious and social mores that marginalize women. For the émigré Bulgakov, sex and sin were inseparable. Though he holds fast to the belief that Eros is a positive force—it is "ecstatic, creative, inspiring"—he concedes that it would be simpler "if it remained solely spiritual."[35] As Valliere and others have pointed out, in his mature period—in contrast to his pre-emigration years—Bulgakov was not able to resolve the antagonism between divinely inspired Eros and sex in the human realm.[36]

As a result, the Mother of God that emerges in Father Sergius's later writings is a picture of both maternity and virginity, flesh-affirming and flesh-transcending womanhood, as is the standard in conventional Christianity. While Bulgakov assures women that they can embrace the Mother of God as one of their own, he underscores that she was actually not like them at all. Praising Mary's perpetual (physical, not just spiritual) virginity, Bulgakov reminds his readers that Mary alone is the New Eve and that her maternity is "incompatible with the contemporary physiology of the human being." Human mothers can relate to the Mother of God only up to a point, and since "in sexual conception and birth the true essence of spiritual motherhood is darkened" they cannot in fact experience the full spiritual joy of Godmotherhood.[37] Thus, what Bulgakov seems to give so generously to women with one hand, he takes with the other. His reliance on essentialist notions of gender creates a distance between Mary and real women, rescinding their agency and pushing them to the margins of his Sophiological project.

Ultimately, however, Bulgakov recovers a gender balance in his vision of the divine-human dialogue through his distinctly Marian ecclesiology. Given that no human body can contain divine femininity the way Mary's did, Bulgakov locates Sophia's earthly presence in the *ecclesial* body. Building on the tradition that the Church bears a feminine, indeed Marian, character, Father Sergius argues that divine Eros can be experienced though collective, maternal-filial "churchly love." He interprets the Song of Songs as a love song between Christ and the Church *and* Son and Mother, describing the ecclesial community as a maternal collective, where "every human soul is also the Mother and Bride of Christ, seeking its heavenly Groom and joining with Him."[38] Aflame with motherly love, Bulgakov writes, the members of the *ecclesia* unite with God.[39]

## THE VIRGIN MARY IN BERDIAEV'S SOPHIOLOGICAL ANTHROPOLOGY

While Bulgakov's émigré-period Mariology (and Sophiology more generally) was denounced as "modernist" by the traditionalist Orthodox establishment, it was also contested by some more liberally minded émigrés in Paris.[40] An alternative vision of Mary emerges in the writings of Nikolai Berdiaev, whose views on the metaphysics of gender and sexuality led to a very different emphasis on the role of the Mother of God for modern Orthodox culture.

Berdiaev was a native of Kiev and an aristocrat, and, like his longtime friend Bulgakov, began his intellectual pursuits as a Marxist. He too returned to Christianity under the sway of Silver Age metaphysics, and was a well-known religious thinker by the time he joined Bulgakov in exile in 1922. With his boundless energy and broad intellect, Berdiaev was the driving force behind some of the most significant activities of Russian émigré Orthodoxy: he edited the journal *The Way* (Put'), ran the Religious-Philosophical Academy, and organized famous salons at his home in Clamart for the Russian and French religious intelligentsia. Berdiaev's philosophical position, often called "Christian existentialism," promotes the values of freedom, individuality/ personhood (*lichnost'*), and creativity as the basis of a new Christian ethics. His writings were popular not only in Russian, but also in French- and

English-speaking circles, for their relevance to wide-ranging issues such as the meaning of history, the crisis of humanism in the technological age, and the dangers of totalitarianism. One of Berdiaev's core concerns was to establish a new Christian anthropology. It is precisely in this context that he turned to the Mother of God.

As was the case for Bulgakov, Berdiaev's conception of Mary was inexorably linked to his understanding of Sophia. Though not a Sophiologist per se, Berdiaev saw himself as an heir to Solov'ev and espoused many of that philosopher's fundamental positions.[41] For Berdiaev, Sophiology was a critical juncture in the development of modern Russian religious thought because it foregrounded the organic-mystical connection between God and creation that is too often ignored in Christian culture.

The contours of Berdiaev's Mariology become most clear when compared to Bulgakov's. In "On Sophiology" ("O Sofiologii," 1929), a review of Father Sergius's *The Burning Bush*, Berdiaev lauds his friend's boldness and creative power.[42] He commends Bulgakov's portrayal of the Mother of God, confirming that she is the greatest manifestation of created Sophia, the summit of creation's wisdom. However, Berdiaev also warns that Bulgakov's Sophiological-Mariological vision misses the mark, and may even be dangerously misleading. Berdiaev insists that the contemporary religious thinker's task is to focus on humanity: "Sophiology must be linked to anthropology."[43] For him, Bulgakov's Trinitarian Sophiology is too cosmological; it leaves humans "enveloped by a divine and cosmic energy."[44] A major problem for Berdiaev is that Bulgakov's Sophiology is too "feminine," or rather, too Marian and too maternal.

Like many of his predecessors and contemporaries (including Bulgakov), Berdiaev approached the metaphysics of gender from the basic premise that masculine (male) and feminine (female) are complementary opposites. This binary structure is consistent with Berdiaev's overall philosophy, where divine/creaturely, spirit/nature, order/chaos—and masculine/feminine—must be reconciled to achieve wholeness (Solov'evan "total unity"). While Bulgakov's vision of unity involved a certain interpenetration of two poles where neither loses its unique character, Berdiaev argued for sublimation. For him, the divine, spiritual, and orderly must sublimate—or "transfigure"—the creaturely, natural, and chaotic world.

Berdiaev's conception of gender and sexuality is even more categorical than Bulgakov's. The domain of feminine, the Berdiaev writes, must be sublimated by the masculine. The cosmos, the soul of the world, with its "mystical, animal-like warmth" is inherently feminine, and must be transfigured by humanity, which is a masculine principle endowed with virtues of freedom, creativity, and individuality.[45] Berdiaev felt that Bulgakov's Sophiology obfuscated this essential hierarchy by giving the feminine cosmic realm parity with, or even prominence over, the masculine *anthropos* (Greek term for "human").

Berdiaev saw this masculine/feminine dynamic at work in the human realm as well, and this binary opposition informs the interplay of Eros, sexuality, gender, and spiritual ethics at the core of his anthropology. In *Destiny of Man* (Sud'ba cheloveka, 1927), for example, Berdiaev ardently defends the erotic impulse as the divine spark that fuels true religious life, and argues for its reinstatement into Christian culture.[46] He links Eros, which has a positive spiritual value, to the masculine virtues of reason, individuality, and the spirit. The opposite of Eros is sex, its degraded counterpart, which is connected to generation and the natural world—all of which bear "feminine" traits. The fundamental tragedy of human existence, Berdiaev writes, is the antagonism between Eros and sex. Postlapsarian human beings are "bisected," divided into the "sick, wounded, disharmonious creatures" of man and woman.[47] Sex must be transfigured, he insists, spiritualized so that the divine wholeness in each individual can be restored. Only then will men and women return to their pre-eternal purity. That is why Berdiaev's ideal image of humankind is the androgyne, the sexless figure who transcends gender.[48]

Though Berdiaev recognizes that the conflict between sex and Eros exists in all people, he asserts that it is much stronger in women than in men. The pull of sex is inherent to women, Berdiaev writes; it is "primary, deep, all-pervasive . . . her sexual life is her entire life, it takes her over entirely," while in men sex is "secondary, more superficial and more differentiated into a special function."[49] A woman endangers a man's spiritual health; she drags him down, "enslaving him to sex and race."[50] The real culprit for Berdiaev is the generative process, and thus women—and mothers specifically—are overwhelmingly responsible for perpetuating fragmentation and death in the world.

Berdiaev's position on women's sexuality, marriage, and family echo not only views well established in patristic writing and traditional Christian culture, but also the anti-procreative strain of Russian religious philosophy, articulated most enthusiastically by Nikolai Fedorov (1827–1903) but present in Solov'ev as well.[51] Berdiaev defines the two warring essences in human beings as the "personal" (*lichnoe*) and the "generative" (*rodovoe*).[52] The personal essence is transcendent, while the generative is debased; the personal leads to union with God, the generative to perpetual death. There are two conflicting forms of love: "personal erotic" (*lichnaia polovaia*) and "procreative" (*rodovaia*).[53] True love is the highest expression of individuality, while procreative love is the most severe form of egoism. The urge to procreate is the selfish desire to continue one's line, its cravings stymie self-realization. Erotic love brings a person to the "perfection of individuality," while "the love of generation, which gives birth—fragments individuality."[54] Spiritual love can conquer nature, and virginity can end the cycle of life and death. The key word in Berdiaev's religious anthropology is virginity, *tsel'nost'*, which in Russian also means wholeness.[55]

The primacy of virginity lies at the core of Berdiaev's conception of Sophia, and, accordingly, of his Mariology. To him, "the feminine" is split between two opposite poles: one is earthly, fallen womanhood with its generative impulses, and the other is its celestial counterpart of pure, holy femininity. Even though Solov'ev argued that true Eros is expressed in *unconsummated* love, Berdiaev felt that his teacher over-sexualized Sophia. Instead, Berdiaev's most trusted authority on divine femininity was the medieval German mystic Jakob Boehme (1575–1624), who envisioned the *Jungfrau Sofia* (Virgin Sophia) as the epitome of female purity, and portrayed her without any of the erotic suggestion found in Russian Sophiology.[56] Only this understanding of a virginal Sophia, Berdiaev argues, can inspire the *anthropos* to overcome the pull of sex and transform it into divine Eros.

For Berdiaev, the ultimate example of Sophianic perfection in the world is the purest of women—the *Ever-Virgin* Mary (*Prisnodeva Mariia*). "In the Christian attitude toward sex," he writes, "the only profound statement has been through the cult of virginity connected with the veneration of the Virgin Mary."[57] Boehme is again Berdiaev's main source, because he understood Mary's main feature to be virginity, not motherhood.[58]

Skeptical of anything remotely generative, Berdiaev expresses concern about Bulgakov's exaltation of *Bogomaterinstvo*, emphasizing that womanhood is exemplified by Mary's Sophianic chastity that triumphs over the "wrong kind" of femininity.[59] Mary's virginity can lead individuals and society to God. Men must long for Mary as their beloved; women must emulate her purity. But, Berdiaev stressed, the Virgin must always be sublimated to the Logos, the divine masculine principle. This is another instance where he considers Russian Sophiology to be misleading: it tends to subordinate the masculine spirit to the feminine soul.[60] For Berdiaev, a case in point is Bulgakov's Sophiology, which risks letting "Godmotherhood overshadow Godmanhood," and Mary eclipse Christ.[61]

As a model for the spiritualized Christian collective, Berdiaev writes, the Virgin is the chaste body of the church whose salvific virtue extends outward. In *The Philosophy of the Free Spirit* (1927), he lyrically praises Mary's ability to reveal true divine beauty in the world:

> The Virgin Mary appears as the virginal principle … Sophia is Beauty. Beauty is the Heavenly Virgin. The illumination and transfiguration of the created and

natural world is the manifestation of Beauty. And when great art penetrates into the beauty of the cosmos, it sees beyond the ugliness of the natural world and sees the virginity, the sophianicity of the world, the divine idea of what it should be.[62]

For Berdiaev, the Blessed Virgin inspires the authentic creativity that can lead humanity to transfigure the cosmos and move the world closer to God.

## BOGOMATERINSTVO IN SKOBTSOVA'S POETIC AND SOCIAL ORTHODOXY

Though Berdiaev's Marian emphasis may have diverged from Bulgakov's in significant ways, a comparison of their writings reveals how both men, known for their progressive Orthodox thought, were in fact strongly bound to certain trappings of inherited traditions. Their adherence to conventional beliefs about gender and sexuality weakened their advocacy of humankind's spiritual dignity, and thus compromised the overall coherence of their religious visions. An alternative picture of Mary in the Paris School emerges in the works of Elizaveta Skobtsova, who was able to overcome some of these limitations and thus offer a more robust model of "the feminine" for modern Orthodoxy.

Skobtsova was born to an upper-class family in Riga, but received her intellectual, spiritual, and political formation in both St. Petersburg and the Black Sea town of Anapa, home to her family's ancestral estate.[63] She began writing poetry as a precocious teenager in the 1910s while frequenting the capital's modernist literary salons. Her political consciousness grew in the years leading up to the revolution, and she spent 1917–1918 serving various political posts as a member of the Socialist Revolutionary Party. Though she occasionally struggled with her faith, Skobtsova eventually embraced a self-styled version of radical Christianity. Following the Bolshevik takeover and during the chaos of the Civil War, Skobtsova decided to leave Russia. In 1924, she and her husband settled in Paris with their three small children.

In emigration, Skobtsova fully entrenched herself in the Orthodox community of the Paris School. She wrote religious essays, poetry and fiction, painted and embroidered icons, and held leadership roles in various émigré social-benevolent organizations. Bulgakov and Berdiaev were part of her intellectual and spiritual inner circle; Father Sergius was her confessor, and she was a regular participant at Berdiaev's Religious-Philosophical Academy. Because of her nonconformist nature, Skobtsova's decision to become a nun in 1932 surprised many. From that point forward, "Mother Maria," as she was called, continued her creative efforts and embarked on large-scale community welfare projects. The Mother of God was the unifying figure of Skobtsova's mature oeuvre, the point where her artistic, poetic, and social work converge.

In her youth, Skobtsova had first encountered the phenomenon of the "divine feminine" in the verse of her Symbolist friends Alexander Blok and Viacheslav Ivanov. Their influence is clear in many of Skobtsova's poems from her Russian period, which depict a benevolent and cosmic maternal presence. In poems such as "Will I listen to quiet prayers?" ("Budu li tikhim molitvam vnimat'?")[64] from her 1914 collection *The Road* (Doroga), Skobtsova's lyrical narrator invokes the "luminous Mother" whose bright protecting veil—the starry sky—illumines the path of her life. In this and other poems, Skobtsova paints a picture of a mystical, omnipresent female divinity by freely combining imagery from Symbolism, Christian Mariology, and the Russian folk conception of Mother Damp Earth (*mat' syra zemlia*).

In her Parisian years, the feminine divine force in Skobtsova's lyrical and theological imagination became explicitly Marian and was anchored in the concept of motherhood. She knew Bulgakov and Berdiaev's writings on the Mother of God, and engaged their Mariologies as she developed her own. Though she supported many of Berdiaev's core positions, Skobtsova disagreed strongly with the philosopher's anti-procreative stance. Polemicizing with him in essays such as "Birth and Creation" ("Rozhdenie i tvorenie," 1931), Skobtsova defends the generative principle as the locus of creativity and freedom.[65] Her approach to Mary was more akin to Bulgakov's, whose notion of *Bogomaterinstvo* became her main operative term. However, she noted the theologian's reticence about the spiritual significance of human motherhood.[66] Skobtsova's unique Godmotherhood gave Orthodoxy a model of Mary with an immediacy and presence in daily life missing from the Mariologies of her male colleagues.

For Skobtsova, the Mother of God provided insight for mending the fragmented state of the modern world. In essays such as "The Second Gospel Commandment" ("Vtoraia evangel'skaia zapoved'," 1939), she decries the over-individualistic ethos of both secular and Christian culture that emphasizes personal, independent striving for God.[67] Mother Maria felt that her generation's main task was to save both the Orthodox Church and society around them by formulating a new theology of community and social engagement.

Her vision for Orthodox reform began from a familiar starting point. While a gender dynamic is key, Mother Maria eschewed the biologically or sexually defined framework relied on by Bulgakov and Berdiaev. Rather, her notions of "masculine" and "feminine" can be inferred from her scriptural basis, that is, from her readings of Christ's two commandments in Matthew 22:37–39 and the events of the Crucifixion. In "The Second Gospel Commandment" Skobtsova reminds her readers that the first Gospel commandment—"Love the Lord your God with all your heart and with all your soul and with all your mind"—calls on the individual to strive for personal knowledge of God. Christ's self-sacrifice at Golgotha epitomized love of God, and thus reveals "masculine" love. The second Gospel commandment—"Love your neighbor as yourself"—calls for love of the other. Mary showed perfect love for the other at the cross, and thus represents "feminine" love. For Skobtsova, Christ and Mary together, Godmanhood *and* Godmotherhood, fulfill Christ's directive. When there is love for God *and* love for other, Skobtsova writes, people "commune through one Divine Love" and the world moves toward total unity.[68] For Mother Maria, the spiritual exercise of *imitatio Christi* (imitation of Christ) must be supplemented by *imitatio Matris* (imitation of the Mother); each person must follow the path of both the God*man* and the God*mother*.

What constitutes this Marian love? Skobtsova gives her fullest explanation in the 1939 essay, "On the Imitation of the Mother of God" ("O podrazhanii Bogomateri").[69] Here, she portrays Mary at the cross not as the stoic, motionless mourner of conventional Orthodox iconography, nor as the emotionally rapt mother known in Catholicism as the *Mater Dolorosa*. Rather, Mary is a bold, active presence. Her Marian touchstone is the double-edged sword (*oboiudoostryi mech'*), the "cross and sword" motif taken from the elder Symeon's prophesy to Mary that "a sword shall pierce your heart also" (Lk 2:22–40). According to the exegetical tradition, the cross of Christ is the sword that pierces his mother's heart; Symeon's prophesy foretells Mary's impending anguish, but also indicates her participation in Christ's mission. Skobtsova adds an explicitly social dimension to this exegesis. For her, the unity of the sword and cross represents the indivisibility of the first and second Gospel commandments, and the necessary integration of personal and collective spiritual pursuits.

At Golgotha, Skobtsova writes, Mary revealed the heart of the Christian social ethos. The Mother of God is for Skobtsova "the great symbol of any genuine relationship among people" because she exemplifies radical, transformative compassion for the other.[70] Mary's suffering was not just her own, Skobtsova insists; Godmotherhood teaches an inherently public lesson. Just as Christ's self-sacrifice gave the world a new moral code, so did Mary's suffering at the foot of the cross. "The two-edged sword," she writes, ". . . teaches us all something and obliges us to something."[71] At Golgotha, Mary charged humanity with a new task by demonstrating how to act toward the other: "It is precisely on the route of Godmotherhood," she writes, "that we must find the justification and substantiation of all our hopes, find the religious and mystical meaning of true human communion."[72] At the cross, Mary annihilated her own will and became entirely receptive to the other. The cross pierced her heart like a sword, and she transformed maternal anguish into compassion. This is "the true measure of love," Skobtsova insists, "the limit to which the human soul should aspire." One must accept the neighbor's cross like Mary did, willingly participate in another's Golgotha "by opening our own heart to the stroke of the double-edged sword." Mary's sword teaches how to truly love one's neighbor, and thus can be the main tool for creating relationships and ordering communities.[73]

By circumventing the topic of sexuality entirely, Skobtsova is able to propose that Godmotherhood is a model not just for women, but all people. Taking up Bulgakov's idea that each human soul unites in itself the image of both Christ and Mary, Skobtsova describes each person as "a diptych of the Mother of God with her Child," the *Bogochelovek* and the *Bogomater*'.[74] Whereas Bulgakov follows the conventional line of reasoning that Christ is the model for men and Mary is the model for women, Skobtsova stresses that all human beings—female *and* male—are essentially bound to *both* Christ and Mary, and must engage both: "The Son of God and his Mother—these are the age-old archetypes, symbols by which the soul orients itself on its religious paths."[75] Imitating Mary is just as fundamental to human nature as imitating Christ: "It is completely natural for humanity to strive to realize in itself the image of the Mother of God in human Godmotherhood."[76]

For Skobtsova, radical Marian love can transfigure society by bringing people into communion with each other, and thus into communion with God. As was the case for Bulgakov and Berdiaev, the Mother of God was central to Skobtsova's ecclesiology, only her Marian vision of the church bears a distinctly *social* character. Mary's active material compassion binds the *ecclesia* together, Skobtsova writes.[77] From the time of the crucifixion, the Mother of God has co-suffered with her children, the ecclesial community, and to this day the Marian church continuously recapitulates the drama of Golgotha:

> As the Mother of Godmanhood—the church—is pierced even now by the suffering of this body of Christ, the suffering of each member of this Body. In other words, all the countless crosses that humanity takes on its shoulders to follow Christ also become countless swords eternally piercing her maternal heart. She continues to co-participate, co-suffer with each human soul, as then on Golgotha.[78]

In compassionate acts, the church, the collective, and Mary become one: "Godmotherhood—in Her and with Her—belongs to the whole church. The Mother Church—in Her and with Her—participates in Godmotherhood."[79] The entire community participates in the Son's self-sacrifice and the Mother's compassion, Skobtsova writes. Every person who imitates Mary takes part in her work, and redefines the community as a tight-knit mystical family. Each individual maternally embraces all of society: "the human soul thereby adopts the whole body of Christ for itself, the whole of Godmanhood, and every human being individually."[80] When you truly love another person, Skobtsova writes, you do not just recognize the divine image in them, you give birth to Christ within yourself.

Though Skobtsova believed that Mary's Godmotherhood exists in all people, she felt that her own experience of motherhood, particularly of maternal suffering, gave her special insight into this mystery. Having lost two of her three children—Nastia, her youngest, died from meningitis in 1926, and Gaiana in 1936 from typhus—she was intimately familiar with maternal pain. As expressed in many of her intensely personal poems of the 1930s, Skobtsova looked to the Mother of God for inspiration to transform her own deep, personal anguish into active love for the other.[81] For example, in "Mother, you and I have a pact" ("Mat' my s toboiu dogovor") from the cycle *Protecting Veil* (Pokrov), Skobtsova poetically renders her intimate relationship with the Mother of God and their material service to creation. Armed with radical compassion, Skobtsova's lyrical narrator joins Mary in her prophetic maternal work of gathering the "children" around her.

> Мать, мы с тобою договор,
> Завет мы заключим любовный, —
> Птенцов из гнезд, зверей из нор
> Принять, любить, объять покровно.
>
> И человеческих свобод
> Тяжелый и священный камень
> Под самый Божий небосвод
> Своими вознести руками.[82]

> [Mother, you and I have a pact,
> We'll make a covenant of love, —
> That the birds in nests, the animals of caves,
> We'll accept, love, embrace in our *pokrov*.
>
> And humanity's freedom,
> That heavy and sacred stone,
> Up to vaults of heaven,
> We'll raise with our own hands.]

In her "covenant of love" with Mary, Skobtsova's lyrical "I" succors humanity and nature, and together they establish a new law—the law of motherly love—to reign on earth. The narrator's tender maternal embrace is the Sophianic act that transforms the cosmos by bringing it to God.

Skobtsova's commitment to transfigurative Marian love was not only rhetorical; she enacted it in everyday life, and even in her manner of death. She called her monastic profession "all-embracing motherhood" and felt it was her duty to take care of everyone around her who was in need. [83] As a nun, Mother Maria devoted most of her time to social outreach, opening a network of halfway houses, canteens, and nursing homes to care for the destitute émigrés. When France was occupied by the Nazis, Skobtsova saw that those who needed her most were Parisian Jews. She joined the Resistance, and her home on Rue de Lourmel became a safe haven for the persecuted. For this, Mother Maria was soon arrested and sent to the Ravensbrück concentration camp where she paid the ultimate price for her radical maternal protection. Ravensbrück survivors recalled how Skobtsova continued her compassionate service even in these most extreme conditions. Her obligation was the same as it had been before—to enact Marian love and create community with those around her. Skobtsova's final creative effort encapsulates her hope and faith, her aesthetic credo and spiritual cause. With her last strength she embroidered an icon of the Mother of God tenderly holding the crucified infant Christ in her arms.[84]

CONCLUSION

In their Marian writings, Bulgakov, Berdiaev, and Skobtsova negotiated tradition and innovation in order to articulate a new vision of contemporary Orthodox culture. The figure of Mary continued to be a potent source of inspiration for Orthodox thought in the West as it faced the shifting geopolitical, spiritual, and sociocultural realities of the later twentieth century. In the 1950s, the lay theologian Pavel Evdokimov (1901–1970) engaged the burgeoning feminist movement by integrating Carl Jung's ideas with those of Bulgakov's to describe Mary as the "feminine archetype" and all women as bearers of special "female charisms" (spiritual gifts).[85] Toward the end of the twentieth century, Behr-Sigel became an important voice in Christian feminism. Picking up the thread present implicitly in Skobtsova's work, Behr-Sigel rejected the gender essentialism of her predecessors, and pursued the ecclesiastical and social implications of the idea of Mary as a model for *all* humanity.[86]

Thus the "creative renewal" of Orthodox Mariology can be traced from the Silver Age and through the span of the twentieth century, a period when the faith faced acute questions about its role in modern life. Even in the twenty-first century, with increased debate about gender, sexuality, family, and society in Orthodox circles in Russia and abroad, Mary continues to be a main juncture between religious beliefs and their expression in the lives of the faithful. With her complex, multifaceted presence, the Mother of God remains at the center of the Christian imagination as both an instance of joint orthodoxy, but also, to use Behr-Sigel's words, a figure who allows the "freedom . . . to interpret and appropriate the mystery according to times and places."[87]

## Notes

1. Elisabeth Behr-Sigel, *The Ministry of Women in the Church* (Redondo Beach, CA: Oakwood Publications, 1991), 182.

2. Solov'ev discusses Sophia in *Chteniia o bogochelovechestve* (Lectures on divine humanity), published in *Sobranie sochinenii*, ed. S. M. Solov'ev and E. L. Radlov (St. Petersburg: Prosveshchenie, 1912), 3:1–181.

3. The literature on Russian Sophiology is voluminous. For a comprehensive analysis of Solov'ev's Sophiology, see Judith Deutsch Kornblatt's *Divine Sophia: The Wisdom Writings of Vladimir Solovyov* (Ithaca, NY: Cornell University Press, 2009). On Sophia in Silver Age writing more broadly, see Kristi Groberg's "The Feminine Occult Sophia in the Russian Religious Renaissance: A Bibliographical Essay," *Canadian-American Slavic Studies* 26, no. 4 (1992): 197–240. The Russian scholar Oleg Riabov has written several large-scale studies on philosophies of gender throughout Russian history. See especially his *Russkaia filosofiia zhenstvennosti: XI–XX veka* (Ivanovo: Iunona, 1999) and *Zhenshchina i zhenstvennost' v filosofii serebrianogo veka* (Ivanovo: Ivanovskii gosudarstvennyi universitet, 1997).

4. Especially notable are the efforts of the lay theologian Pavel Evdokimov (1901–1970), a student of Bulgakov's, whose interest in Simone de Beauvoir led him to engage with Western feminism. See in particular his *Woman and Salvation of the World: A Christian Anthropology on the Charisms of Women*, trans. Anthony P. Gythiel (Crestwood, NY: St. Vladimir's Seminary Press, 1994), first published in French in 1958. For an overview of the impact of the women's movement in Orthodoxy in North America, see "Women in Orthodox and Oriental Orthodox Traditions," in *Encyclopedia of Women and Religion in North America*, ed. Rosemary Skinner Keller, Rosemary Radford Ruether, and Marie Cantlon, vol. 2 (Bloomington: Indiana University Press, 2006): 509–532.

5. Key studies on Mary in Christian culture and society include Marina Warner's *Alone of All Her Sex: The Myth and Cult of the Virgin Mary* (New York: Alfred A. Knopf, 1976); Rosemary Radford Ruether's *Mary: The Feminine Face of the Church* (Philadelphia, PA: Westminster Press, 1977); and Jaroslav Pelikan's *Mary through the Centuries: Her Place in the History of Culture* (New Haven, CT: Yale University Press, 1996).

6. See Michael Aksenov-Meerson's *Trinity of Love in Modern Russian Theology: The Love Paradigm and the Retrieval of Western Medieval Love Mysticism in Modern Russian Trinitarian Thought (from Solov'ev to Bulgakov)* (Quincy, IL: Franciscan Press, 1998), especially xiv–xvi.

7. The question of Sophia's gender is not unambiguous. As Kornblatt points out, while "Sophia" stands for mystical, idealized femininity, Solov'ev's writings also indicate that her gender can actually be rather fluid (*Divine Wisdom*, 38).

8. See especially Florenskii's "Letter Ten: Sophia," in his *Pillar and Ground of the Truth: An Essay in Orthodox Theodicy in Twelve Letters*, trans. Boris Jakim (Princeton, NJ: Princeton University Press, 1997).

9. From the hymn honoring the Mother of God, "It is Truly Meet," heard frequently in the Orthodox cycle of services.

10. Ibid., 281.

11. The topic of gender in Silver Age circles has been addressed by Olga Matich in *Erotic Utopia: The Decadent Imagination in Russia's Fin de Siècle* (Madison: University of Wisconsin Press, 2005) and Jenifer Presto, *Beyond the Flesh: Alexander Blok, Zinaida Gippius, and the Symbolist Sublimation of Sex* (Madison: University of Wisconsin Press, 2008).

12. Maternity is a central point of interest for both secular and religious feminist critics. See, for example, the works of Catholic feminists Rosemary Radford Ruether (see note 5 above) and Elizabeth Johnson's *Truly Our Sister: A Theology of Mary in the Communion of Saints* (New York: Continuum, 2006). The psychoanalytic critic Julia Kristeva has addressed Mary and motherhood in "Stabat Mater," *Poetics Today* 6, nos. 1–2 (1985): 133–52 and "Motherhood According to Giovanni Bellini" in *Desire in Language: A Semiotic Approach to Literature and Art* (New York: Columbia University Press, 1982), 237–69.

13. On Bulgakov's pre-emigration life and works, see Catherine Evtuhov's *The Cross and the Sickle: Sergei Bulgakov and the Fate of Russian Religious Philosophy* (Ithaca, NY: Cornell University Press, 1997).

14. For instance, in 1924, Metropolitan Antonii (Khrapovitskii) attacked Bulgakov's Sophiology in an article in *Novoe vremia*, an émigré newspaper published in Belgrade.

15. Bulgakov's 1937 volume, *Sophia, Wisdom of God: An Outline of Sophiology*, offers a good synopsis of his mature Sophiology. Citations here are to the 1993 reprint by Lindesfarne Books, Hudson, NY.

16. See Paul Valliere's seminal essay, "Sophia as the Dialogue of Orthodoxy with Modern Civilization," in *Russian Religious Thought*, ed. Judith Deutsch Kornblatt and Richard F. Gustafson (Madison: University of Wisconsin Press, 1996), 176–92, as well as his monograph, *Modern Russian Theology: Bukharev, Soloviev, Bulgakov; Orthodox Theology in a New Key* (Grand Rapids, MI: Eerdmans, 2000).

17. Though Bulgakov and his ideas were pushed to the margins of Orthodoxy, he is finding an increasing number of advocates both in Orthodox and non-Orthodox circles. Today, Bulgakov's contributions are seen as pivotal for Christian thought by scholars such as Paul Valliere, Archbishop Rowan Williams, Michael Plekon, Brandon Galaher, Paul Gavrilyuk, Miroslav Tataryn, and others.

18. See, for example, Valliere's analysis in *Modern Russian Theology*, 320–28; articles by Andrew Louth, "Father Sergii Bulgakov on the Mother of God," *St. Vladimir's Theological Quarterly* 49, nos. 1–2 (2005): 145–64, and Robert Slesinski, "Sergius Bulgakov on the Glorification of the Mother of God," *Orientalia christiana periodica* 73, no. 1 (2007): 97–116. A major contribution to scholarship on Bulgakov's Mariology is Thomas Allan Smith's 2009 English translation of Bulgakov's *Kupina neopalimaia: Opyt dogmaticheskogo istolkovaniia nekotorykh chert v pravoslavnom pochitanii Bogomateri* (Paris: YMCA Press, 1927).

19. See especially the sections "The Incarnation of Divine Motherhood," "The Ever-Virgin," "The Bride That Is Not a Bride," and "Liturgics and Iconography," in Brandon Gallaher and Irina Kukota, trans. and eds., "Hypostasis and Hypostaticity: Scholia to *The Unfading Light*," *St. Vladimir's Theological Quarterly* 49, no. 1 (2005): 5–46.

20. Citations here are to Thomas Allan Smith, trans., *The Burning Bush: On the Orthodox Veneration of the Mother of God* (Grand Rapids, MI: Eerdmans, 2009).

21. See Bulgakov's *The Burning Bush*, 69–76, and Gallaher and Kukota, "Hypostasis and Hypostaticity," 34.

22. Bernice Rosenthal, "The Nature and Function of Sophia in Sergei Bulgakov's Prerevolutionary Thought," in *Russian Religious Thought*, ed. Judith Deutsch Kornblatt and Richard F. Gustafson (Madison: University of Wisconsin Press, 1996), 154–75.

23. Bulgakov, *The Burning Bush*, 80–84.

24. Ibid., 82.

25. Ibid., 83.

26. Ibid., 83.

27. Ibid., 82.

28. Ibid., 80.

29. Ibid., 85.

30. Ibid., 87.

31. Published in Sergius Bulgakov, *Churchly Joy: Orthodox Devotions for the Church Year*, trans. Boris Jakim (Grand Rapids, MI: Eerdmans, 2008).

32. Ibid., 18.

33. Ibid., 22.

34. Ibid., 19.

35. Bulgakov, *The Comforter*, trans. Boris Jakim (Grand Rapids, MI: Eerdmans, 2004), 323.

36. See Valliere's discussion of Eros in Bulgakov's emigration-period writings in *Modern Russian Theology*, 366–71. A. P. Kozyrev addresses the topic in light of the discovery of Bulgakov's unpublished essays about gender and sexuality from the mid-1920s, "Muzhskoe i Zhenskoe v Bozhestve" and "Muzhskoe i Zhenskoe." See *S. N. Bulgakov: Religiozno-filosofskii put': Mezhdunarodnaia nauchnaia konferentsiia*, ed. A. P. Kozyrev and M. A. Vasil'eva (Moscow: Russkii put', 2003), 333–95.

37. Bulgakov, *The Burning Bush*, 97.

38. More on Marian interpretations of the Song of Songs in the Western tradition can be found in Rachel Fulton's *From Judgment to Passion: Devotion to Christ and the Virgin Mary, 800–1200* (New York: Columbia University Press, 2002).

39. See Bulgakov's *The Burning Bush*, 103–5; *The Comforter*, 326–28; and *The Bride of the Lamb*, trans. Boris Jakim (Grand Rapids, MI: Eerdmans, 2002), 525–26.

40. A traditionalist reaction to Bulgakov's Mariology-Sophiology is Bishop John (Maximovich)'s *The Orthodox Veneration of the Mother of God* (Platina, CA: St. Herman Press, 1978), while Georges Florovskii's "The Ever-Virgin Mother of God: The Teaching about Virgin Mary," in *Creation and Redemption* (Belmont, MA: Nordland, 1976) and Vladimir Lossky's "The All-Holy," and "Mariology," in *The Orthodox Church in the Ecumenical Movement*, ed. C. G. Patelos (Geneva: World Council of Churches, 1978), 187–98, are more moderate. On the controversy surrounding Bulgakov's Sophiology in general, see *St. Vladimir's Theological Quarterly* 49, nos. 1–2 (2005), which contains: "The Charges of Heresy against Sergii Bulgakov: The Majority and Minority Reports of Evlogii's Commission and the Final Report of the Bishops' Conference," 47–66, and Alexis Klimoff's essay, "Georges Florovsky and the Sophiological Controversy," 67–100.

41. Mikhail Sergeev argues that Berdiaev was more of a Sophiologist than he himself acknowledged. See his chapter, "Sophia in Philosophical Discourse" in *Sophiology in Russian Orthodoxy: Solov'ev, Bulgakov, Losskii, and Berdiaev* (Lewiston, NY: Edwin Mellen Press, 2006).

42. Nikolai Berdiaev, "O Sofiologii: Retsenziia na knigu Prot. Sergiia Bulgakova: Lestvitsa Iakovlia; Ob angelakh," *Put'* 16 (1929): 95–99. The article reviews all three books of Bulgakov's so-called "minor trilogy" (*The Burning Bush*, 1927; *Friend of the Bridegroom*, 1927; and *Jacob's Ladder*, 1929).

43. Nikolai Berdiaev, *Freedom and the Spirit*, trans. Oliver Clarke (London: G. Bles, 1935), 300.

44. Berdiaev, "O Sofiologii," 97.

45. Ibid.

46. Nikolai Berdiaev, *The Destiny of Man*, trans. Natalie Duddington (New York: Harper, 1960), 188. See especially the section "Sex, Marriage, and Love," 232–42.

47. Ibid., 83.

48. Ibid. A good discussion of the androgyne in Russian religious thought is in Matich's *Erotic Utopia*, 71–77.

49. Ibid., 237.

50. Ibid., 245.

51. Important patristic texts on marriage, family, and women's sexuality are the fourth-century treatises by Gregory of Nyssa and John Chrysostom, both called "On Virginity." Matich addresses the anti-procreative strain in modern Russian religious thought in *Erotic Utopia*. On Berdiaev specifically, see Eric Naiman's "Historectomies: On the Metaphysics of Reproduction in a Utopian Age," in *Sexuality and the Body in Russian Culture*, eds. Jane T. Costlow, Stephanie Sandler, and Judith Vowles (Stanford,

CA: Stanford University Press, 1993): 255–76, and Robin Aizelwood, "Berdiaev and Chaadaev: Russia and Feminine Passivity," in *Gender and Sexuality in Russian Civilization*, ed. Peter I. Barta (London: Routledge, 2001), 121–40.

52. Berdiaev, "Metafizika pola i liubvi," cited from a collection of Berdiaev's writing, *Eros i lichnost': Filosofiia pola i liubvi*, ed. V. P. Shestakov (Moscow: Promitei, 1989), 22.

53. Ibid., 26.

54. Ibid.

55. For a discussion on virginity in the early church, see Elizabeth Castelli's "Virginity and Its Meaning for Women's Sexuality in Early Christianity," *The Journal of Feminist Studies in Religion* 2, no. 1 (Spring 1986): 61–88.

56. See especially Berdiaev's article, "Iz etiudov o Iakove Beme: Etiud II. Uchenie o Sofii i androgine. Ia. Beme i russkie sofiologicheskie techeniia," *Put'* 21 (1930): 34–62.

57. Berdiaev, *The Destiny of Man*, 241.

58. Berdiaev, "Iz etiudov o Iakove Beme," 37.

59. Berdiaev, *Freedom and the Spirit*, 301.

60. Ibid.

61. Berdiaev, "O Sofiologii," 89–99.

62. Berdiaev, *Freedom and the Spirit*, 301.

63. The authoritative biography of Skobtsova is Sergei Hackel's *A Pearl of Great Price* (Crestwood, NY: St. Vladimir's Seminary Press, 1981).

64. Mat' Mariia (Elizaveta Skobtsova), *Ravnina russkaia: Stikhotvoreniia i poemy, p'esy-misterii, khudozhestvennaia i avtobiograficheskaia proza, pis'ma*, ed. A. N. Shustov (St. Petersburg: Iskusstvo, 2001), 45.

65. *Rozhdenie i tvorenie* was republished in Mat' Mariia, *Zhatva dukha: Religiozno-filosofskie sochineniia*, ed. A. N. Shustov (St. Petersburg: Iskusstvo, 2004).

66. See Skobtsova's essay, "O sude Solomona i o materinstve," where she challenges some of the ideas in both "Hypostasis and Hypostaticity" and *The Burning Bush*. The essay—unpublished in Skobtsova's lifetime—has been transcribed and translated into English in Natalia Ermolaev, "Motherhood, Modernism, and Mariology: The Poetry and Theology of Elizaveta Skobtsova (Mother Maria)" (PhD diss., Columbia University, 2010).

67. "The Second Gospel Commandment," in *Mother Maria Skobtsova: Essential Writings*, trans. Richard Pevear and Larissa Volokhonsky (Maryknoll, NY: Orbis Books, 2003), 59.

68. Ibid, 59.

69. Skobtsova, "On the Imitation of the Mother of God," in *Mother Maria Skobtsova*, 61–74.

70. Ibid., 68.

71. Ibid., 67.

72. Ibid.

73. Ibid., 71–72.

74. Ibid., 69.

75. Ibid., 70.

76. Skobtsova, "Pochitanie Bogomateri," in *Zhatva dukha*, 186.

77. Skobtsova, "On the Imitation," 69.

78. Ibid.

79. Skobtsova, "Pochitanie Bogomateri," 186.

80. Skobtsova, "On the Imitation," 71.

81. See Skobtsova's book of poems, *Stikhi* (Berlin: Petropolis Press, 1937).

82. Mat' Mariia, *Ravnina russkaia*, 187.

83. Cited in Hackel's *Pearl of Great Price*, 16.

84. Skobtsova and her collaborators, including her son Iura, were arrested in 1943. Skobstova died in the Ravensbrück gas chamber on 31 March 1945 (see Hackel's "Martyrdom" chapter in *Pearl of Great Price*). In May 2004 Mother Maria and her collaborators were canonized as saints of the Orthodox Church.

85. See especially Paul Evdokimov's *La femme et le salut du monde: Chrétienne les charismes de la femme* (Paris: Casterman, 1958).

86. Behr-Sigel is perhaps best remembered for her support of women's ordination. See, for example, "Mary and Women," in *Discerning the Signs of the Times: The Vision of Elisabeth Behr-Sigel,* ed. Michael Plekon and Sarah Hinlicky (Crestwood, NY: St. Vladimir's Seminary Press, 2001), and her book with Bishop Kallistos Ware, *The Ordination of Women in the Orthodox Church* (Geneva: World Council of Churches Publications, 2000).

87. Behr-Sigel, *Ministry of Women*, 182.

# 9

## The Madonna Painter
### Pimen Maksimovich Sofronov and Marian Iconography
### (1898–1973)

ROY R. ROBSON

IN 1970, THE ICON SCHOLAR and lawyer Ivan Czap described a recent trip to Western Europe, where he had sought out the work of his old friend, Pimen Maksimovich Sofronov. Czap wrote that he cherished "the lasting memory of the first time I saw an icon by Sofronov. That was almost twenty years ago, in France ... In the Mediterranean areas he is called 'the Madonna painter.' You will understand why when you look upon his depictions of the *Bogoroditsa*."[1] Unfortunately, Czap did not elaborate on exactly who gave Sofronov this exalted title, nor did he explain its context.

Careful consideration of Sofronov's works, however, can explain just what Czap likely meant with his kind words. Perhaps more than any other Russian iconographer of the twentieth century, Sofronov beautifully captured the multiple tensions of his era: ancient and modern, master and student, and especially the fluid relationship between traditional designs and individual style. By subtly altering Mary's body pose and redirecting her gaze, Sofronov simultaneously glorified and humanized the Theotokos.[2] As his career progressed, Sofronov increasingly included elements from Roman Catholic traditions that also emphasized this characterization of Mary. Paradoxically, the inclusion of non-Orthodox Christian elements may define this Old Believer as a modernist icon painter in both form and philosophy.

## *PRORISI*: PAINTING *INSIDE* THE LINES

Sofronov's early training resembled that of generations of other Old Believer iconographers—he learned from a master through the use of patterns handed down for generations. Sofronov was born in 1898 in the village of Tikhotka, in the Prichudia region of Estonia near Lake Peipus. By the time Pimen Maksimovich was born, the region was already well known for its iconography, especially the studio of Gavriil Efimovich Frolov. At twelve years old, and following the death of his father, Sofronov was apprenticed to Frolov, who in turn became a father figure. In fact, Sofronov's iconographic style can be traced directly to Frolov's influence.[3] Living and working in Frolov's studio, Sofronov absorbed the style and techniques maintained by Fedoseevtsy Old Believers, and indeed spent a short time at the well-known Preobrazhenskoe Cemetery in Moscow. Along with Frolov's other apprentices, Sofronov learned to transfer the outline of iconographic images onto prepared boards by using cartoons called *perevody* or *prorisi*. His contemporary and noted icon restorer F. A. Kalikin described the process this way:

> If an icon painter had to make a replica of an icon outline, he delicately ground some black paint with garlic juice, then he made an outline of the whole composition of the icon with a squirrel-hair brush, the outline being neither thinner nor thicker than the original. When the outline was completed, he took a blank sheet of paper, put it onto the just-outlined icon and holding it with his left hand, he opened a part of the sheet with his right hand and slightly breathed on it to moisten a portion of the outline. Then he rubbed the moistened paper with his right hand and the black paint mixed with garlic juice left a negative imprint on the white paper. This very imprint of the negative outline is called the *proris*.[4]

The *proris* was thus a negative imprint of the original outline. The iconographer could then pinprick this outline hundreds of times, allowing the image to be transferred to a new gesso-prepared board by rubbing the paper with a cloth bag full of charcoal dust.[5]

The use of *prorisi* faithfully transmitted the main outlines of an icon, and a *prorisi* might be handed down from generation to generation. *Prorisi* thus tracked design across multiple generations and cataloged influential artists because the *prorisi* were often signed. A name provided provenance to authenticate an image, while also calling attention to individual artists, a practice widely scorned for finished icons. One signed *proris* from Sofronov's collection reads "this image done by Mikhail Dmitriev, son of Padtsov." Another was inscribed "done in the city of Vitebsk, in the home of Ioann Petrovich Iudin. In the year 7384 [1875] since the beginning of the world, the month of July on the 13th day. The icon was brought to the Edinovertsy church by the Priest Kliment." In a few cases, iconographers experimented with their *prorisi*, pushing beyond traditional boundaries and toward Western-style artist sketches. One, signed "Merzlekov," shows a highly personalized, naturalistic style. Later, Ivan Czap noted the inherent tension between traditional and individual style in his homage to Sofronov:

> Every icon of course bears the imprint of the artist's personality—yet in an ordered, controlled way. For with us Orthodox, the spirit of the individual personality is sensed always through the discipline of tradition, which rules every painter of icons. The freedom allowed the artist is never one which obtrudes a personal note; only the traditional teaching of the Church comes through loud and strong, while the artists [sic] hand guides the understanding. This is the proof, indeed, that as in the Incarnation the Spirit sanctified our material world, so too in the non-naturalistic discipline of the iconographic scheme the divine world has a "real" reflection in the icons.[6]

Sofronov collected *prorisi*, including those done by Frolov, other apprentices, and past iconographers. He used them both for his own work and to help his teaching.

Sofronov also recognized the artistic value of his icons. In 1929, he sold a series of "teaching icons" to Helge Kjellin, a professor at the University of Riga. Each one showed the steps in the process of painting an icon of the Mother of God of Tenderness. The first panel had just an outline as copied from a *proris*. The second and third panels illustrated the technique of layering colors. The fourth was a finished icon.[7] At the Grebenshchikovskaia Community, the Icon Society, and the Kondakov Institute, Sofronov joined his students in exhibiting his works to the public, vividly illustrating the idea that icons should exist as art for public consumption and education. Icons lined the wall and leaned on stands rather than hanging as one would see them in a church or home. This offered people the opportunity to study the images up close.

From 1929 to 1939, Sofronov seemed to be continually on the move. In addition to painting and teaching at his home base—the Grebenshchikovskaia Old Believer community in Riga—Sofronov also taught icon-painting to a number of prominent White Russian émigrés. These contacts led to more teaching at the Icon Association in Paris and the Kondakov Institute in Prague. Most notably, Sofronov became acquainted with Grand Duchess

Marina Petrovna Galitzine and Princess Natalia Grigorevna Iashvil, and through them he began to move in the highest circles of émigré aristocracy.[8] In Prague, Sofronov wrote a short treatise on iconographic technique that complemented a pamphlet he published in Paris in 1931.

Based on their relationship in Paris, Grand Duchess Marina Petrovna recommended Sofronov to King Alexander I of Yugoslavia. In preparation for his first royal commission, Sofronov studied icons and churches across Serbia and Macedonia. As a result, he concluded that the Serbian style was "more heterogeneous" than that of Russia,[9] but the "murals in the ancient monasteries of Serbia and Montenegro were an important influence in perfecting my comprehension and painting of icons and murals. What astonishing treasures of religious art! I cannot help but feel that Byzantine art came to Russia via Serbian and Bulgarian masters."[10] After the assassination of King Alexander, Sofronov found a patron in the Serbian Orthodox Patriarch Varnava. Under the patriarch's patronage, Sofronov founded a school for iconography at the monastery in Rakovitsa, Yugoslavia.[11] Through his commissions and teaching Sofronov continued to meet prominent émigrés, including the future Saint John of Shanghai, who had just been consecrated as bishop by Patriarch Varnava.

In 1939, Vatican Librarian (and later Italian Prime Minister) Alcide de Gasperi invited Sofronov to Rome to paint an iconostasis as the centerpiece for a future exhibition of "sacred missionary and eastern art."[12] Arriving shortly before the outbreak of World War II hostilities, Sofronov and his wife Nadezhda lived first at Grottaferrata, the home of a Greek-rite Basilian monastery with a deep Byzantine artistic tradition. Both Pius XI and the new pope, Pius XII, supported Sofronov's work. In turn, he painted an icon of the head of Saint John the Baptist to be presented to Pius XII. By 1940, Pimen Maksimovich and Nadezhda Sofronov had moved to a small house in Rome.

Other Russian artists helped Sofronov during this period of intense work and suffering over his wife's declining health. Of these, Alessio Issupoff, Gregorio Maltzeff, Vadim Falileev, and Ekaterina Kachura-Falileeva seemed to have had the strongest links to Sofronov—Issupoff painted an oil portrait of Sofronov, Maltzeff portrayed both husband and wife in portraits, and Vadim Falileev gave Sofronov two of the linotypes for which he had become known. Sofronov also long prized a small watercolor painting of an angel that Kachura-Falileeva presented him as a Christmas card. These artists' mixture of Roman Catholic, Byzantine, medieval, and modern styles deeply affected Sofronov. His sketches began to mix traditional *prorisi* with far more Westernized depictions. Studies of a woman and of female eyes well-illustrate this trend (see fig. 9.1).

FIGURE 9.1 Pimen Sofronov, study of female face. Photo by Roy R. Robson.

In these years, Sofronov also showed a remarkable interest in many non-Orthodox artistic techniques. Unable to leave Rome because of the war, nursing his dying wife, and cut off from his Old Believer compatriots,

Sofronov continued to refine his style in the years 1940–1947. He used this time to study Western Christian art from the ancient period to the nineteenth century, incorporating elements that he thought harmonized with the Old Russian technique. For example, Sofronov became enamored of art in the Basilica of Santa Maria in Trastevere. Often called the first church in Rome to be dedicated to Mary, the church has a particularly wide range of Marian depictions. The most important is an exquisite thirteenth-century Pietro Cavallini mosaic, the Coronation of the Virgin. Sofronov particularly loved the twelfth-century exterior mosaics, especially the central figure of Mary nursing Christ (Maria Lactans); he sought out other versions of this image in Rome and also made similar sketches of his own. He bought a copy of *Musaici antichi delle chiese di Roma* (Ancient Mosaics of the Churches of Rome) from which he took a print of the church's exterior, framing it and even retouching the frieze when it became damaged.[13] In fact, his retouching of the print from *Musaici antichi delle chiese di Roma* hinted at other influences too. Instead of reproducing the damaged portion of the picture, Sofronov employed a technique that he developed in Rome. In that picture, as in important commissions from the Vatican, Sofronov nodded to the modernist style by including Impressionist-inspired swirls and visible brush strokes—neither of which fit the canon of Orthodox iconography.

Shortly after the war ended, Bishop Vitalii (Maximenko), abbot of the Holy Transfiguration Monastery in Jordanville, New York, invited Sofronov to live at the monastery for a period of three years. It is likely that Bishop Vitalii had learned of Sofronov from Father Kyprian Pyzhov, the monastery's most well-known iconographer. Pyzhov had learned to paint icons in Nice from Sofronov's pupil, Tamara Elchaninova (wife of the renowned Father Alexander Elchaninov). Prior to Sofronov's immigration to the United States in 1947, most Orthodox churches had icons brought from the "old country" in the so-called Italianate style. In a letter sponsoring Sofronov's emigration, Vitalii called Sofronov an "outstanding, indispensable specialist of the Old Russian Arts."[14] Privately, however, the bishop also warned "that you may be disappointed in using your knowledge of icon painting in the USA. Ancient icon painting is a completely new thing for America and to what extent you will be able to get the local church circles to be interested is hard to say in advance."[15]

In 1953, Sofronov won his first major commission in the United States at the Saints Peter and Paul Russian Orthodox Church in Syracuse, New York. Perched atop a hill overlooking the city's traditionally Irish neighborhood, the church became the starting point for Sofronov's career in America. It took Sofronov two years to finish painting in Syracuse and it provided an example for other churches. Established in short order, Sofronov enjoyed fifteen years of continual commissions. They included Saint Vladimir Russian Orthodox Church, Trenton, New Jersey (1955–1957); Saint Vladimir's Russian Orthodox Church, Miami, Florida (1956); Holy Trinity Russian Orthodox Church, Brooklyn, New York (1958–1960); Three Hierarchs Russian Orthodox Church, Ansonia, Connecticut (1960–1962); Saint Andrew's Russian Orthodox Church, St. Petersburg, Florida (1963); and Saint Anthony's Orthodox Church, Bergenfield, New Jersey (1968). Through this series of church interiors, Sofronov successfully spread his vision of "ancient icon painting" by working for Orthodox congregations from nearly every non-Greek jurisdiction in the United States. In the early 1960s, Sofronov suffered a dramatic fall from scaffolding in Ansonia and, afterward, was limited in his painting to individual icons or the lower levels of church walls. His final mural work was in the tomb his old friend Bishop (later saint) John (Maximovitch) in San Francisco.

## THE MADONNAS OF THE PAINTER: TRADITION AND INNOVATION

Over more than fifty years of painting, Pimen Sofronov subtly but dramatically changed the way he portrayed the Theotokos. Taken together, influences from Old Believer, Serbian, medieval, Renaissance, and modern styles helped Sofronov to negotiate tradition and modernity, East and West. Three important Sofronov works illustrate his development: the All-Hymned Mother (O vsepetaia mati) in Chevetogne; another version of the same icon at the Vatican; and the Church of Saints Peter and Paul in Syracuse, New York. Sofronov's views and portrayal of the Theotokos can best be seen by studying the icons' texts, Mary's gaze, and Sofronov's introduction of western themes and techniques.

Successive versions of a treasured Old Believer icon O All-Hymned Mother illustrate the transformation of Sofronov's work. Three traditional elements of the icon stand out. First is the ornate crown worn by Mary—while not unknown, Old Believer icons of Mary tended not to show Mary with a crown. In addition, on the O All-Hymned Mother icon, small cherubim replace the traditional stars on Mary's shawl. Finally, also take note of the inscription of a prayer, artfully arranged around the shawl. It reads: "O all-hymned Mother, worthy of all praise, who brought forth the Word, the Holiest of all Saints, as you receive this our offering, rescue us all from every calamity, and deliver from future torment those who cry with one voice: Alleluia."[16]

As theology, the icon makes an interesting statement. The crown and prayer emphasize the exalted place of Mary among humans, the "all-hymned" intercessor. By replacing the stars with cherubim on her shawl, however, the icon de-emphasizes Mary's virginity. At the same time it calls attention to her as throne of Christ, as in the ninth ode of the Nativity canon: "What a strange and wonderful mystery do I see. The cave is Heaven; the Virgin—throne of the cherubim." Christ's position appears midway between the austerity of the Kazan and the intimacy of the Vladimir (Eleousa) icon traditions. The child looks neither directly at us (as in the Kazan) nor at his mother (as in the Vladimir). Instead, Christ gazes into the distance even while he wraps a tiny leg around his mother's arm.

FIGURE 9.2 Pimen Sofronov's 1930–1931 version of the O All-Hymned Mother icon, Benedictine Monastery of Almy-sur-Meuse. Photo by Roy R. Robson.

Sofronov likely used a *proris'* in his collection for his 1930–1931 version of O All-Hymned Mother, painted for the Benedictine Monastery of Amay-sur-Meuse (see fig. 9.2). The overall quality of the icon is exceedingly high. A comparison of the *proris* to the final icon illustrates Sofronov's artistic choices. A comparison of these icons shows Sofronov's personal choices at work. In the *proris* (as in other versions of the icon), the Christ child tucked one leg around Mary, while the other stayed hidden in his garment. Sofronov introduced the "crossed leg" style by showing Christ's right foot. This served to foreshadow Christ's suffering on the cross. Likewise, Sofronov chose not to show the Christ child's right hand pushing against Mary's shoulder, reminiscent of the icons showing Christ "at play." Sofronov hid the right hand, implying Christ's embrace of his mother.

Sofronov most vividly departed from tradition in depicting both Mary and Christ's eyes. In the versions done by his mentor, Mary gazes toward Christ, while he looks to the middle ground as described above. Sofronov, however, painted Mary looking outward, nearly at the viewer and perhaps toward the future. Christ engages our eyes directly, linking us unswervingly to him. Showing extreme grace and care, Sofronov thus intensified the dual nature of Christ (human child and all-knowing God), while simultaneously highlighting the extraordinary role of Mary as Birthgiver of God, suffering mother, and throne of God.

A decade later, a fascinating icon version of O All-Hymned Mother exemplifies how Sofronov altered his depictions of Mary based on his experiences in Yugoslavia and Rome (see fig. 9.3). This icon, which Sofronov finished in 1940, was one of two for the Deisis row of the iconostasis at the Congregation for the Oriental Churches. The image brings together elements of different iconographic prototypes, subtly synthesizing them while adding new elements. It generally follows the structure of the Umilenie (Tender Mercy, Eleousa) design that Sofronov also knew as the Slovenskaia (Slovenian). Hearkening back to the earlier O All-Hymned Mother, however, Sofronov painted words around Mary's veil. The script is so artfully wrought that the text first appears as decoration. Only on closer inspection does the prayer become noticeable (see fig. 9.4). In a gesture to his Roman Catholic patrons, Sofronov replaced the prayer "O All-Hymned Mother" (O Vsepetaia Mati) with a Church Slavonic version of a prayer beloved by the Roman church: "Rejoice, O Virgin Mother of God, the Lord is with you; blessed are you among women and blessed is the fruit of thy womb."

Directed neither toward her son nor toward the viewer, Mary's gaze is both loving and sad, as if knowing the pain her son will endure. In his earlier O All-Hymned Mother icon, Sofronov broke with tradition by painting

**FIGURE 9.3** Pimen Sofronov's Tender Mercy or Slovenian icon of the Mother of God, iconostasis at the Congregation of the Oriental Churches, Rome, 1940. Photo by Roy R. Robson.

Christ gazing directly at the viewer. In this case, however, the child looks at his mother, holding her face in one hand, a scroll in the other. Both Mary's and Jesus's eyes have round, dark pupils and corneas, with bright blue-white sclera. The eye shape, color, and contrast help to heighten the emotional intensity of the icon, a technique that Sofronov developed in Yugoslavia

**FIGURE 9.4** Detail of Sofronov's Slovenian icon, showing text painted onto Mary's veil.

based on Serbian and Macedonian models. Christ's legs are again crossed, prophesying the Crucifixion and employing a symbol of death dating from antiquity.[17] Sofronov hid one of Christ's feet in his robes, themselves swept up as a "fluttering himation," one of the "principal characteristics" of images showing Christ leading the righteous out of hell.[18] In this way, Sofronov used iconographic language to portray all three major events of Jesus' life: birth, death, and resurrection.

Sofronov also used color and brush in important new ways. The bright blue of Mary's inner robe both reminds the viewer of Mary's virginity and frames the two figures. Instead of the flat color or gold leaf typically used as background, Sofronov experimented here by layering ochre, brown, gold, and red. He painted a brown penumbra behind the halos and showed his brushwork, a modernist technique that uncharacteristically reminds a viewer of the iconographer's presence.

In total, this icon illustrates a number of Sofronov's new directions. First, he sought to integrate elements from more than one traditional design into a single monumental icon. Second, Sofronov emphasized Mary's human attributes ("blessed are you among women") rather than her role as the cherubic throne, "worthy of all praise." Third, Sofronov incorporated influences from South Slavic iconography (especially the eyes) with a color palette and brush technique likely derived from his close association with other Russian painters in war-torn Rome. It was a master work: one of the finest icons Sofronov ever painted, inspiring "a feeling of devotion by [its] faultless and delicate execution."[19]

Sofronov's experience in Yugoslavia and Italy clearly influenced his perceptions and portrayals of Mary for the rest of his career. On the walls of his first American commission, Saints Peter and Paul (Syracuse, New York), Sofronov portrayed Mary extensively, to the near exclusion of the church's patron saints. To the left of the iconostasis, for example, Sofronov painted the Dormition of the Theotokos; to the right, the Nativity of the Lord. Both, of course, focus on the image of Mary. More important, however, were two huge ceiling icons. The first one portrayed Christ on the Road to Golgotha, covering one half of the barrel vault over the nave. Mary is one of three main elements of the icon, the other two being Jesus and, remarkably, Veronica offering her veil to Christ. In Roman Catholic tradition, Christ's sweat, wiped on the cloth, left an image of his face. There is, however, no Orthodox tradition related to Veronica. (And, notably, Sofronov did not identify Veronica on the icon, although Mary and Jesus have their traditional names shown.) Sofronov apparently liked the imagery, using it repeatedly in American churches. In this icon, Sofronov painted Mary with almost caricature-like emotions, lacking the fine detail of his smaller icons. The image portrays a strong sense of pathos; Mary gazes toward her son, wiping tears from eyes darkened with grief. Sofronov heightened the sense of Mary's human emotions through her gesture, her eyes, and the lack of theological adornment on her robes— no stars, cherubs, or prayers. Even seen at a distance, the image shows the intensified feeling and expressive eyes that Sofronov had developed over the previous fifteen years. It testifies to Mary's emotional response to seeing her son brought low by carrying his own cross, lacking any symbolism or gesture to remind us of her exalted status.

The other monumental main image of Mary—a huge dome icon of the Protection (Pokrov) of the Mother of God—could not be more different in design or tone from the Road to Golgotha (see fig. 9.5). Dominating

FIGURE 9.5 Sofronov's Protection (Pokrov) of the Mother of God icon, ceiling of Saints Peter and Paul Russian Orthodox Church, Syracuse, New York. Photo by Roy R. Robson.

the church, this icon portrays the Mother of God as both intercessor and protectress. Standing on a cloud, she looks down from the dome while two angels hold her veil. Two more angels hover on the clouds next to Mary, while the company of saints gestures to her. Far above, Christ resides in glory at the top of the inner dome. Desiring an even more exalted image of Mary than he had used many years before in the O All-Hymned Mother icon, Sofronov emphasized symbols sometimes seen on the Pokrov icon, but also employed images of Christ Enthroned. These included a blue aureola, clouds, and seraphim surrounding Mary as they would the throne of Christ. Around the dome, he painted the words of the Pokrov holiday expostilarion (sung in the ninth ode of the canon and always reserved for Mary): "O all-holy Lady, Virgin Theotokos, cover us with thy wondrous omophorion, preserving the hierarchs and people from all evil, as the all-wondrous Andrew beheld thee praying in the Church of Blachernae. And send down thy great mercy upon us, O Lady."[20] With this design, Sofronov employed the church's most prominent architectural element, its dome, to glorify Mary.

In these two icons, Sofronov realized his own view of Mary. His mentor, Gavriil Frolov, would likely have condemned Sofronov for painting the Road to Golgotha. First, it illustrated an apocryphal event not recognized by the Orthodox churches. Worse, Sofronov portrayed Mary with pathos that verged on cloying. Mary's eyes, stance, and gesture were all far-removed from the loving but remote Theotokos of Sofronov's early iconography. The Pokrov icon, to the contrary, hews more closely to tradition. Sofronov's composition complements the icon's theology—the troparion for the holiday notes that we live "beneath the precious veil" of the Theotokos. The saints, who represent all humanity, dramatically fill the dome. Moreover, by employing the large aureola, clouds, and seraphim, Sofronov stretched, but did not break from traditional designs. In this case, Sofronov's great genius was to use the icon at all: ceiling icons of Pokrov are exceedingly rare.[21]

## PAINTING *OUTSIDE* THE LINES: SOFRONOV, MODERNISM, AND HIS LEGACY

A close analysis of Sofronov's Marian imagery helps us to understand how he perceived the Theotokos, but also how his portrayal of Mary might affect other artists and believers. Sofronov both introduced and spread the "ancient art" of iconography throughout America—contemporary Orthodox churches now regularly seek out traditionalist iconographers rather than those painting in "Italianate" styles. Thousands of believers have gazed at Sofronov's icons of Mary. In doing so, they have contemplated Sofronov's idiosyncratic mixture of tradition and modernity, and Eastern and Western styles.

At different points in his career, Sofronov's suffered criticism both as a traditionalist and for breaking with tradition. Early in his career, the iconographer Julia Reitlinger complained that Sofronov knew "nothing from the artistic point of view,"[22] while one of his early students remembered that "Pimen Maksimovich himself, though he did not have much taste or culture, was a very apt master, and I learned much from him that I used later."[23] In Italy, Gregorio Maltzeff likely also found inspiration in Sofronov's work. Maltzeff had become known for his Western-style iconography, including an iconostasis he painted for the Pontifical Russian College in 1935–1936. The Benedictine monk Jérôme Leussink, who knew both artists, explained that Maltzeff painted "in an entirely different way" than Sofronov, and that Maltzeff's techniques did "not require much work."[24] After meeting Sofronov, however, Maltzeff altered his depiction of Mary toward Sofronov's style of iconography. Maltzeff had painted his icons of Mary in the Western style for the Russian Pontifical College, but sometime during World War II he began to incorporate some of the techniques he saw in Sofronov's work. One extant icon of the Theotokos, circa 1941–1943, clearly shows Maltzeff's turn toward tradition leavened with modern techniques, including working on board with *kovcheg* (a recessed central area found on some icons). Likewise, Maltzeff's last major commission, the rebuilt St. Maria Damascena on Malta (1949–1950), also illustrates his return to traditional iconographic forms.

In Rome, Sofronov also trained two iconographers who would later go on to important careers. Sofronov and his wife, neither of whom spoke Italian, arrived in Rome at about the same time as Jérôme Leussink. Sofronov took on Leussink as an apprentice, and then helped him paint the chapel at the Congregation of Oriental Churches.[25] Sofronov also taught Father Robert de Caluwe, an Eastern-Rite Catholic priest who had been studying at the Pontifical Russian College in Rome. After the war ended, Leussink returned to the Benedictine Monastery of Chevetogne (earlier located at Amay-sur-Meuse). Caluwe moved to Finland, where he spurred a renaissance of interest in traditional iconography and trained subsequent generations of iconographers. A recent scholar has highlighted Sofronov's influence on northern European iconographers:

[The structure of discipleship is a guarantee of belonging to the tradition, in other words of being a legitimate participant in revivalist Byzantine icon production. When ... Uniate Father de Caluwé, is understood as the inheritor of a tradition carried on by the Old Belief Confessors Gavriíl Frolóv and Pimen Sofronov, it is evident that the chain, or more precisely the disposition, the mental and ideal structure of certain agents is under construction and moving towards consecration through the Old Belief Confessors, the keepers of the original tradition.[26]

After his injury falling from a scaffold, Sofronov intensified his teaching and prepared exhibitions of his work in New York, Los Angeles, and Glassboro, New Jersey. His most important student of the period was Father Dmitri Borisovich Alexandrow, whom he frequently visited in the Russian artist colony of Churaevka (Southbury, Connecticut). The two shared a commission to paint the iconostasis of Holy Trinity Church in Vineland, New Jersey. As Sofronov slowed his pace, however, Father Dmitri accepted new work. He went on to paint murals for two important Russian Orthodox buildings: the Russian Orthodox Cathedral of St. John in Washington, DC, and Saint Vladimir's Memorial Church in Jackson, New Jersey. Sofronov's sense of scale and emotional intensity often appear in the work of Father Dmitri (later Bishop Daniel).

By the last five years of his life, Sofronov had largely stopped producing icons according to the *prorisi* that he had both collected and drawn over his long career. Perhaps because of his worsening blindness, Sofronov's last pieces tended to lack the power and detail of his work even as late as 1968. He dabbled with acrylic paints and painted on melamine and canvas instead of preparing boards. Relying on decades of experience, Sofronov drew from memory and habit. Shortly before Sofronov's death, an anonymous student described the process, saying, "I never saw an instance where Sofronov, while working, used references or copied from reproductions of icons. His works are the fruit of seventy-five years of labor and in his work he does not copy the visible world— he sees a different spiritual world with the eyes of his consciousness."[27] Thus the "Madonna Painter's" artistic gaze, affectionately described here by his student, had incorporated both the handed-down traditions of his Old Believer forebears and also the shape-shifting influences of modernism in an attempt to glorify and humanize his most precious iconographic subject, Mary.

NOTES

1. Archives of the Orthodox Church in America, Czap Collection, folder R170, "Impressions of the Icons of Pimen Sofronov."

2. The term "gaze" brings up a number of snarled theoretical questions. A very good cross-cultural overview is David Morgan, *The Sacred Gaze: Religious Visual Culture in Theory and Practice* (Berkeley: University of California Press, 2005), especially 58–64. Nicoletta Isar's analysis of interaction between viewer and icon in Orthodox Christianity is highly convincing. See Nicoletta Isar, "The Vision and Its 'Exceedingly Blessed Beholder': Of Desire and Participation in the Icon," *RES Anthropology and Aesthetics* 38, no. 1 (Autumn 2000): 56–72. Relatedly, Bernard Faure argues for a revision of Western views of Buddhist icons that would more fully include the ritual aspects and leave behind the commodification of images in "The Buddhist Icon and the Modern Gaze," *Critical Inquiry* 24, no. 3 (Spring 1998): especially 774–77. For a contrasting view, see Andrea G. Pearson, "Gendered Subject, Gendered Spectator: Mary Magdalen in the Gaze of Margaret of York," *Gesta* 44, no. 1 (2005): 47–66.

3. Galina Ponomareva, "P. M. Sofronov i I. N. Zavoloko" (paper presented to the First International Conference "Zavolokinskii Chtenie," Riga, Latvia, 16–17 December 2005).

4. Gleb Markelov, ed., *Kniga ikonnykh obraztsov: 500 podlinnykh prorisei i perevodov s Russkikh ikon XV–XIX vekov* (St. Petersburg: Ivan Limbakh, 2001), preface.

5. Notably, Léonid Ouspensky and Vladimir Lossky did not prescribe the use of *prorisi*: "An experienced iconographer either draws [the image] from his head, if the subject is well known to him, and guided by the meaning of the image, lays out the composition and the figures as he wills, or, if the theme is little known to him, he uses the help of other icons, iconographic manuals, preliminary sketches and so forth." Léonid Ouspensky and Vladimir Lossky, *The Meaning of Icons* (Boston: Boston Book and Art Shop, [1956]), 53.

6. Czap Collection, folder R170.

7. Ulf Abel and Vera Moore, *Icons* (Stockholm: Nationalmuseum, 2002), 195–96.

8. For more on Sofronov's early career in Riga, see Ilze Kreituse, "Vecticībnieku ikonu gleznniecība Rīgas Grebenščikova vecticībnieku draudzes lūgšanu nama kolekcijā," *Mākslas Vēsture un Teorija* 6–7 (2006): 52–64.

9. Letter of Sofronov to Iashvil, April 1934, reproduced in Kari Kotkavaara, *Progeny of the Icon: Émigré Russian Revivalism and the Vicissitudes of the Eastern Orthodox Sacred Image* (Abo: Abo Akademis Förlag, 1999), xxx.

10. Pimen Sofronov, "The Source of Orthodox Art and the Painting Project in Holy Trinity Church" (program for the consecration of the Holy Trinity Church in Brooklyn, NY, 1956), 36–38.

11. One of Sofronov's students at the monastery school was Andrei Georgievich Bartoshevich, the future Archibishop Anthony who later taught iconography at the Russian Cadet Corps in Bela Tserkva. See Bernard le Caro, "A Short Biography of Archbishop Antony (Bartoshevich) of Geneva and Western Europe (+ 1993)," OrthodoxEngland.org, http://orthodoxengland.org.uk/vl_antony_b.pdf.

12. See Alcide de Gasperi, *Scritti e discorsi politici* (Bologna: Società il Mulino, 2007), 2:1:180–81; Gasperi specifically described Sofronov's iconostasis in a long article for *L'Osservatore Romano* on 9 November 1940 and reprinted in de Gasperi, 2:2:1995–96. Cardinal Celso Costantini, with the explicit support of Pope Pius XI, had planned the exhibition as a way to celebrate his idea that Catholicism should not impose Western artistic styles in non-European lands. Sofronov thus represented a midpoint between European and Asian styles as championed by Costantini. See also Morgan, *The Sacred Gaze*, 177–79.

13. *Musaici antichi delle chiese di Roma* (n.p., 1900). This volume is very hard to find—OCLC notes only one copy worldwide, at Princeton University.

14. Sofronov Collection [Private], Letter of Reference for Pimen Maksimovich Sofronov by Archbishop Vitalii (Maximenko), 21 August 1947.

15. Sofronov Collection [Private], Letter of Archbishop Vitalii (Maximenko) to Pimen Sofronov, 17 March 1947.

16. Mari-Liis Paaver, "Koikidest ulistatud Ema . . .," *Kunst.ee* 4 (2004): 89. V. K. Tsodikovich relates the icon to pagan earth rituals in "Semantika i proiskhozhdenie ikonografii bogomateri 'O vsepetaia mati'" (paper presented to the Sixth Scientific Conference on the Problems of Russian Art Culture of the Seventeenth to the First Half of the Eighteenth Century, Moscow, 20–23 December 1999). Summary of the paper available in Russian on Nesusvet: http://nesusvet.narod.ru/ico/books/tezis2/tsodikovich.htm.

17. Chrysanthe Baltoyanni, *Icons: Mother of God in the Incarnation and the Passion* (Athens: Adams Editions, 1994), 83.

18. Ibid. Plates 33 and 34 of this volume show a similar technique in a fifteenth-century Greek icon of the "Virgin Glykophilousa." My thanks to Matthew Milliner of Princeton University for pointing out these design elements.

19. Sofronov Collection [Private], Letter of Eugene Cardinal Tisserant to Prof. Pimen Sovronoff [*sic*], Prot. N. 305/37, 15 October 1940. Art prints of this icon and two others by Sofronov have been published by the Centro Russia Ecumenica in Rome.

20. Translation from the October Menaion: http://www.st-sergius.org/services/services810.htm.

21. The prominent iconographer Father Theodore Jurewicz (himself a student of Father Kyprian Pyzhov and thus in Sofronov's artistic lineage) confirms that, if not unique, this use of the Pokrov icon has little precedent. Personal conversation, Erie, PA, 11 August 2012.

22. Elizabeth Roberts, "'A True Theologian:' The Icon-Painter Sister Joanna (Julia Nikolaevna Reitlinger), 1898–1988," in *Aesthetics as a Religious Factor in Eastern and Western Christianity*, ed. Wil van den Berken and Jonathon Sutton (Leuven: Peeters, 2005), 298.

23. E. E. Klimov, "Vospominaniia," *Baltiiskii arkhiv* 10 (2005): 213–394, quoted in Ponomareva, "P. M. Sofronov." (First International Conference "Zavolokinskii Chtenie," Riga, Latvia, 16–17 December 2005.) Klimov continued his career in Canada, where he emigrated in 1949, until his death in 1990.

24. Letter from Jérôme Leussink to Prior Théodore Belpaire, 19 December 1939. Archives Amay-Chevetogne, fonds Belpaire, Lettres de Leussink.

25. For a fuller description of this collaboration, see Roy R. Robson, "Art and Politics at the Vatican Congregation for the Oriental Churches, 1917–45," *Russian History* 38, no. 1 (2011): especially 47–55.

26. Juha Malmisalo, *In Pursuit of the Genuine Christian Image: Erland Forsberg as a Lutheran Producer of Icons in the Fields of Culture and Religion* (Helsinki: University Printing House, 2005), 52–53.

27. "To the Icon Painter Pimen Sofronov," unpublished manuscript, n.p., n.d. [1973?], signed "a student of P. M. Sofronov." Private collection.

# 10

## The Marian Ideal in the Works of Tatiana Goricheva and the Mariia Journals

Elizabeth Skomp

### STAGNATION, MARY, AND THE SOVIET WOMEN'S MOVEMENT

IN THE EARLY IN THE early days of the Soviet experiment, the "Woman Question" was publically proclaimed to have been answered. Subsequently, for several decades the Soviet women's movement lacked visibility and force.[1] But near the end of Leonid Brezhnev's rule, resistance to and frustration with the conditions in which women lived gave rise to a new wave of Soviet women's activism. As several scholars have noted, two currents emerged in the nascent movement of the late 1970s and early 1980s.[2]

The first stage of this movement was led by Tatiana Mamonova, primary editor of the 1979 almanac *Woman and Russia* (Zhenshchina i Rossiia). Mamonova's feminist identity was an explicitly secular one, and her pronounced attention to reproductive rights and female sexuality, as well as her understanding of feminism as "an essential part of the world democratic movement," revealed her to be an activist sympathetic to Western feminist ideals.[3] Following Mamonova's expulsion from the Soviet Union in 1980, some of her colleagues who remained in Leningrad, including Tatiana Goricheva, Natalia Malakhovskaia, and Iuliia Voznesenskaia, formed a "Russian independent women's religious club" called Mariia. Its orientation and mission, initially focused more narrowly on Russia than Mamonova's broader vision had been, was also more conservative. Positions such as the group's espousal of conventional gender roles led one scholar to note that they might easily be seen as manifesting "feminine, rather than feminist, values."[4] The women of the Mariia group articulated those values in their journal of the same name, of which three issues appeared in *tamizdat* (published abroad) in 1981 and 1982, while a total of six issues appeared in *samizdat* (self-published) form.[5]

Less thoroughly analyzed than the history of late Soviet feminism is the specific content of the *Mariia* journals and their treatment of the Mother of God, for whom the group and journal are named. The first issue of *Mariia* addressed the women of Russia and outlined the group's reasons for selecting Mary as an exemplar given the unenviable position of Russian women during the late Brezhnev years, but the choice of Mary also had roots in earlier texts. As this essay will show, the group's focus on a Marian model for women originated in the convictions of Tatiana Goricheva, who extensively explored the Mother of God in her works both prior to the appearance of the *Mariia* journals and after their publication ceased. Despite the Mariia group's lack of a common theoretical body of knowledge, there are striking affinities between the attributes of the Mother of God that emerged in Goricheva's writings and the everyday women's concerns that the other *Mariia* writers articulated, including motherhood, sacrifice, creativity, humility, and a rich inner life. This harmony of ideas would prove short-lived, for almost as soon as the club's three leaders arrived in Vienna as exiles in July 1980, their divergent views on religion and feminism drove them apart.[6] Indeed, links between the Mariia group and later women's activism in Russia are less evident in the sphere of religion than in their emphasis on maternity and a conventional understanding of femininity and masculinity.[7]

Though their educational background varied—Goricheva (b. 1947) was a graduate of the philosophy faculty of Leningrad State University; Natalia Malakhovskaia (b. 1947) graduated from the philological faculty; and Iuliia Voznesenskaia (b. 1940) studied at the Leningrad Institute of Theater, Music, and Film—the group's leaders came to the blossoming Russian women's movement with common experience in one important respect. All were former participants in Leningrad's Second Culture, "a movement of a new generation of writers and artists, both men and women, who wanted to make their own contribution to Russian culture" but either by choice or out of necessity had to do so outside official venues of publication.[8]

Many participants in the Second Culture called themselves Christians. As the titling of the Mariia group indicates, its core members identified themselves as religious, though not all were believers.[9] Voznesenskaia had been baptized in the Orthodox Church at the age of thirty-three while she was active in the Second Culture movement, but some of the avowedly Christian participants in the Mariia group identified with other denominations. Contributor Tatiana Beliaeva, for instance, was a practicing Baptist in Leningrad and converted to Orthodoxy as an émigré.[10] Reasons for participation in religious activity were varied; while Christianity had functioned as a form of dissidence for some adherents of the Second Culture, Malakhovskaia has asserted that many of the Mariia women were deeply drawn to the spiritual strength and the power of prayer that they found in religious practice, not least because it helped them to cope with the stress of KGB searches and interrogations.[11] When the *Mariia* journals were published, Malakhovskaia was unaffiliated with any particular church and was not baptized.[12] After emigrating, she became involved with the Catholic Church in Austria but later distanced herself from church-based religion.

Though Goricheva had been baptized as a child, she decided to undergo a second baptism at twenty-six.[13] Yet at the time of her adult conversion, Goricheva knew little about Christianity. She began to attend the Nikolskii Cathedral, one of the few churches that remained open in Leningrad, and friends provided her with some religious education as she undertook her first reading of the Gospels.[14] In charting the trajectory of her conversion, Goricheva described the "pre-Christian" period of her life as a time when her motto of "everything is permitted" eventually led her to despise herself.[15] She detailed her difficult first confession and her subsequent path to absolution via prayer to the Mother of God in her memoir *Talking about God Is Dangerous* (Opasno govorit' o boge):

> I had to tell [the elder (*starets*)] my whole biography: a life based on pride and a quest for praise, on arrogant contempt for other people. I told him about my drunkenness and my sexual excesses, my unhappy marriages, the abortions and my inability to love anyone. I also told him about the next period of my life, my preoccupation with yoga and my desire for "self-fulfilment," for becoming God, without love and without penitence.[16]

Prior to her conversion, Goricheva frequented "Saigon," the notorious café that functioned as a center of unofficial cultural activity in Leningrad. Though Goricheva has described it as an ideal locus of freedom, happiness, and intellectual interchange, it was also a site of unorthodox, bohemian behavior and exceptionally relaxed social norms.[17] The maven of underground culture bore little resemblance to the later avid Orthodox believer; Galina Grigoreva, a member of the Mariia club who attended church with Goricheva and sometimes participated in her religious-philosophical seminars, noted that the Goricheva of "Saigon" and the more intensely Orthodox Goricheva were two very different people.[18]

Goricheva's retelling of her conversion and confession yoked those events firmly to the Mother of God. "From Letters to a Spiritual Brother" (Iz pisem k dukhovnomu bratu) introduced the significance of the Marian ideal for Goricheva.[19] While Goricheva visited the Piukhtitsy Convent in Estonia in 1979, "under the protecting veil [pokrov] of the Mother of God," she meditated on her past and described the comfort and consolation she felt there while inhabiting a monastic cell and gazing at an icon of the Mother of God.[20] In a subsequent diary entry, she recalled the consolatory power of a Marian apparition that she espied in the clouds immediately after making the difficult confession of the sins she had committed over the last six years.[21] The direct links among confession, forgiveness, and the Mother of God were reiterated visually and verbally—the neophyte Goricheva had to repeat the prayer "Rejoice, O Virgin" (Bogoroditsa, Devo, raduisia) five times daily for four years in order to receive absolution—as well as in less easily quantifiable ways.

Goricheva apparently embraced the Marian ideal partly to renounce an earlier way of life and also because of her yearning for the protective, sheltering qualities of the Mother of God. Glimpsing the icon in her cell upon awakening from a nightmare, Goricheva experienced the novel feeling of being at home.[22] Equally significant was the comfort she took in viewing Mary as a guiding mother who was a daily presence at the convent and who, according to one nun, "did everything" at the monastery.[23] For Goricheva, prayer to the Mother of God not only fulfilled the directive she had received from her confessor. It also played an important role in impelling her toward self-knowledge via the practices of creativity and obedience to God, thanks to the elevating power of the Bogoroditsa.[24]

Goricheva's "'Rejoice, Redemption of the Tears of Eve'" (Raduisia, slez evinykh izbavlenie), which takes its title from the akathist to the Theotokos, began to explore that elevating power more fully. Composed as the author observed the holiday of the Dormition of the Mother of God and initially printed in the almanac Woman and Russia, the essay anticipated the Mariia group's central focus on the Bogomater'. Goricheva announced that "in this letter I am only beginning a conversation about Her." Indeed, the first and third issues of Mariia would contain a section entitled "Letters on Prayers to the Mother of God" (Pis'ma po molitvam k Bogomateri).[25]

In "Rejoice, Redemption of the Tears of Eve," Goricheva identified the Mother of God as providing a path both to knowledge of self and knowledge of God.

Along that path, daily contemplation of and prayer to Mary would reveal the power of love and sacrifice.[26] Her newfound understanding of the Mother of God as an ideal representation of femininity was the foundation for her meditation on the Marian ideal. Crucial to this ideal femininity were Mary's purity and chastity (*tselomudrie*), and so Goricheva undertook a brief etymological discussion of the latter term in order to emphasize that a chaste person is also a whole (*tselyi*) and wise (*mudryi*) one. This idea of the non-conflicted wholeness of the Mother of God and a lack of divisive dualism between body and spirit later would appeal strongly to several of the *Mariia* writers.[27]

A secular component also accompanied Goricheva's path to self-understanding. Revisiting her reading of Jung's Electra complex and two archetypes of female consciousness—imitation (*podrazhanie*) of the mother and rebellion against the mother—she categorized herself as conforming to the second of these categories. The characteristics Goricheva identified in herself included an anti-maternal and anti-female stance, a focus on intellect and will, a preference for masculine role models, and a suspicion toward the material, instead developing an inclination toward the spiritual. Emulating the Mother of God would mean overcoming the rebellion against the Mother and instead striving to follow her example.

Goricheva ascribed her previous mindset not only to the Jungian model but also to her education and rearing (*vospitanie*) within the Soviet system, namely its valorization of a non-gendered personality ideal.[28] Soviet education did not account for the existence of a "separate but equal" path for women. Further, it taught students to "worship the head and be suspicious of the heart." Its value system contained a persistent admonition to control one's own destiny and construed sacrifice only as negative. As a result, Goricheva and the classmate to whom her meditative letter is addressed left school completely despising all "female' tasks," in other words, the chores of everyday life.[29]

A related (and frequently discussed) theme addressed by Goricheva in this text and later by other *Mariia* contributors was the gap between the publicly proclaimed emancipation of women and their actual social status. She contended that women had not been emancipated; instead, men had been feminized. As a result, she wrote, women were forced to assume all roles, and their subsequent overburdening caused them to become contemporary martyrs. Malakhovskaia's "The Maternal Family" (Materinskaia sem'ia), a contribution to *Woman and Russia*, adopted a similar rhetorical stance but claimed that woman was equal to the task: she "must become everything—so she does become everything" (Ona dolzhna stat' vsem—tak ona vsem i stanovit'sia).[30] It further bemoaned the fact that, though women had equal political and legal rights, they did not possess the "moral rights" of men.[31]

Just as Goricheva's "Rejoice, Redemption of the Tears of Eve" protested the false idea of women's emancipation, "The Maternal Family" lamented the propagandization of a false equality between men and women, and its author further developed the argument by discussing the problem of creative work.[32] Malakhovskaia asserted that the Soviet system prevented women from simultaneously fulfilling the roles of mother and creator. She critiqued self-abnegating women who surrendered their own identity to assume the identity of their child or sacrificed their creative potential in order that their husbands might succeed, arguing that women possessed a superior capacity for cultural creation.[33] She then explained her ultimate aim by describing creativity in apparently Christian terms: "The word bursts out of your soul ... [it is a] mortal sin to kill it in yourself, not to give it life. In order to become a creator, woman must display her energies, unknown to men, heroic energies. But she will come to this—in order to create a new culture, which will change life."[34] In the conclusion to her article, Malakhovskaia imagined the truly liberated women as "not only the physical, but also the spiritual creator of the future world."[35] Though the article bears no obvious religious subtext, its degree of correspondence to the discussion of female creativity in the *Mariia* journals with respect to motherhood and Christianity is striking. As if to emphasize this correspondence, a small illustration—one of only three in the volume— that is reminiscent of an icon appears beneath Malakhovskaia's article. The graphic depicts two black-clad, berobed figures that are apparently a mother and child; the former's head is inclined toward the latter.

Malakhovskaia, Voznesenskaia, and the majority of the other contributors to the *Mariia* journals spoke from the perspective of struggling mothers who sought visible social change. By contrast, though Goricheva did argue forcefully in her writings for the betterment of the position of women, she entered the *Mariia* project with a comparatively large degree of separation from mundane, everyday realities or *byt*. Insofar as Malakhovskaia and other group members accepted the *Bogomater'* as an ideal, it was largely an earthly and maternal one. While Goricheva in part viewed the Mother of God as a maternal figure by whom one might be mothered, many of her *Mariia* colleagues envisioned Mary from the opposite perspective: as a mother to be emulated. The two primary strands of thought in the Mariia group could be reconciled with relative ease because of the centrality of Mary's maternal role in Orthodoxy.

With respect to philosophy and theology, Goricheva was the intellectual leader of the Mariia group. Possessing an undergraduate degree in philosophy and experience leading religious and philosophical seminars, Goricheva came to the group with a body of knowledge that, while by no means comprehensive, was not shared by the other participants.[36] Apart from Goricheva, members of the Mariia club were largely unfamiliar with theology and had little knowledge of the Bible, as almost all came from atheist families and many had come of age during Nikita Khrushchev's anti-religious campaign.[37] Some participants had attended the religious-philosophical seminars begun by Goricheva and her then-husband Viktor Krivulin in 1973 and thus had at least a basic familiarity with the works of religious thinkers such as Pavel Florenskii, Sergius Bulgakov, Nikolai Berdiaev, and others.[38] The seminar eventually took shape as the dissident religious group "37," and the group also produced a *samizdat* journal of the same title.[39]

Within the Mariia group, Goricheva had the most fully developed (and most imaginative) understanding of the Mother of God. Indeed, she would later characterize the Mariia participants as "neophytes."[40] For Goricheva, who had read widely, if not always deeply, in theological texts, the *Mariia* journals served as an ideal forum in which she could develop religious ideas, especially as her dual interests in Mary and the women's movement appeared to coincide. Malakhovskaia had interpreted Goricheva's participation in *Woman and Russia* in this light, claiming that the latter "used the almanac for propagandization of her religious ideas."[41] The heterogeneity of belief within the Mariia group notwithstanding, Goricheva's Orthodox faith accounted for the general religious orientation that informed the journal. Other contributors saw *Mariia* simply as a continuation of *Woman and Russia* under a different name and with a more obvious religious slant. For the women in the latter category, issues of women's daily life and especially the plight of Soviet mothers were of paramount importance.

## MARY AS COUNTERCULTURAL FEMININE SYMBOL

The cover of each of the journal's issues underscored the twin goals of the Mariia club and the central role of the Mother of God. Designed by Natalia Lazareva, the emblem printed on the title page consisted of a Venus symbol that enclosed a flower and the letters "F" and "C." The journal contained no exegesis of the symbol's meaning, though in an article responding to Lazareva's arrest, the journal's authors characterized the flower as a "flower of life" (*tsvetok zhizni*).[42] As a symbol of fertility, it could be interpreted in creative and procreative terms alike. Though the Mariia group's "flower of life" bore little resemblance to flowers more typically associated with Mary such as the lily or the rose, it clearly contained at its center a mandorla, the almond-shaped symbol of medieval origin that represents Mary and

FIGURE 10.1 Emblem of the Mariia group (from the cover of the *samizdat*, or self-published, journal). Courtesy of Natalia Malakhovskaia.

motherhood by symbolizing the womb of the Mother of God. The capitalized Latin letters "F" and "C" apparently pointed to "feminism" and "Christianity" (see fig. 10.1).

The Mother of God had evident pride of place in the journal's first issue. In its preface, addressed to the "women of Russia," the *Mariia* writers explained, "We named our club and journal for the One from whom came salvation for the world, in the name of the earthly and heavenly intercessor of Russia."[43] They imagined Mary as one who "descend[ed] into the hell of female existence" and returned with "despairing" and "hopeless" souls. In short, the Mariia group saw the *Bogomater'* as perhaps the only entity capable of the miracle that rescuing Soviet women from their plight would require.[44]

Further, the writers of *Mariia* envisioned Russia during the late Stagnation period as being on the verge of "spiritual, moral, and physical" ruin. Their portrayal of this impending disaster touched on some of the crucial social problems of the day: "A monstrous wave of nihilism and stupefaction is sweeping away all cultural and spiritual values: families are falling apart, the people are drowning in drunkenness, crime is growing catastrophically and the birth rate is dropping, the general demoralization of society is crossing all possible borders."[45] With the country facing either ruin or resurrection, they argued, the possibility of salvation lay in the hands of women, and the portrayal of the domestic landscape in such urgent and dire terms sought to justify the existence of the journal it prefaced.

Against this backdrop, *Mariia*'s authors returned to the earlier arguments made by Goricheva and Malakhovskaia in *Woman and Russia*. They claimed that the stark reality of Soviet life belied the vaunted Soviet gender equality that existed only on paper; Tatiana Goricheva thus described Soviet society as a "pseudomatriarchal antiutopia" and asserted that the structure of the family was a tool for enforcing authoritarianism.[46] She explicitly identified everyday life as a "Gulag," and Iuliia Voznesenskaia echoed this idea in her article "Domestic Concentration Camp" (Domashnii kontslager').

Goricheva's discussion of the "pseudomatriarchal antiutopia" took Lenin's oft-quoted statement about the ability of any cook to rule the country and applied it in nightmarish form to the Soviet reality in which she lived. The "laws" of fate and superstition that actually governed Soviet society had, in her view, led to the "existential paralysis" of Soviet citizens.[47] Seeking a solution, Goricheva called for "the liberation of women from the traits of 'female' psychology," which included "passivity, silence, and slavish dependency on home and family" and argued that no social revolution would liberate women if it remained unaccompanied by a spiritual revolution.[48] The "female psychology" she described as inculcated in Soviet women contrasted sharply with the Marian attributes of freely chosen humble silence and obedience to God.

In "Witches in Space" (Ved'my v kosmose), Goricheva reiterated the importance of achieving self-knowledge (*samopoznanie*), an idea that she had explored in personal terms in "Rejoice, Redemption of the Tears of Eve" and "From Letters to a Spiritual Brother."[49] Her *Mariia* texts moved beyond the predominantly individual reflection of her earlier works to offer social commentary and aimed to serve as a guide to other women. Women's self-recognition would, importantly, enable them to comprehend reality as well as to create it.

Voznesenskaia's "Domestic Concentration Camp" stressed the "democratic principles of creation" that, along with love, creative cooperation, and openness to diverse points of view formed the foundations of the Mariia group.[50] The author's overt objective was to set the Mariia women apart from "ego-dominated" human rights groups and the Second Culture. In a subsequent response to a questionnaire from the journal *Alternatives* (Alternativy), the authors sought to differentiate *Mariia* from other Leningrad *samizdat* journals with religious concerns, such as *37* and *Chasy* (Hours). They noted that women's issues lay beyond the purview of these journals in terms of both scope and "the aloof, philosophical-reflecting tone of Leningrad *samizdat*."[51] At the same time, they sought to distinguish the collegiality that lay behind *Mariia* as deep, Christian, and chaste, with its authors bound together by shared female pain, intrepidness, and a capacity for sacrifice.[52]

While acknowledging the centrality of the "women's theme" in Russian culture and philosophy and noting the persistent Russian literary veneration of woman, "in whom alone is seen salvation and light," they also envisioned the intersection of the holy and the everyday. They imagined the Mother of God as "covering Russia with her veil [*pokrov*], traveling through our land in the guise of a simple Russian woman, descending into the very hell of Russian life."[53] They further identified a special mission for women in Russia: "to return the human to himself or herself and to God, to oppose violence with love … to force a return to the values of the heart and spirit."[54] It was clear that this female mission would be realized by the Mariia women, who would emulate the Mother of God by performing her work on earth.

"Letters on Prayers to the Mother of God" (Pis'ma po molitvam k Bogomateri) served to educate readers on the virtues of the Mother of God and guide them by suggesting ways to understand Mary and emulate her. Apart from the introduction to the first journal issue, this segment of *Mariia* also engaged most specifically and directly with the idea of the Mother of God. In "On Spiritual Mendicancy" (O dukhovnom nishchenstve), Goricheva discussed the virginity of the Mother of God and emphasized her humility, state of expectation (*ozhidanie*), and beautiful but concealed inner life.[55] Further, Mary's self-identification as a handmaiden or servant of God, a person "completely open to God" and "completely obedient to Reality" was to be understood in positive terms that contrasted sharply with the contemporary Soviet female "slave of a slave" decried in that journal issue's preface.[56]

For Goricheva, the lack of freedom that characterized Brezhnev-era Soviet secular reality for women was accompanied by spiritual death. "Recovery of the Dead" (Vzyskanie pogibshikh) characterized the previous three decades of Soviet experience as a state of "non-being" (*nebytie*) and lamented the severed connection with the Russian cultural and religious past.[57] The Mother of God again presented a salvatory and consolatory alternative to Soviet reality that could heal the aforementioned rift; because of her proximity to the "torments of female existence," she could "hear every sigh" and "wipe away every tear." In defining the Mother of God as the "first Christian woman and the mother of faith, just as Abraham is the father of faith," Goricheva feminized and Marianized a Kierkegaardian precept. By stating that "in each person's life the path from Abraham to Mary is repeated: from an existential religion of the absurd to a joyful and blessed life in faith," Goricheva not only stressed her view of the correct orientation of religious belief but also suggested that a turn to Marian devotion would involve the concomitant rejection of the absurdity of Soviet life.[58] Similarly, the notion of treading a Marian path was a central theme of contributor E. K's "On the Way of the Cross of the Mother of God" (O krestnom puti Bogomateri), indirectly addressed to Tatiana Goricheva in emigration. This writer emphasized the sufferings of Mary as well as her maternal qualities; as mother to all, Mary would lead earthly "wretched orphans" to the truth. By traveling the way of the cross, human beings would learn to "live in the spirit of chastity, humility of mind, patience, and love."[59]

In "From a Letter to Leningrad" (Iz pis'ma v Leningrad), Goricheva recounted her post-emigration efforts to explain to feminists in Vienna why the Church was the only place where contemporary Russian women could find true freedom, consolation, and strength.[60] She maintained that Mary presented a live, viable ideal for Russian women, while in the West, she had been transformed into a dead moral ideal.[61] The perceived vibrancy of this Marian model also suggested the possibility of change in Russia, including renewed attention to gender roles. Earlier Goricheva had argued for the reversal of Soviet collective *vospitanie* so that men and women would be identified as distinct and separate entities. The Mariia group believed that women possessed unique, gendered attributes that were not socialized but innate, and such a belief served to explain why the Mariia writers emphasized the Mother of God as intercessor rather than advocating a direct appeal to God or Christ. These writers averred that Marian veneration would enrich women in particular. Men, however, were not excluded from the Mariia group, as evidenced by male-authored letters (including one penned by Alexander Solzhenitsyn) to the journal and a male-authored contribution to the third volume.

The *Mariia* writers condemned the Soviet system for stripping men and women of the roles they would otherwise naturally assume. Further, they saw the Soviet regime's eradication of the spiritual and the natural as having created sexless human beings; alternatively, Goricheva characterized *homo Sovieticus*—the average Soviet person—as a hermaphrodite.[62] Because women were refused the possibility of fulfilling their role in personal and family life (admittedly an essentialist view), the Mariia women called for the reinstatement of traditionally understood gender roles. Correspondingly, Voznesenskaia also saw true female fulfillment as possible only if women were "allowed to be women" and not "terrible sexless creatures."[63]


## MARY, FEMINISM, AND MOTHERHOOD

There was consensus within the Mariia group that this female fulfillment necessarily included motherhood. Though contributor Tatiana Mikhailova wrote that she "consider[ed] woman above all a mother," she also lamented the fact that women were forced to be mothers both to their children and to their husbands.[64] They could escape the latter role, she believed, if men would assume their role fully and shoulder more familial responsibility. In contrast, Goricheva approached the fulfillment of the mother-role from another angle, asserting that women were denied the possibility of fully satisfying their maternal instinct because dire socioeconomic conditions prevented them from having the number of children they might desire. Despite these limitations on the mother-role, Sofia Sokolova ascribed to motherhood a unique path to development of the self, a special type of self-realization that no totalitarian regime could remove and that would involve strength and enrichment "spiritually, morally, and emotionally."[65] Indeed, Goricheva had defined the emancipation of woman as chiefly a "spiritual-ontological problem" rather than merely a political issue.[66]

   The journal's contributors continued to seek the female reassumption of a proper and "true" womanly role. Voznesenskaia, for instance, called for "real men and real women" to stem further societal deterioration.[67] Accordingly, the third issue of *Mariia*, published in 1982, addressed the Marian qualities of humility and obedience (*smirenie i poslushanie*) as virtues.[68] It is important to note, however, that the contributors to *Mariia* did not intend to advocate passivity and inactivity. Instead of submission to husbands, they encouraged submission to God, and they understood humility as "a realization of one's great mission."[69] In the third issue of *Mariia*, Goricheva's "Hope above Hope" (Nadezhda sverkh nadezhdy) praised the silence, seriousness, and humility of the Mother of God and identified the latter as the most important of the Christian virtues. At the same time, Goricheva was careful to emphasize that "Russian Christians understand by experience that *smirenie* has nothing in common with abjection [and] slavery."[70]

   The Mariia women appeared to introduce humility and obedience as coping strategies for their contemporary sociocultural context. Though they viewed the Soviet system as having disfigured and destroyed all that is human, they nonetheless vowed that their own experience would not be in vain:

> Let it teach us to seek salvation not in external reforms and changes, let it turn our gazes into the depths of the heart and open to us that which is given . . . only to woman: the ability to love and sacrifice everything for the sake of love, the ability not to seek in this love "something of one's own," the ability to listen to God and follow him, the ability to live by the heart, and not [solely] by reason.[71]

Since radical social change was not a viable possibility, internal change served as a way of gaining agency within an externally repressive regime.

Proponents of such an approach might easily be disparaged if they advocated an inward turn and the exclusion of the external world. But the women of the Mariia group actively sought to engage the external world via a transformation in female identity: "a new woman must be born in Russia— free and independent; however, not using her freedom to harm those close to her, but transforming it into a creative impulse [*tvorcheskii poryv*], a woman, who has risen to the understanding of her great [*vysokii*] task, who has become conscious of the century's pain like her own personal pain, managing to make someone else's suffering her own fate."[72] According to this formulation, the correct use of freedom would involve both co-suffering—a central attribute of the Mother of God—and creation or creativity.[73]

Iuliia Voznesenskaia's address to the (female) readers of *Mariia* at the end of the journal's first issue identified some of the group's central areas of concern and exemplified their concept of co-suffering and co-participation in both the domestic and international communities.[74] In addition to gaining a fuller understanding of the position of Soviet women, they established an agenda that aimed to address such problems as hunger, drunkenness, women's legal rights, female joblessness, the position of women in Central Asian republics, the growing Solidarity movement in Poland, and their opposition to the occupation of Afghanistan. The group's understanding of suffering and community manifested Marian emulation via an engagement with social and political problems.

Though the *Mariia* writers were deeply concerned with social issues that affected the status of women, their larger goal of (re)infusing Soviet life with spirituality was never far from the rhetorical center of any article. This problem was particularly acute for mothers who struggled with the routine demands and pressures of everyday life. Though the articles on *byt* in the second issue of *Mariia* represented varied viewpoints about the utility of *byt*, all attempted to grapple with *byt* and to rehabilitate it. Even if these discussions of everyday life rarely mentioned the Mother of God directly, the themes of the articles echoed the parts of the journal with a more explicitly Marian focus. Goricheva's "Anti-Universe of the Soviet family" ("Antivselennoi sovetskoi sem'i") argued that "everyday life [*byt*] displaces spiritual being [*bytie*]."[75] In her treatment of the same issue, Natalia Malakhovskaia asserted that an obsession with *byt* (what she termed "bytomania") had negative implications for child-rearing and demonstrated too great an emphasis on the material rather than spiritual aspects of existence. As a consequence, she argued, many women took the misguided step of sacrificing themselves for their children and husbands.[76] Malakhovskaia envisioned female community and solidarity as one way of addressing the problems of *byt*.

Alla Sariban introduced a new dimension to the discussion in her article "Woman and *Byt*" (Zhenshchina i byt). For Sariban, *byt* was neither homogeneous nor monolithic. She advocated separating from women's labors those tasks that could become a source of creative work (*tvorchestvo*) instead of monotony and tedium. The primary such area she envisioned was child-rearing, a task she believed should have a spiritual component, stating: "The absence of this sacred relationship to the maternal mission, which has become ordinary for us, is not only ruinous for children, but also greatly impoverishes a woman's life, reducing it from the plan of *bytie* to the plan of routine *byt*, that is, non-existence."[77] However, since the complete eschewal of *byt* was a utopian fantasy, she suggested that women could avoid enslavement to it by choosing to limit *byt* to the smallest possible area of their existence and "to seek a source of life in transcendence, religion, to which the female soul is so sensitive."[78]

Recognition of and respect for women's creativity and creative powers could also help to correct the imbalance between *byt* and *bytie*. In "Domestic Concentration Camp" Voznesenskaia identified women's primary role as "the creation of love as a new spiritual reality" or "creation of the new in all areas of life."[79] Voznesenskaia viewed women as having a much wider sphere of creation than men, whose creativity she saw as limited to the work environment. Using this definition, women's creativity could then be understood in biological, social, and aesthetic terms.

The relationship between motherhood and female creativity is a complex one. Helene Deutsch's assertion that "the urge to intellectual and artistic creation and the productivity of motherhood spring from common sources" and that "one should be capable of replacing the other" echoes the Mariia women's view of such endeavors as interrelated in a fundamental and natural way.[80] Thus, in unfolding her analysis of female creative production, Voznesenskaia first established the primacy of women's roles in both bearing and raising children.

Acknowledging women's responsibility for the spiritual education of their children, the Mariia women ascribed considerable importance to this labor. Voznesenskaia also argued for the legitimacy of female-authored creative works (a campaign instigated by the sexism some members of the group had encountered in the Second Culture and by the disdain of some male dissidents for women's writing and thought).[81] When plans for a women's journal (*Woman and Russia*) began to coalesce, there was an evident need to reclaim and differentiate the feminine space in the creative sphere. Malakhovskaia recalled standing on the spit of Vasilevskii Island with Mamonova, Goricheva, and Voznesenskaia and hearing about how Goricheva garnered praise for her "masculine mind," while Voznesenskaia received accolades for her "masculine poems."[82] Indeed, one scholar has identified the striving for creative self-realization as a distinguishing characteristic of both strands—religious and secular—of the resurgent women's movement of the Stagnation period.[83]

Creativity also activated and illustrated aspects of the Marian ideal. Goricheva's post-*Mariia* work *The Russian Woman and Orthodoxy* (Russkaia zhenshchina i pravoslavie) made explicit the connections among humility, self-knowledge, and the creative act: "humility, if it is true, reveals the human individual, gives it the possibility of fully participating in synergetic co-creation with God."[84] Her 1993 essay "On the Kenosis of Russian Culture" (O kenozise russkoi kultury) emphasized the importance of following a godly path—the way of the cross (*krestnyi put'* or *stradaniia*)—not in pursuit of resurrection but in order to be renewed through creative love.[85] This Marian path for earthly women relates directly to the idea of creation that the Mariia writers stressed and to the transformative potential of suffering. In *Daughters of Job* (Docheri Iova), originally published in 1986, Goricheva returned to this theme by interpreting Mary's "yes" (*fiat*) not as passive (an interpretation that she attributed to feminists) but as "the highest creativity, a movement of the Holy Spirit, eternally active and fruitful [*plodonosiashchego*]".[86]

For Tatiana Goricheva, engagement with the Mother of God was part of a protracted personal religious search. Indeed, of all the members of the Mariia group, she alone continued to devote significant effort to religious and philosophical writings that extended and developed her ideas about the Mother of God, while the group's other leaders pursued scholarly and belletristic work in related spheres. Following exile from the Soviet Union, Malakhovskaia went on to publish a monograph and fiction about the folkloric figure Baba-Iaga, as well as a volume of poetry, and Voznesenskaia has published several novels, some in the genre of Orthodox fantasy.

In retrospectively considering the Mariia group's activities and the contents of the journals, Malakhovskaia would later distance herself from certain ideas expressed in them. After emigrating, she says, she came to better understand her own religiosity as a religion of the Mother.[87] Her understanding of the Mother of God was not as delimited by Orthodoxy as Goricheva's; Malakhovskaia was interested in connections between Mary and the archetypal goddess-figure.[88] Only in emigration did Malakhovskaia begin to study feminist theology, and she learned German in order to be able to read theological texts.[89]

Though the *Mariia* journals may be understood as an emerging voice amid the persistent clamor of dissident outcry in Stagnation-era Leningrad, the exile or imprisonment of the group's leaders ensured the dissipation and fragmentation of its message within Soviet borders. The disintegration of the group did not, however, inevitably indicate a corresponding ephemerality in its members' beliefs, such as the multifaceted nature of female creativity, the Mother of God as a feminine model, and an inclusive redefinition of community. Just as she had argued in the preface to the first issue of *Mariia*, Goricheva remained convinced in emigration of Mary's salvatory potential. In *Daughters of Job*, Goricheva termed the present day the "age of the Mother of God" and described it as a "time of contradictions, extremes and apocalyptic elements," suggesting that Mary alone might offer a redemptive alternative.[90] Since that time, the pull of the Marian ideal has remained equally strong; when asked in a 2008 interview to define the true place of women in contemporary Russian society, Goricheva responded: "I think that the Mother of God shows us an example: her humility, [capacity for] sacrifice [*zhertvennost'*] and strength."[91]

## NOTES

1. For a short review of literature on Soviet feminist activity, see Barbara Alpern Engel, "Women in Russia and the Soviet Union," *Signs* 12, no. 4 (1987): 781–96.

2. See, for example, Alix Holt, "The First Soviet Feminists," in *Soviet Sisterhood*, ed. Barbara Holland (Bloomington: Indiana University Press, 1985), 237–65; Tatyana Mamonova, "Introduction: The Feminist Movement in the Soviet Union," in *Women and Russia: Feminist Writings from the Soviet Union*, ed. Tatyana Mamonova (Boston, MA: Beacon Press, 1984), xiii–xxiii; and Rochelle Ruthchild, "Sisterhood and Socialism: The Soviet Feminist Movement," *Frontiers: A Journal of Women Studies* 7, no. 2 (1983): 4–12.

3. Quoted in Holt, "The First Soviet Feminists," 241.

4. Julie Curtis, "Iuliia Voznesenskaia: A Fragmentary Vision," in *Women and Russian Culture: Projections and Self-Perceptions*, ed. Rosalind Marsh (New York: Berghahn Books, 1998), 179.

5. To understand the risk involved in publishing the *Mariia* journal, it is important to note that individuals who produced, disseminated, or simply possessed *tamizdat* or *samizdat* material were subject to prosecution under Article 70 (Anti-Soviet Agitation and Propaganda) of the Soviet penal code.

6. See Tat'iana Goricheva, *Tol'ko v Rossii est' vesna!: O tragedii sovremennogo Zapada; Dnevniki 1980–2003* (Moscow: Russkii khronograf, 2006), in which Goricheva wrote about her

fraying relationship with Malakhovskaia and Voznesenskaia after their arrival in Vienna in July 1980: "Naturally, my point of view on almost all questions does not coincide with the points of view of the other 'feminists.' And the gulf between us is growing" (29).

7. For a discussion of the continued conflation of femininity and motherhood in the post-Soviet period, see Rebecca Kay, *Russian Women and Their Organizations: Gender, Discrimination and Grassroots Women's Organizations, 1991–96* (New York: St. Martin's Press, 2000), 65–82.

8. Anna-Natal'ia Malakhovskaia, "O Zarozhdenii russkogo feministicheskogo al'manakha 'Zhenshchina i Rossiia' (Interv'iu s Mariei Zav'ialovoi)," *Solanus* 14 (2000): 68.

9. Galina Grigoreva avers that all participants who came to Mariia via the Second Culture were Christians. Interview with Galina Grigor'eva, Collection of feminism documents, Nauchno-informatsionnyi tsentr "Memorial," St. Petersburg, Russia, 9.

10. Interview with Natal'ia Malakhovskaia, Collection of feminism documents, Nauchno-informatsionnyi tsentr "Memorial," St. Petersburg, Russia, 48.

11. Ibid., 25.

12. Ibid., 27.

13. Tatiana Goricheva, *Talking about God Is Dangerous: The Diary of a Russian Dissident* (New York: Crossroad, 1987), 21.

14. Tat'iana Goricheva, "Zhenshchina-filosof v pravoslavnom khrame: Beseda s Tat'ianoi Gorichevoi," *Voda zhivaia*, 27 February 2008, accessed 11 August 2011, http://rusk.ru/st.php?idar=26040.

15. Tat'iana Goricheva, "'Radiusia, slez evinykh izbavlenie'," in *Zhenshchina i Rossiia: Al'manakh*, ed. Tat'iana Mamonova (Paris: Des femmes, 1980), 24–25.

16. Goricheva, *Talking about God*, 22.

17. Iu. M. Valieva, comp., *Sumerki "Saigona,"* Tvorcheskie ob'edineniia Leningrada (St. Petersburg: Samizdat, 2009), 139.

18. Interview with Galina Grigor'eva, 16.

19. Tat'iana Goricheva, "Iz pisem k dukhovnomu bratu," *Grani* 123 (1982): 166–89.

20. Ibid., 168.

21. Ibid., 170–71. Goricheva later avowed suspicion of Marian miracles and apparitions, claiming that in Orthodoxy, the miracle lay in life itself. She eventually came to accept these apparitions after witnessing Marian devotion in Ecuador. See Goricheva, *Tol'ko v Rossii*, 198, 201.

22. Ibid., 171.

23. Ibid., 173–74.

24. Goricheva, "'Radiusia'," 26.

25. Ibid., 27. For "Pis'ma po molitvam k Bogomateri," see *Mariia* 1 (1981): 31–34, and *Mariia* 3 (1982): 60–64.

26. Ibid., 21.

27. Ibid., 26.

28. Ibid., 23.

29. Ibid., 24.

30. Natal'ia Malakhovskaia, "Materinskaia sem'ia," in *Zhenshchina i Rossiia: Al'manakh*, ed. Tat'iana Mamonova (Paris: Des femmes, 1980), 39.

31. Ibid., 32.

32. Ibid., 36.

33. Ibid., 37.

34. Ibid.

35. Ibid., 40.

36. For a brief discussion of the seminar led by Goricheva and her then-husband Viktor Krivulin in the context of "near-Orthodox" religious communities and the "religious seekership of Soviet intellectuals," see Olga Cherpurnaia, "The Hidden Sphere of Religious Searches in the Soviet Union: Independent Religious Communities in Leningrad from the 1960s to the 1970s," *Sociology of Religion* 64, no. 3 (October 2003): 377–88.

37. Author's e-mail interview with Natal'ia Malakhovskaia, 25 June 2011. On gender, religion, and atheism under Khrushchev, see Irina Paert, "Demystifying the Heavens: Women, Religion, and Khrushchev's Anti-Religious Campaign, 1954–64," in *Women in the Khrushchev Era*, ed. Melanie Ilič, Susan E. Reid, and Lynne Atwood (New York: Palgrave Macmillan, 2004), 203–21.

38. Direct references to these thinkers are strikingly absent from the *Mariia* journals, although some of their ideas are present in diluted or reflected form, particularly in connection with Christianity and social activism. Similarly, though there is no evidence that the group's members were familiar with the works of Mother Mariia Skobtsova, there is a remarkable resonance between Skobtsova's essay "O podrazhanii Bogomateri" (On the imitation of the Mother of God, 1939) and the social agenda that the Mariia women articulate in their writings, which Natalia Ermolaev discusses in the present volume. Goricheva became familiar with Skobtsova's works in emigration and cites her in volumes such as *Docheri Iova* and *Tol'ko v Rossii est' vesna!*

39. Goricheva, *Talking about God*, 48. For a brief discussion of the "37" group, see Jane Ellis, *The Russian Orthodox Church: A Contemporary History* (Bloomington: Indiana University Press, 1986), 390–96. On the origins of the journal of the same name, see Viktor Krivulin, "'37,' 'Severnaia pochta,'" in *Samizdat (Po materialam konferentsii "30 let nezavisimoi pechati 1950–80 gody," Sankt-Peterburg 25–27 aprelia 1992 g.)*, ed. Viacheslav E. Dolinin (Pavlovsk: Memorial, 1993), 74–81.

40. Tat'iana Goricheva, *Docheri Iova: Khristianstvo i feminizm* (St. Petersburg: Alga-Fond, Stupeni, 1992), 48.

41. Malakhovskaia, "O Zarozhdenii," 74.

42. "Soobshchenie o novoi atake sovetskikh vlastei na zhenskoe dvizhenie," *Mariia* 3 (1982): 96.

43. Malakhovskaia has claimed that she thought up the name for the journal, since after the exile of Mamonova *Zhenshchina i Rossiia* would have to be renamed and also transformed from an almanac into a journal. Commenting that "there are many female names in Russia, and more women in Russia than KGB workers," she reasoned that if this journal were to be banned, it could be relaunched or reinvented under a different name; in addition, "Mariia" had an attractive "fairytale nuance." She concluded that for Goricheva, "the name 'Mariia' had a very discrete religious orientation and namely that interpretation" stuck in readers' minds. See Malakhovskaia, "O Zarozhdenii," 79.

44. "K zhenshchinam Rossii," *Mariia* 1 (1981): 7.

45. Ibid., 7.

46. Tat'iana Goricheva, "Ved'my v kosmose," *Mariia* 1 (1981): 10; Goricheva, "Antivselennaia sovetskoi sem'i," *Mariia* 2 (1982): 35.

47. Goricheva, "Ved'my v kosmose," 10.

48. Ibid., 11, 12.

49. Ibid., 10.

50. Iuliia Voznesenskaia, "Domashnii kontslager'," *Mariia* 1 (1981): 17, 18.

51. "Otvety na anketu zhurnala 'Alternativy,'" *Mariia* 1 (1981): 24.

52. Ibid., 25.

53. Ibid., 26.

54. Ibid., 28.

55. Tat'iana Goricheva, "Pis'ma po molitvam k Bogomateri," *Mariia* 1 (1981): 31.

56. Ibid., 34; "K zhenshchinam Rossii," 7.

57. Goricheva, "Pis'ma po molitvam k Bogomateri," 33.

58. Ibid., 34.

59. E. K., "O krestnom puti Bogomateri," *Mariia* 3 (1982): 60.

60. Tat'iana Goricheva, "Iz pis'ma v Leningrad," *Mariia* 3 (1982): 62.

61. Ibid., 63. The idea of Russia as a site of great spiritual potential and a source of hope, contrasting sharply with a morally bankrupt, consumerist, and spiritually dead West, was a theme Goricheva would revisit frequently in emigration, most directly in Tol'ko v Rossii est' vesna!, a selection of her diary entries from her travels between 1980 and 2003.

62. Goricheva, "Ved'my v kosmose," 10.

63. Voznesenskaia, "Domashnii kontslager'," 16.

64. "Diskussiia na temu 'Feminizm i Marksizm,'" *Mariia* 1 (1981): 22.

65. Sof'ia Sokolova, "Slabyi pol? Da, muzhchiny," *Mariia* 1 (1981): 43.

66. Goricheva, "Ved'my v kosmose," 9.

67. Voznesenskaia, "Domashnii kontslager'," 19.

68. Malakhovskaia later commented that she found the articles on *smirenie* "unacceptable." Interview with Natal'ia Malakhovskaia, 38.

69. "Iz pis'ma o leningradskikh diskussiiakh kluba 'Mariia' kontsa 1980 g.," *Mariia* 3 (1982): 37. If this definition of humility seems to indicate a reversion to earlier gender relations, so does Galina Khamova's (pseudonym of Galina Grigor'eva) call in her article "Rezkie repliki" (Sharp words) for the right of women not to work outside the home if they so chose. The first section of that article concluded with the capitalized plea: "MY KHOTIM *BYT'* MATERIAMI, ZHENAMI, KHOZIAIKAMI—ZHENSHCHINAMI, NAKONETS!" (We want to *be* mothers, wives, housewives—and finally, women!) Grigor'eva's status as a sometime single mother may explain her argument that a single mother should be able to stay home with her children and not be considered a "parasite."

70. Tat'iana Goricheva, "Nadezhda sverkh nadezhdy," *Mariia* 3 (1982): 32.

71. "K zhenshchinam Rossii," *Mariia* 1 (1981): 7.

72. Ibid., 8.

73. On the capacity of the Mother of God to co-participate, co-feel, and co-suffer with each human soul, see Maria Skobtsova, "On the Imitation of the Mother of God," in *Mother Maria Skobtsova: Essential Writings*, trans. Richard Pevear and Larissa Volokhonsky (Maryknoll, NY: Orbis, 2003), 69.

74. Iuliia Voznesenskaia, "K nashim chitatel'nitsam," *Mariia* 1 (1981): 79–84.

75. Goricheva, "Antivselennaia sovetskoi sem'i," 36.

76. Natal'ia Malakhovskaia, "V nenasytnoi utrobe," *Mariia* 2 (1982): 40.

77. Alla Sariban, "Zhenshchina i byt," *Mariia* 2 (1982): 45.

78. Ibid., 46.

79. Voznesenskaia, "Domashnii kontslager'," 14.

80. Quoted in Susan Rubin Suleiman, "Writing and Motherhood," in *The (M)other Tongue: Essays in Feminist Psychoanalytic Interpretation*, ed. Shirley Nelson Garner, Claire Kahane, and Madelon Sprengnether (Ithaca, NY: Cornell University Press, 1985), 358.

81. The presence of sexism within a dissident group as a catalyst for the development of feminist activity has a cross-cultural corollary in the emergence of the women's movement of the 1960s from the civil rights movement in the United States. See Sara Evans, *Personal Politics: The Roots of Women's Liberation in the Civil Rights Movement and the New Left* (New York: Vintage, 1979).

82. Interview with Natal'ia Malakhovskaia, 6.

83. Sof'ia Chuikina, "Uchastie zhenshchin v dissidentskom dvizhenii (1956–1986)," *Gendernoe izmerenie sotsial'noi i politicheskoi aktivnosti v perekhodnoi period: Sbornik nauchnykh statei*, ed. Elena Zdravomyslovaia and Anna Temkina (St. Petersburg: Tsentr nezavisimykh sotsiologicheskikh issledovanii, 1996), 69.

84. Tat'iana Goricheva, *Russkaia zhenshchina i pravoslavie: Bogoslovie, filosofiia, kul'tura* (St. Petersburg: Stupeni, 1996), 84.

85. Tat'iana Goricheva, "O kenozise russkoi kul'tury," in *Khristianstvo i russkaia literatura: Sbornik statei*, ed. V. A. Kotel'nikov (St. Petersburg: Nauka, 1994), 63.

86. Goricheva, *Docheri Iova*, 29.

87. Interview with Natal'ia Malakhovskaia, 26.

88. Ibid., 28. In direct opposition to Malakhovskaia, Goricheva has rejected the idea that the Mother of God is connected to *mat' syra zemlia* (Mother Damp Earth) or other pagan traditions (*Docheri Iova*, 50). The editors of *Zhenshchina i Rossiia* critiqued the Mariia group, seeing it as limited and excluding sectors of society that were neither Russian nor Christian. See "Actions and Counteractions," in *Women and Russia: Feminist Writings from the Soviet Union*, ed. Tat'iana Mamonova (Boston, MA: Beacon Press, 1984), 235–44.

89. Ibid., 52.

90. Goricheva, *Docheri Iova*, 63.

91. Goricheva, "Zhenshchina-filosof."

# 11

## Following in Mary's Footsteps
### Marian Apparitions and Pilgrimage in Contemporary Russia

STELLA ROCK

THIS CHAPTER EXPLORES PILGRIM ENCOUNTERS with the Mother of God in the sacred places of contemporary Russia. Such encounters, especially the "experiences of radical presence" that are Marian apparitions, conflate a specific earthly location with the "no-place" of transcendence.[1] Mary is, for her devotees, universally accessible, but in certain places she seems more present. The Mother of God often announces her presence to Orthodox devotees via miraculously revealed images rather than apparition, but these sanctify place in similar ways. How Russia's sacred topography is shaped by relations between humans and the Mother of God and how Russian pilgrims experience and interpret her presence will be examined via case studies of two very different shrines—one embryonic and marginal, the other a nationally significant pilgrimage center.

Holy Trinity-Saint Seraphim Diveevo Convent in the Nizhnii Novgorod region is a large and well-established institution that attracts over 200,000 pilgrims annually.[2] Although Saint Seraphim is the primary draw for contemporary pilgrims, Diveevo may be categorized as a Marian apparitional shrine. By contrast, Gorokhovo is the near-empty site of a former village in Kirov region, where an icon of the Kazan Mother of God is believed to have appeared. The majority of pilgrims encounter this uninhabited place with its partially derelict church as they pass through it on their way to another shrine. In both places Mary makes her presence felt, sometimes radically so.[3] How do these contrasting shrine environments impact upon, embody, channel, and facilitate pilgrim experiences of Mary's presence?

## RUSSIAN PILGRIMAGE TO MARY IN EUROPEAN CONTEXT

Marian pilgrimage has attracted increasing attention from researchers in various disciplines. While some studies have acknowledged that which is of primary importance to the pilgrim—the opportunity to interact with the sacred—few have focused on the nature of this relationship, preferring instead to explore the material causes and consequences of Marian devotion, concentrating on power, gender, social and economic relationships, and identity formation.[4]

Modern pilgrimage in Western Europe is predominantly Marian. Marian apparitional shrines do not dominate numerically, but the immense popularity of shrines such as Lourdes, Knock, and Fatima in contemporary pilgrimage culture—and the development of new apparition sites such as Medjugorje and Clearwater—testifies to their importance.[5] The desire to be where the Mother of God has been, at sites "where the transcendent breaks into time and comes face-to-face with humans," exercises perhaps the most powerful pull on modern (or postmodern) Catholic pilgrims.[6] Not all apparitions will generate pilgrimage, especially if unsupported by the institutional church; nevertheless, they have considerable potential to do so "because the holy person who is assumed to have appeared on earth imbues the apparition site with a special, long-lasting aura of sanctity."[7]

As yet there is no academic overview of functioning Russian Orthodox shrines, but publications aimed at contemporary pilgrims confirm Vera Shevzov's and Jill Dubisch's observations that Orthodox experience of the Mother of God is predominantly connected with icons rather than apparitions.[8] However, while Marian icons are central to Orthodox worship, Mary does not dominate the Russian pilgrimage market. In one guidebook for pilgrims 30 percent of the icons and relics listed were Marian, in another 17 percent, and in one volume not a single Marian icon was listed.[9] Moreover, although Marian apparitions have been recorded in modern Russia,[10] there is no major Orthodox shrine in Russia that is sanctified by the appearance of the Mother of God in quite the same way that—say—Lourdes and Fatima are, although the local administration has harbored aspirations to construct something similar around the Kazan Mother of God Monastery. Some hope that Kazan will work with an "elite" club of six pilgrimage sites (Częstochowa, Lourdes, Fatima, Loreto, Altötting, Mariazell) to create a special pilgrim path across the Marian shrines of Europe, claiming it to be the oldest Marian apparitional shrine in Europe. An especially venerated copy of the Kazan icon remains, however, the focus of the shrine.[11]

Mary's visits to Russia sometimes leave "actual" footprints that are venerated in a number of places,[12] but—as in the example of Kazan—they generally generate icons. As Shevzov points out, these icons have been viewed as "the imprints of [Mary's] footsteps" over the Russian land, and they are often named after the specific place in which they appeared.[13] These images initially sanctify the landscape where they are found, or bestow special favor on one community, but may then be moved to, or replicated in, a different location. One should not overstress the apparent differences between Catholic apparition-focused and Orthodox icon-centered veneration, however. Catholics may seek Mary's presence in, for example, touch relics of Our Lady of Guadalupe, or travelling statues of Our Lady of Fatima, and Catholic apparitional images also have the potential to become more important than the locus of Mary's appearance.[14]

Despite the portability of Orthodox sanctity, and the transcendence of Christian divinity, specific locations are important. To appeal to a saint on their own territory (where their icon miraculously appeared, for instance) is especially efficacious. A key combination of person and place allows Orthodox believers to most effectively access the holy, as Greene's exploration of responses to the Soviet campaign against relics powerfully demonstrates: believers could tolerate the exposure and ridicule of their local wonderworkers, but not the physical removal of their remains.[15] Furthermore, as contemporary pilgrim guidebooks make clear, in most instances significant images and relics are contained within the walls of a monastic institution. This offers pilgrims proximity to an environment imbued with holiness.

Although Robert Orsi has identified "the ongoing eruption of presence into the [modern] spaces of its denial," post-Reformation, post–Vatican II European space has been substantially disenchanted.[16] In contrast, presence has remained central to Orthodox religiosity, and sanctity in the physical environment (such as apparitions confer) is no rarity. The persistence of pilgrimage in Soviet times—when the material fabric of shrines might be desecrated, removed, or destroyed—confirms that, for Russian pilgrims, holiness is also deeply embedded in places associated with a saint's life or death.[17] Repeated religious activity may also contribute to making a place sacred, rendering it *namolennyi* (from *namolit'*—to pray fervently) and—crucially—the spiritual is tangible in and present in the material of every icon.[18] As one pilgrim discovered, there are "miracles in almost every town. Every holy place has its own miracles. There is an image of the Kazan Mother of God in all churches existing in Rus', because—it's well known—she also protected Rus' from the Poles during the Time of Troubles."[19] Amid such wealth, one might argue, temporary spiritual manifestations in other material places—trees, cupolas, fields, streets—exert no extraordinary pull.

## RESONANT HISTORY AND LAY VISIONARIES AT GOROKHOVO

The vast majority of pilgrims encounter Gorokhovo during a grueling one hundred and fifty kilometer procession of the cross to Velikoretskoe, which pauses at the shrine mid-morning on its third day. This six-day round trip to the centuries-old shrine of Velikoretskoe—an otherwise obscure village in Kirov region (Viatka diocese)—now attracts twenty to thirty thousand participants annually, although not all of these will walk the whole way.[20] Those who do make it into Gorokhovo will have covered fifty kilometers the previous day, and will have been walking since three a.m. This diverse body of pilgrims, from all over Russia and the "near abroad," pours into the shrine on 5 June annually, but much smaller groups of local pilgrims, in which women predominate, process to the shrine on feasts of the Kazan icon of the Mother of God. The few pilgrims visiting at other times also have no option but to approach the shrine on foot, passing the village cemetery, since there are no longer any passable roads into or out of what was once a flourishing village with a school.[21]

Gorokhovo is now uninhabited, and the only buildings standing are a recently restored church dedicated to the Kazan icon of the Mother of God and a large wooden hut built by volunteers working on the church since 1998. A short stroll from the church is a natural spring, also dedicated to the Kazan icon, at which two wooden bathing huts and a water-dispensing fountain have been constructed. According to a lay activist heavily involved in Gorokhovo's restoration, oral tradition suggests that an icon of the Mother of God of Kazan miraculously appeared here. Although written testimony of this has yet to be found, he points out that when the local wooden church was rebuilt in stone in the early nineteenth century, its main dedication was changed from the three holy hierarchs to the Mother of God of Kazan. Some "great event," he surmises, clearly influenced this decision.[22]

Gorokhovo is therefore a "found object" shrine rather than an apparitional one, sanctified by the miraculous appearance of a Marian image, but according to some pilgrims Mary herself often appears here. She appears annually to a fifty-year-old pilgrim from Tolyatti, for example, as he approaches the shrine during the procession to Velikoretskoe. "Every year I see an image of the Holy Mother of God at the village of Gorokhovo, which appears in the sky for a few minutes and then disappears. For me this is an unbelievable sight and a joy." Other pilgrims recount that true believers, or the pure of heart, will witness a vision of Mary in Gorokhovo, or on the cupola of the church as they approach Gorokhovo. "Pilgrims say a lot of things," one of the women working at the local cathedral observed drily, when questioned about these apparitions. Some clergy are similarly circumspect—the only local Marian apparition for which there is any evidence, they point out, is that accorded Saint Trifon of Viatka.[23]

The apparitions experienced by pilgrims at Gorokhovo are not unusual, however—numerous pilgrims in Diveevo perceive Saint Seraphim on the cupola of the cathedral during important feasts, for example. Some pilgrims are keen to recount Marian encounters in times of danger rather than moments of especial grace: a middle-aged pilgrim in Solovki shared her childhood recollection of being saved from a bear by a beautiful lady she now realizes was Mary; a terminally ill pilgrim in Pskov-Pecherskii Monastery recounted her vision of Christ and the Mother of God, "just like icons," in the corner of the operating theatre. Such personalized, protective interactions with laity rarely generate pilgrimage, but—if accepted by shrine guardians—they may eventually enter the clerically approved, authoritative narrative of a related shrine.[24]

For pilgrims, visions that occur at a shrine are confirmation of the special power or grace of the holy place, or a reward for the faith and efforts of the visionary. Inna Naletova interprets one pilgrim's declaration that she could not see an icon weeping because she had not walked with the pilgrims who carried it to Diveevo shrine as evidence of the "kenotic communities" formed on pilgrimage.[25] While Naletova interprets her pilgrim as placing the emphasis on walking *together*, it may, however, have been on the very act of walking (in a two week procession); a similar interpretation was offered for a photographer's inability to capture the circular rainbow that appeared around the sun during Velikoretskoe's festal liturgy. While the photographer's expensive camera failed, many pilgrims photographed the rainbow successfully on low-quality mobile phones. This, a local priest explained, was because the rainbow was especially for those who had escorted the icon of Saint Nicholas from Kirov to Velikoretskoe through muddy fields and forests. Saint Nicholas would hardly allow distant newspaper readers to share in this reward.[26]

Gorokhovo has a long history as a "spiritual oasis" for pilgrims on the way to Velikoretskoe.[27] It was one of the villages visited by the icon of Saint Nicholas in the nineteenth and early twentieth centuries during its annual progress from the regional capital of Viatka (now Kirov) to its miraculous birthplace.[28] During the 1950s, when the procession became an unauthorized mass pilgrimage led by local believers rather than clergy, pilgrims continued to gather and pray at Gorokhovo—one of only two such stopping places identified by the local commissioner for the Council of Russian Orthodox Church Affairs.[29] Only since the late 1990s has Gorokhovo been the focal point for its own processions of the cross, although many pilgrims joining these have already encountered the shrine during the Velikoretskoe procession.

In contrast to the Velikoretskoe pilgrimage, Gorokhovo's processions are far less strenuous. On the Kazan icon of the Mother of God feasts of 4 November and 20/21 July buses take pilgrims from Kirov to a local village, from where they process ten or so kilometers to Gorokhovo with an icon of the Mother of God of Kazan.[30] Until these processions were blessed by the local bishop in 1999 they took the form of unofficial lay-led pilgrimages, where participants prayed in the then almost entirely ruined church, and bathed in the spring. Clerical participation was initially limited and sporadic, but in recent years a local priest has ensured that all may confess and receive communion during the pilgrimage. The summer procession has recently been extended to include an overnight stay, with an all-night vigil followed by a liturgy celebrated on the morning of the feast. In 2011, pilgrims pitched tents in the long grass, or slept in cement dust on the unfinished floor of the church.[31]

The topography of Gorokhovo is simple, with the church acting as both focal and access point. Pilgrims follow the clergy from the dirt track into the empty body of the church where, during the annual pilgrimage to Velikoretskoe, a short prayer service (*moleben*) with a hymn (akathist) to Saint Nicholas and an office of the dead (*panikhida*) are celebrated. Beyond the church, across a field and down a woodland track, a water blessing ceremony with an akathist to the Kazan Mother of God is simultaneously celebrated at the spring. Current pilgrim activity at the shrine is dictated as much by the volume of pilgrims as by any perceived tradition. The thousands of Velikoretskoe pilgrims must choose to attend the *moleben* in church or follow other clergy down to the holy spring. Participants in the Kazan processions can access all clerically led prayers, since one priest serves all two hundred or so pilgrims.[32] The Kazan icon carried on these latter processions is also venerated at frequent intervals throughout the pilgrimage.

In addition to icon veneration in situ, clerically led prayers, and sacraments, pilgrims may access the sacred via the natural features of the shrine. Bathing is an important aspect of post-Soviet pilgrimage, and nowadays Gorokhovo spring is reputed to work miracles. In recent years pilgrims bathing there have apparently been cured of asthma, leg pain, infertility, eczema, even cataracts. It is particularly efficient at curing eyes, one local pilgrim tells me, because it is dedicated to the Kazan icon, and because it contains a high level of natural silver.[33] The spring now flows poorly, but pilgrims queue to collect water and to bathe in the rudimentary huts separating men and women. Water from the spring is taken home by pilgrims as a "portable, palpable" source of divine grace.[34]

Another significant focal point is a fresco fragment high up on the external wall of the bell tower, an image of Mary with the child Jesus flanked by figures

FIGURE 11.1 Mother of God fresco, Gorokhovo. Photo courtesy of Sandra Reddin.

too partial and faint to identify, but described as angels in literature aimed at pilgrims (see fig. 11.1).[35] This image has strong emotional significance for many pilgrims, who pray intensely, sometimes weeping, before the bell tower wall. It is via this damaged image that the Mother of God interacts with most pilgrims, displaying increased (or, rarely, decreased) clarity from year to year. Some maintain that the image has appeared only since pilgrims began to visit Gorokhovo, claiming that when they first visited, twelve or more years ago, there was nothing to be seen. Pilgrims tend to perceive the image as becoming clearer as they resanctify the place with prayers and processions, and Mary's strengthening image is also interpreted as an indication that she is pleased with their collective efforts and/or hears their prayers.[36]

In addition to this spiritual labor, procession participants also contribute physically to the restoration of the shrine. Velikoretskoe pilgrims recount how, one year, they passed a load of bricks that lorries had been unable to transport into Gorokhovo due to the lack of roads. The procession leaders asked pilgrims to each take just one brick with them. In 2011 local pilgrims formed a human chain to move bricks into the body of the church and stack them ready for the builders.

Although the church exterior is now completely rebuilt, rendered and painted white, an area around the fresco has been left as rough brick, testifying to the church's former state of desecration. According to local believers, during the Soviet period Mary's image was plastered over, whitewashed, even hammered off, but miraculously continued to reappear despite all attempts to erase it. The image has both political and spiritual symbolic significance because most pilgrims are conscious—and some are acutely conscious—of the Velikoretskoe procession as the resurrection of a tradition that "the Bolsheviks" attempted, and failed, to eradicate. Mary's appearance to pilgrims on a desecrated church, in a deserted village, offers a powerful message of hope. For one pilgrim her indestructible fresco shows that Russia is under the protection of the Mother of God and that no one can take that protection away.[37]

Gorokhovo's church was closed in the 1930s and partially dismantled for building materials in the 1960s. Some pilgrims recount that bricks were taken to build the local school, which is now completely destroyed, while the church alone stands, although according to one local journalist proximity to the school building is what saved the church from being blown up entirely. In this latter version, the bricks were taken to a neighboring village to build a farm that still stands, although the village itself, like Gorokhovo, no longer exists.[38] Locals also recount that the man who threw down the church bells swiftly perished, and the appearance of lit candles, together with the sounds of vigil services emanating from the ruined building, encouraged local inhabitants to gradually abandon the village.[39] The church's ruined state resonates strongly with local believers, who continue to experience a variety of divine sounds and visions within and without its walls. One pilgrim, whose father lived in Gorokhovo before she was born, recalls meeting a woman in the ruined church in 2000 whose parents were also former residents of Gorokhovo. She "felt something must happen" and drew her companion's attention to the aperture where once the altar stood. While she could not see anything herself, her companion perceived there an image of the Kazan icon of the Mother of God.[40]

For all its historical resonance this deserted village, with its almost empty church and woodland spring, is a particularly detached and peaceful place. As a researcher of Spanish apparitions has pointed out, successful vision sites often have an "otherness, otherworldliness, nonhumanness, semiwildness" about them, characteristics that are perhaps "more appropriate for spontaneous, and less tamed, manifestations of grace."[41] Believers may approach Mary here in unregulated fashion, although this is already changing as the shrine becomes more firmly integrated into diocesan life. Nevertheless, here pilgrims find the time and space to personally interact with Mary, in ways that reflect the diversity of believers' relationships with the Mother of God.

These relations are not necessarily uncomplicated, or even benign. One male pilgrim, who spent an unusually long time praying on his knees and repeatedly venerating the icon which had been carried in procession, explained that he is a "realist" who joins the Kazan processions to resolve problems and to ensure that nothing bad happens. When he once failed to do so Mary punished him with a "blow" on the very day of the November pilgrimage.[42] Another pilgrim who participates in processions seeking help in daily life expressed her difficulty relating to Mary (perhaps, she speculates, because of a difficult relationship with her earthly mother) and could not say how the shrine was connected with the Mother of God. One woman, who feels particularly supported by Mary after making a vow before her Kazan icon, continues to make the journey annually simply because of her love for the Mother of God. In Gorokhovo Mary may be "mum" (*mama*), "intercessor" (*zastupnitsa*), or a divine being who independently punishes and then forgives the penitent, as well as the provider of an indestructible, irremovable "Protecting Veil" (*Pokrov*) over Russia.[43]

## MARIAN APPARITIONS AND THE SACRED TOPOGRAPHY OF DIVEEVO

If the Gorokhovo shrine is notable for its emptiness and wildness, the Holy Trinity-Saint Seraphim Diveevo convent is impressive in its regulated abundance. With huge cathedrals, several churches, a prominent bell tower and extensive grounds restored, landscaped, and constructed piecemeal since 1990, Diveevo is a magnet for contemporary pilgrims. It hosts high-profile visitors from the worlds of politics and culture, and also has powerful friends among the dead: the canonized Romanovs are intimately connected with the historic development of the shrine. Although Diveevo is situated in a difficult to access, rural area of Nizhnii Novgorod oblast, the convent has become one of the most significant and popular pilgrimage centers in Russia. Important feasts attract up to 10,000 pilgrims, and the convent feeds 3,000 pilgrims a day in summer months.[44] While adult women pilgrims predominate on ordinary days, feast days attract a more diverse crowd.

Diveevo may be categorized as a Marian apparitional shrine, although its primary devotional focus is Saint Seraphim (canonized in 1903). Seraphim's relics were brought to the convent in 1991, and most pilgrims testify that they are visiting the saint himself, that they have been called by him personally or that their journey to the shrine and time there has been supervised by him in some way.[45] Mary's direct intervention is prominent in the shrine's creation narrative and in its complex sacred topography, however, and many pilgrims are acutely aware of her actual or potential in-place presence.

The convent's chronicle, compiled at the end of the nineteenth century and first published in 1896, begins with an explanation that Diveevo is the Mother of God's fourth domain (*zhrebii* or *udel*) on earth. Mary's ownership of the convent is stressed in all publications aimed at pilgrims. One woman, visiting for a month with her three small children, explained that the Mother of God was given her first domain at the feast of Pentecost, when all the apostles were given lands to evangelize and she was allotted Georgia. She did not manage to reach it, as "some sort of event" meant that she landed instead on Athos, which became her second domain. Her third domain was the Kievan land, and then Diveevo. This pilgrim could not remember where she had read the story, but it is a reasonable rendition of the chronicle narrative that is repeated in most, if not all, publications about the shrine.[46] "And there won't be another," one woman who visits Diveevo three times a year elaborated; "it's written in the Gospels. We can't understand this but it is so—[Diveevo is] the final domain in the world."[47]

Pilgrim literature also stresses that the founding and development of Diveevo's religious community were closely supervised by Mary. Her instructions were first delivered in a series of dreams to a young widow, the nun Alexandra, tonsured at Kievan Florovskii Convent but dispatched by Mary to wander the shrines of Russia in search of a place to found a new cloister. In 1760, on her way to visit Sarov Monastery, the location of the future religious community was indicated to Mother Alexandra by the Mother of God as she dozed by a wooden church in the village of Diveevo. With the blessing of Mary herself, in the 1770s Alexandra had a stone church built here in honor of the Kazan icon of the Mother of God, and a community eventually grew up around it.[48] Mary assured Alexandra that on this fourth domain would flourish "a great convent, the like of which has never been, and will never be, in the whole world," a promise that allowed believers to hope that the 1927 closure of Diveevo convent was not final.[49] Some publications also suggest that the Mother of God repeated this promise of future greatness in 1988, appearing to the last surviving Diveevo nun and declaring that "[your monastic] cell and this place will raise up the whole of creation."[50]

According to the chronicle, before her death in 1789 Alexandra entrusted Sarov monks Pakhomii and Seraphim—then a young hierodeacon—with the spiritual supervision of her sisterhood. After Pakhomii's death, Seraphim's first attempt to intervene in the life of the community in order to relax the particularly strict rule was firmly if politely rebuffed by the then-superior Ksenia, who saw no reason to change what the elder Pakhomii had organized. Seraphim continued to send women to Ksenia's community, but did not again attempt to direct them until the Mother of God appeared to him in 1825, rebuked him for neglecting Alexandra's request, and ordered him to take up his responsibility for the Diveevo sisters "since it is by My will that she gave it you."[51]

Rather than instructing Seraphim to challenge Ksenia's authority, the
Mother of God ordered Seraphim to build the great cloister she had promised
in a nearby location in the village of Diveevo, with eight named sisters—
all of whom had never married—taken from the original sisterhood. The
chronicle—citing the writings of N. A. Motovilov—relates how Mary gave
the new sisterhood a new rule "the like of which had never before existed
in any cloister" and declared that henceforth the community would only
accept maidens and that she herself would be the abbess. The promise of
greatness originally made to Mother Alexandra's community was therefore
transferred to Seraphim's new "windmill" community, the virginal core of the
contemporary convent thus named because Mary also instructed Seraphim
to build the sisters a wooden windmill.[52] Meanwhile, Mother Ksenia retained
authority over Mother Alexandra's original Kazan sisterhood and continued
to accept widows.

Narratives published by the convent also stress that in developing the built
and spiritual structures of the community, Saint Seraphim followed Mary's
express directions, which she conveyed to him in apparitions, rather than his
own human thoughts or any earlier example.[53] During this 1825 apparition
Mary struck the ground with her staff to create a healing spring, and also gave
instructions for the building of Diveevo's most famous feature, the *kanavka*, a dry
moat and rampart intended to frame and protect the new community's territory

FIGURE 11.2 *Kanavka* at Diveevo, 2008. Photo courtesy of Sandra Reddin.

(see fig. 11.2). In Seraphim's words, this *kanavka* is the "very path where the Queen of Heaven walked, taking the convent into her domain. There the little feet [*stopochki*] of the Queen of Heaven have passed."[54] Anyone who walked the *kanavka* and prayed to the Mother of God as directed would have "Athos and Jerusalem and Kiev," so a holier place can hardly be imagined. Moreover, Mary is believed to walk the bounds of her domain once every twenty-four hours, so her presence is continually refreshed.[55] The last authenticated sighting of her on the *kanavka*, by a bishop, was one evening in 1927.[56]

Despite the apparent importance of this structure, the sisters did not start construction until 1829, and rushed to complete it in cursory fashion before Seraphim's death in 1833. According to contemporary convent publications, instead of constructing a moat as instructed, three arshins deep with ramparts three arshins high (these measurements are understood as symbolic of the Trinity—in contemporary terms three arshins is just over two meters), in many places they dug only one or two arshins down.[57] Less than ten years after Seraphim's death his windmill community was united with the Kazan community by the Holy Synod and the structure of the fortifications apparently altered for ease of access. Carriages even drove along the *kanavka* and this relaxed attitude to the Mother of God's fortifications existed until the community became a convent under Abbess Maria at the beginning of the 1860s. Mother Maria removed the offending bridges and access points, cleared the moat of rubbish, and sprinkled the ramparts along which the sisters walked with sand.[58]

For all Mother Maria's efforts to return the *kanavka* to its former state, during restoration of the contemporary convent Abbess Sergiia discovered that the *kanavka* had never been completed according to instructions. Despite the shallow depth of some sections, no further digging had been done after 1833—and "the task of fulfilling the commandment of the Mother of God and Father Seraphim lay on the shoulders of the sisters participating in the revival of the convent."[59] Post-Soviet redevelopment of the shrine, rather than simply replicating what existed before the convent's 1927 closure, reflects a contemporary interpretation both of these apparitions and of the apocalyptic prophesies attributed to Seraphim.

CONTEMPORARY CONSTRUCTION AND THE EXPERIENCE OF PRESENCE:
MATERIALITY, AUTHENTICITY, AND INNOVATION

After the convent's closure the *kanavka* was almost entirely filled in, but continued to draw pilgrims who were able to follow trees planted along the original line of fortifications. One priest visiting from Moscow in the summer of 1971 walked round those parts of the *kanavka* still accessible at 5 A.M., managing to pray seventy or eighty of the one hundred and fifty "Rejoice, O Virgin Theotokos" prayers prescribed by Saint Seraphim.[60] While Mary is believed to walk nightly around the *kanavka*, or at dawn when the birds begin to sing, this priest may simply have been trying to evade detection rather than coincide with her visit: *samizdat* records tell us the police carried out surveillance of the *kanavka*, and that pilgrims were sometimes arrested.[61]

Work on the current *kanavka* began in 1997, when the sisters were permitted to begin their meticulous construction on territory that had until then been in the hands of the local administration. Despite all efforts to finish the *kanavka* before the centenary celebrations of Saint Seraphim's canonization in 2003, the fortifications were not quite completed: a memorial listing Diveevo soldiers killed in the war, and a memorial to the unknown soldier, stood exactly where the *kanavka* dug in 1833 ended. These memorials were eventually relocated and in 2006 the last gap in the fortifications was filled in.[62]

While Seraphim's original "orphans" skimped in their digging, the current convent administration under Mother Sergiia made sure that the contemporary structure was built to the heavily symbolic specifications identified in historical documents. The completed fortifications left a wide entrance near the site where—according to Seraphim—a cathedral in honor of the Mother of God would one day be built. A 2009 convent publication, recalling the promise that Diveevo would one day be a *lavra*, notes that their building program plans the construction of this prophesied church, and work on the Annunciation Cathedral of the Most Holy Mother of God began in 2012.[63] In publicizing Mary's promises and fulfilling prophesies about the convent's internal and external structures, the current administration is hurrying toward greatness: "and it is possible that this time is already near."[64]

The geography of Diveevo is also resonant with Mary's continued activity. "There are many holy places in Rus', but only in Diveevo is the Mother of God with us every day," explains one Orthodox journalist; although she is mostly invisible, she is sometimes perceptible in an aroma as wondrous as that of the Garden of Eden.[65] Mary's daily timetable is uncertain—one pilgrim speculated that she walks the *kanavka* in the morning rather than at night, since at dawn she bathes at the Kremenki spring (eight kilometers from Diveevo) before making her way to the convent. This spring is promoted as the site of two apparitions: one by Saint Seraphim who told local peasants that "the Most Holy Mother of God, before she walks the *Kanavka*, washes her face in the water of this spring," and the other a weeping face of the Mother of God in reddened spring waters, lamenting those killed in Stepan Razin's rebellion.[66]

The fact that Mary visits Diveevo nightly is why, another pilgrim explains, it is desirable for visitors to spend at least one full twenty-four hour period there: in doing so they will, in some way, experience Mary's divine presence.[67]

One of the most important ways of interacting with Mary is by repeating her circadian walk around the *kanavka*. "As Saint Seraphim said, the Most Holy Mother of God herself walked around the *kanavka* with her own little feet," one woman observed, "and it's possible for me, a sinner, to touch her grace, her grace-filled footsteps, in order to gain even a little bit of her grace and strength."[68] Pilgrims begin this ritual by kissing a marble crucifix and complete the circuit by kissing a marble cross with a relief of the Mother of God of Tenderness. These crosses are an innovation, erected in 2004 (together with another cross which marks the eastern-most point of the fortifications) to mark the future "holy gates" through which the sisters will access the great cenobitic institution promised them.[69] Walking round the *kanavka* slowly, pilgrims attempt to say one hundred and fifty prayers to the Mother of God, a ritual promoted in convent literature as "a means of uniting oneself with the Purity of the Ever-Virgin [Mary], commensurate with one's abilities." This circumnavigation is even compared with the liturgy, "leading the soul of the one praying to the greatest mystery of our salvation" and spiritually strengthening them on other paths in life.[70]

Pilgrims experience walking in Mary's footsteps differently—it may be as easy and comforting "as if someone carried me in their arms," as one woman commented on a popular website about Diveevo,[71] but it may also be spiritually challenging:

> The holy *kanavka*, along which the Mother of God herself treads, is also the most difficult "examination" of conscience.... Not everyone has got through this path. Some have become ill, others have started to yell (*krichat'*).[72]

Shrieking or shouting uncontrollably (along with seizures, violent hiccupping, and making animal noises) is traditionally understood as a symptom of demonic possession often manifested in proximity to a holy object or ritual,[73] and, as this pilgrim implies, those walking the *kanavka* may find themselves attacked by demonic forces rather than united with the Mother of God. Observing a woman praying through supernaturally strong hiccups and yawns, an Orthodox journalist observed that "it was difficult to watch ... I hope she made it to the end. And the devil will not become too comfortable in her still young, but evidently already deeply sinful, body."[74]

As a structure marked out and repeatedly touched by the feet of the Mother of God herself, the *kanavka* is a type of contact relic. Appealing to Mary from the very soil she patrols once every twenty-four hours is considered especially efficacious, and many pilgrims believe that all (good) desires will be fulfilled if one completes the cycle of recommended prayers. Pilgrims sometimes walk barefoot, and desperate petitioners may even circumnavigate the length of the *kanavka* on their knees.[75] A regular pilgrim to Diveevo described the *kanavka* as a "very powerful" holy thing that had been seen from space as a column of fire, and related the story of "an invalid" who, two years previously, had completed the ritual on crutches and been healed.[76] While pilgrims share stories of significant healings facilitated by walking the *kanavka*, there are also smaller, more intimate revelations of Mary's presence. Before the walkway was paved, pilgrims sometimes discovered her teardrops along the sandy path:

> Went round the *kanavka*, completed the prayer rule, even sang (quietly) and one woman gathering up the sand suddenly says that she had found one of the Mother of God's little teardrops—a dark blue pebble I think: well there's a thing. And I was already ready to leave, when in the last pinch I see a dark blue pebble well there's a thing. [sic] the Mother of God's tear. Put it in [my] top pocket and then show it to Mother, [the nun] who allotted us an obedience in the green-house, saying to her:
> —Look, I found a dark blue pebble in the sand on the *kanavka*.
> —That is a great kindness of the Virgin Mary, she's really marked you out.[77]

Some pilgrims choose to follow the nuns' regular evening procession around the *kanavka* with a copy of Saint Seraphim's beloved icon of the Mother of God of Tenderness. Pilgrims are not only following Mary's image: some believe that Mary herself invisibly lead the sisters and they are following closely in divine footsteps. The precise location of these footsteps has proved contentious, but when disagreements over the reconstructed *kanavka* temporarily gave rise to an "alternative" evening procession, Mary was naturally felt to be walking with the nuns rather than the protesters. Some pilgrims simply found this "new" *kanavka* hard to get used to, and talk with nostalgia about the "old."[78]

Mary's presence is nevertheless felt beyond the limits of the monastically regulated contemporary *kanavka*—in the trees that helped pilgrims identify and follow the *kanavka* during the Soviet period, for example. Pilgrims sometimes saw icons of the Mother of God in these trees, or perceived her face in their bark. They became so valuable that they had to be protected from pilgrims wanting to take pieces of bark home with them. Many of these trees were felled during the reconstruction work, and at the entrance to the *kanavka* the sisters hung a sign that explained "the pagan essence of this ritual." This did not deter some pilgrims from walking below the neatly tiled embankment and pausing at an especially revered tree in order to lay their palms or foreheads against the trunk.[79]

This newly constructed *kanavka*—a clearly delineated, paved walkway, fenced with iron railings—bears no resemblance to the grassy embankment that early twentieth-century pilgrims followed, or to the dusty tree-lined path that Soviet pilgrims navigated by. "How grace-filled every little stone and blade of grass is here, blessed by the Mother of God and perpetually blessing all those who visit these places," declared one visitor to Diveevo in 1926. Pilgrims in this period took flowers from the *kanavka*, and earth, which "sometimes protected them from attacks of the enemy."[80] "Herbs of the Mother of God" were apparently still being collected in Diveevo by elderly women in the region in the late 1950s.[81] Flowers and earth continue to be sought as souvenirs, but pilgrim access to them is increasingly constrained by both the physical boundaries of the new walkway and convent regulations.

While pilgrims are now forbidden to take bark, grass, flowers, twigs, or leaves from the *kanavka*, the convent recognizes that earth on which the Mother of God has walked is "dearer than gold," and a large wooden box of earth excavated from the *kanavka* is set aside for pilgrims to take home with them.[82] A notice erected by the convent in the 2000s (but no longer in place in 2010, although the box remained) informed pilgrims that "earth from the Holy Kanavka is sacred [*sviatynia*]. One should take a handful and keep it in a holy place near the icons. When sick one may apply the earth to the sore place or put it in spring water and drink [it]. Do not tread on earth from the Holy *Kanavka* with your feet."[83] According to a pilgrim from Rostov-on-Don, *kanavka* earth may also be eaten—sweet-tasting and spread on bread—in times of sickness or temptation.[84] Earth may even be sprinkled in a protective barrier around oneself: "After all, the Mother of God walks daily on this little earth [*zemel'ke*]. And She imbues this earth with Her grace, so wherever this earth is, all uncleanliness recoils from that place."[85]

Convent literature stresses this apotropaic or protective role of Mary's *kanavka*.[86] Mary's merciful compassion is a trope common to both Russian Orthodox and modern Catholic apparitional piety,[87] but in appealing to her from her own territory, Diveevo pilgrims are almost guaranteed protection from both earthly trials and divine retribution: "if we appeal with heartfelt prayers to the Heavenly Queen, to the true Intercessor of the Christian family, to the Helper of the helpless, then we will not remain unheard."[88]

CONCLUSION

Although Mary may be appealed to from anywhere, and encountered in her icons in any church, in some places she is perceived as present with an unusual degree of proximity. Gorokhovo and Diveevo have been sanctified by an image of Mary and her apparitions respectively, although some pilgrims to these shrines are unaware of their Marian connection, and Saint Seraphim remains the main focus of Diveevo. Her historic connections with these sites are recorded and reinforced by the built environment, and visiting pilgrims experience her contemporary presence—visible and invisible—in the material fabric of the holy place and sensory engagement. Via both miraculous image and manifestations to individuals, Mary reassures pilgrims that she values their efforts and is listening to their petitions.

Mary's daily visitations to Diveevo effectively transform the shrine environment into a contact relic, which pilgrims interact with in tangible and intimate ways. The topography evokes both the historical apparitions and Mary's circadian visits. Pilgrims may bathe in the spring Mary washes in, collect her tears, discern her fragrance. The "spiritual and prayerful center point of Diveevo convent," the *kanavka*, testifies to Diveevo's status as national powerhouse of grace governed by Mary herself.[89] More importantly in terms of pilgrim experience, it allows pilgrims to "literally" walk in Mary's footsteps, a mimetic ritual that brings them into intimate proximity with the divine. Pilgrim experience has become increasingly managed by the shrine guardians, however, in a reconstructed environment promoted as closer to divine intentions. In some areas this has proved controversial and has reduced access to elements pilgrims perceive as grace-giving.

In contrast, Gorokhovo's sacred topography—although changing—is far less regulated, and pilgrim behavior is less clearly channeled. Pilgrims may approach Mary via clerically led activities, but a significant part of Gorokhovo pilgrimage is bathing in the holy spring and interacting on a one-to-one basis with a fresco of the Mother of God. The man-made fabric of the shrine is minimal in comparison to Diveevo, and the single church—dedicated to the Kazan icon of the Mother of God—retains evidence of its once ruined state. While this wildness and ruination has negative resonances, it significantly adds to pilgrim experience. The section of the external church wall around the miraculously indestructible fresco has been left unrendered, a fragment of former desecration that both testifies to the resilience of the community's Orthodox belief and assures the faithful of Mary's perpetual presence.

NOTES

1. Robert Orsi, "Abundant History: Marian Apparitions as Alternative Modernity," in *Moved by Mary: The Power of Pilgrimage in the Modern World*, ed. Anna-Karina Hermkens, Willy Jansen, and Catrien Notermans (Burlington, VT: Ashgate, 2009), 215–25. Orsi's work has been a particular

inspiration in the writing of this chapter, but I am also grateful to Simon Coleman, Jeanne Kormina, Alexei Lidov, Vera Shevzov, Ann Shukman, and Katya Tolstaya for constructive feedback on earlier drafts.

2. Author field notes, July 2008: the convent's pilgrimage center helps house 200,000 pilgrims a year, a figure that does not include those who make their own arrangements with local families or private hotels.

3. The case studies are based on publications written for and by pilgrims, plus participant observation and interviews with pilgrims in Diveevo primarily in June 2010, during the Kazan icon of the Mother of God procession to Gorokhovo in July 2011, and during the annual Velikoretskii procession in 2009 (this latter research funded by the British Academy) and 2010.

4. Orsi, "Abundant History," 215–25. See, for example, Sandra Zimdars-Swartz's *Encountering Mary: From La Salette to Medjugorje* (Princeton, NJ: Princeton University Press, 1991); Sanne Derks, *Power and Pilgrimage: Dealing with Class, Gender and Ethnic Inequality at a Bolivian Marian Shrine* (Berlin: LIT Verlag, 2009); Hermkens, Jansen, and Notermans, eds, *Moved by Mary*. Michael P. Carroll's *The Cult of the Virgin Mary: Psychological Origins* (Princeton, NJ: Princeton University Press, 1986) categorizes apparitions either as illusions or hallucinations.

5. In Mary Lee Nolan and Sidney Nolan's unsurpassed survey, *Christian Pilgrimage in Modern Western Europe* (Chapel Hill: University of North Carolina Press, 1989), 11 percent of shrines studied were classed as apparitional and 18 percent as "found object" (generally images), the vast majority of both being Marian, 257–59. On "postmodern" apparitions, see William H. Swatos, Jr., "Our Lady of Clearwater: Postmodern Traditionalism," in William H. Swatos and Luigi Tomasi, eds., *From Medieval Pilgrimage to Religious Tourism: The Social and Cultural Economics of Piety* (Westport, CT: Praeger, 2002), 181–92; Angela K. Martin and Sandra Kryst, "Encountering Mary: Ritualization and Place Contagion in Postmodernity," in *Places through the Body*, ed. Heidi J. Nast and Steve Pile (New York: Routledge, 1998), 207–29.

6. Orsi, "Abundant History," 216.

7. Nolan and Nolan, *Christian Pilgrimage*, 266–67.

8. Vera Shevzov, *Russian Orthodoxy on the Eve of Revolution* (New York: Oxford University Press, 2004), 214; Jill Dubisch, *In a Different Place: Pilgrimage, Gender and Politics at a Greek Island Shrine* (Princeton, NJ: Princeton University Press, 1995), 240. Studies of medieval and early modern Catholic pilgrimage reflect a similar pattern, which supports the supposition that the attraction of apparition sites is a late modern phenomenon: see William A. Christian Jr., *Apparitions in Late Medieval and Renaissance Spain* (Princeton, NJ: Princeton University Press, 1981), 16–18; David Freedberg, *The Power of Images: Studies in the History and Theory of Response* (Chicago: University of Chicago Press, 1991), 99–135; Caroline Walker Bynum, *Christian Materiality: An Essay on Religion in Late Medieval Europe* (New York: Zone Books, 2011), 108–11. While no comprehensive overview of modern Russian pilgrimage exists, significant contributions have been made by Jeanne Kormina (see note 12 below); Inna Naletova (see, for example, "Orthodoxy beyond the Walls of the Church: A Sociological Inquiry into Orthodox Religious Experience in Contemporary Russian Society" [PhD diss., Boston University, 2007]); and Alexander A. Panchenko (see, for example, "Ivan i Yakov—strannye svyatye iz bolotnogo krai [religioznye praktiki sovremennoi novgorodskoi derevni]," in *Religioznye praktiki v sovremennoi Rossii*, ed. K. Russele [Rousselet] and A. Agadzhanian [Moscow: Novoe izd-vo, 2006]), 211–35. For further works by Russian scholars, see Stella Rock, "Touching the Holy: Orthodox Christian Pilgrimage Within Russia," in *International Perspectives on Pilgrimage Studies: Itineraries, Gaps and Obstacles*, ed. Dionigi Albera and John Eade (New York and London: Routledge, 2015), 47–68.

9. *Sputnik palomnika: Putevoditel' po sviatym mestam; Chudotvornye i mirotochivye ikony, sviatye moshchi, tselebnye istochniki* (Moscow: Trifonov Pechengskii Monastery, Kovcheg, 2002) catalogs over 240 relics of saints, 82 Marian icons, and 27 icons of Christ and the saints. Twenty-one of the 152 springs listed are dedicated to the Mother of God, plus a few unnamed springs located in a monastery or church dedicated to the Mother of God. E. Goncharov, *Molitvennyi putevoditel' palomnika* (Voronezh: Izd-vo Borisova, 2007) lists twenty-eight shrines dedicated to other saints,

five to Marian icons, one to the life-giving cross; Svetlana Kuzina's *Putevoditel' po sviatym mestam Rossii: Gde i kak molit'sia o schast'e, zdorov'e i den'gakh* (Moscow: Astrel', 2009) contains not a single Marian shrine. Dmitrii Orekhov's guidebook *Sviatye istochniki Rossii* (St. Petersburg: Amfora, 2009) contains twice as many springs dedicated to various saints as to Mary. A. A. Panchenko's study of northwestern rural shrines identifies 10 percent as having a feast day connected with icons of the Mother of God: *Issledovaniia v oblasti narodnogo pravoslaviia: Derevenskie sviatyni Severo-Zapada Rossii* (St. Petersburg: Aleteiia, 1998), 73.

10. See Vera Shevzov, "On the Field of Battle: The Marian Face of Contemporary Russia," in the present volume; Ieromonakh Alipii, "Pod Pokrovom Bozhiei Materi," *Eparkhialnyi Viatskii Vestnik* 7, no. 123 (2000): 4.

11. D. Khafizov, "Mesto iavleniia Bozhiei Materi v Kazani: Palomnichestvo i perspektivy mezhdunarodnogo turizma," 2007, last accessed 04 February 2014, available online at www.tourfactor. ru/conference-2007/34-palomnichestvo-pilgrimage/55--n-.html. In fact Czestochowa reflects an image-centered spirituality, as the official shrine site makes clear: "This sanctuary was not built after a Marian apparition as is usually the case for major holy sites. Without the painting [of Mary], Jasna Góra would be nothing but a building complex," last accessed 11 August 2011, www.jasnagora.pl. On developing the pilgrimage center and gaining observer status in the network of Marian shrines, see also publications on the official sites of the mayor of Kazan: "V Kazani stroiat pravoslavnyi palomnicheskii tsentr," *Gorod Kazan'*, published in July 2008, http://www.kzn.ru/old/page383.htm/show/4053; and "Mer Kazani Il'sur Metshin: 'Vozrozhdenie palomnichestva—shag k dukhovnomy rostu . . .,'" Ofitsial'naia stranitsa Il'sura Metshina, last accessed 12 July 2017, http://metshin.ru/ru/blogs/26 ; see Shevzov, "On the Field of Battle" in the present volume for further detail on the return of the Kazan icon.

12. Jeanne Kormina, "Pilgrims, Priest and Local Religion in Contemporary Russia: Contested Religious Discourses," *Folklore* 28 (2004): 25–40; Panchenko, *Issledovaniia*.

13. Shevzov, "On the Field of Battle."

14. On Guadalupe, see International Divine Mercy Affiliates, last accessed October 2011, www.feastofmercy.net/affiliates.shtml, for example; on Fatima, see David Morgan, "Aura and the Inversion of Marian Pilgrimage: Fatima and Her Statues," in Hermkens, Jansen, and Notermans, eds, *Moved by Mary*, 49–65. The miraculous medal has become more important than the chapel in Paris where Mary appeared in 1830, for example, although the chapel is nevertheless a place of pilgrimage (see the Chappelle Notre Dame de la Médaille Miraculeuse site: http://www.chapellenotredamedelamedaillemiraculeuse.com/langues/english/making-a-pilgrimage/). However, the image on the medal is not an accurate representation of Sister Catherine's vision, just as the statue of Our Lady of Lourdes did not seem to Bernadette anything like her lady. See Carroll, *The Cult of the Virgin Mary*.

15. Robert H. Greene, *Bodies Like Bright Stars: Saints and Relics in Orthodox Russia* (DeKalb: Northern Illinois Press, 2010).

16. Orsi, "Abundant History," 220. On Vatican II's impact on Marian devotion, see Robert A. Orsi, *Between Heaven and Earth: The Religious Worlds People Make and the Scholars Who Study Them* (Princeton, NJ: Princeton University Press, 2005). See also William A. Christian, *Visionaries: The Spanish Republic and the Reign of Christ* (Berkeley: University of California Press, 1996), 315.

17. Stella Rock, "'They burned the pine, but the place remains all the same': Pilgrimage in the Changing Landscape of Soviet Russia," in *State Secularism and Lived Religion in Soviet Russia and Ukraine*, ed. Catherine Wanner (Oxford: Oxford University Press, 2012), 159–89.

18. On *namolennost'*, see Zh. Kormina, "'Sviataia energetika namolennogo mesta': O iazyke pravoslavnykh palomnikov," in *Natales grate numeras? Sbornik statei k 60-letiiu Georgiia Akhillovicha Levintona*, ed. A. K. Baiburin and A. L. Ospovat, Studia Etnologica 6 (St. Petersburg: Izd-vo Evropeiskogo universiteta, 2008), 251–65. An edited version of this article is available in French translation as "La langue des pèlerins orthodoxes: 'L'énergie sacrale d'un lieu chargé de prière,'" in *Pèlerinages en Eurasie et au-delà*, ed. Kathy Rousselet, *Slavica Occitania* 36 (Toulouse: Toulouse University, 2013), 203–18. Clemena Antonova, in *Space, Time, and Presence in the Icon: Seeing the World with the Eyes of God* (Burlington, VT: Ashgate, 2010), suggests that while theologians and clerical elites accept a "partial

real presence" of form rather than essence, popular usage implies "full real presence," 100–101; Gabriel Hanganu, "Eastern Christians and Religious Objects: Personal and Material Biographies Entangled," in *Eastern Christians in Anthropological Perspective*, ed. Chris Hann and Hermann Goltz (Berkeley: University of California Press, 2010), 33–55; see also Vera Shevzov, *Russian Orthodoxy*, 223.

19. L., female b. 1956, interview by author, Kirov, 26 July 2011.

20. Newspapers cite police estimates of the numbers of pilgrims leaving Kirov and entering Velikoretskoe. Many participants simply escort the icon out of Kirov, and a large number arrive in Velikoretskoe by bus.

21. Until 1956 the village was the center of the Malo-Dolgovskii village council: S. P. Kokurina, ed., *Entsiklopediia zemli Viatskoi*, vol. 1, bk. 2 (Kirov: Oblastnaia pisatel'skaia organizatsiia, 2002). The school closed in 1972, and the last inhabitants left at the end of the 1970s.

22. Male lay activist, interview by author, Gorokhovo, 5 June 2010. Andrei Gorokhovskii writes that the icon miraculously appeared "in the woods, by the pond" at the beginning of the nineteenth century: *Akh, Gorokhovo, Gorokhovo* (Kirov: Loban, 2011), 7. In an interview in December 2013, the hieromonk who led the November 2013 procession also noted that a miracle-working icon of the Kazan Mother of God appeared in Gorokhovo "sometime around" the eighteenth century, and that the wooden hut has been replaced by two stone buildings.

23. "V Velikoretskom krestnom khode ezhednevno proiskhodiat chudesa," *ProGorod* 23, no. 328, 5 June 2010, 2; field notes recorded in 2007 by Evgeniia Riabova; author's field notes recorded in 2009 and 2010; Fathers Alexander Balyberdin (then diocesan secretary) and Andrei Dudin (director of the diocesan archive), interviews by author, Kirov, June 2010.

24. Local television broadcast, Nizhnii Novgorod, August 2002; elderly female pilgrim, interview by author, Diveevo, 11 June 2010; author field notes Solovki, 2004; E., female b. 1952, interview by author, Pskov, 14 June 2010. Mary is reported to have appeared to the sick and disabled in the late sixteenth and early seventeenth century and advised them to go to the Pskov-Pecherskii Monastery for miraculous healing: Tikhon (Sekretarev), *Vrata nebesnye: Istoriia Sviato-Uspenskogo Pskovo-Pecherskogo monastyria* (Pechory: Sviato-Uspenskii Pskovo-Pecherskii monastyr', 2008), 608–9. Diveevo convent apparently collects testimony about contemporary miracles, intending to continue the published convent chronicle, which currently ends in 1927: Aleksandr Kobets, *Novye chudesa prepodobnogo Serafima Sarovskogo* (Moscow: Velikoross, 2001).

25. Inna Naletova, "Pilgrimages as Kenotic Communities beyond the Walls of the Church," in *Eastern Christians in Anthropological Perspective*, ed. Chris Hann and Hermann Goltz (Berkeley: University of California Press, 2010), 240–66.

26. Author field notes, Velikoretskoe, June 2009.

27. Nikolai Perestoronin, "Gorokhovo," *Viatskii Krai*, 28 September 2010.

28. See, for example, *Kalendar' Viatskoi Gubernii na 1887* (Viatka, 1886); in 1924 the icon stopped for celebrations at Gorokhovo on 6 June; see Gosudarstvennyi arkhiv Kirovskoi oblasti (hereafter GAKO), f. 300, op. 2, d. 14, l. 3.

29. GAKO, f. R-2169, op. 45, d. 11, l. 29. See also Rock, "'They burned the pine.'"

30. On the significance of this feast, see Vera Shevzov, "Scripting the Gaze: Liturgy, Homilies and the Kazan Icon of the Mother of God in Late Imperial Russia," in *Sacred Stories: Religion and Spirituality in Modern Russia*, ed. Mark D. Steinberg and Heather J. Coleman (Bloomington: Indiana University Press, 2007), 61–92. By 2013, buses were apparently no longer being provided for pilgrims by the diocese, and pilgrims had to make their own way to the procession's starting point or to the shrine itself.

31. "Kazanskoi na poklon," *Viatskii nabliudatel'*, 4 August 2000, 8; "Iz luzy—na krestnyi khod v Gorokhovo," *Viatskii eparkhial'nii vestnik* 8 (2005): 214. By 2013 the November procession started on 3 November and pilgrims stayed overnight in the church and in a recently built stone house.

32. Father Andrei Dudin, interview with author, Kirov, November 2010. In 2013 the November procession attracted around two hundred pilgrims and over six hundred took part in the July pilgrimage. The diocese provided two priests to hear confessions and serve the liturgy. Confirmed with diocesan clergy who have led the July or November processions.

33. Lay activist, interview with author, Gorokhovo, 5 June 2010; "Krestnyi khod na Velikuiu," *Viatskii eparkhialnyi vestnik* 6, no. 260 (2009): 4; L., female b. 1956, interview by author, Kirov, 26 July 2011. No reference to Gorokhovo's holy spring in Soviet archival sources or in diocesan publications from the nineteenth and early twentieth centuries was discovered during the preparation of this essay.

34. On the Byzantine "blessings" of pilgrimage, such as water, wax, and oil, see Gary Vikan, *Byzantine Pilgrimage Art* (Washington DC: Dumbarton Oaks Research Library and Collection, 1982).

35. Gorokhovskii, *Akh, Gorokhovo*, 28.

36. Interviews by author in Gorokhovo, July 2011 with the following: forty-seven-year-old male from Kirov; V., male from Kirov b. 1956; group of female pensioners from Kirov oblast. Field notes recorded in 2005 by Vasilii Iarovikov, Iuliia Smirnova, Evgeniia Riabova: my thanks to local historian Vladimir Korshunkov for these and other field notes from 2006 and 2007.

37. For an example of Gorokhovo perceived as a Kitezh-like symbol of indestructible Orthodox Russia (the legendary city Kitezh sank beneath a lake to escape Tatar-Mongol attack), see Perestoronin, "Gorokhovo"; I., female aged fifty-three; S., female b. 1963 also referred to Mary's protecting veil (*pokrov*) over the Viatka land and Russia, interviews by author in Gorokhovo, 20 July 2011.

38. Matvei Galetskii, "K 'Kazanskoi' na poklon," *Viatskii nabliudatel'* 32, no. 101, 4 August 2000, 8; N., female, aged twenty-five, and S., female b. 1963, interviews by author in Gorokhovo, 20 July 2011; see also V. Bakun, "Gorokhovskaia Atlantida," *Iur'ianovskie vesti* 101, no. 9242, 22 August 2002, 3.

39. Field notes recorded in 2005 by Iarovikov, Smirnova, Riabova; Gorokhovskii, *Akh, Gorokhovo*, 29. Alternatively, the man who threw down the cross swiftly perished: Galetskii, "K 'Kazanskoi' na poklon".

40. L., female b. 1956, interview by author, Kirov, 26 July 2011.

41. Christian, *Visionaries*, 315. By the time of proofing in 2017, Gorokhovo is significantly less wild and empty. Large bronze statues of Jesus and St Nicholas (emphasizing the connection with Velikoretskoe) as well as prominent stone constructions were observed during author field work in June 2016.

42. Male, aged forty-seven, interview by author, Gorokhovo, 21 July 2011.

43. For Mary as a powerful, independent, and vengeful figure in a Catholic context, see Sanne Derks, "Religious Materialization of Neoliberal Politics at the Pilgrim Site of the Virgin of Urkupiña in Bolivia," in Hermkens, Jansen, and Notermans, eds, *Moved by Mary*, 117–32. Of eight pilgrims to Gorokhovo (one of whom was interviewed by the author in Kirov) who answered the question "what does the Mother of God mean to you?," two pilgrims described her as mother or mum; one as a figure to whom one could always turn to for help; one as intercessor; one as the *Pokrov* of Viatka and Russia and intercessor; one as a force who punished and then forgave; one as a slightly scary enigma (*zagadka*); and one did not know.

44. See, for example, "Svetlana Medvedeva sovershila palomnichestvo v Diveevskii monastyr," *Nizhegorodskaia mitropoliia*, 6 August 2008, last accessed 12 July 2017, http://nne.ru/news/svetlana-medvedeva-sovershila-palomnichestvo-v-diveevskij-monastyr/ ; author field notes, July 2008.

45. Observations based on fieldwork trips to the Feast of the Translation of Saint Seraphim's Relics in Diveevo in 2002 and 2008 and interviews conducted mostly in June 2010. See also Iulia Mikhailovna Shevarenkova, "Diveevkie legendy," *Zhivaia Starina* 4 (1998): 25–27, and Arina Valer'evna Tarabukina's article in the same issue, "Sviatye mesta v kartine mira sovremennykh 'tserkovnykh liudei'," 28–30 (based on fieldwork from 1997 and 1995 respectively). The same perception of Seraphim's personal involvement in pilgrimage is evidenced in the narratives of Soviet pilgrims to Diveevo and neighboring Sarov: for example, see "Iz perepiski dvukh sviashchennikov," *Grani* 108 (1978): 124–51; Professor Ivan Mikhailovich Andreev (a pilgrim in 1926), "K Batiushke Serafimu," in *K batiushke Serafimu: Vospominaniia palomnikov v Sarov i Diveevo (1823–1927)*, ed. T. S. Moskvina (Moscow: Otchii Dom, 2006), 583–84.

46. *Letopis' Serafimo-Diveevskago monastyria Nizhegorodskoi gubernii Ardatovskago uezda*, ed. Arkhimandrite Serafim (Chichagov) (Moscow: Izd-vo Moskovskogo Bogoroditse-Rozhdestvenskogo zhenskogo monastyria, 1996), 1–6. See also, for example, the convent-produced *Sviato-Troitskii*

*Serafimo-Diveevskii zhenskii monastyr': Putevoditel'* (Nizhnii Novgorod, n.d.). The third *udel* is, more specifically, the Kievan Caves Lavra. For a detailed history of the convent's development, based on archival research, see Ol'ga Bukova, *Zhenskie obiteli prepodobnogo Serafima Sarovskskogo: Istoriia desiati nizhegorodskikh zhenskikh monastyrei* (Nizhnii Novgorod: Knigi, 2003), 159–377. Bukova's research supplements and challenges the historical accuracy of the chronicle's narrative—on which pilgrim literature is primarily based—on various points. My thanks to Christine Worobec for providing this source.

47. L., from Kirov, aged fifty, interview with author, Diveevo, 11 June 2010.

48. *Sviato-Troitskii*, 3.

49. *Letopis'*, 6; see, for example, Helen Kontzevitch, *Saint Seraphim, Wonderworker of Sarov, and His Spiritual Inheritance* (Wildwood, CA: Saint Xenia Skete, 2004; first published in Russian in 1981), 179.

50. "Desiatiletnii iubilei vozrozhdennoi obiteli," Portal "Divnoe Diveevo," last accessed 25 March 2010, www.diveevo.ru/24/.

51. *Letopis'*, 58–59, 179, 182.

52. *Letopis'*, 182. Bukova cites an official report from 1839 that dates the establishing of this second community to 1827 and notes that it is surrounded by a ditch instead of a fence. By 1839 there were already 103 unmarried women in the windmill community, and 112 widows and unmarried women in the older community. Bukova, *Zhenskie obiteli*, 190.

53. *Kanavka Tsaritsy Nebesnoi* (Diveevo: Sviato-Troitskii Serafimo-Diveevskii monastyr', 2009), 8.

54. As reported by Sister Ksenia Vasil'evna in *Letopis'*, 258. In her discussion of pilgrims' use of diminutives, Kormina notes *stopochki* as the imprints left on stones by divine feet in Kormina, "Sviataia energetika," 251.

55. *Sviato-Troitskii*, 25; *Letopis'*, 258; *Kanavka*, 3.

56. Author field notes, 2008; see also *Kanavka*, 24. This vision is depicted on the northern wall of the convent's new hospital church in honor of the Icon of the Mother of God the Healer (Tselitel'nitsa), which was consecrated in October 2008 although work was completed only in March 2010: Ivan Ivanovich Mager, "O rosposiakh novogo khrama v Diveeve," *Moskovskii zhurnal* 8, no. 236, 15 August 2010.

57. One arshin is equal to seventy-one centimeters.

58. *Kanavka*, 11–15.

59. Ibid., 31.

60. "Iz perepiski dvukh sviashchennikov." According to Sergei Fomin, the letter was written by Father Vladimir Ivanovich Smirnov (1903–1981) to Father Ioann Efimovich Potapov (1897–1972): *V Gosti k batiushke Serafimu* (Moscow: Palomnik, 2007), 506–7.

61. "Novye koshchunstva vlastei v sviatykh mestakh," *Posev* 4 (1981): 5.

62. *Kanavka*, 40.

63. From the Greek *laura*. In Russia this is an honorific title indicating a large and especially significant monastic community (such as the famous Trinity-St Sergius Lavra near Moscow).

64. Ibid., 33–34, 54. On the building of the new cathedral, see, for example, "Sobor Blagoveshcheniia Presviatoi Bogoroditsy," Portal "Divnoe Diveevo," last accessed 02 January 2013, available at http://www.diveevo.ru/1022/.

65. Anton Zhogolev, "Poias Bogoroditsy," *Blagovest* (Samara), 1 September 2006, 31. L. from Kirov, b. 1956, smelled incense while walking round the *kanavka*, and concluded it issued from the icon carried by the nuns (interview by author, Kirov, 26 July 2011).

66. E., female under forty years old, interview by author, Diveevo, 11 June 2010. Two women who have been selling tea by the spring since 2002 say that during the Soviet period people bathed there and "always" said the Mother of God bathed there. See also "Istochnik 'Iavlennyi' v Kremenkakh," Chetvertyi udel Presviatoi Bogoroditsy, last accessed 13 Dec 2010, www.4udel.nne. ru/springs/17.

67. L. from Kirov, aged fifty, interview by author, Kirov, 2 June 2010.

68. O. from Krasnoiarsk, interview by author, Diveevo, 10 June 2010.

69. *Kanavka*, 42: a single wooden cross marked the beginning of the prerevolutionary *kanavka*.

70. *Kanavka*, 64–5; see also Palomnitsa Tat'iana, "*Sovety palomnikam Serafimo-Diveevskogo*," Portal "Divnoe Diveevo," last accessed 13 Dec 2010, available online at www.diveevo.ru/54/.

71. Comment left by pilgrim Iuliia on "Kanavka Tsaritsy Nebesnoi v Diveevskom monastyre," Portal "Divnoe Diveevo," accessed 13 Dec 2010, www.diveevo.ru/19/.

72. Natal'ia Sizova, "Putevye zametki: Rus' prikrovennaia," Portal "Divnoe Diveevo," last accessed 13 Dec 2010, www.diveevo.ru/59/.

73. Christine D. Worobec, *Possessed: Women, Witches, and Demons in Imperial Russia* (DeKalb: Northern Illinois University Press, 2001), 7, 67.

74. Zhogolev, "Poias Bogoroditsy."

75. I., female under forty from Moscow, interview by author, Diveevo, 10 June 2010. See also Olga Izheniakova, "V glush': V Diveevo; Za veroi i chudesami," *Argumenty i fakty*, no. 3, 19 January 2005; Zhogolev, "Poias Bogoroditsy."

76. L. from Kirov, aged fifty, interview by author, Kirov, 2 June 2010.

77. B. Skvortskov, "Vot i posetili my Diveevo," Portal "Divnoe Diveevo," last accessed 13 Dec 2010, available online at www.diveevo.ru/55/.

78. O., female from Moscow, b. 1971, e-mail interview by author, 20 December 2010; see also, "Liudi zdes' prosypaiutsia," *Dvinskaia Pravda*, no. 23, 11 February 2005; Zhogolev, "Poias Bogoroditsy"; N., female from Moscow, b.1977, interview by author, Moscow, 25 July 2013.

79. A male pilgrim from Nizhnii Novgorod, aged twenty-eight, recalled a guide telling him in 1992 that pilgrims would periodically report that they saw icons in the trees, although their companions might not be able to perceive them (interview by author, Kremenki, 11 June 2010); on the face of the Mother of God imprinted in bark, see Olga Novikova, "Turist ili palomnik?," *Pravoslavnaia vera* 18, no. 398, 2009 (last accessed 14 July 2017, available online https://eparhia-saratov.ru/Articles/article_old_7269); "Privolzhskii polpred uveren, shto s regional'nymi vyborami 'osobykh problem ne budet'—Nizhnii Novgorod 11 iiunia," *VolgaInform*, 11 June 2004; "Shto my videli," *Nizhegorodskie novosti*, no. 84, 11 May 2001; Tat'iana Rusinova, "Torzhestvo pravoslaviia," *Nizhegorodskie novosti*, no. 144, 6 August 2004 ; I. Ivanov, "Paskha posredi leta: Zametki palomnikov o torzhestvakh v Diveevo," *Vera-Eskom*, issue 1, no. 445, August 2003 (last accessed 16 Feb 2011, available online at www.rusvera.mrezha.ru/445/3.htm); Kobets, *Novye chudesa*, 102. On the healing properties of trees and earth at Diveevo, see also Stella Rock, "Seeking Out the Sacred: Grace and Place in Contemporary Russian Pilgrimage," *Modern Greek Studies Yearbook* 28–29 (2012–2013): 193–218, and Iulia Mikhailovna Shevarenkova, "Sviatyni Serafima Sarovskogo v Nizhegorodskom krae: Kul't kanavki," *Traditsionnaia kul'tura* 1, no. 3 (2001): 93–98.

80. Dr. A. P. Timofievich, "V gostiakh u Prepodobnogo Serafima," in *K batiushke Serafimu*, 564; Protoierei Stefan Liashevskii, "Diveev monastyr' v miatezhnye gody," in *Letopis' Serafimo-Diveevskogo monastyria* (Palomnik: Moscow, 2005), 668.

81. A., born 1953 in a village in the Nizhnii Novgorod region, recalls "grannies" at the local cemetery talking about walking to Diveevo to venerate the holy places and collect such healing herbs from the *kanavka* when she was aged five to seven. Unrecorded conversation with author in Velikoretskoe, 1 December 2013, subsequently confirmed in writing.

82. I. Viazovskii, "Chetvertyi udel," *Vera-Eskom*, issue 1, no. 393, August 2001, (last accessed 16 Feb 2011, available online at www.rusvera.mrezha.ru/393/9.htm; Kobets, *Novye chudesa*, 101; "Sovety palomnikam Serafimo-Diveevskogo monastyria," Portal "Divnoe Diveevo," last accessed 13 Dec 2010, available online at www.diveevo.ru/54/.

83. Diveevo Sviataia Kanavka (Volgograd: Parish of Uriupinskaia icon of the Mother of God, 2008), film.

84. N., woman, born 1949, interview by author, train to Arzamas, 9 June 2010.

85. Viazovskii, "Chetvertyi udel."

86. There is not space here to discuss the *kanavka* as a shield against the Antichrist; the similarities between Diveevo and other Marian apparitional cults in terms of the apocalyptic themes

and conspiracy theories evoked by devotees are unfortunately beyond the scope of this essay. Shevarenkova has highlighted the relationship between the *kanavka* as the girdle of the Mother of God and the apotropaic ritual of engirdling a church: see "Diveevskie legendy."

87. Senni Timonen, "The Cult of the Virgin Mary in Karelian Popular Tradition," in *Byzantium and the North*, ed. Paavo Hohti (Helsinki: Acta Byzantina Fennica, 1987), 101–19; Sergei S. Averintsev, "The Image of the Virgin Mary in Russian Piety," *Gregorianum* 75, no. 4 (1994): 611–22; Zimdars-Swartz, *Encountering Mary*, 247, 255.

88. *Kanavka*, 64.

89. Ibid., 3.

# 12

## On the Field of Battle
### The Marian Face of Post-Soviet Russia

VERA SHEVZOV

IN FEBRUARY 2012, MEMBERS OF the now infamous female performance art group, Pussy Riot, staged a three-part production that they subsequently deemed a "Punk Prayer Service" (Pank moleben).[1] Combining footage from live "staging" in the Epiphany (Elokhov) and Christ the Savior cathedrals in Moscow in a montage internet clip, the group's "political gesture" *qua* prayer had an explosive effect that reverberated worldwide and caught even the performers off guard.[2] While this performance touched a wide array of political, artistic, and religious sensibilities, its incendiary effect and emotional resonance in Russia can be attributed in large part to Mary, the mother of Jesus, widely revered in that country as the Birthgiver of God or *Bogoroditsa*.[3]

While it may have been the first public appeal to Mary from within Russia to garner widespread international attention, Pussy Riot's Punk Prayer was not the first public overture to Mary in post-Soviet times. Indeed, since the emergence of the Russian Orthodox Church as a formidable presence in Russian society following the millennial celebration of the Christianization of Rus' in 1988, the image of Mary increasingly permeated the media as an emblem of public Orthodoxy, especially throughout the 1990s and early 2000s.[4] Drawing on Russia's Orthodox Christian heritage, the Moscow Patriarchate has attempted to establish its public presence and relevance by "guiding" civil society socially, culturally, and politically "in the interests of uniting its forces in service to the fatherland and the nation."[5] In doing so, it has directed its efforts largely at cultivating a broad civic identity that at least resonates with, if not confessionally embraces, Orthodox symbols and values—efforts that critics have interpreted as an aggressive clericalization of society.[6] As part of this mission—itself a reflexive response to the experience of Soviet state atheism—many clergy and laity have played an active role in re-scripting social and political memory and promoting values that, in their estimation, will ensure the viability of Orthodoxy in the life of Russia as a state and nation in the future.[7] One of the most powerful mediums in this enterprise has been the image of the *Bogoroditsa*.

The *Bogoroditsa* and her icons are among contemporary Russia's most valuable cultural assets. Although not based directly on scripture, much of Russia's Marian culture is grounded in Orthodox tradition, which lends sacred authority to her images and the stories associated with them. Popular myths about Mary's relationship with Russia—supposedly one of her favorite places of sojourn on Earth, with her icons serving as one of the "imprints of her footsteps on the [Russian] land"—combined with a rich, ancient liturgical and patristic heritage provide the foundation for her enduring presence in Russian history and culture.[8] As a result, Mary and her icons add authoritative weight to any message or policy that Orthodox clergy, lay believers, or, as in the case of the Pussy Riot incident, even non-Orthodox citizens, wish to communicate or implement. Neither the *Bogoroditsa* nor her icons are easily dismissed.[9]

Mary and her icons are deeply ingrained in the history of Russia's historical imagination. As the nineteenth-century Russia thinker Dmitrii Samarin noted, Orthodox believers in Russia widely understood the Mother of God as a figure who directs Russia's history: "Neither God the Father, nor the Son, but she authoritatively intervened in the course of events."[10] For Orthodox believers, Russia's history was (and is) a biblically informed, "enchanted" history in which events called for discernment before they could be fully grasped. Insofar as Mary and her icons were often associated with the interpretation of major events and with the survival of Russia as a state and people, the image of the Mother of God became inseparable from Orthodox historical memory and collective hope during times of national crisis. Indeed, in prerevolutionary Russia, commemorations associated with certain nationally revered Marian icons offered clergy the occasion to speak about the past, to reflect upon history and its meaning for the purposes of Russia's present and future.[11] Given this deeply embedded association between Mary and the fate of Russia, it is not surprising that in a 2009 poll on the occasion of celebration of the Day of the Russian Flag (22 August), respondents routinely associated its blue color with Mary and her protection of the country.[12] Consequently, Mary and her icons provide a cache of sacred memory aids on which church officials and believers can draw to orient themselves in the post-Soviet world.

The image of the Mother of God has historically dominated the landscape of the miraculous in Russia, so much so that, according to numerous icon-related narratives, even non-believers recognized her power.[13] Perceived miraculous events have generated stories and memories; accordingly, Marian icons provide *loci* of narrative formation that engage the viewer's imagination on a wide variety of contemporary moral, social, political, and economic levels. Moreover, sustained by storytelling, Russia's Marian culture is dynamic and fluid, and can accommodate changing circumstances. Retaining an aura of antiquity (or "medievalism," depending on one's perspective), stories associated with Mary and her icons can be modified and augmented in order to maintain their relevance in any given time period.

The Moscow Patriarchate has capitalized on these features of Orthodox Marian culture as it has attempted to shape a common national and civic identity rooted in what it defines as "traditional values" and a shared interpretation of Russia's past. Its public appeals to the *Bogoroditsa* as a protectress and vanguard are reinforced by a vibrant grassroots Marian culture. One of the most vivid testimonies to the Church's efforts and to Mary's cultural comeback in the public sphere is the extent to which she, her icons, and the stories associated with them attracted the attention of the post-Soviet media, especially in the 1990s and early 2000s. "News" associated with the *Bogoroditsa* routinely appeared in print, on television, and on the web in the two decades following the fall of communism, which helped to link her image with everyday life while reinvigorating a seminal symbol from Russia's historical, cultural, and religious past.

Drawing primarily on sources from post-Soviet media, this essay examines the ways in which both clergy and laity within the Orthodox Church galvanized the cult of the Mother of God as they have tried to reclaim Russia from its atheistic Soviet past, making Orthodoxy a cultural, political, and social "identity marker" for Russia's citizens.[14] Focusing on Mary's image with regard to such issues as land and territory, historical and collective memory, statehood and civil society, as well as Russia's survival in light of a perceived demographic crisis, this essay traces the Church's creative engagement of Mary and her icons in its attempts to promote national and civic unity. The essay then turns to several key controversies in which images of the Mother of God prominently figured, as many Russian citizens insisted on their own interpretations of a post-Soviet "Orthodox Russia" or resisted the incursion of the institutional church and Orthodoxy into the public sphere altogether.

## THE MARIAN MAPPING OF POST-SOVIET RUSSIA

On one level, the Marianization of post-Soviet Russia begins geographically, with an exercise in cognitive mapping. Place and space historically are not arbitrary categories in Orthodox Marian culture. Marian icon stories commonly depict the Mother of God choosing where to reside: icons mysteriously appear at certain sites; they resolutely return to a particular place when moved, or cannot be moved at all.[15] Accordingly, many of Russia's most revered images of the Mother of God are named after the cities and towns with which their foundational narratives are associated. They are "reminders of geographical points in our homeland," as one priest from the Belgorod diocese noted.[16] Furthermore, insofar as some of Russia's most well-known miracle-working Marian icons are associated with military victories, Mary's protection of Russia as territory—however its boundaries were defined in a given period—has been part of the lore of Russian culture from at least the twelfth century.[17]

The contemporary connection of Russia's best-known Marian icons with place encourages people to imagine Russia's expansive geographic territory in sacred, Marian terms: the Tikhvin icon of the Mother of God blesses Russia's northern regions; the Iveron icon blesses the south; the Pochaev and Smolensk icons guard Russia on its western frontier; the Kazan icon is positioned in the East. "In the center," stated one reporter from Iakutia, "shines the image of the Vladimir icon of the Mother of God, inscribed by the Evangelist Luke on a board from the table on which the holy family ate."[18] By means of Marian images, Russia has been reincorporated into a publicly revived narrative concerning history and divine Providence that had been laid to waste during Soviet times.

The imaginative Marianization of Russia's territory is endless in its potential variations and meanings, depending in part on the icons used as signifiers. In 2003, for instance, in an article that appeared in the newspaper *Red Star* (Krasnaia zvezda), the official newspaper of the Ministry of Defense, the St. Petersburg priest and promoter of Marian miracle-working icons Gennadii Belovolov presented a reworked, post-Soviet version of the more traditional Marian map.[19] It replaced Marian icons from Russia's pre-Petrine past with images whose foundatioinal narratives concerned events in the late nineteenth or twentieth century. Belovolov's map included the Leushino icon of the Mother of God to the north, which, according to a version of its widely circulated story, was deemed "the Savioress [*Spasitel'nitsa*] of Russia" by the well-known late nineteenth-century priest, John of Kronstadt.[20] To the west, Belov situated the Valaam icon of the Mother of God, whose visual representation has been associated with "mystical symbolism of monarchical authority."[21] He placed the Port Arthur icon of the Mother of God, associated with the Russo-Japanese War (1904–1905), on Russia's eastern borders; in the south, he situated one of Russia's most recent iconographic representations of the Mother of God, the so-called icon of the Holy Cross (Sviato-Krestovskaia). This icon's story is based on an apparition of the Mother of God reportedly witnessed during the 1995 siege of a hospital by Chechen terrorists in the town of Budyonnovsk (named "Holy Cross" prior to 1921), located seventy miles north of Russia's border with Chechnya.[22] The well-known image of the Mother of God named She Who Reigns (Derzhavnaia), associated with the 1917 abdication of the Emperor Nicholas II, occupies the map's center, replacing the image of the Vladimir icon in more traditional Marian mappings.[23]

Among the most noteworthy features of this array of images is that all but the most recent Sviato-Krestovskaia icon of the Mother of God date to the reign of Emperor Nicholas II. Betraying nationalist monarchist inclinations, Belovolov's map correlated the integrity of Russia with the period immediately preceding the fall of the Romanov dynasty. The map symbolically linked post-Soviet Russia with a mythically conceived time understood by many Orthodox believers to have been violently disrupted by seventy years of Soviet atheist rule. Moreover, each of the Marian iconographic types he chose as guardians of Russia's borders was in its inception new in Russia's constellation of specially revered and miracle-working images of the Mother of God; symbolically, in this configuration, they presaged a new period in Russia's history. In such mythically strategic arrangements of some of Russian Orthodoxy's most well-known icons of the Mother of God—be they ancient or modern—those such as Belovolov have imagined a "magical" or "mystical" Marian cross over Russia. It was as if the Mother of God herself "blessed Russia with the sign of the cross, safeguarded it on four fronts, as an indestructible wall, and preserved it from the evils and destruction . . . of the past century."[24]

When asked about such Marian mappings of Russia, a member of the Moscow Patriarchate noted skeptically that if one actually looked at a map, the geographic distribution of these cities did not lend itself to the formation of a cross.[25] By far, not all contemporary Orthodox Christians embrace such imaginative mappings. Nevertheless, such musings regarding Mary and territory facilitate the reforging of an imagined sacralized bond among land, nation, and people. Public Orthodox rituals involving Marian icons endorsed by the Moscow Patriarchate—such as aerial or maritime processions and blessings of large areas of land—only reinforce such sensibilities.

In 2007–2008, the Foundation of the Flag of Saint Andrew and the Russian Athos Society, with the support of the patriarch of Moscow and all Rus', Alexei II (Ridiger), organized a dramatic year-long procession called "Under the Star of the Birthgiver of God." Its purpose, in part, was to remind people that the "land of Russia" was Mary's "earthly domain" (*zemnoi udel*).[26] The massive performative act began in six cities in Russia and two foreign cities, each of which was associated with a particular icon of the Mother of God: Vladivostok (She Who Reigns); Iakutsk (Life-Giving Source); Barnaul (Kazan icon); Rostov-on-Don (Iveron icon); St. Petersburg (Tikhvin icon), Arkhangelsk (Smolensk icon); Athos (Athos icon) and Jerusalem (Jerusalem icon). Representing the eight rays of the star of Bethlehem, these processional tributaries converged in Moscow after they had symbolically re-sacralized Russia's vast territory. These processions marked the land through prayer and through the construction of crosses as monuments at strategic locations along the way.[27] As a woman from the Moscow region claimed about this project, "Only prayer sanctifies the land."[28] Similarly, a reporter noted that this "act" harkened back to the ancient Russian understanding of processions as "a means of protecting the Fatherland from seen and unseen enemies."[29]

By actively promoting a territorial and geographical association between the *Bogoroditsa* and Russia, Orthodox believers laid claim to a vast terrain that modern sensibilities would otherwise deem neutral and civically shared. In so doing, Orthodox Christians—clergy and laity alike—attempted to create what sociologist Anthony D. Smith has referred to as a "sacred communion of citizens," a notion of nation that rests on a "felt and willed communion of all those who assert a particular moral faith and feel an ancestral affinity."[30] The image of the Mother of God and the combined actions of prayer and procession in this sense are no less political than they are religious—meant to "facilitate unity of the peoples of Russia, and of secular and spiritual authorities."[31] Ultimately, Marian mappings have international implications as well. As one priest from Vladivostok, who in 2004 was involved in a maritime procession with an icon of the Mother of God in the Sea of Japan, concluded, "we are geographically located on the boundaries of two countries, two worlds, two civilizations"; the image of Mary, he maintained, helps people to think about the "spiritual faces" of these two worlds.[32]

## MARY AND POST-SOVIET ORTHODOX MEMORY

Semantically-laden territory becomes symbolically potent insofar as it links place, image, history, and memory. Contemporary imaginative mappings of Russia reflect three interrelated levels of historical preoccupation within church and society that contributed to the post-Soviet revitalization of Marian culture: Russia's "deep past" (*glubokoe proshloe*), its more recent Soviet past, and more contemporary events.

Perhaps the most salient example of the Church's preoccupation with its "deep past"—the pre-Petrine centuries with which the foundational stories of the icons on the "classical" map are associated—can be seen in the establishment of Russia's new national holiday, the Day of National Unity. Commemorating Russia's emergence from the Time of Troubles at the turn of the seventeenth century, the holiday is associated with domestic political turmoil, the

FIGURE 12.1 Commemorative postage stamp, 2012. Four-hundred-year anniversary of the "Restoration of the Unity of the Russian State" following the Time of Troubles. The Kazan icon of the Mother of God is pictured in the background. Photo courtesy of Dmitry Ivanov.

intervention of foreigners, the liberation of Moscow from occupying Polish forces in 1612, and the preservation of statehood.[33] Presenting the Time of Troubles as a period with direct meaning for contemporary Russia, Patriarch Alexei II maintained that it was "a turning point in the history of the Russian state, since it was then that its future was being decided."[34] Since 2005, the Day of National Unity has been celebrated on 4 November, a date designed to coincide with the celebration of the Kazan icon of the Mother of God on the Russian church's liturgical calendar (see fig. 12.1). An example of a civil-religious holiday, 4 November is presented as two-fold: "a spiritual celebration" and a "great national holiday," much as it was in the nineteenth century when both church and state commemorated this icon.[35]

The architect of the new holiday was the subsequent patriarch of Moscow, Kirill (Gundiaev), who, as Metropolitan of Smolensk and Kaliningrad and chairman of the Russian Orthodox Church's Department of External Church Relations, also chaired Russia's Interreligious Council.[36] Proposed by Russia's Interreligious Council in 2004, the holiday was ostensibly a response to the school hostage crisis in Beslan that year. In its official statement, the Interreligious Council claimed that the events in Beslan marked the launching of "undeclared war" by Islamic separatists against Russia and that Russia could win this war only if it stood civically united.[37] Members of the Interreligious Council hoped the new holiday would promote a sense of national unity by awakening the sense of a shared past. The new holiday was supposed to "fill a gap" in the memory of that past.[38] Patriarch Alexei II reiterated this idea when he stated that the new holiday was dedicated to the "revival of historical memory among our people"—a memory, he maintained in 2007, which was purposefully distorted during Soviet times.[39]

Since becoming patriarch in 2009, Kirill has been increasingly more active with respect to the scripting of Russia's history, supporting, for instance, an annual interactive historical exhibit to mark the Day of National Unity, some of which have since been combined into a permanent exhibit "Russia—My History" housed in Moscow's VDNKh's exhibition center.[40] Also using the occasion of the commemoration of Marian icons, he has publically cultivated the sensibilities that promote the formation of Orthodox collective memory in particular.[41] In a sermon delivered in 2009 on the occasion of the celebration of the Vladimir icon of the Mother of God, for instance, the patriarch summed up the role that such Marian icon-related celebrations play in fostering public Orthodox memory. Just as every person has the right to interpret history, he maintained, so do believers have the right to see God's workings in their own lives and in the life of their homeland. If believers "gaze" on history in the spirit of their forefathers, he noted, the past will be more comprehensible and calamities can be avoided in the future. Such feasts as the celebration of the Vladimir icon, in his estimation, help "to understand, to feel … the relationship of God to humanity."[42]

A second level of historical preoccupation contributing to the revival of Marian culture in post-Soviet society concerns the more immediate Soviet past and attempts to come to terms specifically with the revolutionary events of 1917. In this context, the Mother of God named She Who Reigns (Derzhavnaia) has emerged as a prominent symbol. The history of the Derzhavnaia's special veneration extends back to 1917 and the experiences of a peasant woman, Evdokiia Ivanovna Andrianova, who, like the young girl Matrona in the case of the Kazan icon, was reportedly directed in a dream to search for the icon. The key detail in this story was the date of the icon's discovery—15 March (2 March) 1917, the day of the abdication of Tsar Nicholas II—a coincidence that the well-known Orthodox publicist Protodeacon Andrei Kuraev has referred to as "a gesture of the heavens."[43] By October of that year, in the midst of revolutionary turmoil, Nikolai Likhachev, the priest in the town of Kolomenskoe outside of Moscow who had helped Andrianova search for the image, published the narrative of the icon's discovery with the blessing of Metropolitan Tikhon of Moscow, who in a month's time became patriarch.[44] Influenced by the historic events of his day, Likhachev rescripted Andrianova's account, shifting the focus of the story from her to the "suffering Russian people," who, in his version, Andrianova represented. Thus, Mary appeared not to Andrianova individually, but to "the people" through her.[45]

Such myth-making continued to shape the life of the Derzhavnaia icon in subsequent years. Accounts about the icon were informed as much by the depiction of Mary in this icon as by Andrianova's own experiences. The icon—modern Russian Orthodoxy's version of Maria Regina—depicts the Mother of God seated on a throne holding a scepter and orb as symbols of imperial power with the Christ child on her lap (see fig. 12.2).[46] In some retellings of this icon's story, Mary gains a voice of her own and initiates the association between her icon and the fall of the monarchy.[47] For instance, in one account she states to Andrianova, "I will take the throne and scepter into my own hand. … You need to distribute copies of this image among people for their aid."[48] The well-known spiritual elder Archimandrite Ioann Krestiankin (1919–2006), for instance, told the story of the icon in this way.[49] More recent references to the Derzhavnaia icon reflect decades of such retellings. In a 2008 essay entitled "At the Crossroads of Domestic History," published in the journal *Molodaia gvardia* (Young guard), the publicist and monarchist Valerii Shambarov presented the Mother of God as having "taken the scepter and orb that fell from the hands of the emperor into her

FIGURE 12.2 Icon of the Mother of God named She Who Reigns (Derzhavnaia). Eighteenth Century. Church of the Kazan Icon of the Mother of God, Kolomenskoe. Photo by Vera Shevzov.

own . . . [she became] the sole and consistent ruler of Russia." Political lines continually change, he wrote, "but all authorities are temporary and exist only as long as she tolerates them."[50]

Since its official return from the State Historical Museum to the Orthodox Church in 1990 much of the discourse surrounding the Derzhavnaia icon concerns history—namely, the 1917 revolutions and their Soviet aftermath.[51] Churchmen have linked the icon's return to the "liberation" of Russia from its most recent—that is, Soviet—historical "yoke."[52] While it is tempting to dismiss the story of the Derzhavnaia icon as monarchist propaganda, much of the liturgical and homiletic rhetoric that surrounds the icon is more complex; it demands more from the devotee and even the secular viewer than right-wing conservative loyalties. While it is the favorite icon of many monarchist extremists and patriotic fringe groups, mainstream Orthodox clergy do not routinely use the occasion of the icon's celebration to advocate the return of the monarchy. They associate it more with questions of collective responsibility, the nature of history, and the faculties one needs in order to discern the meaning of that history.[53]

In a controversial 2015 statement on the occasion of the annual historical exhibit "Orthodox Rus'" in the Moscow Manege in honor of the Day of National Unity, Patriarch Kirill, for instance, spoke about the Derzhavnaia's protective role in Russia's history. That year's exhibit—"Orthodox Rus': My History from the Great Turmoil to the Great Victory (1896–1945)"— included the display of the original Derzhavnaia icon for public veneration. Claiming that the "best minds of Russia" understood the finding of the Derzhavnaia icon as a sign of Mary's leadership and protection (*pokrov*) of Russia following the abdication of Emperor Nicholas II, the patriarch recast the Church's usually staunchly anti-Stalinist narrative in a more rehabilitative tone, which garnered widespread reaction in the press. Despite the terror, and despite the "evil actions" of those in power, the patriarch argued, the nation had made great strides toward modernization during the first two decades of Soviet rule, which, in his estimation, should not be minimized. His assertion that "the successes of ... the state leader who stood at the helm" should not be minimized despite his "evil actions" led almost immediately to public debates about contemporary church-state relations, patriarch Kirill's current political motives, and the Church's ethical reasoning and positioning regarding current and future state policy.[54]

Finally, in terms of history and memory, the Orthodox Church has also been preoccupied with contemporary events and with history as it is being made. If the Kazan icon encourages the recollection of events from the sixteenth and seventeenth centuries, and the Derzhavnaia icon prompts thinking about 1917 and its aftermath, the recently established icon of the Mother of God of the Holy Cross (Sviato-Krestovskaia) focuses on contemporary events (see figs. 12.3 and 12.4). On 18 June 1995 Chechen separatists killed more

FIGURE 12.3 Kazan icon of the Mother of God, Kazan Cathedral, St. Petersburg, Russia.

FIGURE 12.4 Mass-produced rendition of the icon of the Mother of God named Holy Cross (Sviato-Krestovskaia), Sofrino. Photo by Dick Fish.

than 128 civilian hostages—including women and children—who were held in Budyonnovsk. During the attack on the city, people testified to a Marian sighting in the sky, where she stood despondently to the right of the cross.[55]

Local church officials commissioned an icon to be painted on the basis of testimony given by those who reportedly witnessed the apparition.

In order to lend this new image of the Mother of God authenticity, its composition was compared to the well-known Akhtyrka and Seven-Sword (Semistrel'naia) icons of the Mother of God, the subjects of Worobec's and Smith's essays respectively in this volume.[56] At the same time, the foundational narrative of the Sviato-Krestovskaia icon echoes those that inform Russia's most well-known pre-Petrine Marian icons. In many of those stories, catastrophe was averted when the antagonists reportedly had a vision of the Mother of God.[57] The stories associated with the Sviato-Krestovskaia image often take a similar line: the rebel leader Shamil Basaev freed the hostages and left the hospital compound only when the Chechen terrorists also reportedly witnessed the apparition.[58] In addition, stories associated with the Sviato-Krestovskaia image routinely emphasize that the site on which the hospital in Budyonnovsk stood had been a monastery up until the 1930s. That monastery had been constructed in memory of Grand Prince Michael of Tver, who was executed by the Golden Horde in 1317 and eventually canonized. Accounts of the Sviato-Krestovskaia icon speak of Grand Prince Michael as "the first martyr of the northern Caucasus."[59] The contemporary events in Budyonnovsk in 1995, consequently, are framed in these layers of "deep history."

Just as Orthodox churchmen and believers might link events from the deep past to new Marian iconographic types in order to lend them legitimacy, so too do believers turn to the past in order to sacralize recent events. In November 2010, for instance, one church in the Moscow diocese chose 4 November (22 October)—the day of the Kazan icon and the Day of National Unity—to commemorate the casualties of the Bolshevik Revolution, the Civil War, and of all those compatriots who perished in Russia and abroad in the twentieth century. By doing so, this local community ritually linked Russia's recent past with its deep past, thereby signaling the potentially unifying power of Orthodox memory, and revitalizing the capacity of a Marian image to generate such commemoration.[60]

VISUAL REFERENTS

Given that Mary, her icons, and the narratives with which they are associated often prompt historical reflection, their effectiveness as collective memory aids depends in large part on the way in which these narratives are publicly scripted. What is the nature of post-Soviet Orthodox public discourse surrounding Mary and her icons? What are some of the recurrent themes publically associated with them?

Public discourse regarding Marian icons in the first decades of post-Soviet Russia exhibited two broad, sometimes competing tendencies regarding national identity. One emphasized an identity associated with Russia as a diverse, multiethnic, and multireligious state; the other focused more specifically on an ethnic Russian identity, inseparably linked with Orthodox Christianity. A vivid example of the first trend can be seen in the case of the Kazan icon of the Mother of God and the commemoration of the Day of National Unity described earlier. In his sermon on 4 November 2010, Patriarch Kirill recounted the events in what has come to be the standard shared narrative associated with this holiday among church and state officials. According to the sermon, during the Time of Troubles Russia found itself on the brink of destruction as a nation; poverty and chaos reigned; foreigners occupied the country, and were poised to rule, thanks to the support of many of Moscow's elite "boyar clans" whose loyalties to Russia were questionable.[61]

While foreign threat is a common theme in Russia's Marian lore, the feast of the Kazan icon along with the new civic holiday in particular offers the occasion to recast that threat in contemporary terms. In addition to globalization, information technology, and the prioritization of personal economic wealth as potential dangers to Russia's spiritual and political sovereignty, some officials have pointed to terrorism as the main threat.[62] Still others cast NATO forces in the guise of the contemporary "foreigner."[63] In 2006, Nikolai Lisovoi, publicist and senior specialist at the Institute of Russian History, maintained that Russia was under siege by "the spiritual model of the Western-European person."[64]

According to Patriarch Kirill, however, "foreigners" were not the ultimate problem during the Time of Troubles. The real issue of that time was the self-generated "confusion of consciousness" among Russia's population—a theme the patriarch has often reiterated in a not-so-subtle allusion to his reading of post-Soviet trends. "No one knew what to do"; people, consequently, were ready to embrace foreigners in the hope that they would ensure the nation's prosperity and well-being.[65]

The Kazan icon and the Day of National Unity, therefore, commemorate the purported collective will to overcome social and political turmoil and the threat of foreign domination. The promoters of the Day of National Unity have maintained that such an act of collective will could only result from the solidarity of all its citizens, regardless of their "ethnic or social [sense of] belonging."[66] The alleged "miracle" in 1612 was not so much in Russia's unlikely victory over a powerful military enemy but in the collective realization that the real threat to Russia was domestic divisions and in the mustering of strength to overcome those divisions.[67]

Consequently, through the association of the Kazan icon with the Day of National Unity, the image of Mary in post-Soviet Russia has become embroiled in the discourse concerning "civic responsibility" and the unity of civil society (*grazhdanskoe obshchestvo*).[68] Church and state officials have emphasized the diversity of the militia that was responsible for Russia's "victory" during the Time of Troubles. Patriarch Alexei II noted that Russians, Tatars, Bashkirs, Mordovians, Chuvash, and other ethnic groups joined forces to prevent the loss of their lands; the head of the Muslim Religious Directorate in the Nizhnii Novgorod region, Umar Idrisov, in turn, estimated that 30 percent of the troops involved in the liberation of Moscow in the seventeenth century were Muslims. The beginning of the restoration of Russia, therefore, depended on this unity of peoples.[69] The creation of Russia as "a great and sovereign power," maintained President Vladimir Putin, depended on the strength of this popular will[70]—which according to the story of the Kazan icon was reinforced by Mary.

While not downplaying the populist element in the story, Orthodox churchmen have concurrently emphasized the role that the institutional church and the Orthodox faith played in galvanizing this unified civic spirit. Highlighting related details in the story of the Kazan icon, some clergy have reminded their listeners (or readers) that Russia's independence, liberation, and political successes could not have happened without collective prayer. .[71] In his sermon in November 2010, Patriarch Kirill was more direct in his assessment. Reflecting the current political and social aspirations of the Orthodox Church in Russia, he argued that the Patriarch of Moscow at the time, Germogen, filled the existing power vacuum. The institutional church, Patriarch Kirill pointed out, provided the source of leadership and guidance at that critical historical juncture. As one priest from the Cathedral of the Kazan Icon of the Mother of God in Moscow's Red Square confirmed in 2011, "the formation of the Russian state [at that time] took place under the canopy of Orthodoxy. . . . Thanks to the influence of Orthodoxy, each people ... preserved its own traditions."[72] Another priest and member of the Union of Russian Writers, Aleksei Zaitsev from the Chelyabinsk region, went so far as to claim that the events the holiday commemorates demonstrate that national unity is not dependent on state officials, suggesting the state played a secondary role in the nation's well-being.[73] As the visual marker of this turning point in Russia's history, therefore, the Kazan icon has been publically positioned as a unifying symbol for a multi-confessional and multiethnic Russian state, which the Patriarch "guides."[74]

Post-Soviet Orthodox discourse regarding Marian icons has also often addressed the themes of loss, return, and restoration. When considered in light of these themes, Orthodox discourse tends to focus more on Russians as a distinct ethnic group. Following the Bolshevik Revolution, countless icons were destroyed, sold, or displaced with émigrés who sought refuge abroad. In the turmoil, many specially revered icons of the Mother of God lost the chain of narrative that their *lives* provided, and their fates were unknown or largely forgotten during the Soviet period. As a result, when prerevolutionary specially revered icons of the Mother of God have been unexpectedly located or returned from abroad, believers have marked the event as "miraculous" and have chronicled the return as an exercise in broader historical reflection, especially with respect to the Soviet past.[75]

Clergy took the occasion of the finding or return of an icon to instill a sense of collective responsibility among ethnic Russians in particular for a perceived historical calamity and to prompt listeners to consider the conditions and circumstances that led to it. For instance, on the fifth anniversary of the highly publicized return of the Tikhvin icon of the Mother of God from Chicago to Russia in 2004—an event that drew more than one and a half million worshippers in Moscow and St. Petersburg alone—Patriarch Kirill set the icon's post-1917 odyssey in a biblical framework.[76] Comparing Russians to the Israelites and attributing their fate to the violation of a divine covenant, the patriarch emphasized the collective responsibility of Russia's citizens for the Soviet period; the nation collectively chose this path according to the priorities it set and the values it chose. In response, God abandoned Russia to its own devices, and the icon's departure was a sign of this leave-taking. Its return, Patriarch Kirill pronounced, confirmed the gradual restoration of "faith and fidelity" among Russians and the slow repair of a broken covenant.[77]

The finding or return of specially revered icons of the Mother of God also offered churchmen the occasion to weave together two strands of Russia's history in the twentieth century—Soviet Russia and Russia Abroad—which is one feature of Patriarch Kirill's vision of the "Russian World" (*Russkii mir*) on which President Vladimir Putin eventually drew. In one example from 2009, an official delegation of the Russian Orthodox Church Abroad brought the miracle-working Kursk-Root icon of the Mother of God, in its possession since 1920, on a visitation to Russia. The visit, which took place two years after the ratification of the Act of Canonical Unity between the Moscow Patriarchate and the Russian Orthodox Church Abroad (May 2007), was described as a "pledge of unity" among all Orthodox Christians worldwide of Russian heritage.[78] The year-long procession "Under the Star of the Birthgiver of God" mentioned earlier commemorated this unification as well. In addition to icons that were linked with the geographic locality where the eight "rays" of the procession originated, each processional group carried a copy of the Derzhavnaia icon that was made especially for this ambitious undertaking. The procession commenced with a special prayer service before the Vladimir icon of the Mother of God and was part of the broader unification event that Patriarch Alexei termed "the gathering of the Russian peoples." The eight processions eventually converged in Kolomenskoe, the birthplace of the Derzhavnaia icon. The year-long act ended with a combined procession from Kolomenskoe to Moscow's Christ the Savior Cathedral in order to commemorate the first anniversary of the reconstitution of a unified Russian Orthodoxy, for which birthplace, residence, and citizenship were no longer criteria for "authentically" belonging.[79]

## MARY AND THE FUTURE OF RUSSIA

The institutional church's attempts to shape collective memory, inform historical discourse, and consolidate a national and civic identity that embraces Orthodoxy involve more than just Russia's past and present. The Moscow Patriarchate has also shown its active investment in Russia's future.[80] Of particular concern for the Church in this realm was Russia's perceived demographic crisis in the late 1990s and early 2000s—the estimates of which pointed to a 30 percent decrease in the Russian population by mid-century.[81] The Church embraced the issue as an Orthodox cause, with the metropolitan of Kaluga and Borovskii, Kliment (Kapalin), going so far as to consider supplementing Orthodox conceptions of marriage with the idea of a "feat [podvig] in the name of Russia's future."[82] Maintaining that the demographic crisis was caused above all by "a broken value system" and a "darkening of moral consciousness," the Moscow Patriarchate as early as the 1990s stepped up its rhetoric concerning "traditional values," and embarked on promoting motherhood, family, and anti-abortion legislation.[83]

As a woman who is revered as a virgin and who, according to Orthodox tradition, was a single mother of a single child (following the presumed death of Joseph), it is difficult to champion Mary as a model for childbearing and traditional family values. Nevertheless, reminiscent of the Maternity Medal and the order of "Mother-Heroine" that the Soviet State instituted in 1944 as part of a broader range of pro-natal policies, in 2006 the Orthodox Church established an annual award—the "Patriarchal Decoration of Motherhood" (Patriarshii Znak Materinstva)—that honors mothers who have distinguished themselves through the spiritual and moral upbringing of at least five children.[84] Although Mary would not have qualified for this award, her image, ironically, was imprinted on the medal women received. In addition, the high-profile All-Russia Demographic Program "Sanctity of Motherhood"—the publicly proclaimed goal of which was to make having three children socially "fashionable"—has a logo that resembles the Mother of God with her child, although the organization's patron saint is Evfrosiniia, the wife of Dmitrii Donskoi and a mother of twelve.[85]

Despite the difficulties that the image of the Mother of God poses as a symbolic patron of a birthing campaign, both church and state officials have drawn her and her icons into public discussions of motherhood, childrearing, and abortion. In a 2009 published greeting on the feast of the Nativity of the Mother of God, Iuvenalii (Poiarkov), the metropolitan of Krutitsk and Kolomna, encouraged childbearing by reminding readers of the biblical appraisal of offspring as a divine blessing (and their absence as a curse), and promoted childrearing as a sacred social service.[86] In 2008, the Orthodox Church's Synodal commission on youth unsuccessfully proposed the idea of instituting a state-wide holiday in honor of pregnant women (Den' beremennykh) that would correspond to the Church's celebration of the Feodorov icon of the Mother of God (29 August). The highly revered familial icon of the Romanov dynasty, and a reported favorite of the last empress, Alexandra Feodorovna, had garnered widespread veneration even before the 1917 revolutions for its supposed powers in matters concerning fertility, pregnancy, and birthing.[87] Advocates of the proposed new holiday argued that it would enhance the social status of pregnant women by modifying negative stereotypes and prejudices concerning pregnancy.[88]

Counting on the emotional impact of Mary's image on women's attitude toward childbearing and birthing, Orthodox clergy and lay activists supported the placement of her icons in maternity hospitals. In 2009, a priest from the city of Volzhskii in Volgograd, for instance, noted that an icon of the Mother of God hangs in one of the city's maternity hospitals. Beside the image, a sign states: "Every woman in childbirth resembles the Mother of God. Love her and fear offending her."[89] Significantly, this image was placed near the hospital's service entrance and not in the actual maternity ward; its primary viewers physicians, nurses, and other hospital personnel whose disposition toward mothers and newborns is, from the Church's point of view, critical for enhancing childbirth and fostering the earliest mother-infant bonds.

Similarly, a grassroots initiative lasting some three years (2006–2009) focused on furnishing maternity hospitals throughout Russia with the icon of the Mother of God named Helper in Childbirth (Pomoshchnitsa v rodakh). Members of the short-lived pro-life center "Joy of Motherhood" (Radost' materinstva)—again, overseen by a male Orthodox activist—visited more

**FIGURE 12.5** Mass-produced icon of the Mother of God named Helper in Childbirth. Photo by Dick Fish.

than sixty cities and distributed some three thousand such icons throughout Russia during this period.[90] With its iconographic roots stemming from post-Tridentine depictions of the Immaculate Conception, this type first appeared in Russia by way of Ukraine. Its several variations include the currently well-known image depicting Mary with long hair draping over her shoulders, head uncovered. Her hands cup an infant Christ child enclosed in a womb-like mandorla, thereby signifying the relationship between a mother and her unborn fetus (see fig. 12.5). The akathist in honor of the icon, composed by the priest Vladimir Andreev, whose paternal experiences reportedly led to the special veneration of such an icon in the city of Serpukhov (some sixty miles south of Moscow), hails Mary for easing women's "difficult lot" and relieving the pains associated with labor and birthing.[91] Typically, such icons hang in hospital chapels, prayer rooms, or other strategic locations. In one maternity facility in Irkutsk, for instance, the icon was hung over the door through which women passed on their way to the birthing room.[92] Since the 2006 campaign, the icon of the Mother of God named Helper in Childbirth continues to be the icon of choice that Orthodox Christians donate to maternity facilities throughout Russia and that is listed on websites for expectant mothers or women who seek to have children.[93]

Perhaps the most dramatic Marian event tied to the campaign to avert Russia's demographic crisis was the bringing of the relic of the Virgin Mary's belt (cincture)—professed to heal infertility—from the Vatopedi Monastery on the all-male enclave of Mount Athos to Russia in the fall of 2011.[94] Sponsored by the "Fund of the Apostle Andrew the First-Called," whose main mission is to help preserve the historical, cultural, and spiritual values of Russia, and supported by its affiliate organization "The Sanctity of Motherhood," the travels of Mary's belt to sixteen cities occurred in the span of some five weeks (20 October–27 November 2011). According to Church estimates, the relic drew some three and a half million people for veneration, 800,000 of these in Moscow alone.[95] While the Fund of the Apostle Andrew had brought relics to Russia in the past—including those of John the Baptist and the Evangelist Luke—Mary's belt was exceptional for its massive turnout and for the extent of media attention it received. The patriarch of Moscow, Kirill, dubbed the belt's visit "the event of the year;" people, especially women, made long journeys to venerate the belt, sometimes waiting more than twenty hours in line.[96] "Not one event," Patriarch Kirill observed, "either political or sports-related, has gathered as many people as this image of the Most Holy Birthgiver of God."[97]

While the belt's visitation generated public debate on a wide range of issues—faith and obscurantism, poverty, Russia's inadequate medical infrastructure and failing economic conditions—the issue of fertility and Russia's demographic crisis remained prominent.[98] According to the director of the national organization "The Sanctity of Motherhood," Natalia Iakunina, the sponsorship of this visit was her organization's small "mite" given to the cause of Russia's demographic crisis.[99] In addition to its display for public veneration, the belt was also taken to local maternity centers that offer legal, financial, and psychological counseling to pregnant women. Popular talk shows featured women who had difficulty conceiving and who claimed to put trust in the power of Mary's belt to help them in their efforts.[100] Patriarch Kirill supported the legendary association between the relic and conception by publicly noting that women who suffer from infertility and who wore facsimiles of the belt and participate in fervent prayer may indeed conceive after venerating it.[101] As a signal that the belt's visit was "a success" in demographic terms, a year later during a national forum dedicated to family policy, Natalia Iakunina reported that some of the cities to which the belt had been brought—including St. Petersburg, Ekaterinburg, and Krasnoiarsk—had seen an increase in birth rate.[102]

Ultimately, however, discussions about fertility and conception that surrounded the belt fed the broader debate over the role of Orthodoxy and the institutional church in the future of Russia. In particular, Patriarch Kirill publicly presented this Marian event as testimony to the power of Orthodoxy in contemporary post-Soviet society and to Russia's identity as an Orthodox nation. "For this reason alone it was necessary to have the belt of the Most Holy Mother of God brought to Russia."[103] In turn, the ultra-nationalist, neo-communist political activist, member of the Writers' Union, and editor of the weekly newspaper *Zavtra* (Tomorrow), Aleksandr Prokhanov, interpreted the outpouring of devotion to the belt of the Virgin in terms of national security, especially with respect to the ideological, cultural, and "metaphysical expansion of the West."[104] The event, he argued, testified to an existing defense system in Russia—faith—that was as significant as its Air and Missile Defense Systems. The human energy associated with that faith, he mused, creates an "invisible shield" around Russia, which will deflect "the rockets of the enemy" and transform them into mere "bodiless flashes."[105] The image of Mary, as such rhetoric illustrates, has played a strategic role in post-Soviet discourse on the "spiritual security" of the nation.

## MARIAN CONTESTATIONS

Associated with the growing influence of Orthodoxy in Russia's public sphere, Mary and her icons have also become entangled in the cultural, political, and religious fracas that the public face of Orthodoxy has increasingly generated. Intimately linked with Russia's political and cultural past, and also with Orthodox memory of that past, the image of Mary evokes a sense of sacred, authoritative invincibility that competing factions in church and society often attempt to harness or disarm for their particular causes.

From its inception, the Day of National Unity, for instance, signaled Mary's involvement in what have become known as Russia's "memory wars." For many non-Orthodox and Orthodox citizens alike, the Kazan icon is symbolic of what has been termed the "merging" (*srashchanie*) of church and state in Russia and of the Church's desire to script broader public memory and historical thinking. As one professor of history from Moscow State University argued when the holiday was first instituted, the Day of National Unity has "a religious significance and those who stand behind it should honestly own up to the fact that we are celebrating the day of the Kazan icon."[106]

The new holiday's replacement of 7 November (the anniversary of the Bolshevik Revolution) as a national holiday irritated communists, communist-sympathizers, and many citizens who, often out of inertia, enjoyed the old holiday. In their estimation, the introduction of the new holiday was a deliberate attempt to marginalize the Bolshevik Revolution in the annals of Russia's history. As Gennadii Ziuganov, leader of Russia's Communist Party, stated to his colleagues in the Duma who ratified the holiday, "You have decided to spit into the grave of your grandfathers, your forefathers."[107] Instead of the unifying symbol it was meant to be, the Kazan icon, consequently, proved divisive from the outset.

Critics also challenged the claim that the holiday—and thus the Kazan icon—could foster a common national identity and social unity.[108] They argued that the Time of Troubles was a period of extreme social and political upheaval and questioned the claim that Orthodox hierarchs inspired and sided with "the people."[109] Other skeptics turned to the history of the Kazan icon, pointing to its initial association with the colonization of Kazan in the sixteenth century. As one publicist remarked, the Kazan icon might more accurately be called "the anti-Kazan'" icon, since its initial official veneration was spawned as a rebuff to Kazan's Muslim population.[110] In this vein, Tatar nationalists criticized the Day of National Unity, referring to the Kazan icon' as "a symbol of colonial yoke."[111]

Perceived as yet another arbitrary and artificially imposed holiday in a state floundering to cultivate a sense of national identity after decades of Soviet rule, the Day of National Unity stirred heated debate. As the holiday's political agenda and the institutional church's role in its orchestration became increasingly evident, the Russian public no longer regarded the holiday's correspondence with the Kazan icon as coincidental. Instead, the public celebration of this and other Marian icons has since provided an occasion for the institutional church to engage public criticism by challenging what Patriarch Kirill has referred to as "attempts to rewrite Russia's history."[112]

FIGURE 12.6 Image of the Mother of God named Rus' Resurrecting (Voskreshaiushchaia Rus').
Photo by Dick Fish.

Despite official church efforts to promote Orthodox memory as Russia's national memory, the Moscow Patriarchate at the same time has been leery of comparable mythmaking at the grassroots level, especially from Orthodoxy's extremist quarters. Institutional church caution can be most vividly seen in the fate of the image of the Mother of God named Rus' Resurrecting (Voskreshaiushchaia Rus'; see fig. 12.6). Dating to 1998, the image was based on a vision reportedly experienced by Olga Pavlenko from the city of Piatigorsk (Stavropol region) while she listened on tape to an akathist in honor of the Marian feast of the Pokrov while sick at home on the day of this widely celebrated Russian Orthodox feast. Reportedly during this vision, the walls and ceilings seemed to disappear as the *Bogoroditsa*, dressed in a shimmering white robe, descended in a blinding white light. According to Pavlenko, Mary held a protective veil or *pokrov*, with which she covered the earth below. This shimmering covering held tiny gold crosses that reportedly glistened in light. As Mary descended, Pavlenko claimed she saw these tiny crosses—"symbols of grace"—fall from Mary's veil and descend on people below. Each person seemed to react to this grace in his or her own way. Some began to run from the Mother of God, covering their eyes and ears. Some began to darken, while others radiated light.[113] The story also included the common trope—Mary choosing a place to reside. The *Bogoroditsa* not only reportedly directed Pavlenko to have an image of her made in the form she appeared in the vision, but she also identified where the icon was to be placed—near the relics of Saint Seraphim of Sarov in the Holy Trinity Church of the Seraphim-Diveevo Monastery, a community described by Stella Rock in this volume.[114]

Reportedly supported by a well-known elder at the Sanaksarsk Monastery (Mordovia), Olga Pavlenko's vision led to a groundswell of veneration of this image, which traveled on grassroots initiative to churches and monasteries particularly in Ukraine—Kiev, Pochaev, Odessa, and Crimea.[115] In 1999, the image even hung in the Diveevo convent's Holy Trinity church for ten days before church officials reportedly directed the abbess to remove it.[116] Fueled by publications in the non-church press, the distribution of mass-produced paper images, increasingly influential internet iconographic copies, and an attempt in 2003 to secure the Orthodox Church's official approval, the veneration of the image remains contested.[117]

Various factors contributed to Orthodox institutional objections to the veneration of the image: perceived iconographic irregularities in the way in which Mary is depicted; the tiny crosses that appear to be linked with peoples' "darkening" or demise; the seeming elevation of Mary to a goddess figure; an iconographic style reminiscent of "occult" artists such as Nicholas Roerich; and the personal profile of Olga Pavlenko, who was quickly branded by some churchmen as a psychic (*ekstrasens*) whose relationship to Orthodoxy was tenuous.[118] Evidently not versed in Russia's tradition of Marian icon stories, which usually depict Mary as a strong-willed woman, the critic Alla Dobrosotskikh objected to Mary's authoritative demeanor in Pavlenko's purported vision: "Could the most submissive of women," she argues, "have spoken in such a manner?"[119]

Perhaps most objectionable to Orthodox Church officials, however, was the image's heavy nationalist overtones and its embrace by religious fringe groups. In 2002, for instance, Svetlana Frolova, the self-ordained "Mother Fotiniia the Light-Bearer," founded a community in the Nizhnii Novgorod region named in honor of the Rus' Resurrecting image. Mother Fotiniia petitioned Patriarch Alexei II in 2005 to ordain her to the priesthood and subsequently gained notoriety for promoting Vladimir Putin as a saint, while likening Patriarch Alexei II to Pontius Pilate.[120] The image of the Mother of God named Rus' Resurrecting gained similar support from the "True Orthodox Church in Russia" under the direction of Metropolitan Rafael (Prokopiev-Motovilov) and many so-called "tsar-worshippers."[121] These groups embrace extremist myths about Russia and its history that remain censored by the Moscow Patriarchate. Because of the image's broad dissemination and its association with right-wing, anti-Semitic and anti-Islamic fringe groups, some Orthodox clergy regarded the image as part of a conspiracy to undermine Orthodoxy. Finally, in 2004, the patriarch of Moscow, Alexei II, officially censored this image of the Mother of God named Rus' Resurrecting, relegating it to the ever-growing category of "uncanonical icon-making," or "pseudo-icons." Doing so, he placed it in the same category with images of Rasputin and Tsar Ivan the Terrible.[122]

## THE *BOGORODITSA* AND THE PUSSY RIOT CHALLENGE

In 2012, Pussy Riot's Punk Prayer presented the Orthodox Church with its most formidable public challenge to date. Ironically, insofar as it was a response to Patriarch Kirill's demographic and memory politics, Punk Prayer testified to the Church's successes in reclaiming an influential presence in post-Soviet society.[123] A tribute to the power of Mary's image to galvanize and stir political, religious, and cultural sensibilities in post-Soviet society, Punk Prayer drew on the image of the *Bogoroditsa* to check the moral authority of Church leaders and to challenge key institutional church efforts on several fronts: the cultivation of church-state relations, the scripting of public and historical memory, and legislation on LGBTQ rights, gender equality, reproductive rights, and family politics.[124]

Although Western audiences recognized the Punk Prayer as protest art to which they have become accustomed since the 1960s, Russia's citizens were largely jarred by the performance and were critical of its form. A majority of Orthodox believers regarded the iconoclasm of the Punk Prayer as sacrilege not so much for its words as for its staging in a church. The performance's use of a sacred place—a feature less common to the American postmodernist avant-garde of the 1980s and 1990s that nonetheless drew freely on Christian symbolism—in particular violated the religious sensibilities of many adherents of Russia's Orthodox faith.[125] Pussy Riot's use of well-known church hymnody ("Rejoice, O Virgin" from Sergei Rachmaninoff's *All Night Vigil*, 1915) and its Orthodox prayer-like form and lyrics only exacerbated the perceived lines between sacred and profane.[126] While some Orthodox clergy resisted labeling the act as sacrilegious on the technical grounds that nothing was stolen, insofar as the performative act was based on the appropriation (or "theft") of sacred space for the purposes of a political and artistic "gesture" and online video clip, reaction to the performance resonated with criticism regarding acts of perceived cultural appropriation often heard in the West as well.[127] Even many non-believers and progressive believers deemed the act inappropriate and in poor taste, despite public attempts to "de-sacralize" the performance venue by disclosing the Christ the Savior Cathedral's dubious legal status and the various commercial ventures on its site.[128] Iconoclastic and perceived sacrilegious acts, however, are rarely religiously neutral and often are signifiers of views collectively understood as no less sacred than the beliefs they challenge. Consequently, despite its irreverence, the Punk Prayer stirred its hearers in large part because of its appeal to the *Bogoroditsa*.

While members of Pussy Riot traced their inspirational roots to Western-inspired feminist philosophy, art-performance, and punk rock—and indeed their Punk Prayer resonated with these traditions abroad—in Russia, the Punk Prayer reverberated with Orthodox Marian culture.[129] First, it appealed to the image of the Mother of God as a powerful historical force; it assumed that the Mother of God has the independence, authority, and means to intervene in events—the same assumption commonly praised and upheld by Orthodox clergy and laity in their celebration of such well-known images as the Kazan and Vladimir icons of the Mother of God. The parallels one Russian blogger drew are noteworthy. The faithful, he wrote, have historically called on the Mother of God for help "on the field of battle." In the case of Pussy Riot, the field of battle is a cultural one, involving women's rights, political activism, and church-state relations. Why are these, he rhetorically asked, less significant than the battle between the Novgorodians and the Suzdalians?[130]

Further, Punk Prayer as a verbal icon resonated with the image of Mary as one who brings people to their senses, usually in order to avert disaster.[131] Liturgically, the *Bogoroditsa* is portrayed as "bringing light to darkness, driving away falsehood, and destroying corruption."[132] As a cry of protest for something "to finally move in our spiritual-less country," Punk Prayer was fashioned as a liturgical appeal to the Mother of God for no less.[133] In addition, the Prayer drew on the assumption that Mary, as stated in the Matins service in honor of the Kazan icon, "is the longed-for helper of the world" and that her help is available to all.[134] Modern Orthodox Marian culture has been essentially a populist culture. At the same time, in stories associated with her and her icons, Mary is not depicted protecting everyone, but only those who are loyal to her. By questioning the loyalty and worthiness of Russia's current church and state leadership, the performers of the Punk Prayer positioned their act as a desperate yet hopeful appeal to the Mother of God. According to Ekaterina Samutsevich, the group drew on the tradition of turning to Mary as they strove to convey a feeling of hopelessness and dejection.[135]

Indeed, in his commentary on the "Punk" performance, professor of philosophy Andrei Miasnikov argued that some church and state officials found the performance disquieting because it tapped into their genuine faith in the power of the Mother of God. The performance, in his estimation, would have been less threatening had it appealed to the people to rise in revolt rather than to the image of the *Bogoroditsa* in whose name Russia's church and state leadership have formulated actions and policies.[136] Similarly, the dissident Orthodox priest Gleb Yakunin (1936–2014) confirmed the sincerity of the prayer, suggesting that the Mother of God had taken the performers "under her special protection." In the long run, he mused, the group's act would promote the "victory of genuine Orthodoxy."[137]

The Punk Prayer has also resonated with the prominent place of women in the history of Marian iconic lore. Although it has yet to be examined comprehensively in feminist terms, Russia's modern Marian culture is heavily based in women's experiences. Stories associated with Marian icons often challenge conventional notions of hierarchy and authority, especially in terms of gender. Moreover, women's experiences were frequently precursors to events that then became subjects of Orthodox memory. Ironically, the foundational narrative of the Kazan icon—which church and state officials have promoted as a symbol of national unity—concerns a young girl and a mother who initially were ignored by church and civic officials and who acted on conviction despite being ignored and dismissed.

Although some Russian feminist organizations did not initially support Pussy Riot, the Punk Prayer resonated among some of Russia's more feminist-minded Orthodox individuals.[138] Former Moscow University professor Elena Volkova, for instance, has noted that the appeal of the Punk Prayer to Mary to "become a feminist" refers to Mary's living presence outside the conventionalizing frame of her traditional icons—a theme explored some thirty years ago by feminist artist Yolanda Lopez in her trilogy on the Virgin of Guadalupe.[139] According to Volkova, the Punk Prayer petitions especially for protection of abused women, "who are beaten in rooms where [her] icons hang, who are bought and sold, and whose bodies are used as soulless meat." The appeal for Mary to become a feminist, maintained Volkova, is to pray as follows: "Instill in those who kiss your image and who venerate your belt a basic respect for women."[140] As another woman reportedly noted, "The Most Holy Mother of God has always been a feminist; she has always struggled for the rights of the offended and oppressed."[141]

Punk Prayer's tightly woven mix of the impious and the reverent, the traditional and the modern, and the sacred and the profane, has resulted in its association with a wide range of trends in Russia's cultural history. Patriarch Kirill, along with such widely viewed television programs as Boris Korchevnikov's "I Don't Believe" ("Ne veriu!") and Arkadii Mamontov's "Provocateurs" ("Provacatory"), unequivocally situated the Punk Prayer in the tradition of the fierce anti-religious campaigns of the 1920s–1930s.[142] In such a reading, Punk Prayer echoes the imagery of Mary in widely distributed anti-religious posters and such publications in the 1920s as the magazine *Bezbozhnik u stanka* (The atheist at the workplace), which accompanied the mass destruction of churches and public derision of religious sensibilities. Similarly, from this perspective, Punk Prayer is cast in the same vein as the contemporary and controversial exhibits "Careful, Religion!" (2003) and "Forbidden Art" (2007), despite the fact that this art was displayed in a museum. At the same time, radical Christians, such as the former hiermonk Illarion (Roman) Zaitsev, defended the authenticity of the Punk Prayer as prayer (and hence the use of sacred place), encouraging believers to view its untraditional form in terms of the demands of the times, comparable to some of the devotional acts of Russia's contemporary motorcycle clubs ("bikers").[143] Orthodox Christians, such as church historian Elena Beliakova, while aware of the sanctity of place, dismissed its use in the case of the Punk Prayer performance. Beliakova maintained that since the Moscow Patriarchate promotes certain churches as cultural centers, church officials should anticipate conflicts and tensions in their use. Therefore, instead of linking Pussy Riot with anti-religious activists of the 1920s, she placed Punk Prayer as a genre in the tradition of Alexander Pushkin's poem "Gavrilliada" (the subject of Sarah Pratt's essay in this volume). Beliakova reminded readers that

Pushkin's youthful folly also did not lend him to seek a blessing from church officials for the poem's composition.[144]

Other commentators seemed unaware of the potential for location to qualitatively alter meaning. Sociologist Alek Epshtein, for instance, saw no distinction between acts that were staged outside of the cathedral and the Punk Prayer. Consequently, he situated the *Bogoroditsa* of the Punk Prayer in the tradition of late nineteenth- and early twentieth-century artists such as Kuzma Petrov-Vodkin, who, in such works as the *Petrograd Madonna* discussed by Wendy Salmond in this volume, drew on the image of Mary in their rendering of motherhood in a new socio-political context.[145] Similarly, artist Aleksandr Kosolapov, author of the controversial image of the Kazan icon of the Mother of God "Icon-Caviar," compared the refrain "Mother of God, Chase Putin Away" to Silver Age poet Vladimir Mayakovsky's famous refrain: "Bolt your pineapple, stuff your face with quail / Your last day, bourgeois, has come without fail!"[146] Despite a mixed reception in Russia's art world, the Punk Prayer performance has been deemed by some as the "best and most powerful postmodern work in recent times."[147]

While many listeners in the West have embraced the Punk Prayer as a familiar form of political art that promotes human and civil rights as well as gender equality in the face of political oppression, in Russia the "Prayer" reverberated differently. The Punk Prayer domestically carried its own quint-essentially Russian pitch.[148] Reflecting on their Punk Prayer performance from a penal colony in Mordovia in January 2013, Nadezhda Tolokonnikova acknowledged this by speaking not so much about the Western intellectual and artistic trends that inspired the work, but about its inherently religious quality (despite the insistence of her co-performer Ekaterina Samutsevich that the performance was strictly political).[149] Noting her longtime interest in Russian religious philosophy, she viewed herself and the Punk Prayer within the tradition of such nineteenth- and twentieth-century thinkers as Nikolai Berdiaev, Vladimir Solov'ev, and Vasilii Rozanov, who though often critical with respect to the institutional church, nevertheless contributed to sustaining Orthodoxy in a modern age.[150]

In 2001, sociologist of religion Alexander Agadjanian noted the powerful role that media discourse played in transforming Orthodox Christianity from a marginalized, "forbidden" religion during Soviet times to a widely embraced public religion. This transformation helped forge a national identity in the aftermath of the "shocking breakup of the social system." If, as he suggests, media discourse became "the main territory for the reception, reinterpretation and application of religion in contemporary Soviet society," it certainly has served the same function for Mary.[151]

The mediatization of Orthodoxy in general and Mary in particular in the first decades following the collapse of the Soviet Union have had mixed results for the Orthodox Church. On the one hand, keenly aware of the power of mass media in shaping values, attitudes, and political, economic, and social policies, church officials have embraced mass media for its educational and missionary potential, encouraging Orthodox journalists to use the media as a means of "preaching and implementing Christian moral ideas."[152] Media in this context can be seen as promoting the Church's efforts of "Orthodoxizing" Russian society. The common references in the press to the Mother of God and to Russia as her "domain" (*udel*) or "house" (*dom*), for instance, promote a sense of belonging among Russia's citizens, encouraging individual and collective "living conversation" with the *Bogoroditsa*.[153] Contemporary Orthodox churchmen hope that such "conversation" will at least dovetail with confessional identity. The unexpected public response to the 2011 visitation of the Virgin's belt from Mount Athos showed, if nothing else, that people had something to say to her.

On the other hand, as Professor of Religious Studies Gordon Lynch has pointed out, mass media fosters the "deregulation of religious ideas and symbols," moving them beyond the boundaries of the institutional church into the marketspace of ideas, associations, and objects. Consequently, as Pussy Riot performer Katya Samutsevich so aptly confirmed, these ideas and symbols no longer effectively "belong" exclusively to the Orthodox Church.[154] As a public or even civil religion, Orthodoxy—however it is conceived—becomes the domain of the people, not all of whom share or even know the language, hermeneutical principles, or unwritten codes that inform and help boarder cultural define the faith community. Media, therefore, has accelerated the processes of secularizing Orthodox symbols as much as it has contributed to the church's broader cultural missionizing agenda. As the Pussy Riot affair so poignantly demonstrated, media has also become a forum where the image of the *Bogoroditsa* can be renegotiated and transformed in unanticipated ways outside the boundaries of the interpretive community of faith. While perhaps perceived by some as un-Orthodox in form and intent, such reworkings often speak no less strongly to and have no less effect on the history of that community.[155]

## NOTES

1. A portion of the research included in this essay was conducted with the support of the National Council for Eurasian and East European Research, the National Endowment for the Humanities, and Smith College. This essay is part of a forthcoming larger project on the political, social, cultural and religious uses of the image of Mary, the Mother of God, in modern and post-Soviet Russia. Any views,

findings and conclusions expressed in this publication do not necessarily represent the views of these funding agencies. I am also grateful to Heather Coleman for her helpful comments on a draft of this essay. Note that technically "Pank Moleben" means "Punk Prayer Service." Throughout this essay, however, it will be referred to as "Punk Prayer," which has become the standard recognized translation.

2. For the group's description of their action as a "political gesture," see "Pussy Riot: Art or Politics?," in *Pussy Riot! A Punk Prayer for Freedom*, by Pussy Riot (New York: The Feminist Press at the City University of New York, 2013), 15–17. For the performers' surprise at the explosive reaction to their act, see, for example, "Chego khoteli i chego dobilis' Pussy Riot," Polit.ru, 16 April 2012, http://polit.ru/article/2012/04/16/discussion; "V kontse bylo slovo," *Profil'*, no. 29, 13 August 2012, 10–11; "Osoboe mnenie," *Ekho Moskvy*, 12 October 2012, http://www.echo.msk.ru/programs/personalno/939598-echo/. Unless otherwise noted, URLs in this essay were last accessed on 1 July 2017.

3. For a translation of the "Punk Prayer Service," see Pussy Riot, *Pussy Riot!*, 13–14.

4. The proliferation of miracles associated with icons of the Mother of God in Russia beginning especially in the early 1990s, along with the emergence of her image in Russia's post-Soviet devotional and political discourse, parallels Marian phenomena in other parts of the world, though the phenomena in Russia usually go unmentioned in discussions concerning the European or the global Marian subculture. See, as examples, Maureen Orth, "The World's Most Powerful Woman," *National Geographic* (December 2015): 30–59; E. Ann Matter, "Apparitions of the Virgin Mary in the Late Twentieth Century: Apocalyptic, Representation, Politics," *Religion* 31, no. 2 (2001): 125–53; Sandra Zimdars-Swartz, "The Marian Revival in American Catholicism: Focal Points and Features of the New Marian Enthusiasm," in *Being Right: Conservative Catholics in America*, ed. Mary Jo Weaver and R. Scott Appleby (Bloomington: Indiana University Press, 1995), 215–40.

5. Vsevolod Chaplin, "Active Neutrality," *Nezavisimaia gazeta*, 10 November 1999. Quoted in Nikolas K. Gvosdev, "Unity in Diversity: Civil Society, Democracy, and Orthodoxy in Contemporary Russia," in *Burden or Blessing: Russian Orthodoxy and the Construction of Civil Society and Democracy*, ed. Christopher Marsh (Boston: Institute on Culture, Religion and World Affairs, Boston University, 2004), 28.

6. The discussion of the clericalization of Russian society began in earnest in Russia's press in 2003, in connection with plans to introduce a mandatory course on "The Foundations of Orthodox Culture" in public schools. For example, see Mikhail Shakov, "Klerikalizatsiia Rossii ne grozit: Moskovskii Patriarkhat lish' sozdaet vidimosti svoei vliiatel'nosti," *NG Religiia*, no. 3, 19 February 2003; Anatolii Cherniaev, "'Pogublennaia dukhovnost'," *Svobodnaia mysl'*, no. 4 (April 2006): 136–48. Concern over this trend received wide attention again in 2007 when ten members of the Russian Academy of Sciences drafted a letter to President Putin in which they voiced concerns about the "active penetration of the church into all spheres of social life." See E. Alexandrov et al., "Politika RPTs: Konsolidatsiia ili razval strany?," *Novaia gazeta, prilozhenie "Kentavr"* 3, 22 July 2007; "Kod da istiny: Eksperty 'PG' obsuzhdaiut rol' Tserkvi v grazhdanskom obshchestve i svetskom gosudarstve," *Rossiiskaia gazeta*, 7 August 2008, http://www.rg.ru/2007/08/07/cerkov-spor.html. Since 2007, public discussion and debates about the clericalization of society in Russia have become increasingly more heated.

7. For distinctions between individual, social, collective, and public memory, see Edward S. Casey, "Public Memory in Place and Time," in *Framing Public Memory*, ed. Kendall R. Phillips (Tuscaloosa: University of Alabama Press, 2004), 17–32.

8. E. Poselianin, comp., *Bogomater': Polnoe illiustrirovannoe opisanie eia zemnoi zhizni i posviashchennykh eia imeni chudotvornykh ikon* (St. Petersburg: P. P. Soikina, 1900), 10. Sofiia Snessoreva, comp., *Zemnaia zhizn' presviatoi Bogoroditsy i opisanie sviatykh chudotovrnykh ee ikon, chtimykh pravoslavnoiu tserkov'iu, na osnovanii sviashchennogo pisaniia i tserkovnykh predanii, s izobrazheniiami v tekste prazdnikov i ikon Bozhiei Materi* (1898; repr., Iaroslavl: Verkhne-Volzhskoe knizhnoe izd-vo, 1994), 81.

9. While the confessional identities of the five Pussy Riot performers in the Cathedral of Christ the Savior have been a subject of wide speculation, Nadezhda Tolokonnikova publicly acknowledged that she is not a baptized Orthodox believer; although Katya Samutsevich's father maintained that his daughter was baptized as a child, Samutsevich herself avoided publicly discussing her faith,

maintaining that the issue was irrelevant to the purpose of the performance. "Otets Samutsevich ne znal o Pussy Riot," *Rossiiskaia gazeta*, 2 August 2012, http://www.rg.ru/2012/08/02/sud-site.html; Elena Masiuk, "Dvushechka," *Novaia gazeta*, no. 7, 23 January 2013, 3–4. Maria Alyokhina, however, was know as an engaged member of the Orthodox community.

10. Dmitrii Samarin, "Bogoroditsa v russkom narodnom pravoslavii," *Russkaia mysl'*, kn. 3–4 (1918): 8.

11. Vera Shevzov, *Russian Orthodoxy on the Eve of Revolution* (New York: Oxford University Press, 2004), 244–54; Vera Shevzov, "Scripting the Gaze: Liturgy, Homilies, and the Kazan Icon of the Mother of God in Late Imperial Russia," in *Sacred Stories: Religion and Spirituality in Modern Russia*, ed. Mark D. Steinberg and Heather J. Coleman (Bloomington: Indiana University Press, 2007), 61–92; Vera Shevzov, "Cast in Marian Light: Liturgy and Orthodox Memory in Late Imperial and Post-Soviet Russia," in *The Place of Liturgy in Russian Cultural History*, ed. Ronald Vroon, Sean Griffin, and Jeffrey Riggs (Slavica: forthcoming); T. A. Listova, "Bogoroditsa, Moskva, i nekotorye napravleniia religiozno-politicheskoi zhizni Rossii," *Etnograficheskoe obozrenie*, no. 4 (2010): 159.

12. Listova, "Bogoroditsa," 158; Vasilii Larionov, "Andrei Isaev: Rossiane assotsiiruiut sebia s etim flagom," *Izvestiia*, no. 155, 22 August 2008, 2; M. A. Men', "Pravda, vernost' i muzhestvo," *Ivanovskaia gazeta*, no. 152, 22 August 2009; Elena Kuzmina, "Nash belo-sine-krasnyi," *Novgorodskie vedomosti*, no. 24, 24 August 2010.

13. As examples, see N. Ia., *Russkim pravoslavnym khristianam: Povestvovanie o chudotvornoi ikone Presviatoi Bogoroditsy Fedorovskoi-Kostromskoi* (St. Petersburg: Strannik, 1869); Poselianin, *Bogomater'*, 285.

14. For the notion of "identity index," see Aleida Assmann, "Re-framing Memory: Between Individual and Collective Forms of Constructing the Past," in *Performing the Past: Memory, History, and Identity in Modern Europe*, ed. Karin Tilmans, Frank van Vree, and Jay Winter (Amsterdam: Amsterdam University Press, 2010), 38.

15. *Slava Bogomateri: Svedeniia o chudotvornykh i mestno chtimykh ikonakh Bozhiei Materi* (Moscow, 1907), 38–40; 92–93.

16. "Propoved' blagochinnogo Belgorodskogo okruga protiereia Olega Kobets, nastoiatelia Spaso-Preobrazhenskogo kafedral'nogo sobora goroda Belgoroda v den' prazdnovaniia iavleniia Smolenskoi ikony Bozhiei Materi," *Smolenskii sobor*, 15 October 2010, http:www.smsobor.ru/pastor/conversation/2152.html.

17. D. S. Likhachev, *Russkie letopisi i ikh kul'turno-istoricheskoe znachenie* (Moscow: Izd-vo Akademii Nauk SSSR, 1947), 278.

18. Natal'ia Rusina, "Kazanskaia ikona Presviatoi Bogoroditsy: Khranitel'nitsa vostochnykh granits Rossii i goroda Neriungi," *Iakutiia*, no. 122, 6 July 2000; Ianov Krotov, "Moskva—Vtoraia Kazan'," *Vremia MN*, no. 007, 1 June 2000; Dmitrii Aleshin, "Istoriia: Tikhvinskaia ikona vernulas' domoi," *Argumenty i fakty*, no. 28, 14 July 2004, 11; "Sviatynia: K nam vernulas' ikona Kazanskoi ikony Bozhiei Materi," *Komsomol'skaia pravda*, no. 162, 31 August 2004, 2.

19. Gennadii Belovolov, "Torzhestvo vzbrannoi voevody," *Krasnaia zvezda*, no. 157, 27 August 2003, 6. For another example of the Marianization of Russia's territory, see Vadim Lebedev and Iuliia Deminkova, "Taina Fatimskogo chuda," *Novaia gazeta*, no. 30, 27 April 2000.

20. For the narrative of the Leushino icon of the Mother of God, see *"Az esm' s Vami i Niktozhe na Vy": Povestvovanie o chudotvornoi ikone Presviatoi Bogoroditsy* (Chernigov: Danevskii Sviato-Georgievskii zhenskii monastyr, 2001). The narrative associated with this icon has come under harsh public scrutiny among some Orthodox circles, which has led to the questioning of the icon's authenticity. See V. P. Filimonov, *Ikona Bozhiei Materi "Az Esm' s Vami i Niktozhe Na Vy"* (Vologda: Izd-vo Vektor, 2010), http://anti-raskol.ru/pages/780. Despite the controversy and doubts raised about the icon, Russia's main manufacturer of ecclesiastical merchandise, Sofrino, continues to sell reproductions of this iconographic type.

21. N. V. Dmitrieva, comp., *O Tebe raduetsia: Chudotvornye ikony Bozhiei Materi* (Moscow: Izd-vo Sretenskogo monastyria, 2004), 37–43.

22. For an account of the Port Arthur icon of the Mother of God, see Andersin-Lebedeva, *Skazanie ob ikone Port-Arturskoi Bogomateri* (Odessa: Tip. Eparkhial'nogo doma, 1916); for an account

of the icon of the Mother of God of the Holy Cross, see *Skazanie o iavlenii Presviatoi Bogoroditsy v. g. Budennovske 18 iiunia 1995 goda i napisanii ikony Ee Sviato-Krestovskoi* (Moscow: Izd-vo, 1999).

23. For a collection of devotional, ethnographic, and historical materials associated with the icon of the Mother of God named She Who Reigns, see Sergei Fomin, ed., *Derzhavnaia pravitel'nitsa zemli russkoi* (Moscow: Palomnik, 1999).

24. Belovolov, "Torzhestvo vzbrannoi voevody."

25. "Sviatynia: K nam vernulas," 2.

26. Sviateishii Patriarkh Moskovskii i Vseia Rusi Aleksii II, "Patriarshee poslanie v sviazi c otkrytiem programmy 'Pod zvezdoi Bogoroditsy,'" 17 May 2007, http://www.patriarchia.ru/db/print/243142.html.

27. For a site commemorating this program, see "Pod Zvezdoi Bogoroditsy: Mezhdunarodnaia programma," http://star.icxcnika.ru/. For the itinerary of the event, see "O programme 'Pod zvezdoi Bogoroditsy,'" *Livejournal* (blog), last accessed 10 January 2011, http://mavar-dina.livejournal.com/136557.html. For devotional descriptions of the event, see "Rus' Derzhavnaia: Krestnyi khod vseia Rusi," *Pravoslavie v Tatarstane,* 9 September 2008, http://www.kazeparhia.ru/smi/?ID=16003; Nikolai Golovkin, "Krestnyi khod vselenskogo masshtaba," Stoletie.ru, 12 July 2007, http://www.stoletie.ru/obshchestvo/krestni_hod_vselenskogo_masshtaba.htm.

28. Serafima Darina, "Pod zvezdoi Bogoroditsy," *Slavianka* 27, no. 3 (May–June 2010), last accessed 15 June 2012, http://www.slavianka.com/old/article-50.html?id=137.

29. Ul'iana Grishina, "Po Rusi," *Literaturnaia gazeta,* no. 46, 21 November 2007, 12; Golovkin, "Krestnyi khod vselenskogo masshtaba."

30. Anthony D. Smith, "The 'Sacred' Dimension of Nationalism," *Millennium: Journal of International Studies* 29, no. 3 (2000): 792.

31. Ibid.

32. Tamara Kliberova, "Dubovyi krest—na dno Iaponskogo moria," *Vladivostok,* 6 April 2004. The local press often reports rituals involving Marian icons and the blessing of Russian territory. See, as an example, Oksana Zemskaia, "'Derzhavnaia' ikona khranit Rossiiu," *Nizhegorodskie novosti,* no. 45, 14 March 2009; Iuliia Borisova, "Sviataia puteshestvennitsa," *Amurskaia pravda,* no. 147, 14 August 2010.

33. For a detailed account of the icon's *life,* see "Povest' o chestnom i slavnom iavlenii obraza prechistoi Bogoroditsy v Kazani," in *Patriarkh Ermogen: Zhizneopisanie, tvoreniia, istoricheskie predaniia, chudesa i proslavlanie,* ed. E. A. Smirnova (Moscow: Pravoslavnaia entsiklopediia, 1997), 41–58; *Skazanie o iavlennoi Kazanskoi ikone Bozhiei Materi, byvshikh ot neia chudesakh, ustanovlenii povsemestnago prazdnovaniia ei v Rossii v 1649 g.* (Moscow: Izd-vo. E. Konovalova, 1907).

34. "Slovo Sviateishego Patriarkha Aleksiia na otkrytii pamiatnika Mininu i Pozharskomu v Nizhnem Novgorode," Patriarchia.ru, 4 November 2004, http://www.patriarchia.ru/db/print/55730.html; Irina Sizova, "Chem stolet'e interesnei dlia istorika, tem dlia sovremennika slozhnee," *Riazanskie vedomosti,* no. 215, 4 November 2009; Dmitrii Steshin "Chto my prazdnuem 4 noiabria?" *Komsomol'skaia pravda,* no. 165, 3 November 2009.

35. N. I. Florinskii, *O tom, po kakomu sluchaiu otechestvennaia tserkov' nasha prazdnuet presviatoi Bogoroditse 22-go oktiabria* (Vladimir: Gub. tip., 1864); P. I., "Pouchenie v den' prazdnovaniia chudotvornoi Kazanskoi ikone Bozhiei Materi," *Saratovskiia eparkhial'nyia vedomosti* (1877): 580–85. For contemporary references to the celebration of 4 November in similar terms, see Egor Kholmogorov, "Iskupitel'naia zhertva ili politcheskii suisid?," *APN Nizhnii Novgorod,* 21 January 2005, http://apn-nn.com/76402-200116.html; Ekaterina Abramova, "4 noiabria: Dvoinoi prazdnik," *Iaroslavskii region,* no. 43, 3 November 2010; Svetlana Pashkina, "Odin makhal flagami, drugie shli s ikonami," *Zolotoe kol'tso,* no. 209, 8 November 2011.

36. The Interreligious Council is a pan-confessional organization consisting of leaders and representatives from the four "traditional" faiths in Russia—Russian Orthodox, Muslim, Jewish, and Buddhist. It was established in 1998 on the initiative of the Moscow Patriarchate, and especially Metropolitan Kirill (Gundiaev), who at the time oversaw the Patriarchate's Department for External Church Relations, in order to coordinate efforts both with respect to civil society and with respect to the state in matters concerning religion and faith. For Patriarch Kirill's role as architect of the new

holiday, see the comments by the well-known priest Vsevolod Chaplin, "Den' narodnogo edinstva, god 2014-yi," *Vsemirnyi Russkii Narodnyi Sobor*, https://vrns.ru/society/3401.

37. For the September 2004 statement of the Interreligious Council, see "Segodnia my dolzhny byt' ediny kak nikogda." *Russkaia narodnaia liniia*, 23 September 2004, "http://pravoslavnye.ru/monitoring_smi/2004/09/23/segodnya_my_dolzhny_byt_ediny_kak_nikogda/; "Den' Narodnogo Edinstva: Edinenie—simvol prochnosti strany, *Kurskaia pravda*, no. 165, 3 November 2009.

38. "Segodnia my dolzhny byt' ediny."

39. "Slovo Sviateishego Patriarkha Aleksiia"; "Patriarshee slovo v den' prazdnika Kazanskoi ikony Bozhiei Materi," Patriarchia.ru, 4 November 2007, http://www.patriarchia.ru/db/print/317100.html.

40. See "Rossiia—moia istoriia. Istoricheskii park na VDNKh," http://myhistorypark.ru/.

41. See, in particular, Patriarch Kirill's address to the World Russian People's Council on 1 October 2012, Patriarchia.ru, http://www.patriarchia.ru/db/text/2502801.html. For an example of the emphasis placed on memory in a sermon on a Marian feast, see Protoierei Andrei Alekseev, "Propoved' v prazdnik Kazanskoi ikony Bozhiei Materi," 4 November 2016, http://mail.dmdonskoy.ru/node/3146.

42. "Slovo Sviateishego Patriarkha Kirilla za Bozhestvennoi liturgii v den' prazdnika Vladimirskoi ikony Bozhiei Materi," Patriarchia.ru, 3 June 2009, http://www.patriarchia.ru/db/text/665838.html.

43. Andrei Kuraev, *Shkol'noe bogoslovie*, accessible at *Azbuka vospitaniia*: http://azbyka.ru/tserkov/lyubov_i_semya/vera_i_deti/kuraev_shkolnoe_bogoclovie_37-all.shtml.

44. Nikolai Likhachev, "Skazanie o iavlenii ikony Bozhiei Materi pri Voznesenskoi v sele Kolomenskom tserkvi, Moskovskago uezda," *Dushepoleznyi sobesednik* 9 (1917): 314–16.

45. See, for example, O. A. Platonov, "Derzhavnaia—chudotvornaia ikona presviatoi Bogoroditsy," *Bol'shaia entsiklopediia russkogo naroda*, http://www.rusinst.ru/articletext.asp?rzd=1&id=357&abc=1.

46. For a discussion of Eastern and Western Christian depictions of the Maria Regina image of the Virgin Mary, see Bissera V. Pentcheva, *Icons and Power: The Mother of God in Byzantium* (University Park: Pennsylvania State University Press, 2006), 21–26.

47. Irina Kartavtseva, "Vokrug Kremlia s Derzhavnoi," in Fomin, *Derzhavnaia pravitel'nitsa*, 70–71.

48. E. B., "'Derzhavnaia' v Diveeve," in Fomin, *Derzhavnaia pravitel'nitsa*, 61–67.

49. Arkhimandrit Ioann (Krestiankin), "Pod Derzhavnym Pokrovom," in Fomin, *Derzhavnaia pravitel'nitsa*, 126–27; Platonov, "Derzhavnaia."

50. Valerii Shambarov, "Na perekrestakh otechestvennoi istorii," *Molodaia gvardiia*, no. 19 (October 2008): 286–87. For the evolution of the various narrative strands in the *life* of the icon named She Who Reigns, see Muzei imeni Andreia Rubleva, "Derzhavnaia ikona Bozhiei Materi: 95 let iavleniiu," 15 March 2012, *Livejournal* (blog), http://expertmus.livejournal.com/95360.html.

51. Anna Il'inskaia, "Iavlenie ikony," in Fomin, *Derzhavnaia pravitel'nitsa*, 79–89.

52. Arkhimandrit A. V. Vasil'ev, "Ikona Bozhiei Materi 'Derzhavnaia'," *Slovo: Pravoslavno obrazovitel'nyi portal*, 3 May 2009, http://www.portal-slovo.ru/art/41032.php.

53. See, for instance, Protoierei Dimitrii Smirnov, "Vsenoshchnoe bdenie pod prazdnovanie 'Derzhavnoi' ikony Bozhiei Materi," *Blagoveshchenie: Biblioteka Pravoslavnogo khristianina*, 14 March 1991, http://www.wco.ru/biblio/books/dimitrs12/H03-T.htm.

54. "Glava gosudarstva i Predstoiatel' Russkoi Pravoslavnoi Tserkvi otkryli vystavku 'Pravoslavnaia Rus'" v Moskve," Patriarchia.ru, 4 November 2015, http://www.patriarchia.ru/db/text/4263139.html; Kateryna Shchotkina, "Stalin and the Russian Orthodox Church," *Euromaidan Press*, 19 November 2015, http://euromaidanpress.com/2015/11/19/stalin-and-the-russian-orthodox-church/; "V RPTs otvergli upreki v opravdanii Stalina patriarkhom Kirillom," *Interfax*, 11 November 2015, http://www.interfax.ru/russia/478611.

55. Gennadii Petrov, "U sviatogo kresta otmolennye pomianutye," Budennovsk.org, 16 June 2017, http://budennovsk.org/?p=141570; Sightings of the Mother of God have also been associated with the South Ossetian War in August 2008. See Oleg Bedula, "Pomoshch' s nebes," Osradio.ru, 9 September 2008, http://osradio.ru/osetija/print:page,1,8982-pomoshh-s-nebes.html.

56. Poselianin, *Bogomater'*, 513–14.

57. Gail Lenhoff, "Temir Aksak's Dream of the Virgin as Protectress of Muscovy," *Die Welt der Slaven* 49 (2004): 39–64.

58. *Skazanie o iavlenii Presviatoi Bogoroditsy*; "Chudesnoe zastupnichestvo Bogoroditsy," *Stavropol'skaia gazeta*, 27 June 2012.

59. Dmitrieva, *O Tebe Raduetsia*, 317–20.

60. Vitalii Petrov, "Bez smuty," *Rossiiskaia gazeta*, no. 249, 3 November 2010, 1; "V Den' narodnogo edinstva v Moskve proshla panikhida po vsem zhertvam revoliutsii i grazhdanskoi voiny," *Radonezh*, 4 November 2010, http://radonezh.ru/news/v-den-narodnogo-edinstva-v-moskve-proshla-panikhida-po-vsem-zhertvam-revolyutsii-i-grazhdanskoy-10859.html.

61. "Slovo Sviateishego Patriarkha Kirilla posle Bozhestvennoi liturgii v prazdnik Kazanskoi ikony Bozhiei Materi," Patriarchia.ru, 4 November 2010, http://www.patriarchia.ru/db/text/1311883.html; Patriarch Kirill, "O dukhovnom smysle preodoleniia smuty," Pravoslavie.ru, 3 November 2012, http://http://www.pravoslavie.ru/57181.html; "Patriarshaia propoved' v prazdnik Kazanskoi ikony Bozhiei Materi posle Liturgii v Uspenskom sobore Kremlia," Patriarchia.ru, 4 November 2015, http://www.patriarchia.ru/db/text/4263946.html.

62. Sergei Maksudov, "Minin i Pozharskii vmesto Marksa i Engel'sa: Den' natsional'nogo edinstva mozhet razdelit' Rossiian," *Nezavisimaia gazeta: Religiia* 1, 6 October 2004; Elena Iakovleva, "Vera protiv Smuty," *Rossiiskaia gazeta*, no. 255, 6 November 2012; Mitropolit Kaluzhskii i Borovskii Kliment, "Pravoslavnaia kul'tura i molodezhnaia sreda," Sedmitza.ru, 28 January 2005, www.sedmitza.ru/index.html?did=20738.

63. Georgii Spiridonov, "My sil'ny esli my ediny," *Iakutiia*, no. 206, 3 November 2005; Veronika Vorontsova, Anna Alekseeva, "Den' narodnogo neznaniia," *Novye izvestiia*, no. 198, 5 November 2014.

64. "Zadacha tserkvi—ne otritsat' no votserkovit' svetskuiu kul'turu, otmechaet pravoslavnyi uchenyi," *Interfaks-Religiia*, 31 October 2006, http://www.interfax-religion.ru/?act=news&div=14828.

65. "Slovo Sviateishego Patriarkha Kirilla posle Bozhestvennoi liturgii; Patriarshaia propoved'."

66. "Pozdravleniia s Dnem narodnogo edinstva," *Vladivostok*, no. 165, 3 November 2006.

67. Andrei Zubov, "Kakoi prazdnik my ob'iavliaem natsional'nym, tak i nachinaet razvivat'sia istorii otechestva," *Tat'ianin den'*, 3 November 2006, http://www.taday.ru/text/30078.html.

68. Nail' Gafutulin, "Gde edinenie, tam pobeda!," *Krasnaia zvezda*, no. 204, 3 November 2006; Episkop Ivanovo-Voznesenskii i Kineshemskii, Iosif, "Prazdnik vnutrennei sily Rossiiskogo naroda," *Ivanovskaia gazeta*, no. 203, 2 November 2007; Marianna Danilova, "Vozvrashchenie k traditsiiam," *Sovetskii Sibir*, no. 214, 3 November 2010; Iuliia Matiushchenko et al., "Prazdnuem: Chto?," *Kuzbass*, no. 203, 1 November 2011; "Den' grazhdanskogo obshchestva," *Novosti Iugry*, no. 170, 3 November 2011.

69. Sergei Siniukov, "Svetlyi prazdnik posle smutnogo vremeni," *Volga*, no. 163, 2 November 2008.

70. "Speech at the Ceremonial Reception for the Day of National Unity," *President of Russia*, 4 November 2005, http://en.kremlin.ru/events/president/transcripts/23252. It is noteworthy that support for the new holiday has grown significantly since its introduction in 2005. If in 2007 only an estimated 39% of Russia's citizens considered the new holiday necessary and meaningful, by 2014, that figure had grown to 63%. "Dve treti rossiian shchitaiut Den' narodnogo edinstva nuzhnym prazdnikom," Tass.ru, 30 October 2014, http://tass.ru/obschestvo/1541986.

71. Slovo Sviateishego Patriarkha Kirilla v prazdnik Kazanskoi ikony Bozhiei Materi v Kazanskom sobore na Krasnoi ploshchadi," Patriarchia.ru, 4 November 2011, http://www.patriarchia.ru/db/text/1665278.html; Ieromonakh Ignatii (Shestakov), "Narodnoe edinstvo: Slovo v den' prazdnovaniia Kazanskoi ikony Bozhiei Materi," Pravoslavie.ru, 4 November 2013, http://www.pravoslavie.ru/65443.html; Zubov, "Kakoi prazdnik."

72. Protoierei Igor Fomin and Natal'ia Smirnova, "Zastupnitsa: Den' Kazanskoi ikony Bozhiei Materi i Den' Narodnogo Edinstva," *Pravoslavie i mir*, 4 November 2011, http://www.pravmir.ru/zastupnica-prazdnik-kazanskoj-ikony-bozhiej-materi-i-den-narodnogo-edinstva/.

73. "Den' narodnogo edinstva. Chto prazdnuem? Kto prazdnuet?" Pravoslavie.ru, 3 November 2011, http://www.pravoslavie.ru/49641.html.

74. Dustrik Markosian, "Pobeda nad smutoi," *Rossiia*, no. 43, 12 November 2009, 11; Aleksandr Slavutskii, "Podvig vo imia otechestva," *Moskovskaia pravda*, no. 242, 3 November 2010, 2.

75. Nikolai Koniaev, *Prazdnik Rossii: Vozvrashchenie dvukh chudotvornykh ikon Bozhiei Materi* (St. Petersburg: Russkii ostrov, 2008).

76. Aleshin, "Istoriia," 11.

77. "Slovo Sviateishego Patriarkha Kirilla za Bozhestvennoi liturgiei v Tikhvinskom monastyre," 9 July 2009, Patriarchia.ru, http://www.patriarchia.ru/db/text/689974.html; Kirill, "Patriarshee poslanie v sviazi s prineseniem.'"

78. Kirill, "Patriarshee poslanie v sviazi s prineseniem"; Marina Gladkova, "V Moskvu pribyla chudotvornaia Kurskaia ikona," *Vecherniaia Moskva*, no. 171, 14 September 2009.

79. "V stolitse proidet moleben o nachale Mezhdunarodnoi dukhovnoi prosvetitel'skoi programmy 'Pod zvezdoi Bogoroditsy,'" Patriarchia.ru, 17 May 2007, http://www.patriarchia.ru/db/text/242924.html; Aleksii II, "Patriarshee poslanie v sviazi s otkrytiem"; "V khrame Khrista Spasitelia zavershilsia krestnyi khod Pod zvezdoi Bogoroditsy," *Klin pravoslavnyi*, http://www.pravklin.ru/publ/5-1-0-28.

80. Mitropolit Kaluzhskii i Borovskii Kliment (Kapalin), "Shkola, semia, Tserkov—zadachi v usloviiakh demograficheskogo i dukhovnago krizisa," 24 January 2005, Sedmitza.ru, www.sedmitza.ru/index.html?did=20657.

81. Sergei Kara-Murza, "Padenie rozhdaemosti v Rossii: Faktor kul'tury," *Molodaia gvardiia*, no. 7 (August 2010): 110–21; Aleksei Reiutskii, "Kak Rossii vyiti iz demograficheskogo krizisa," *Tserkovnyi vestnik*, 26 November 2012, http://e-vestnik.ru/analytics/kak_rossii_vyyti_iz_demograficheskogo_krizisa_6197/. The birthrate steadily increased from 2011–2016, although at the time of this essay's publication, new concerns about another looming crisis have arisen. See, for example, Anatolii Komrakov, "Rossiia podoshla k novoi demograficheskoi iame," *Nezavisimaia gazeta*, no. 147, 18 July 2017.

82. Nikolai Golovkin, "Zashchitnitsa materei Rossii," Pravoslavie.ru, 30 November 2007, http://www.pravoslavie.ru/jurnal/1073.htm.

83. "Vystuplenie Sviateishego Patriarkha Kirilla na pervom zasedanii Patriarshei komissii po voprosam sem'i i zashchity materinstva," Patriarchia.ru, 6 April 2012, http://www.patriarchia.ru/db/print/2143731.html; "Patriarkh: Demograficheskii krizis vyzvan narusheniem sistemy tsennostei," *RIA Novosti*, 22 September 2010, http://www.rian.ru/religion/20100922/278126332.html. Also see comment by Iosif, the bishop of Ivanovo-Voznesenk, "Prazdnik vnutrennei sily Rossiiskogo naroda," *Ivanovskaia gazeta*, no. 203, 2 November 2007; Golovkin, "Zashchitnitsa materei Rossii." Some conservative Orthodox clergy are quite vocal with respect to their views on the demographic crisis. According to the controversial, conservative, and outspoken archpriest Dimitrii Smirnov, no bright future awaits Russia, "no economists can help it," while it is "bathed in the blood of infants." Protoierei Dmitrii Smirnov, "Propoved' v den' pamiati Vifleemskikh Mladentsev," *Zavet*.ru, http://www.zavet.ru/absmirn02.htm. For support of the Church's views from Russia's academic circles, see, for example, V. N. Leskin, "Ideologicheskie osnovy upadka sovremennogo instituta sem'i," *Obshchestvennye nauki i sovremennost'* 2 (2011): 29–42; Kara-Murza, "Padenie rozhdaemosti v Rossii."

84. "Polozhenie o 'Patriarshem znake materinstva,'" Patriarchia.ru, 5 October 2006, http://www.patriarchia.ru/db/text/149326.html. For Soviet pro-natal policies and the various maternity awards, see Lewis A. Coser, "Some Aspects of Soviet Family Policy," *American Journal of Sociology* 56, no. 5 (March 1951): 424–37; David L. Hoffman, "Mothers in the Motherland: Stalinist Pronatalism in Its Pan-European Context," *Journal of Social History* 34, no. 1 (Fall 2000): 35–54; Michele Rivkin-Fish, "Pronatalism, Gender Politics, and the Renewal of Family Support in Russia: Toward a Feminist Anthropology of 'Maternity Capital,'" *Slavic Review* 69, no. 3 (Fall 2010): 701–24. The Church seems to have curtailed promoting the award on a wide scale after negative public reaction to Patriarch Alexei's awarding of the prize in 2007 to Irina Abramovich, mother of five and former wife of oligarch Roman Abramovich. "Alexey II Awards Irina Abramovich for her 'Motherly Ministry,'" *Interfax Religion*, 27 November 2007, http://www.interfax-religion.com/?act=news&div=3991; "11 Safronovykh protive 5 Abramovichei," *Pravda*, no. 139, 14 December 2007, 4.

85. The organization's patron saint, however, is Evfrosiniia, the wife of Dmitrii Donskoi and a mother of twelve. For the website of this organization, see Sviatost' materinstva, http://sm.cnsr.ru.

86. Iuvenalii, mitropolit Krutitskii i Kolomenskii, "K chitateliam gazety 'Kommersant', *Kommersant*, no. 174, 21 September 2009, 6.

87. Natal'ia Sukhinina, "Pomoshchnitsa v rodakh," Pravda.ru, 16 September 2003, http:// health.pravda.ru/gynaecology/oldmethods/16-09-2003/38416-ikona-0/. For a description of the celebration of the Feodorov icon in prerevolutionary Russia, see S. V. Bulgakov, *Nastol'naia kniga dlia sviashchenno-tserkovno-sluzhitelei* (1913; repr., Moscow: Izdatel'skii otdel Moskovskogo Patriarkhata, 1993), 1:317. References to prayer before the Feodorov icon as helping in matters of fertility and childbirth are widely found on forums relating to childbearing and motherhood. As an example, see the forum Materinstvo, http://forum.materinstvo.ru/index.php?showtopic=1268034.

88. Iulia Gonchareva, "V Rossii poiavit'sia Den Beremennykh?," *Moskovskii komsomolets*, no. 254, 14 November 2008, 14; "V Russkoi Tserkvi predlagaiut vvesti v ofitsial'nyi kalendar' Den' beremennykh," *Russkaia beseda*, 17 November 2008, http://www.rusbeseda.ru/index.php?topic=3795.0; Iakov Makartsov, "Den' beremennykh na Viatke," 23 October 2009, *Viatskaia pereprava*, http://sobor-urzhum.ucoz.ru/news/den_beremennykh_na_vjatke/2009-10-23-158.

89. Margarita Pirogova, "Otchet o poseshchenii sektsii 'Sluzhenie Tserkvi v meditsinskikh uchrezhdeniiakh rodovspomozheniia' na XVII Rozhdestvenskikh chteniiakh," 17 February 2009, *Meditsinskii otdel Kazanskoi eparkhii*, http://www.pravoslavie-med.ru/med_i_pravoslavie/ginekologia/otchet/; The icon of the Mother of God named Unexpected Joy is also commonly listed among those to which mothers are recommended to turn in prayer for the welfare of their children. Taisiia S. Oleinikova, *Pokrovitel'stvo presviatoi Bogoroditsy: Pered kakoi ikonoi Bozhiei Materi v kakikh sluchaiakh nado molit'sia* (Moscow: Dar, 2009), 84.

90. Marina Parenskaia, "Bud'te Zdorovy!," *Volga*, no. 103, 17 July 2009; Ol'ga Postnova, "Budushchim Mamam pomogut ikony," *Volga*, no. 92, 20 June 2009.

91. Protoierei Vladimir Andreev, "Ikona Bozhiei Materi 'Pomozhenie rodam,'" *Pravoslavnyi Serpukhov*, http://pserpuhov.sergbond.ru/blagochinie/sviatini/pomozhenie.php; "Akafist Bozhiei Materi pred ikonoi Eia 'V rodakh Pomoshchnitsa,'" Akafist.narod.ru, http://akafist.narod.ru/B/V_rodah_Pomoshnica.htm.

92. Ol'ga Kremlianskaia, "Pomoshchnitsa v rodakh," *Irkutskaia eparkhia*, 31 January 2008, http://iemp.ru/main_news.php?ID=1169&sphrase_id=7172183. Prerevolutionary Russia knew of two visually similar images—"Help in Childbirth" (Pomoshch' v rodakh) and "Aid to Women Giving Birth to Children" (Pomogatel'nitsa zhenam chady razhdati). Both appeared in the Church's 1907 supplement to the Russian language *Menaion* that was devoted exclusively to icons of the Mother of God; both were also designated as icons that helped women in childbirth. *Slava Bogomateri*, 216–17. For the history of this iconographic type, see E. Iu. Suvorova, "Russkie ikony Bogomateri 'Pomoshchnitsa v rodakh' XVIII–nachala XX vv.: Problemy ikonografii," *Iskusstvo khristianskogo mira: Sbornik statei*, ed. Aleksandr Saltykov et al. (Moscow: Pravoslavnyi Sviato-Tikhonovskii Gumanitarnyi Universitet, 2007), 10:417–37.

93. "Aleksinskomu roddomu peredana ikona Bozhiei Materi 'Pomoshchnitsy v rodakh,'" Mirtesen.ru, 16 March 2012; http://mirtesen.ru/pad/4324734124; "Ikona pomoshchnitsa pri rodakh," Beremennost', http://beremennost.net/ikona-pomoshchnitsa-pri-rodakh; "Pomoshchnitsa v rodakh," Khotim detei, http://hotimdetey.ru/article/ikoni/pomoshchnitsa_v_rodah/; "Molitva o pomoshchi v rodakh, ikona 'Pomoshch' v rodakh,'" Bebi.ru, 29 April 2011, https://www.baby.ru/blogs/post/25209445-24875845/.

94. For a history of the origins of the belt or girdle of the Virgin Mary, see John Wortley, "The Marian Relics at Constantinople," *Greek, Roman, and Byzantine Studies* 45, no. 2 (2005): 181–87.

95. "Patriarkh Kirill: Poias Bogoroditsy dal velikuiu nadezhdu," Vesti.ru, 7 January 2012, http:// news.rambler.ru/12371046/; "Poias nadezhdy i spaseniia Rossii," Simvol-very.ru, http://simvol-veri.ru/xp/poyas-nadejdi-i-spaseniya-rossii.html; Elena Iakovleva, "Sviatoe delo: Protoierei Vladimir Vigilianskiii i protodiakon Andrei Kuraev o poiase Bogoroditsy," *Rossiiskaia gazeta*, 1 December 2011, http://www.portal-credo.ru/site/?act=monitor&id=17169.

96. See Patriarch Kirill's annual televised Christmas address for 2012, "Poias Bogoridisty dal velikuiu nadzehdu," Vesti.ru, http://www.vesti.ru/only_video.html?vid=389143; Iakovleva, "Sviatoe delo"; Evgeniia Surpycheva and Iuliia Khozhateleva, "Kak korrespondent 'KP' stoiala v ocheredi k poiasu Presviatoi Bogoroditsy za chudom," *Komsomol'skaia pravda*, no. 175, 23 November 2011, 5.

97. Patriarkh Kirill, "Prineseniia Poiasa Bogoroditsy stalo ubeditel'nym svidetel'stvom togo, chto my zhivem pravoslavnoi strane," Patriarchia.ru, 1 December 2011, http://www.patriarchia.ru/db/text/1794105.html.

98. Tat'iana Makina and Nikolai Shaburov, "Dlia tolpy, kotoraia stoit v ocheredi za chudom religiia neotlichima ot koldovstva," *Moskovskie novosti*, no. 16, 25 November 2011, 1; Vladislav Inozemtsev, "Poias Bogoroditsy vmesto normal'nogo zdravookhraeniia, *Moskovskii komsomolets*, no. 268, 25 November 2011, 4.

99. "Pust' Govoriat," television program moderated by Andrei Malakhov, *YouTube*, 28 December 2011, http://www.youtube.com/watch?v=QtQYoLKSz5M.

100. See, as an example, "Pro zhizn'," television program moderated by Ol'ga Bakushinskaia, 2 November 2011, which can be viewed through the site Video@mail.ru, https://my.mail.ru/mail/lyudmilashapase/video/158/1369.html.

101. Marina Grineva, "Pomolimsia o materinstve," *Samarskie izvestiia*, no. 206, 9 November 2011.

102. Natal'ia Iakunina, "Programmnyi doklad N. V. Iakuninoi na otkrytie Foruma," *Sviatost' materinstva*, 20 November 2012, http://sm.cnsr.ru/ru/news/nfrf/Programmnij_doklad_N_V__Yakuninoj_na_otkritii_Foruma/?news=yes. Also see Alexei Ovchinnikov, "Poias Bogoroditsy prines v Rossiiu bebi-bum," *Komsomol'skaia pravda*, no. 142, 25 September 2012.

103. Patriarch Kirill, "Prineseniia Poiasa Bogoroditsy"; "Slovo sviateishego Patriarkha Kirilla v tret'iu godovishchinu intronizatsii v Khrame Khrista Spasitelia," Patriarchia.ru, 1 February 2012, http://www.patriarchia.ru/db/text/1992020.html.

104. The theme of Russia's "spiritual security" as a matter of national security has been a recurring theme in Russia's political discourse since at least 2005. See Julie Elkner, "Spiritual Security in Putin's Russia," *History and Policy*, January 2005, http://www.historyandpolicy.org/papers/policy-paper-26.html.

105. Alexander Prokhanov, "Protivoraketnyi poias Presviatoi Bogoroditsy," *Zavtra*, no. 48, 30 November 2011, 1.

106. "Metamorfozy: Prazdniki kak instrument politicheskoi bor'by . . . neizvestno s kem," *Moskovskaia pravda*, no. 243, 7 November 2005; Maksudov, "Minin i Pozharskii." The abbot of the Holy Resurrection Ermolinskii hermitage (Nizhnii Novgorod), Varlaam (Borin), offered a similar evaluation. See "Chto dumaiut o Dne narodnogo edinstva nashi sograzhdane?," *Uchitel'skaia gazeta*, no. 44, 3 November 2009, 14.

107. "GOSDUMA priniala v pervom chtenii popravki v trudovoi kodeks," *Telekanal TVTs*, 23 November 2004, http://rudocs.exdat.com/docs/index-397858.html?page=2; also see Ol'ga Vandysheva, "Slava Velikomu Ianvariu!," *Komsomol'skaia pravda*, 24 November 2004, http://www.kp.ru/daily/23409/34339.

108. Inna Lomantsova, "Prizhivetsia ili net?," *Orenburzh'e*, no. 167, 4 November 2009.

109. Aleksandra Glukhova, "Krivye analogii," *Kommuna*, 11 October 2005; Marina Ivleva and Tat'iana Batova, "Net takoi daty—4 noiabria," *Vladivostok*, 3 November 2005; Nikolai Kirsanov, "Gde zhe tut 'Narodnoe edinstvo,'" *Sovetskaia Rossiia*, no. 128, 2 November 2006; Gennadii Starchekov, "Kogda lozh' stanovitsia zakonom," *Pravda*, no. 122, 2 November 2007, 4; N. A. Kirsanov, "Den' Pozora, a ne 'Narodnogo Edinstva,'" *Sovetskaia Rossiia*, no. 121, 3 November 2009, 4.

110. For the stories related to the Kazan icon of the Mother of God, see Shevzov, "Scripting the Gaze"; Krotov, "Moskva—Vtoraia Kazan.'"

111. Iuliia Glezarova, "Chudotvornaia ikona kak simvol Russkogo iga," *Nezavisimaia gazeta*, no. 21 (151), 17 November 2004; "Ikona iz pokoev Papy zhelanna v Kazani ne dlia vsekh," *Mir religii*, 4 August 2004, http://www.religio.ru/news/8623.html; Irina Kurginian, "Karnaval edinstva," *Zavtra*, no. 46, 12 November 2008.

112. Vystuplenie sviateishego Patriarkha Kirilla na otkrytii XVI-ogo Vsemirnogo russkogo narodnogo sobora," Patriarchia.ru, 1 October 2012, http://www.patriarchia.ru/db/text/2502163.html.

113. Galina Andrianova, comp., *Iavlenie Bozhiei Materi v obraze "Voskreshaiushchaia Rus',": Opisanie i svidetel'stva proiavleniia blagodatnoi Eia pomoshchi, Akafist Presviatei Vladychitse Nashei Bogoroditsy v chest' chudotvornyia ikony Eia 'Voskreshaiushchaia Rus'"* (Stavropol: Kavkazskaia zdravnitsa, 2004), 4–8.

114. Andrianova, *Iavlenie Bozhiei Materi*, 4–8.

115. Ibid., 6; O. P. Kliukina, "Vokrug obraza Voskreshaiushchaia Rus," Votserkovlenie.ru, http://www.vocerkovlenie.ru/index.php/gizncerkvi/1302--q-q-.html.

116. Kliukina, "Vokrug obraza Voskreshaiushchaia Rus."

117. Ol'ga Kravets, "Aktual'noe bogoslovie: Materialy, pis'ma i svidetel'stva blagodatnoi pomoshchi Presviatoi Bogoroditsy v obraze Ee Voskreshaiushchaia Rus' pri molitvennom k Nei obrashchenii peredany v komissiiu po kanonizatsii sviatyn' pri Sviashchennom Sinode Russkoi Pravoslavnoi Tserkvi," Blagoslovenie.ru, www.blagoslovenie.ru/client/chudesa/2.htm. For the variety of representations of this image, see "Ikona Presviatoi Bogoroditsy 'Voskreshaiushchaia Rus," PravIcon.com, http://pravicon.com/icon-68.

118. "Ikona Bozhiei Materi 'Voskreshaiushchaia Rus," *Mir Russkoi ikony*, http://ru-icons.ru/icons/51.html; Alla Dobrosotskikh, "Soblazn' 'Osobogo sluzheniia,' ili kak naviazyvaiut pochitanie psevdoikony 'Voskreshaiushchaia Rus," in *Iskusheniia nashikh dnei: V zashchitu tserkovnogo edinstva* (Moscow: Danilovskii blagovestnik, 2003), 259–78; Vladimir Makarov, "Lzhesvidetel'stvo v ikone," in *Chudesa istinnye i lozhnye*, comp. A. V. Moskovskii et al. (Moscow: Danilovskii blagovestnik, 2007), 362–70; Protoierei Maksim Maksimov, "Pochemu v tserkvi poiavliaiutsia netserkovnye iavleniia?," in *Chudesa istinnye i lozhnye*, 372; Tatiana Matiash "Neblagoslovennaia: Pochemu Tserkov ne priznaet ikonu 'Voskreshaiushchaia Rus'?," Anti-raskol.ru, http://anti-raskol.ru/pages/2556; Sviashchennik Vasilii Petrov, "Pochemu Tserkov ne priznaet ikonu 'Voskreshaiushchaia Rus'?," *Apologet*, 24 January 2012, http://apologet.in.ua/apologetika/psevdopravoslavnye-sekty/voskreshayushhaya-rus/2228-pochemu-tserkov-ne-priznaet-ikonu-voskreshayushhaya-rus.html.

119. Dobrosotskikh, "Soblazn' 'Osobogo sluzheniia,'" 262.

120. "V 'Tserkvi matushki Fotinii Sviatonosnoi' Putin obi'iavlen apostolom," Newru.com, 11 April 2005, http://www.newsru.com/russia/11apr2005/st_putin.html; Svetlana Gamzaeeva, "Chetyre voploshcheniiaVladimira Putina," *Nezavisimaia gazeta*, 24 December 2009, http://www.ng.ru/politics/2007-12-24/3_kartblansh.html. For the community "Voskreshaiushchaia Rus," see http://www.webcitation.org/6Dj2MMT1W; Anna Danilova, "Nizhegorodskaia sekta imeni Putina," *Pravoslavie i mir*, 23 January 2012, http://www.pravmir.ru/nizhegorodskaya-sekta-imeni-putina/.

121. For the "True Orthodox Church in Russia," see its official website, http://ipckatakomb.ru/. For its official glorification of the image of the Mother of God named Rus' Resurrecting, see "Deianie Pomestnogo sobora IPTs(R) o proslavlenii ikony Materi Bozhiei 'Voskreshaiushchaia Rus,'" Credo.ru, 16 November 2004, http://www.portal-credo.ru/site/?act=news&id=28554. For the phenomenon of "tsar-worshippers," see Andrei Grigoriev, "Teologiia Tsaria-iskupitelia: Ul'trapravoslavnye apologetiki upodobili Nikolaia II Khristu," *NG-Religiia*, 17 November 2010; S. L. Firsov, *Na vesakh very: Ot kommunisticheskoi religii k novym "sviatym" postkommunisticheskoi Rossii* (St. Petersburg: Vita Nova, 2011). The following discussion is part of a broader essay on this topic. See Vera Shevzov, "Women on the Fault Lines of Faith: Pussy Riot and the Insider/Outsider Challenge to Post-Soviet Orthodoxy," *Religion and Gender* 4, no. 2 (2014): 121–44.

122. "Doklad Patriarkha Moskovskogo i Vseia Rusi Aleksiia II," Arkhiereiskiii sobor Russkoi Pravoslavnoi Tserkvi, 3 October 2004, http://xxc.ru/sobor/docs/doclad_patriarha.htm. Regarding the phenomenon of such "new saints," see Firsov, *Na vesakh very*. On the phenomenon of pseudo-icons, see Iuliia Andreeva, "Psevdoikony nashego vremeni," Pravoslavie.ee, http://www.pravoslavie.ee/docs/pseudoicons.pdf; A. Slesarev, "Sovremennye psevdopravoslavnye ikony," Anti-raskol.ru, http://www.anti-raskol.ru/pages/1251.

123. Technically, members of the band have maintained they were provoked to stage the Punk Prayer when they did by two events: (1) the Patriarchate's "staging" of the visit of the belt of the Mother of God during the highly politically charged time before Duma elections in order to distract believers; and (2) Patriarch Kirill's granting Vladimir Putin a "metaphysical" (*vnezemnoi*) role in Russia's history for his policies during extraordinarily economically difficult years in the 1990s. See "Stenogramma vstrechi predsedatelia Pravitel'stva RF V. V. Putin so Sviateishim Patriarkhom Kirillom i liderami traditsionnykh religioznykh obshchin Rossii," 8 February 2012; see comment by Ekaterina Samutsevich as quoted in "Prigovor Pussy Riot," *Snob.ru*, 22 August 2012, https://snob.ru/selected/entry/51999.

124. These are the main themes addressed in the Punk Prayer lyrics. See Pussy Riot, *Pussy Riot!*, 13–14.

125. Jerry D. Meyer, "Profane and Sacred: Religious Imagery and Prophetic Expression in Postmodern Art," *Journal of the American Academy of Religion* 65, no. 1 (1997): 19–46.

126. For a detailed analysis of the Punk Prayer in light of Orthodox identity and its politics in contemporary Russia, see Vera Shevzov, "Women on the Fault Lines of Faith: Pussy Riot and the Insider/Outsider Challenge to Post-Soviet Orthodoxy," *Religion and Gender* 4, no. 2 (2014): 121–44. For a detailed discussion of the ambiguity of the notion of blasphemy, see S. Brent Plate, *Blasphemy: Art That Offends* (London: Black Dog Publishing, 2006).

127. Claiming that no objects were stolen, some commentators, including clergy, have denied the sacrilegious nature of the performance, basing their logic on the original Latin *sacrilegium*, meaning stealing sacred property. As examples, see Ieromonakh Roman Zaitsev, "Nastoiashchie khristiane moliatsia za etikh devushek," *Novye izvestiia*, 6 July 2012; Andrei Sharyi, "Sviashchennik Iakov Krotov—pank gruppe Pussy Riot," Radio svoboda, 7 March 2012, http://www.svoboda.org/content/article/24508098.html. A broader definition that includes the notion of cultural appropriation as a form of theft (in this case, with respect to the use of sacred space) has elicited comparable charges of sacrilege and offence in other contexts. Such a designation raises a host of questions regarding definition, boundaries, and claims to "ownership" with respect to Orthodox stories, rituals, and other material embodiments of beliefs in post-Soviet society. For issues concerning offence and cultural appropriation, see as examples Conrad G. Brunk and James O. Young, "'The Skin Off of Our Backs': Appropriation of Religion," in *The Ethics of Cultural Appropriation* (Malden, MA: Wiley-Blackwell, 2009), 93–114; Inés Hernández-Ávila, "Meditations of the Spirit: Native American Religious Traditions and the Ethics of Representation," in *Women's Studies in Religion: A Multicultural Reader*, ed. Kate Bagley and Kathleen McIntosh (Upper Saddle River, NJ: Prentice Hall, 2007), 55–64; James O. Young, "Profound Offence and Cultural Appropriation," *Journal of Aesthetics and Art Criticism* 63, no. 2 (Spring 2005): 135–46.

128. See the evaluation, for instance, of opposition leader Aleksei Naval'nyi, "Pro pussi riot," *Livejournal* (blog), http://navalny.livejournal.com/690551.html; Alek D. Epshtein, "Mobilizovannaia Bogoroditsa: Pank-moleben gruppy 'Pussy Riot' v Khrame Khrista Spasitelia," *Neprikosnovennyi zapas*, no. 3 (2012): 130–33; Zhanna Golubitskaia, "'Pis'kin bunt'—osmyslennyi no besposhchadnyi," *Moskovskii komsomolets*, no. 57, 17 March 2012, 6.

129. For examples of the Punk Prayer's resonance with Western feminist readings of the Marian tradition, see Bridget, "Virgin Mary, Mother of God, Become a Feminist," Women in Theology, 18 August 2012, http://womenintheology.org/2012/08/18/virgin-mary-mother-of-god-become-a-feminist/. For a description of the sources of the group's feminist inspiration, see Vlad Tupikin, "Pussy Riot protiv Putina i Flippa Kirkorova, za Takhrir v Moskve," OpenSpace.ru, 11 November 2011, http://pussy-riot.livejournal.com/2857.html.

130. "Skandal vokrug Pussy Riot v eskhatologicheskom perspekte," *Sovremennoe drevlepravoslavie*, 10 April 2012, https://staroobrad.ru/modules.php?name=News2&file=article&sid=836. For a similar view, see "Protodiakon Kuraev ne shchitaet aktsiiu Pussy Riot sviatotatstvom i bogokhul'stvom," Newsru.com, 12 May 2012, http://newsru.com/religy/12may2012/kuraev.html.

131. Arkhimandrit Mefodii Morozov, "Kazanskaia ikona—sviatynia smutnogo vremeni," *Tat'ianin den'*, 4 November 2008, http://www.taday.ru/text/141726.html.

132. "The Service in Honor of the Icon of the Mother of God of Kazan," in *The Kazan Icon of the Mother of God: History, Service, and Akathist Hymn*, ed. and trans. Isaac E. Lambertsen (Liberty, TN: Saint John of Kronstadt Press, 1998), 13.

133. "Pank Moleben, 'Bogoroditsa Putina Progoni' v Khrame Khrista Spasitelia," *Livejournal* (blog), 21 February 2012, http://pussy-riot.livejournal.com/12442.html.

134. "Service in Honor of the Icon," 21.

135. "Interv'iu: Uslovno osuzhdennaia uchastnitsa gruppy 'Pussy Riot' Ekaterina Samutsevich," Credo.ru, 23 November 2012, http://www.portal-credo.ru/site/?act=news&id=96966; "Bogoroditsa, Devo, Putina Progoni," *Livejournal* (blog), 7 March 2012, http://yuhrnikke.livejournal.com/298078.html; Vladimyr Golyshev, "Byt' Khristom, ili eshche raz ob iurodstve Pussy Riot," *Livejournal* (blog), http://stariy-khren.livejournal.com/38124.html.

136. Andrei Miasnikov, "Pochemu opasna pank-gruppa 'Pussy Riot'? Filosofsko-Teologicheskoe rassuzhdenie," *Radio Ekho Moskvy* (blog), 30 August 2012, http://echo.msk.ru/blog/otvagin/924818-echo/.

137. Iakov Krotov, "Programma 'Radio Svoboda: S khristianskoi tochki zreniia,'" *Biblioteka Iakova Krotova*, 16 June 2012, http://krotov.info/library/17_r/radio_svoboda/20120616.htm.

138. For an example of Russian feminist response to Pussy Riot, see, Aktivistki IG Za Feminizm, "PR i diskreditatsiia zheskogo dvizheniia," *Za Feminizm*, 16 April 2012, https://www.zafeminizm.org/147-pr-i-diskreditaciya-zhenskogo-zhvizheniya.html.

139. Karen Mary Devalos, *Yolanda M. López* (Los Angeles: UCLA Chicano Studies Research Center Press, 2008).

140. Elena Volkova, "Pussy Riot School: Urok 2," *Radio Ekho Moskvy* (blog), 13 June 2012, http://echo.msk.ru/blog/lenavanna/898678-echo/.

141. Viktoriia Matveeva, "K chemu Bogoroditse byt' feministikoi?," Pravda.ru, 23 August 2012, http://www.pravda.ru/faith/religions/orthodoxy/23-08-2012/1125806-feminism-0/#. Elena Volkova draws similar parallels in her blog *Pussy Riot School: Urok 2*.

142. "Spetsialn'yi korrespondent: Provokatory," *TK Rossiia-1*, 24 April 2012, https://www.youtube.com/watch?v=-yk4lLQ_9Hg.

143. Roman Zaitsev, "Pravoslavnyi sviashchennik o 'Pussy Riot' i situatsii v RPTs: S kem vy khristiane?," YouTube, http://www.youtube.com/watch?v=KrjuV7mZoRU; Adel Kalinichenko, "Nastoiashchie khristiane moliatsia za etikh devushek," *Novye izvestiia*, no. 117, 6 July 2012.

144. Elena Beliakova, "Oskorbliat chuvstva veruiushchikh mogut tol'ko ikh sobstvennye grekhi," *Radio svoboda*, 24 August 2012, http://www.svoboda.org/content/article/24687146.html.

145. Epshtein, "Mobilizovannaia Bogoroditsa," 127.

146. For Kosolapov's well known-image "Icon-Caviar" styled in the form of the Kazan icon of the Mother of God, see The Tsukanov Art College, http://www.tsukanov-art-collection.ru/picture.html?id=277. For Kosolapov's comments on Pussy Riot, see "Amerikanskii sotsart priznal v Pussy Riot rodstvennye dushi," *INO TV*, 13 September 2012, https://russian.rt.com/inotv/2012-09-13/Amerikanskij-socart-priznal-v-Pussy. Also see comments by art historian Andrei Erofeev, "RPTs poprosit za Pussy Riot," *Dozhd'*, 17 August 2012, http://tvrain.ru/articles/rpts_poprosit_za_pussy_riot-329412/.

147. Mark Lipovetsky, "Na glavnyi vopros sovremennosti otvechaet filolog, avtor 'Paralogii' i 'Performansov nasiliia,'" Litfest.ru, http://litcentr.in.ua/news/2012-05-16-2054.

148. For examples of immediate Western response to Pussy Riot, see Pussy Riot, *Pussy Riot!*, 121–50; Timothy Beal, "Pussy Riot's Theology," *The Chronicle Review*, 28 September 2012; Bridget, "Virgin Mary."

149. According to Samutsevich, given the performance's strictly civic nature, "it would be strange to view it in light of Christian traditions." See "Ekaterina Samutsevich: Milliony dollarov menia ne interesuiut!," *Sobesednik.ru*, 22 October 2012, http://sobesednik.ru/incident/20121022-ekaterina-samutsevich-milliony-dollarov-menya-ne-interesuyut.

150. Masiuk, "Dvushechka."

151. Alexander Agadjanian, "Public Religion and the Quest for National Ideology: Russia's Media Discourse," *Journal for the Scientific Study of Religion* 40, no. 3 (2001): 351.

152. Department for External Church Relations of the Moscow Patriarchate, "Bases of the Social Concept of the Russian Orthodox Church," paragraph 15: Church and Mass Media, http://orthodoxeurope.org/page/3/14.aspx.

153. Jeanette Rodriguez and Ted Fortier, *Cultural Memory: Resistance, Faith, and Identity* (Austin, TX: University of Texas Press, 2007), 30.

154. Gordon Lynch and Jolyon Mitchell, eds., *Religion, Media, and Culture: A Reader* (New York, Routledge, 2012), 1; "Closing Courtroom Statement by Katja," in Pussy Riot, *Pussy Riot!*, 89.

155. Lynch and Mitchell, *Religion, Media, and Culture*, 1–5; Peter Horsfield, "Media," in *Key Words in Religion, Media, and Culture*, ed. David Morgan (New York: Routledge, 2008), 111–23; Stig Hjarvard, "The Mediatization of Religion: A Theory of Media as Agents of Religious Change," *Northern Lights* 6, no. 1 (2008): 10.

# Afterword

JUDITH DEUTSCH KORNBLATT

AMY SINGLETON ADAMS AND VERA Shevzov have titled this volume *Framing Mary: The Mother of God in Modern, Revolutionary, and Post-Soviet Russian Culture*. Although certain aspects of Mary's symbolism remain consistent over time and space, it is clear that no single frame can contain her, that she resists containment within any single genre, medium, space, point of view, political purpose, class, ecclesiastic pronouncement, or ritual approach. From the introduction by the two editors through the twelve individual essays, and from the numerous illustrations to the immensely helpful glossary at the end, she appears both visual and verbal, eternal and temporal, associated with particular locations but constantly mobile, able to incorporate both Eastern and Western iconographic trends, communal and individual, at the juncture between religious beliefs and their expression in the lives of the faithful, mother and creator, intercessor and protector, earthly and transcendent, Russian and universal, central and peripheral, a personal apparition or dream as well as a prescribed iconographic model, liturgical and iconographic, art and religion, gazing and gazed upon, lyric voice and poetic subject, domestic and public, symbol of both Church and State, not to mention virgin and mother. Given her capaciousness, some unanswerable questions might remain at the end of the volume: First, how does the Mary who peers out at us from centuries of Russian religious icons remain "Russian," and, second, how does she remain "religious," considering the often less than spiritual causes for which she has been increasingly invoked?

The simple answer to both these questions is: with great difficulty. When images of this unmarried Jewish mother of a single child are hung in maternity wards in post-Soviet era hospitals to encourage Russian motherhood, skeptical viewers might not help but wonder if Marian devotion is not verging irrevocably far into the political and demographic. What slogans are being used in non-ethnic Russian, predominantly Muslim areas? Or does the Russian power elite in Moscow not sanction fertility in those communities in the same way? Mary is not alone in these trends toward secularization, of course. It is hard to ignore Saint George emblazoned on the doors of Moscow police cars. Or de rigueur photos of government representatives lighting candles, fingers sometimes crossed behind their backs. Furthermore, the trend toward globalization is not new. Over the past two or three centuries, Russian Orthodox icon painters have adopted many Western Catholic, modernist, even postmodernist, models so that traditional reverse perspective, color imagery, and even architectural spaces are often no longer recognizable. Nonetheless, a deeper look at the essays in this volume points to ways in which the Russian Mother of God, both in her concrete manifestations and as abstract *Bogomaterinstvo*, might be specially marked for endurance.

At least three interconnected themes stand out in explanation of this endurance, and are highlighted by the multidisciplinary character of the collection. These are story, mobility, and gaze. Studies of literature, religion, history, and art all engage each of these themes in their own and overlapping ways. And each, ironically, grows from what the editors of the volume refer to as the commonplace nature of the image of Mary in Russian culture.

What about story? Very few, if any, Russian icons of Mary exist without a non-scriptural, popular tale of origin. They are associated with individual people, places, and experiences, and each has a particular history. As such, picture and story are integrally united, and not only in those narrative icons that depict multiple episodes from Mary's biography on the same board or around the periphery of one icon, flattening chronology and hierarchy. Rather, the back story of each image reaches from the biblical period of Mary's own life to the date of the apparition of the image and from there to the eternal present, dynamically marrying contemporary viewer and ancient, sacred image. The non-canonical nature of the stories associated with the appearances of Mary in the Russian countryside, before decisive battles or in resolution of marital disputes, illnesses, and childbirth crises allows the narratives to continue to grow into modern times. They can change and attach themselves to new situations in ways that the more tightly controlled associations with Jesus in the Gospel narratives, for example, cannot. The Vladimir Marian icon cured one young girl centuries ago, you say? So why can't she cure me, now, as well?

Mary's movement across space is as significant as is her evolution through time, expressing the interface of narrative and physical location. Throughout Russian history, an icon associated with one location might have been brought to another, where it can perform its wonders in a new space and situation. The procession from place to place itself takes on meaning, so that each physical step along the journey is blessed, as it were, by the miraculous powers of the image being carried. Again, what Stella Rocks calls the "portability of Orthodox sanctity" is not limited to images of Mary. In her case, however, the pervasiveness of this characteristic related to the *Bogoroditsa* buttresses her ability to survive the forces of secularization and globalization. Even "exiled" to communities in the West, the Russian Mother of God icon can do its sanctified work.

As for gaze, this theme, too, is not limited to Mary. But the penetrating eyes of a Tender Mercy (Umilenie) icon uniquely draw us into a personal, domestic scene as they look out at the viewer instead of at the face of the precious child in his mother's arms. The worshipper or viewer gazes on Mary as she gazes back, uniting us in her love, her pain, her passion. Her home is our home. Her space is our space. Her story is our story.

A number of essays in this volume attest to the fact that ecclesiastic and imperial authorities often struggled to maintain control over the multiplicity of Mary narratives and images. Adams and Shevzov refer to a "laity-driven Marian subculture within Orthodoxy," "shared, collective encounters with Mary," and "the populist underpinning of modern Russia's Marian worship." The Russian Mother of God is an everyday, every-woman intercessor. Her very commonplace nature has ensured her long life in Russian culture. Can satire chip away at her durability? Irony? Crass commercialization? So far, it seems not.

In the near and distant future, will the Russian face of Mary the Birthgiver of God in her many poses remain recognizable? When she gazes out from screens on tiny mobile devices from all corners of the globe will one still feel her healing powers? When she lends her grace to the fostering of Russian hegemony on twenty-first-century propaganda posters will she have the same impact as she had carried on poles between villages in centuries past? Can her stories retain their unique power in punk lyrics, or post-punk lyrics, or whatever music the next years bring us? This volume attests to the fact that the youthful mother with her sad eyes and quiet composure has endured for centuries in a historically and politically volatile Russia. She found a nurturing home for her manifold images in what has always been, in fact, a diverse and multicultural nation. Perhaps her endurance is precisely *because* she is Russian and holy. Or perhaps simply because she is a mother.

# Glossary

## Icons of the Mother of God and Their Stories

This glossary is intended to provide readers with a summary of the commonly accepted versions of their foundational stories related to the icons of the Mother of God relevant to the present volume. Commemoration days indicate the dates on which significant events associated with the icon—its discovery or particular miracles attributed to it, for example—are believed to have occurred. It is important to note that written accounts of such stories may have been composed decades or centuries after the events they describe. Identifying the earliest manuscript(s) of an icon's story and understanding how subsequent versions of its story may have influenced an icon's history as a devotional object is a complex task and sometimes the subject of scholarly debate. Readers interested in particular icon types and the history of their related legends should consult the following: *Slovar' knizhnikov i knizhnosti Drevnei Rusi*, 3 vols. (Leningrad: Nauka, 1987–2003); Andreas Ebbinghaus, *Die altrussischen Marienikonen-Legenden* (Berlin: Otto Harrissowitz, 1990). In addition to the essays in the present volume, the following descriptions were based on: *Ikony Rossii*, www.iconrussia.ru (Zhanna G. Belik and Olga E. Savchenko, who oversee this site, are research fellows at the Andrei Rublev Museum); E. Poselianin, comp., *Bogomater': Polnoe illiustrirovannoe opisanie eia zemnoi zhizni i posviashchennykh eia imeni chudotvornykh ikon* (St. Petersburg: P. P. Soikina, 1900); Sofiia Snessoreva, comp., *Zemnaia zhizn' Presviatoi Bogoroditsy i opisanie sviatykh i chudotvornyh eia ikon*, 3rd ed. (St. Petersburg: Tuzov, 1910); *Pravoslavnaia entsiklopediia*, http://www.pravenc.ru/. To view icon images not pictured in this volume, see pravicon.com (in Russian).

### Abalak icon of the Mother of God (Абалакская икона Божией Матери)

This icon depicts the Mother of God "of the Sign" flanked on one side by Saint Mary of Egypt and on the other by Saint Nicholas; it is named for the village of Abalak outside of the Siberian city of Tobolsk. Its story begins in 1636, when a pious widow named Mariia reportedly saw this icon in a dream, in which a voice directed her to tell her fellow villagers to construct a church in honor of the icon. At first, the widow regarded the directive with skepticism, but then experienced three subsequent visions. In one of them, Saint Nicholas informed her that should she ignore the directive, the priest and some parishioners would die. The widow then told the local bishop, Nektarii (Teliashin) and fellow villagers about her experiences. The church was constructed the same year. According to the story, in 1637, at the request of a peasant, Evfimii, the protodeacon of Tobol'sk Cathedral painted the icon that Mariia had seen in her dream. Believers soon attributed miracles to prayer before the icon. The Abalak icon of the Mother of God icon is of the Sign (Znamenie) type. She faces the viewer with upraised hands and the image of the Christ child appears within a golden mandorla on her breast. The icon is commemorated on 10 December (27 November, O.S. [Old Style]) and 2 August (20 July, O.S.).

### Akhtyrka icon of the Mother of God (Ахтырская икона Божией Матери)

On 2 July 1739, priest Daniil Vasiliev reportedly found an icon of the Mother of God as he worked in the fields near the Protection Church in Akhtyrka (Kharkov province). The priest initially kept the icon in his home. After three years, Father Danilov claimed to have had a series of dreams in which Mary directed him to wash the dusty icon with water and to keep that water for its healing properties. His daughter was the first person reportedly healed (from chronic fever) after drinking the water and from prayers before the image. Convinced of the icon's special qualities, Danilov moved the icon into the parish church. In 1751, after a lengthy investigation, the Holy Synod designated the icon as miracle-working. In 1768 Empress Elizabeth helped fund the construction of the Cathedral of the Holy Virgin on the site where Father Danilov claimed to have found the icon. The original icon was lost or stolen in 1903, when it was sent to St. Petersburg for restoration. The iconographic type is commemorated on 15 July (2 July, O.S.).

### Bogoliubskii icon of the Mother of God (Боголюбская икона Божией Матери)

The Bogoliubskii icon of the Mother of God commemorates Mary's appearance to Grand Prince Andrei Bogoliubskii (1111-1174). As Grand Prince of Vladimir (1157-1174), Bogoliubskii relocated from Kiev to Vladimir in 1155. When he left Kiev, Bogoliubskii took with him an icon of the Mother of God, which later became known as the Vladimir icon. Just outside the future city of Vladimir, the horses carrying the icon stopped and refused to move. Bogoliubskii then reportedly had a vision Mary, who appeared to him with a scroll in her right hand, and directed him to take the icon to Vladimir, construct a church (eventually constructed in honor the Nativity of Mother of God), and establish a monastery on this particular site. Bogoliubskii commissioned an iconographer to paint an icon of Mary as she had appeared to him in his vision. This icon became known as the Bogoliubskii icon. Mary is depicted in this icon without the Christ child, holding a scroll in her right hand with her left hand lifted in gesture upward to Christ, who is depicted in the icon's upper right hand corner. The icon is commemorated on 1 July (18 June, O.S.).

### Feodorov icon of the Mother of God (Феодоровская икона Божией Матери)

Scholars debate the origins of the Feodorov icon of the Mother of God, attributing its commission to different princes of medieval Rus', including Andrei Bogoliubskii and Iaroslav Vsevolodovich. According to its legend, however, the Feodorov icon resided in a chapel and then a monastery near the city of Gorodets (Nizhnii Novgorod province) until 1238, when the monastery was destroyed by the Mongol forces of Batu Khan. The icon was presumed destroyed, but Vasilii Iaroslavich (1236/41–1276), the prince of Kostroma and younger brother of Grand Prince Alexander Nevskii (1221–1263), reportedly rediscovered it perched on a tree some seventeen years later while hunting. The local clergy took the icon to the cathedral church in Kostroma, whose patron saint was the Byzantine warrior Fedor Stratelates. The icon came to bear this patron saint's name. In 1613, the Feodorov icon became associated with the beginning of the Romanov dynasty, reportedly playing a central role in convincing the reluctant mother Ksenia Ivanovna (by this time, the nun Martha) to allow her sixteen-year-old son, Mikhail Fedorovich Romanov, to accept the throne at the invitation of the national assembly (Zemskii Sobor). An indication of the place of honor that the Feodorov icon subsequently held within the Romanov dynasty is evidenced by the fact that when foreign princesses married Russian grand princes and converted to Orthodoxy, they took the patronymic "Feodorovna" in honor of this icon. Hence, the wife of Tsar Paul I and the wife of Tsar Alexander III were both named Mariia Fedorovna; the wife of Tsars Nicholas I and Nicholas II were both named Alexandra Feodorovna. The icon is commemorated on 27 March (14 March, O.S.), and on 29 August (16 August, O.S.).

### Icon of the Mother of God named Do not Lament Me (икона "Оплакивание Христа" or "Не Рыдай Мене, Мати")

Based on the words from a hymn sung during matins on Holy Saturday, "Do Not Lament me, O Mother," this icon type, which was known in Russia from the fifteenth century, depicts Mary mourning over her son, in the tomb. Sometimes compared to the Roman Catholic Pieta, the icon depicts Mary embracing her son,

who inclines his head toward his mother, his eyes closed and arms crossed across
his unclothed body. A cross is usually depicted in the background. There were no
well-known miracle-working icons of this type in prerevolutionary Russia.

### The icon of the Mother of God named Helper in Childbirth (икона Божией Матери "Помощница в родах")

This icon type first appeared in Russia by way of Ukraine. Its several variations
include the currently well-known image depicting Mary with long hair draping over her shoulders, head uncovered. Her hands cup an infant Christ child
enclosed in a womb-like mandorla, which is reminiscent of the "Sign" type of
icon. Typically, women who face difficult pregnancies may particularly revere
the Helper in Childbirth icon. Together with the thematically related icon of the
Mother of God named "Blessed Womb" (Божья Матерь "Блаженное Чрево"),
the icon is commemorated on 8 January (26 December).

### The icon of the Mother of God named Hodegetria (икона Божией Матери "Одигитрия")

The Hodegetria icon (Putevoditel'nitsa; "She Who Shows the Way") is a well-
known Byzantine type of icon of the Mother of God. It depicts Mary holding
the infant Jesus in her left arm and pointing to him with her right hand. The
Smolensk icon of the Mother of God is the most well-known Russian icon of
this type, often thought to be a copy of the widely-known Byzantine Blacherni-
tissa-Hodegetriia icon. While the origins of the Smolensk icon are unknown,
according to its legend, the daughter of Byzantine Emperor Constantine IX
Monomachos brought it to Rus' in 1046, when she married the prince of
Chernigov, Vsevolod Iaroslavovich. Their son, Vladimir Monomakh, eventually brought the icon to Smolensk, where it was housed in the Cathedral of the
Dormition of the Mother of God. It became renowned for the role it reportedly played in preserving Smolensk from destruction by Batu Khan in 1239.
In the ensuing centuries, because of changes in governance and intermittent
military strife, the icon moved frequently between Smolensk and Moscow. The
icon disappeared during the German occupation of Smolensk during World
War II. The icon is commemorated on 10 August (28 July, O.S.).

### The Holy Cross icon of the Mother of God (Свято-Крестовская икона Божией Матери)

In its composition, this icon is reminscent of the Akhtryka icon, with the Mother
of God in a grieving pose, inclining her head toward a cross. The depiction is
based on a vision reportedly witnessed by numerous people during the 1995
siege of a hospital by Chechen terrorists in the town of Budyonnovsk (known as

"Holy Cross" before 1921). The town is located seventy miles north of Russia's border with Chechnya. Between 14–19 June, almost two thousand people—including 150 children—were held hostage in the regional hospital. The hospital was located on the former grounds of a monastery, where, in the fourteenth century, the body of Prince Mikhail of Tver lay in state after he was executed by Ozbeg Kahn of the Golden Horde. On 18 June 1995, several dozen people allegedly saw an Orthodox cross and the Mother of God in the sky, which was understood as a sign of her protection. The icon is commemorated on June 18 (5 June O.S.).

### Iveron icon of the Mother of God (Иверская икона Божией Матери)

The Iveron icon of the Mother of God (a Hodegetria type) is housed in the Iveron Monastery on Mount Athos. According to one of its legends, the icon belonged to a wealthy and pious widow in the city of Nicaea during the reign of iconoclast Emperor Theophilus (813–842). One of the emporor's soldiers reportedly struck the icon with a spear and blood flowed out of it. The widow implored the soldiers not to touch the icon until the next morning. When the soldiers left, she set the icon out to sea to preserve it. Two centuries later, the monks of Mount Athos were said to have discovered an icon floating on the sea, which they associated with stories about the widow. As often reported in icon-related stories, this icon itself "chose" where to reside. A highly respected elder in the monastery, Gabriel, had a vision in which the Mary informed him that she did not want to remain in the church, but instead intended to act as the community's protectress. The icon found its permanent home, therefore, on the monastery gates. This story also earned the icon the name of Gatekeeper (Portaitissa). According to the icon's story, in the seventeenth century, the future Patriarch of Russia Nikon (Minin), arranged to have a copy of this icon brought to Moscow during the reign of Tsar Aleksei Mikhailovich. During the nineteenth century, a highly revered copy of the Iveron icon was housed in a chapel outside the Kremlin walls; believers frequently requested the image be brought to their homes for special prayer services. The Iveron icon is commemorated on 25 February (12 February, O.S.) on 26 October (13 October, O.S.)

### Icon of the Mother of God named Joy of All Who Sorrow (икона Божией Матери "Всех Скорбящих Радость")

The Joy of All Who Sorrow depicts the Mother of God—sometimes with the infant Jesus on her left arm, sometimes standing alone—surrounded by destitute and impoverished people. The iconographic type became widespread in Russia in the late seventeenth century, when Evfimiia, the sister of patriarch Joachim, was reportedly healed by prayer before an image of this iconographic type after being directed to it by a voice—supposedly that of the Mother of God—she heard during prayer. The icon is commemorated on 6 November (24 October, O.S.).

**Jerusalem icon of the Mother of God (Иерусалимская икона Божией Матери)**

This icon is of the Hogeditria type and depicts Mary with the Christ child in her right hand. Like the Vladimir and Smolensk icons of the Mother of God, this icon is also attributed to the hand of the apostle Luke, who, according to its story, painted it fifteen years following Jesus's death. The Byzantine Emperor Leo I (457–474) reportedly brought the icon from Jerusalem to Constantinople. Upon his baptism in Korsun (now Kherson, Crimea), Prince Vladimir accepted this icon as a gift and transferred it to Kiev, and then to Novgorod, where it spent some four hundred years in the Cathedral of St. Sophia. As with many of Rus's most well-known icons, Tsar Ivan IV ("the Terrible") eventually had the icon brought to the Dormition Cathedral in Moscow. In 1812, Napoleonic forces reportedly plundered the cathedral and took the icon to France. The icon is commemorated on 25 October (12 October O.S.).

**Icon of the Mother of God named Life-Giving Spring (икона Божией Матери "Живописный источник")**

Although earlier versions of this icon seem to have differed in their representation, since the fourteenth century, it usually depicts Mary and the Christ child seated in a font situated over a spring from which water flows. The icon's story is connected to Byzantine Emperor Leo I (457–474), who, as a young soldier, helped a blind man, who was lost and in need of refreshment. Leo went in search of water, but was said to have heard a voice directing him to an overgrown spring nearby. The voice also instructed him to rub mud from this source on the blind man's eyes; he did so and the blind man was healed. Subsequently, Emperor Leo I had the site of the water source cleared and constructed a church near it in honor of the Mother of God as the "Life-Giving Source."

**Kazan icon of the Mother of God (Казанская икона Божией Матери)**

The Kazan icon of the Mother of God was the most widely revered icon in late imperial Russia. Its story begins in 1579, some twenty years following the annexation of Kazan by Tsar Ivan IV ("the Terrible") in 1552. Following a fire that had swept the city, in that year, the young girl Matrona had a series of dreams in which Mary directed her to inform the local bishop and city authorities that an icon was buried beneath the ashes. At first, Matrona's mother dismissed these dreams as products of a child's vivid imagination. In Matrona's final dream, however the icon appeared emitting fiery rays, and Matrona reportedly heard Mary's voice state, "If you do not follow my words . . . I will appear in another place, and you will perish." The frightened Matrona begged her mother to follow Mary's directives. This time, the mother reported these events to the local bishop and to the city's officials, who also at first dismissed Matrona's experiences. At this point in the story, Matrona's mother took matters into her own hands. She and Matrona went to the site, where Matrona found the icon buried under ashes, yet intact and undamaged. The first healing attributed to the icon took place as church officials carried the found icon in procession to the local church. The day of the icon's reported discovery, 8 July, soon became a local feast day in Kazan. In 1612, the icon was also credited for Russia's victory over Polish forces on 4 November (22 October, O.S.). In 2005, the Russian government established a new holiday—the Day of National Unity—celebrated on 4 November, which corresponds to the November commemoration day of the Kazan icon. The icon is commemorated on 21 July (8 July, O.S.) and 4 November (22 October, O.S.).

### Kursk-Root icon of the Mother of God "Of the Sign" (Курская Коренная икона Божией Матери "Знамение")

This icon depicts Mary with her hands in the orans posture. They are framed by the Lord of Hosts and the Old Testament prophets, images that some scholars believe were added later to the original icon. A hunter reportedly discovered the icon on 8 September 1295 (the day of the feast of the Nativity of the Blessed Virgin Mary) in the forest at the root of a tree outside the city of Kursk, which had been recently rebuilt after its destruction by Batu Khan in 1237. The story relates how the hunter picked up the icon and a spring burst forth on the site. There, he built a small chapel, where the icon was housed. In 1383, Tatar forces burned the chapel and, according to legend attempted to destroy the icon by splitting it in half. When the local priest gathered the pieces together, the icon allegedly restored itself. Afer some time in Moscow, the icon was returned to the Kursk region to reside at the Znamenskii Monastery, where in 1898, it survived an attempt to destroy it. The icon was evacuated from revolutionary Russia twice. First, in 1920, the bishop of Kursk, Theophan, brought the icon to Thessaloniki and Serbia. It was returned at the request of White Army troops in the Crimea, but evacuated again a year later. Eventually brought to the United States, it first resided in the New Kursk Hermitage in Mahopac, NY and then in the Cathedral of the Sign in New York City. The icon, called the "Hogeditria of the Russian Diaspora" in the West, is commemorated on 8 March (21 March, O.S.) and 8 September (21 September, O.S.).

### Leushino icon of the Mother of God (Леушинская икона Божией Матери)

This icon depicts Mary in a standing position dressed in a blue maphorion over a red chiton. She is holding the Christ child whose arms are in the orans position. This icon was reportedly donated by a merchanct from Gatchina to the Leushino St. John the Forerunner Convent in Novgorod diocese in 1862, then led by Abbess Taisiia (Solopova). Several important copies of the icon were made. To one was added the inscription "I am with thee and no one will offend thee" (Az esm' s Vami i Niktozhe na Vy) and presented to the nineteenth-century priest John of Kronstadt, who called the icon "the Savioress" (Spasitel'nitsa) of Russia. Father John blessed the Petersburg merchant Vasilii Murav'ev with the icon, predicting correctly that Murav'ev would later take vows and pray 1000 days and nights before the image for the salvation of Russia. This icon is commemorated on 24 June (July 7, O.S.).

### The icon of the Mother of God named Tenderness (икона Божией Матери "Умиление")

The Tenderness type of Mother of God icon includes a wide range of other well-known icons of the Mother of God—the Feodorov, Korsun, Tolga, and Vladimir icons, for instance—that depict the tender relationship between mother and child as they embrace cheek to cheek. In some depictions of the Tenderness type, Mary's gaze expresses weariness or sorrow, as if foreseeing her son's fate.

### Novopechora or Sven' icon of the Mother of God (Новопечерская or Свенская-Печерская икона Божией Матери)

This icon is associated with the founding of the Sven' (later Novopechora) Monastery of the Holy Dormition in 1288. According to legend, the icon was made by Alipii, the well-known icon painter of the Kievan Caves Lavra, where it eventually came to be revered as miracle working. While in Briansk, the prince of Chernigov, Roman Mikhailovich, lost his sight and requested that this icon be brought to him from the Kievan Caves Lavra. The icon disappeared in transit and was found on a hill near the banks of the Sven' River. When he heard about the incident, the prince came to the place where the icon was found, prayed before the image, and was healed. The prince founded a monastery in honor of the Mother of God at the same site. Tsar Ivan IV ("the Terrible") donated jewels for the decoration of the icon. He later ordered two stone churches built in honor of saints Anthony and Theodosius, who are depicted on the icon standing on either side of Mary and the infant Christ. The icon is commemorated on 16 May (3 May, O.S.).

### Nursing icon of the Mother of God ("Млекопитательница")

Known in the West as the *Virgo Lactans* and in Byzantium as the *Galaktotrophousa*, this icon depicts Mary nursing her infant son. While known in Russia since the fourteenth and fifteenth centuries, this icon was not one that was widely venerated as miracle-working. The story of one of the most well-known images of this iconographic type in the Christian East was associated with the Cappadocian-Greek monk Saint Savvas "the Sanctified" (d. 532), who lived in a monastery near Jerusalem, and Saint Savva, the archbishop of Serbia (1174–1236); it was housed at the Hilandar Monastery on Mount Athos. This icon is commemorated on 25 January (12 January, O.S.). According to some accounts, in 1860, an unnamed person from the Kursk diocese was healed from a long illness by prayers before a copy of this icon. A variant of this iconographic type that was considered miracle-working in Russia was reportedly discovered in 1650 near Minsk, where a church was constructed in its honor. This icon was locally commemorated on 28 August (15 August, O.S.).

### "O All-Hymned" icon of the Mother of God (икона Божией Матери "О Всепетая Мати"; Арапетская икона)

Scholars have been unable to trace the origins this particular iconographic type, which is not associated with miracle stories. Evidence of its existence in Russia, however, has been traced to the late seventeenth century. Similar to the Lamentation icon, its name derives from hymnody, namely, from the thirteenth *kontakion* of the akathist to the Mother of God: "O All-Hymned Mother, worthy of all praise, who bore the Word." In this icon, Mary, sometimes wearing a crown, holds her infant son, sometimes in a position reminiscent of the Hodigetriia type. Instead of the traditional three stars, three medallions with angels appear on the shoulders and forehead of her maphorion. Characteristically, the hymnographic words after which the icon is named are imprinted in the edge of the maphorion around Mary's face. The icon is commemorated on 19 September (6 September, O.S.).

### The Oranki icon of the Mother of God (Оранская икона Божией Матери)

A copy of the Vladimir Mother of God, this icon eventually became revered as miracle-working in its own right. It was reportedly painted by Archpriest Kodrat of Moscow's Assumption Cathedral in the early seventeenth century at the request of Petr Gliadkov, a landowner from the village Bocheevo in Nizhnii Novogorod diocese. According to the icon's story, five years after receiving the icon, in 1634, Gliadkov had three dreams in which he heard a voice directing him to a hill and telling him to construct a church there in honor of the Vladimir icon of the Mother of God. Gliadkov later found the hill located near the village of Oranki. He reportedly traveled to Moscow to petition the patriarch at the time, for permission to construct a church in honor of the Vladimir icon of the Mother of God on this site, where he later housed the icon. At the same time, a small community of monks settled near the church. A year after the church's construction, the icon reportedly became myrrh-bearing, with numerous believers claiming that they were healed by prayers before this image. In 1642, Petr Gliadkov took monastic vows, taking the name Pavel. By then widely known in the region, the icon began making annual visitations in 1771 to Nizhnii Novogorod and Arzamas. Although it is a copy of the Vladimir icon, the Oranki icon is distinguished by nine saints who are included at the bottom of the icon below the image of Mary: namely, the metropolitans of Kiev and all Rus' Peter (d. 1326), Alexis (before 1296–1378), and Jonah (d. 1461?); the prince of Chernigov, Mikhail Vsevolodovich (1179–1246), and the boyar Feodor; the Tsarevich Dmitrii Ivanovich of Uglich (1582–1591); and the holy fools Maksim of Moscow (d. 1434); Basil the Blessed (1469–1552), and John of Moscow (d. 1589). The icon is commemorated on 3 June (21 May, O.S.).

### The Pochaev icon of the Mother of God (Почаевская икона Божией Матери)

This icon is associated with the Pochaev Monastery in honor of the Assumption of the Most Holy Mother of God in today's western Ukraine. The story tells of two monks who settled on the site of the future monastery in 1340. One of the monks climbed to the top of the mountain and saw the Mother of God standing on a rock, surrounded by flames. The monk reportedly called the other monk; the shepherd Ioann Bosoi ("Barefoot") is also often listed as a witness. Afterwards, the monks and the shepherd reportedly found an imprint of Mary's right foot on the stone where she had stood. Traveling through the region, in 1559, Metropolitan Neophyte of Constantinople reportedly left the local noblewoman Anna Goiskaia an icon of the Mother of God as a gift. Goiskaia later gave the icon to the monastic community as a gift. The icon was placed in a church built on the rock where Mary was purported to have stood; the icon reportedly protected the church from siege in the late seventeenth century. Pochaev icons of the Mother of God often depict Mary's footprint in a stone. The icon is commemorated 5 August (23 July O.S.) and 21 September (8 September O.S.).

### The Port Arthur icon of the Mother of God (Порт-Артурская икона Божией Матери)

In 1903 a Crimean War veteran sailor reported a dream in which Mary was standing on the edge of the sea holding a linen cloth with imprint of the face of Christ (Mandylion). She warned of an impending war on a distant sea shore and directed the sailor to have an icon painted, depicting her as he had seen her in the dream. The resulting icon is also known as "The Victory of the Most Holy Birthgiver of God" (Торжество Пресвятой Богородицы) and, for many believers, foretold Russia's fate in the Russo-Japanese War (1904–1905). Mary instructed the sailor to deliver the icon to Port Arthur but, after a long and complex journey, the icon did not make it to its destination in time to prevent the Russian defeat. Despite the devastating military loss, the icon is considered a protector of Russia. The icon is commemorated on 29 August (16 August O.S.).

### The icon of the Protecting Veil of the Mother of God (икона "Покров Пресвятой Богородицы")

This icon is associated with one of the most revered feast days among Russia's Orthodox believers. The festal icon is based on the vision of Blessed Andrew, the Fool for Christ, in Constantinople's Church of the Virgin of Blachernae as recorded by the presbyter Nicephorous in the tenth century. According to the account, during an all-night vigil, Andrew—a Slav by birth who had been sold into slavery in Constantinople—together with his student Epiphanius, saw the Mother of God spread her veil (*pokrov*), which "shimmered with the radiating grace of God," in protection over those present. Though there is no scholarly consensus regarding the dating of when (or if) Andrew lived, nevertheless, in Russia, the vision is usually dated to the year 910, during the reign of Leo the Wise, and is associated with the Byzantine victory over "the enemy," which sources often designate as the Saracenes. Other historians who favor other dates for the figure of Andrew, identify "the enemy" as the Rus' or the Bulgars. Historians have also referred to the celebration of this feast as "a riddle of Russian liturgics," testifying to the differing accounts of the historical beginnings of the feast's celebration. The composition of the icon, already set in Rus' by the thirteenth century, has two variations. One version depicts Mary above the Royal Doors to the sanctuary, her arms raised in supplicatory prayer. Angels above her hold a protective veil (*pokrov*) over those present in the congregation below. Other versions highlight her role as heavenly protectress. The feast of the Protecting Veil is commemorated 14 October (1 October, O.S.).

### The image of the Mother of God named "Rus' Resurrecting" (образ Божией Матери "Воскрешающая Русь")

This late twentieth-century image depicts the vision reportedly experienced on the feast day of the Pokrov (Protecting Veil) by Olga Pavlenko from the city of Piatigorsk in the Northern Caucasus. Sick at home, Pavlenko was listening to a taped prayer service when the walls of her apartment seemed to melt away and, according to her account, Mary descended in a blinding white light dressed in a shimmering white robe. In her hands, Mary held a veil (*pokrov*), which covered the entire earth below her. Pavlenko reported seeing countless tiny crosses fall from Mary's veil and descend on people below. Each person reacted to these "symbols of grace" in different ways. This post-Soviet vision and its resulting image was initially embraced by many believers, mostly on Russia's southern and western borders. It remains an image contested by church officials, especially because of its nationalistic overtones. This icon is unofficially commemorated on 12 December.

**The icon of the Mother of God named She Who Reigns (икона Божией Матери "Державная")**

> This icon depicts Mary enthroned with the Christ child on her lap and holding the orb and scepter of royal authority. In 1917, the peasant woman Evdokiia Ivanovna Andrianova experienced a series of dreams in which she was reportedly directed to search for this icon in a church in the village of Kolomenskoe. With the help of a parish priest, she discovered the icon on 2 March (15 March, O.S.) 1917. Because the abdication of Tsar Nicholas II took place on the same day, the icon soon acquired both religious and political significance. In the absence of a tsar, believers concluded, Mary would assume sovereignty of Russia. This icon is one of the most publicly displayed icons in post-Soviet Russia. It is commemorated on 2 March (15 March O.S.).

**The icon of the Mother of God named Seven Arrows (Семистрельная икона Божией Матери)**

> Similar in composition to the icon of the Mother of God named Softener of Evil Hearts (Икона Божией Матери "Умягчение злых сердец"), this icon depicts the Mother of God pierced by seven arrows (or swords)—four on her left side and three on the right—representing the pain she experienced through the suffering of her son. As the Softener of Evil Hearts, this icon was inspired by the prophecy of Simeon, who foresaw that Mary's soul would be pierced by a sword (Lk 2:35). In prerevolutionary Russia, a miracle-working icon of the Mother of God named Seven Arrows was located in the Toshin Church of St. John the Theologian outside the city of Vologda. According to the icon's story, a peasant who was ill for many years heard a voice in a dream that directed him to search for an icon of the Mother of God located in the belfry of the Toshin church and to pray before it. He located the icon, which had been used as a floorboard in the bell tower. After the icon was cleaned and a prayer service performed before it, the peasant was healed. In 1830, the same icon was credited for helping to bring an end to a cholera outbreak in Vologda. This icon is commemorated on 26 August (13 August, O.S.).

**The Seven Lakes icon of the Mother of God (Седмиозерная икона Божией Матери)**

> This Hogeditriia type derives its name from the Seven Lakes Hermitage of the Mother of God near Kazan. In 1615, the monk Evfimii brought the icon from Velikii Ustiug to the monastery. It is credited with delivering the city of Kazan from a deadly plague in 1654, when a man radiant with light is reported to have appeared to a pious monk in a dream, telling him that the city's inhabitants should fast for seven days and then meet the icon which was on its way

to the city in a procession from the Seven Lakes hermitage. This icon is commemorated on 9 July (26 June O.S.), 10 August (28 July O.S.), and 26 October (13 October O.S.).

**Tikhvin icon of the Mother of God (Тихвинская икона Божией Матери)**

According to the story of this Hogeditria type of icon, it, too, was among those reportedly painted by the Evangelist Luke, and, in the fifth century, enshrined in the Church of the Virgin of Blachernae in Constantinople. In 1383, fisherman on Lake Ladoga near Novgorod reportedly witnessed the icon hovering over the water, which was later interpreted as a sign of Mary's decision to leave Constantinople for Rus' before the fall of the Byzantine Empire. After its appearance, the icon was found in the town of Tikhvin where, over the centuries, two churches and a monastery were built in its honor. The icon is credited with the monastery's survival. During World War II, the German army removed the icon, which subsequently found a long-term home at the Holy Trinity Cathedral in Chicago. In 2004, the icon's overseer, the archpriest Sergei Garklavs (1927–2015), accompanied the icon "home" to the Tikhvin Monastery of the Dormition of the Mother of God, located near St. Petersburg. The icon is commemorated on July 9 (26 June O.S.).

**Tolga icon of the Mother of God (Толгская икона Божией Матери)**

The story of the Tolga icon of the Mother of God, which is a Tenderness type, is set in the early fourteenth century. According to its legend first recorded in the sixteenth century, the icon was discovered by Prokhor, the bishop of Rostov and Iaroslavl', during a diocesan visitation. Having stopped for the night near the Tolga river, he woke to see a pillar of light in the distance. Taking up his staff, he walked and found the icon suspended in the air. The following morning, Prokhor returned to the site with members of his entourage and found the icon with the staff he left behind the night before. Overwhelmed by the appearance of the icon, Prokhor directed that a church be constructed on that spot, where the Tolga Monastery was later founded. The icon depicts Mary seated on a throne holding her infant son, whom she gently supports and pulls toward her in the Tenderness pose. The icon is commemorated on 21 August (8 August, O.S.).

**Icon of the Mother of God named Unexpected Joy (икона Божией Матери "Нечаянная радость")**

This icon is a Hodegetria type. It depicts a story recounted in 1638 by Dmitrii (Tuptalo), the archbishop of Rostov, in which a man who led a sinful life converses with an image of the Mother of God. Once, while saying his prayers, the man saw the image move before his eyes and wounds open on the hands, legs, and sides of the Christ child. This icon depicts the conversation between Mary and the sinner that ensued. Falling on his knees, the man beseeched Mary to reveal to him who was responsible for her son's wounds. Mary spoke, informing him that he was responsible, along with all other sinners, who repeatedly crucify her son. Similar to Marian miracle stories in the Catholic West meant to show the power of Mary's intercession, the man asked the Mother of God to intercede with her son for his forgiveness. Christ initially refused, but because of Mary's staunch support of the sinner, Christ eventually yielded to her request. The icon is commemorated on 14 May (1 May, O.S.) and 22 December (9 December, O.S.).

**Ustiug icon of the Annunciation (Устюжская икона Благовещения Пресвятой Богородицы)**

One of the few Russian icons from the pre-Mongolian period, the twelfth-century Ustiug icon of the Annunciation depicts Mary at the moment of the appearance of the Angel Gabriel, as recorded in the Gospel According to Luke, and her conception of Christ, who is depicted in a mandorla in her womb. The icon is associated with the life of the holy fool Procopius (d. 1285), and was composed in the seventeenth century. A European tradesman who settled in Novgorod, Procopius was eventually drawn to the Orthodox faith. He subsequently abandoned his business affairs, gave away his possessions, and entered a local monastic community. Unable to shed his previous identity as a businessman, however, he decided to move to the remote region of Velikii Ustiug in Russia's north, where he became known as a fool-for-Christ. There, he was derided by the citizens, who paid no attention to his prophesy that doom would befall the city if its people did not pray and repent. When an unusually violent storm occurred, the people recognized their error and joined Procopius in prayer before this icon. An abundance of holy oil flowed from the icon, which was used to treat various ailments. In 1567, Tsar Ivan IV ("the Terrible") had the icon brought to Moscow and placed it in the Kremlin's Dormition Cathedral. The icon is commemorated on 21 July (8 July, O.S.), the feast day of Saint Procopius.

**Valaam icon of the Mother of God (Валаамская икона Божией Матери)**

This Hogeditria type icon depicts the Mother of God standing on a cloud formation and dressed in a red maphorion over a blue chiton. In her arms is the Christ child, who raises his right hand and, in his left, holds a cross-bearing orb which symbolizes authority. The icon was painted in 1878 by the monk Alipii at the Valaam Monstery, located on an island in Lake Ladoga in Russian Karelia. The first miracle attributed to the icon took place in 1897, when Natalia Andreevna Andreeva was reportedly cured of rheumatoid arthritis. During

World War II, the icon was taken to Finland and is housed at the New Valaam Monastery. This icon is commemorated on 7 August (25 July O.S.) in Finland and 14 June (1 July O.S.) in Russia.

**Vladimir icon of the Mother of God (Владимирская икона Божией Матери)**

An example of the Tenderness type, the Vladimir icon of the Mother of God, according to tradition, was attributed to the Evangelist Luke. According to its story, in the twelfth century, Patriarch of Constantinople Luke Chrysoberges sent the icon as a gift to Grand Prince of Kiev Iurii Dologorukii, who placed it in a convent located in Vyshgorod, outside of Kiev. In 1155, the grand prince's son, Andrei Iurievich Bogoliubskii, took the icon with him to Vladimir, the city after which it was eventually named. In 1395, the icon was brought in procession to Moscow to protect the city from the invasion of the Turko-Mongol ruler Tamerlane. According to legend, at the moment the icon was being greeted in Moscow on 8 September (26 August, O.S.), Tamerlane had a dream in which a luminous woman appeared to him, surrounded by a host of angels brandishing fiery swords. Tamerlane reportedly awoke in fright and fled. The icon was brought permanently to Moscow in 1480 and placed in the Dormition Cathedral. The icon is commemorated on 3 June (21 May, O.S.), 23 June (6 June, O.S.), and 8 September (26 August, O.S.).

# Contributors

**AMY SINGLETON ADAMS**, associate professor of Russian literature, the College of the Holy Cross

**ELENA N. BOECK**, professor of history of art, DePaul University

**NATALIA ERMOLAEV**, assistant director at the Center for Digital Humanities, Princeton University

**JUDITH DEUTSCH KORNBLATT**, professor emerita of Slavic languages and literature, the University of Wisconsin-Madison

**SARAH PRATT**, vice provost for graduate programs and professor of Slavic languages and literatures, the University of Southern California

**ROY R. ROBSON**, division head for arts and humanities and professor of history, Penn State University

**WENDY SALMOND**, professor of art history, Chapman University

**VERA SHEVZOV**, professor of religion and director of the program in Russian, East European, and Eurasian studies at Smith College

**ELIZABETH SKOMP**, associate dean for faculty development and inclusion and professor of Russian, The University of the South (Sewanee)

**ALEXANDRA SMITH**, reader in Russian studies and director of the MSc in theatre and performance programme at the School of Languages, Literatures, and Cultures, University of Edinburgh

**WILLIAM WAGNER BROWN**, professor of history emeritus, Williams College

**CHRISTINE D. WOROBEC**, distinguished research professor emerita, Northern Illinois University

# Index

Blachernae, Church of, 6
Blanchot, Maurice, 156, 157
Blok, Alexander
　Beautiful Lady (Prekrasnaia Dama), 16, 126
　"Collapse of Humanism" (Krushenie
　　gumanizama), 174
　Mother of God, 15
　Petrov-Vodkin, 173, 175–176, 177–78
　"Scythians" (Skify), 173
　Skobtsova, Elizaveta (Mother Maria), 199
　"Twelve, The" (Dvenadtsat'), 173, 177, 182
　western Madonna, 15
Blue Rose group, 168
Boehme, Jakob, 197
Bolshevik Revolution, 10, 20, 25, 26, 123, 144,
　172–77, 191, 198, 283, 286, 292
Bolsheviks, 123, 172, 178
Bonnell, Victoria, 123, 124
Book of Degrees of the Royal Genealogy
　(Stepennaia kniga tsarskogo
　rodosloviia), 9
Borisov-Musatov, Viktor, 168
Brezhnev, Leonid, 227, 228, 236
Briansk, region 38, 51, **52**, 53, 54, 324
Briusov, Valerii, 126, 173
Bruegel, Pieter, 172
Budyonnovsk, Stavropol region, 25, 274,
　282–283, 320
Bulgakov, Sergius, priest, 26, 188
　The Burning Bush (Kupina neopalimaia), 191
　"Hypostasis and Hypostaticity (Ipostas' i
　　ipostasnost'), 191
　"Most Pure Motherhood: Dedicated to
　　Russian Mothers" (Prechistoe materin-
　　stvo) 193
　motherhood, 192–94, 197–99, 201, 203, 233
　The Philosophy of Economy (Filosofiia
　　khoziastva), 190
　Sophiology, 190–95
　Unfading Light (Svet nevechernii), 190
Bykov, Dmitrii, 123
Byzantium, 61, 69

Campanella, Tommaso, 174
Capri School, 123, 139n9
Catholicism, Roman
　iconography, 11, 48, 61–62, 64–65, 68–69,
　　74–75, 209, 212, 220, 314
　Marian devotion, 20, 22, 23, 40, 99, 187, 200,
　　247–48
　Marian processions, 21

sacred space, 41–42
Cavallini, Pietro, 214
Chechnya. See Budyonnovsk.
Chernov, Victor, 17, **18**
Christ
　Akhtyrka icon of the Mother of God, 61,
　　67–72
　Berdiaev, Nikolai, 197
　birth of, 87
　Bride of, 113
　Bulgakov, Sergius, 192–94
　Christology, 6, 187, 191
　Crucifixion, 61, 67–71, 181, 199, 201, 219
　Godman (Bogochelovek), 192, 201
　Godmanhood (Bogochelovechestvo), 16, 126,
　　189, 192, 197, 200–202
　Golgotha, 67
　icons of, 6–7, 24, 44, 100, 154, 155
　Passion of, 67, 68–71, 75, 123, 134, 143n83,
　　158, 159, 315
　Petrov-Vodkin, Kuzma, 170, 174–75, 178
　resurrection of, 71, 68, 69, 113, 137
　"Skazki: Noël," 86
　Skobtsova, Elizaveta (Mother Maria),
　　199–202
　Sofronov, Pimen, 217–19, 220–22
　Solov'ev, Vladimir, 192
　Symbolism, 126
　Tsvetaeva, Marina, 159
　"The Twelve," 173, 176, 182, 184n26
　Volfila, 180
　Word of God (Logos), 134, 189, 192, 197
Christ the Savior, Cathedral (Moscow), 270,
　287, 296
Chudovskii, Evfimii, monk (d. 1705), 64
Church of St. Vasilii Zlatoverskii, Ovruch, 167
Church of the Nativity of the Mother of God
　(Lubensk), 74
church schism, seventeenth century, 61
Civil War, Russian (1917–1922), 17, 148, 151,
　157, 158, 174, 191, 198, 283
communism, 10, 28, 123, 180, 272
Constantinople
　Church of St. Mary of Blachernae, 6, 78n19,
　　222, 327, 329
　Hagia Sophia, 155
　icon of the Protecting Veil of the Mother of
　　God, 327
　Jerusalem icon of the Mother of God, 321
　Marian legacy, 11
　Pochaev icon of the Mother of God, 326